In the Governor's Shadow

In the Governor's Shadow

The True Story of Ma and Pa Ferguson

Carol O'Keefe Wilson

University of North Texas Press

Denton, Texas

10 9 8 7 6 5 4 3 2 1

Permissions:
University of North Texas Press
1155 Union Circle #311336
Denton, TX 76203-5017

The paper used in this book meets the minimum requirements of the American National Standard for Permanence of Paper for Printed Library Materials, z39.48.1984. Binding materials have been chosen for durability.

Library of Congress Cataloging-in-Publication Data

Wilson, Carol O'Keefe, 1950- author.
In the Governor's shadow : the true story of Ma and Pa Ferguson / Carol O'Keefe Wilson. -- First edition.
  pages cm
Includes bibliographical references and index.
ISBN 978-1-57441-553-7 (cloth : alk. paper) -- ISBN 978-1-57441-563-6 (ebook)
1. Ferguson, James Edward, 1871-1944. 2. Ferguson, Miriam Amanda, 1875-1961. 3. Governors--Texas--Biography. 4. Women governors--Texas--Biography. 5. Texas--Politics and government--1865-1950. I. Title.
F391.F47W55 2014
976.4'06092--dc23
[B]
                                    2013041279

The electronic edition of this book was made possible by the support of the Vick Family Foundation.

Book design by **Jimmy Ball Design**

For Jena and Britt

Jack

Alex

and

Kennedy

Contents

Illustrations

Acknowledgments

The reliability of the content of this book is critical to its value. Such a story, written more than a century after it began, could only be written comprehensively and accurately using information from many sources. The safeguarding of the documents, books and other records necessary for this kind of research depends to a very large degree on the work of museums, libraries and other institutions that dedicate themselves to such preservation. Without their diligent work, a successful project of this nature would be almost impossible. I salute the fine work that all of these organizations do to promote and protect the integrity of our history.

Specifically I would like to thank Stephanie Turnham, the Director of the Bell County Museum. This local museum was the starting and ending point for this project. I frequented its library and archives where I always found a smile and a helping hand from the very capable museum staff. My thanks are also due to the Lena Armstrong Library in Belton, the Salado Public Library, and the Temple Public Library. I would also like to acknowledge the staff at the Bell County Clerk and District Clerk's offices for their assistance (in particular Cindy Woodum). Thank you to Betty Sue Beebe, the curator at the museum at the University of Mary Hardin-Baylor. I commend the Dolph Briscoe Center for American History in Austin and the University of Houston, which do an outstanding job of preserving important documents of historical significance and making them available to researchers. Thank you to Betty Cross of Eastland County without whose help I might never have found H. C. (Hosea) Poe's first name and the *Eastland Telegram* for printing my request for information.

A host of friends and associates contributed to the success of this undertaking by offering their services as mentors, readers, advisors and sounding boards. In particular, Mike and Nancy Kelsey allowed me to draft them into positions of assistance when they were generous enough to answer an early request to proofread a portion of my work for local historical accuracy. After they extended that initial kindness, I relied on them heavily for information and moral support which they supplied in abundance, often setting aside their own projects to help me.

Jim Donovan, an exceptional writer, shared with me his valuable insight and talents for which I am most grateful. Patricia Benoit, an author and writer of local history for the *Temple Daily Telegram*, was most helpful in pointing me to some critically important online research tools. Friends who served as readers are Bryan (Buz) Gover, Elaine Foster, Kathy Hennig, Karen Thieme, Doris Kemp, David Yeilding, Jeff and Vicki Lemon, Amy Moore, and Margaret Priest. These parties cheerfully suffered through some very rough drafts.

Michael LeFan, my first editor, deserves special mention. Michael was a childhood victim of polio who refused to surrender to adversity. Typing with his foot, this remarkable gentleman became a writer as well as an inspiration to everyone who met him. I was fortunate to be among that group. Regrettably Michael did not live to see the completion of this project. His contribution to humanity lives on in his inspirational writing as well as in the writings of those he motivated with his unique dignity and courage. He is missed.

Thank you, Ron Chrisman, for believing in this project from the beginning. My sincerest appreciation also goes to Karen DeVinney, my capable and patient editor.

Preserving history takes on many forms. For their tireless efforts in lovingly restoring the Temple Ferguson mansion to its former glory, I would like to acknowledge Jim and Linda Ellis. But for their efforts, we almost certainly would have lost this historical landmark. Thanks are also due to the efforts of Linda Knight and others who worked to save the structure.

Without question, in the absence of the moral support of certain individuals who believed in me when the idea for this project was pure whimsy, this book would never have been completed. Quite simply put, at the time I began this project, the scope of the task was beyond my understanding. If these family members and friends felt that the task of writing a biography of two Texas governors was entirely too ambitious for this novice, they never disclosed those doubts. As the scale of the undertaking became alarmingly clear, it was their encouragement that kept me moving forward.

My brother Michael O'Keefe was my heartiest champion. A successful writer in his own right, he is a mentor and an unfailing inspiration to me. It would be impossible to overstate his contribution to this work. My husband Guy Wilson, a gifted teacher and a true gentleman, patiently endured my obsession in the pursuit of historical accuracy. My dear friend Charlotte Koehler has given her friendship but so much more ... her time, her support, her ear, and her confidence in me are but a few of the gifts she has consistently offered. These individuals backed the idea for this project from conception and offered unwavering support even when called into service as proofreaders and companions on tedious research excursions.

Lifelong friends Debra Lawhorn and Debra Leggett have blessed my life with their love and support. I also offer a hearty thanks to my friends and former work-family at McLane Company for their encouragement throughout this undertaking.

A special thanks to my mother, Charlene (Tommie) O'Keefe, whose faith in me has always been unshakable. Among the many gifts she gave to me was a love and appreciation for reading. My father, Fred O'Keefe, would have been proud of this work had he lived to see its completion. All of my professional accomplishments stemmed from the good education that my parents made a priority.

A final mention goes to my darling daughters and grandchildren and my wonderful son-in-law Brad all of whom bring joy to my life. There is no greater gift a writer can receive than a supportive backdrop of family and friends who supply alternating doses of encouragement, assistance, and creative solitude. Thank you for understanding that.

Introduction

Dan Moody, campaigning for Ross Sterling in 1930, expressed this sentiment regarding the election of Miriam Ferguson when he said, "Let us not have our children, as they turn the pages of history, say that the Fergusons could do what they have done and still be returned to power in Texas." [1]

Dan Moody anticipated our day, a day when we would revisit those years of Fergusonism and try to make sense of them. We are the future citizens of which he spoke and we can now re-examine and comment on that peculiar circumstance with a retrospective advantage.

James and Miriam Ferguson, separately and jointly, held sway over Texas politics as no couple before or since from roughly 1915 to 1940. Considering that James Ferguson's impeachment occurred early in his political career, his ability to maintain significant influence for more than two additional decades following that ousting is remarkable. Adding his wife, a political novice, to the mix only deepens the mystery as to why a majority of Texas voters would endorse such a scheme.

In some respects, the Ferguson tale lacks closure. For the remainder of his life, James Ferguson proclaimed his innocence on the charges that unseated him in 1917. The details of those charges were rather obscure and complicated, perhaps making it difficult for the public to draw a conclusion. Even for those who doubted Ferguson's innocence, once he was removed from office his punishment seemed complete with the admonishment that he could hold no future state office. Some viewed his refusal to accept that fate as unbridled ambition while others saw it as sheer audacity.

Regardless of our assessment of the Fergusons' success as public servants, one point is undeniable: they were largely successful in getting elected because they were extremely popular with voters. This popularity came via an association with the working class of their day, primarily the rural constituency. Though Jim was a cattleman, by the time he entered politics in 1914 he was far removed from the grueling lifestyle associated with farming and ranching. Even so, this early self-characterization as a country-bumpkin-turned-businessman who fluently spoke the language of the farmer took root and came to define him politically. This country-boy association with the Ferguson name was further perpetuated by Miriam when she entered politics. For a large block of voters, this categorization evoked an unshakable loyalty and an ardent belief that the Fergusons were "our kind of folks" and therefore trustworthy.

This simple depiction of the Fergusons as crusaders for the rural community reflects to a great extent on their intertwined political legacies. The nicknames "Ma" and "Pa," as well as "Farmer Jim," seem to further propagate the myth that the Fergusons were somewhat innocuous political players whose only agenda related to farmers. Adjectives such as cartoonish, witty, and colorful are frequently used to describe the pair, but these descriptions are distortive, minimizing the significance of their power and the impact the duo had on the landscape of Texas politics for a quarter-century.

Unquestionably, the Fergusons had a great deal of influence over the tenor of their public image during their lives and, in many ways, they retain that influence to-day. They accomplished this in several ways, beginning with the destruction of most of the documents in their hands at the completion of their terms. Jim's penchant for suing newspapers that printed articles that reflected negatively on him ensured a lim-ited number of such articles. By contrast, Ferguson's own newspaper, printed weekly for seventeen years and widely circulated, was a vehicle for his views that went largely unchallenged. Through this publication and Ferguson's fiery campaign speeches, he successfully muddied the waters as to his guilt on the impeachment charges and other subsequent rumors of wrongdoing.

Adding to the imbalance of data, the Fergusons' elder daughter, Ouida Ferguson Nalle, joined ranks in the family's efforts to craft a positive Ferguson legacy by publishing a biography of her parents. This highly subjective book—published in 1946, two years after Jim's death—continued the cry of "foul" on behalf of her father. We naturally expect a book written by a family member to hold a bias, and Nalle delivers liberally on that expectation. Due to a scarcity of published material about the ex-governors, Nalle's book titled, *The Fergusons of Texas*, is often used by Ferguson researchers. While it certainly has value in humanizing the disgraced governor, it is dishonest as a comprehensive account by virtue of its critical omissions, errors, and distortions. Its subtitle, *Two Governors for the Price of One*, promises more insight into the couple's terms as governors than it delivers. Instead, it exudes a defensive view and simply reinforces the family's belief that the Fergusons were routinely victimized. [2]

Whatever conclusion we might draw regarding the guilt or innocence and the historical contributions of the Fergusons, it is imperative that we do so based on the pertinent facts. Their political platforms in support of the rural community and their stance against the Ku Klux Klan created the impression that they championed the rights of agrarians and blacks, notions that warrant re-evaluation. Their popu-larity and nicknames aside, and their wittiness and family loyalty notwithstanding, their historical significance lies in the fact that they were key players in Texas history. Texas voters honored them with the sacred trust of public office on four occasions. In accepting that honor, they subjected themselves to the expectation of a high standard of conduct and for this reason we have a right to scrutinize their performance and hold them accountable in that regard. Though their personal conduct was interesting and sometimes entertaining, it is their actions in regard to that sacred trust of public office that are most important in determining their proper place in Texas history.

Prologue—A Tainted Victory

The election result on November 4, 1924, was news bigger than the State of Texas. The political tide was turning in the state, and the results of the election reflected that much-needed change, but the most remarkable aspect of the governor's race was not limited to state or even national appeal. It was worldwide news.

Texas voters had elected Miriam Amanda Ferguson governor, a significant feat in the year 1924, particularly in a southern state like Texas. She was not the first female in the role of governor. That distinction belonged to Nellie Tayloe Ross of Wyoming, elected to fill the term of her husband after his death, but Miriam was only weeks behind her in capturing the honor. Nor was Mrs. Ferguson the first female to hold a public office in Texas. In 1918, following the first primary in which Texas women voted, Annie Webb Blanton won the office of Superintendent of Public Instruction after a heated campaign. However, Mrs. Ferguson's election to the state's highest office was no less astonishing. To assume that Miriam's victory was merely a result of the changing times and evidence of women's emergence into the political world, would be a colossal misjudgment. It would be another fifty years before a female who was not related in some manner to a former male governor would attain a gubernatorial office entirely on her own merits.

Yet Miriam's gender was not the most important aspect of her candidacy. She was in fact the antithesis of feminism, and in every respect the most unlikely of candidates. Every facet of Mrs. Ferguson's journey to the governorship had grown out of extraordinary circumstances beginning with the fact that she had no political experience whatsoever. She could boast of no legal or business background or any other qualification for office, an inadequacy to which she freely admitted throughout her campaign. Forty-nine-year-old Miriam, the mother of two grown daughters and grandmother of one grandson, was typical of her contemporaries in 1924. Since her marriage to James Ferguson in 1899, she had been a devoted homemaker but had held dominion over little else. She mastered the efficient operation of her home with much help, leaving control of the family finances solely under her husband's direction.

In an interview in 1914, at the onset of her husband's political career, Miriam made this statement regarding her sentiments on life and the controversial subject of women's suffrage:

For myself, I have led such a sheltered life and such a contented life, that I have really given little thought to the subject of women's suffrage. My husband has always attended to every business care. I have never had to feel the responsibility of any of that sort of thing, and even if I had the right to vote, I do not think that I would care to use the right. [1]

Her self-confessed life of relative leisure, a life that was largely free of any technical responsibilities, had changed little in the ten years since she had given that interview to a newspaper reporter. Her indifference to the contentious topic of women's suffrage was further testament that Miriam Ferguson had no early political aspirations. No person serious about a future political run could afford the luxury of apathy on such a controversial topic.

If her lack of qualifications were not ominous enough in light of her new role, the reason that she had entered the race was even more disquieting. Mrs. Ferguson ran as a proxy candidate in place of her husband James due to his disqualification from holding a state office. The State had impeached James "Jim" Ferguson from the governor's office in 1917, convicting him on a total of ten charges related to the areas of misappropriations of state funds, banking violations, and charges of improperly influencing certain members of the Board of Regents of the University of Texas.

After her husband's disqualification from candidacy in the 1924 governor's race was upheld, Miriam's name supplanted his on the ballot and the pair joined forces to reclaim the governor's chair. The Ferguson name, as it related to politics, suddenly became plural. There was little, if any, deception on the part of the Ferguson team as to their intentions. Miriam deferred to Jim during campaign speeches, and employed his help in filling in the blanks when reporters asked her about "her" platform.

The Fergusons made no pretense about the driving force behind Mrs. Ferguson's bid for election. They pled for a chance to clear the family name of the stain of impeachment, speaking of the suffering they had endured, their quest for "freedom," and their desperate financial situation. Even this plea contained a hidden message; asking for freedom rather than forgiveness removed any hint of acknowledged guilt and carried the implication that the impeachment was the source of their deprivation. Miriam appealed specifically to the mothers in the audience, asking that they vote for her to facilitate the lifting of the dark cloud that tainted her daughters' names. To Jim, reclaiming the governorship—even using his wife as a vehicle to get there—represented the absolution he sought.

It was not in response to this pleading for forgiveness that caused voters to back the ill-equipped candidate, nor was it popularity or the support of newly enfranchised women that catapulted Mrs. Ferguson to the top in the primary, and later, the general election. In fact, Jim had rebuked suffragists in 1916 as they struggled to obtain a referendum to vote, leaving many to detest and distrust the Ferguson name. Instead, elements of imperfect timing coupled with vote splitting in the primaries had created a quagmire, a perfect storm of political disharmony that rendered a result in candidates that was pleasing to few. [2]

The immense compromise on the part of Texas voters in 1924 that led them to elect a candidate they knew was unsuitable is explainable with three letters: KKK. Many Texans feared the growing power of the Ku Klux Klan whose power and influence grew rapidly after its reemergence in Texas in 1920. In particular, the group's dominance in local law enforcement and other positions of authority troubled many Texans. By 1924, a voting majority vowed to unseat Klan members at all costs. This they did, but in doing so they placed their trust in the hands of a team that amounted to the coupling of the disqualified with the unqualified.

There were Ferguson loyalists who were more than ready to support the pair, but not enough to prevail in the absence of the Klan issue. Even many Ferguson enemies, at least temporarily, cast aside the scars of past discord in support of the Ferguson camp. For example, Martin Crane, a former State's Attorney General and the attorney who had prosecuted Jim in the impeachment trial, offered his support to Miriam. On the other hand, many lifelong Democrats, believing a Ferguson vote was simply unconscionable, resorted to voting for Republican George C. Butte in the general election. [3]

For their part, the Fergusons were totally incapable of acknowledging, perhaps even to themselves, that they were merely the victors in a choice that amounted to a lesser of two evils. The ending of a seven-year stint in the purgatory which they believed legislators had visited upon them as a result of the impeachment, was too sweet a prize to dilute with any such rational thought. They reveled in their victory and took note of their detractors as they prepared to take back the reins of state government.

All eyes were on Texas in 1925 as Mrs. Ferguson took the oath of office. It was not her intention to do so, but by virtue of her election she represented women in their growing desire for acceptance in roles outside of helpmate and mother. Her true goal was entirely personal. The family name that she had fiercely fought to protect could be restored; with the momentum of goodwill created by the defeat of the KKK, she had been given that golden opportunity. Singularly, Jim had made a mess of things. Could they, in concert, produce a better result? Jim Ferguson would find sanctuary as an advisor in the shadow of his wife's governorship; their second chance would begin at this pivotal moment. Their collective ability as leaders, their sincerity of purpose, and, above all, their integrity, were on the line. As recipients of the chance for redemption for which they had so humbly begged, would the Fergusons proceed with actions that would prove them worthy of that hard-fought public trust?

They would not.

Chapter 1
Tangled Family Roots

Although Jim Ferguson and Miriam Wallace lived only a few miles from each other as children, in lifestyles they were worlds apart. Their family roots were slightly intertwined, but it seems that their paths seldom crossed until they were young adults. Each was born to a hardy pioneer family in Bell County in the final years of the state's Reconstruction period, and raised in a rural environment typical of that era. However, for the most part, the similarities in their lives ended there.

Bell County, near the center of Texas but slightly east, benefits from at least one enduring source of recorded history from its earliest days. The son of one of the original pioneers in the area, Judge George W. Tyler was born in 1851 in what would later become neighboring Coryell County (formed 1854). He attended Salado College and received a law degree from Lebanon Law School in Tennessee before setting up a private practice in Belton. During his long life, Tyler accumulated a vast collection of notes and documents that pertained to life in early Bell County. Possessing an interest in local history, Tyler surely used his career in law, his public service as a State Senator from 1888 to 1892, and his extensive community involvement, as opportunities to expand his assemblage of data. Compiled and edited by Charles W. Ramsdell after Tyler's death in 1927, this collection of notes became the basis for a book titled, *History of Bell County.* This work, first published in 1936, chronicles the days when the first white settlers came to the area to carve out new lives in virtual isolation. In the preface, the author speaks of the "gifts of nature" that blessed the land and attracted the newcomers. These gifts included resilient farmland and plentiful water sources which were essential elements for the early settlers who came in search of cheap acreage. Tyler tells of the junction of three streams that came to be known as the Three Forks at Little River, the county's most prominent landmark. The Leon, the Lampasas and the Salado converge to form the Little River, a fertile area that attracted Indians, Spaniards, and later, white settlers. The abundance of stories about Indian conflicts with Anglo settlers included in Tyler's writing, offers evidence of the early clashing of these overlapping cultures. [1]

Listed among the names of the founding families that settled this vast county are both Ferguson and Wallace, each appearing several times in Tyler's account of Bell County's formative years. [2] Most Bell County settlers logically staked their claims near the spring or river's edge, where timber and grasses were abundant and the soil rich. The Wallace and Ferguson families followed that course with differing degrees of success. Small communities emerged from the joint efforts of those early settlers, often beginning with churches and makeshift schools. One of the first of these to materialize in Bell County was Nolandsville (also sometimes shown as Nolanville), established in 1850 and later renamed Belton. Belton was, and still is, the county seat, and for many years was the dominant city in the county. One local historian later referred to Belton with the befitting title of the "Grandma of Bell County." [3]

If Belton could be called the grandmother of the county, Salado, some nine miles south, would certainly be considered one of her oldest children. An ambitious plan to build a great school on a hill overlooking the picturesque Salado Creek spawned the development of the Salado community. That plan came to fruition in 1860 when founders incorporated the stately structure under the name Salado College, a name that is misleading, at least by today's standard. The fine school included elementary levels but was, in reality, a preparatory school and not a college. [4]

With the prestigious institution serving as a keystone, the Salado community quickly developed. Enterprising settlers tapped the area's environmental gifts such as the fast-moving waters of Salado Creek that were ideal for powering mills. These milling services were important to local farmers but also increased commerce by attracting farmers from surrounding counties. The community enjoyed roughly two decades of rapid growth and prosperity before its exclusion from railroad routes halted its progress and sent its population into a decline. Salado was an important and progressive town during its heyday and its citizens made a valuable contribution to the developing Bell County. The emphasis that Salado founders put on education early in their societal development is commendable. Today, Salado is a charming village that remembers and honors its proud history, particularly the historic mills that once held great significance to its development, the illustrious school that once graced the hill, and its distinction as a stopping point on the bygone stagecoach line. [5]

The toil of those early settlers had hardly begun when a most egregious interruption in the form of the Civil War fell upon them. They were by vast majority secessionists, a point well made in 1860 when an impassioned speech against secession, made from the balcony of Salado's Stagecoach Inn, brought a light pelting of stones. The speaker was the governor of Texas, General Sam Houston. He fared no better when he took his speech to Belton where a man threatened to shoot him from the perch of packing boxes that represented his makeshift platform. Needless to say, Bell County voters were not swayed by the governor's sentiment and later voted heavily in favor of secession. [6] They then backed their conviction with might; Tyler spoke with pride of Bell County's participation in the war effort, saying, "Bell County, at the beginning of the war, did not exceed four thousand in white population, yet the muster rolls of her soldiery credited her with more than one thousand men and boys who donned the Confederate gray. No county or country, we believe, ever made a better showing of loyalty to home and fireside." [7]

But not all southerners donned the gray. The Civil War has often been characterized as a war of brother-against-brother and the saying was quite literal in the Ferguson family. The relationship between (future governor) Jim Ferguson's father, James Eldridge Ferguson, a Methodist minister, and his brother Wesley G. Ferguson was forever severed when Wesley declared his Union sympathies in 1861.

Reverend James Ferguson married Fannie Phillips Fitzpatrick in Victoria, Texas, in 1855, but moved to Houston and began preaching before the onset of the war. Though Wesley lived in Bell County where James moved at the end of the war, their fierce differences were too acute to ever be discharged. So unyielding was Reverend Ferguson's conviction that he saw, even after the war's end, only disappointment and shame in his Brother Wesley's allegiance to the Union. James proudly fought for the Confederacy, and though details of his service and the years immediately following it are obscure, we know that he made his way back to East Texas by late 1863, a point demonstrated by the birth of the couple's second son in August of 1864. The growing Ferguson family moved to Bell County in 1867, where James purchased a small farm and grist mill on the banks of Salado Creek and resumed his ministry. [8]

Reverend James Ferguson's estranged brother Wesley died in 1868, leaving a widow, Eliza Garrison Ferguson, and two young daughters, Annie and Mary, ten and four years of age, respectively. The punishment imposed upon Wesley by his family for the disgrace he had inflicted upon the family name, was an eternal one. Today, a secluded tombstone sits behind a home in rural Bell County marking the grave of Wesley Ferguson, buried in isolation from other family members who retained their honor in the family with their unshakeable Southern loyalty.[9]

Joseph Wallace, Miriam's father, also fought for the Confederacy. At the war's conclusion he returned to, and took possession of the Wallace family farm in Bell County. In 1869 he married Eliza Ferguson, the widow of Wesley Ferguson, a union that distantly connected the Ferguson and Wallace households and created, for Joseph Wallace, an instant family. Eliza's daughters, Annie and Mary, would be both half-sibling to Eliza's future offspring with Joseph, and cousins to the children of Reverend James and Fannie Ferguson.

In the early 1870s, the inhabitants of Bell County were still wrestling with the demoralizing effects of Reconstruction and the rampant lawlessness that followed as they labored to make a living off the land. One writer of early Bell County history, Bertha Atkinson, offered her perspective on the days after the Civil War with this statement: "The political condition throughout Texas during the Reconstruction period was almost unbearable. It might well be said that the citizens had no political rights. The trials and dangers of Reconstruction days were even more devastating to the country and exasperating to the southern spirit than the period of the war had been." [10]

During this protracted period of uncertainty and under the influence of the resilient spirit that prevailed in its wake, James Edward Ferguson and Miriam Amanda Wallace were born some six miles and four years apart.

The young James Edward Ferguson, born on the farm on Salado Creek on August 31, 1871, to the circuit-riding Methodist minister, James Eldridge Ferguson, and his wife Fannie, was an unlikely candidate for anything requiring the benefit of a stable and prosperous family life. He was the sixth child to his mother, Fannie, but not her last. One more sibling, a boy named Alexander, would be born almost three years later to a family that could ill-afford the addition. With the birth of the family's last child in early 1874, two-year-old Jim became the charge of his sister Kate, who was twelve years his senior. Two earlier babies had died at birth, but the surviving family of seven struggled to live on the meager wages of a frontier minister. Fannie and the children worked the family farm and grist mill on Salado Creek in the frequent absence of the elder Ferguson. In doing so, they often found themselves at the mercy of the unpredictable Texas weather. Frequent droughts produced a double hardship: they compromised the level of the swift creek water needed to power the mill and caused parched crops to wither.

Nature's elements were not the only obstacles facing these Texans in the years after the war. They labored to overcome the after-effects of their lost cause, often at the mercy of Union garrisons sent to take over the existing local governments and address the interests of freed slaves. This, coupled with the confiscation of their possessions, left many Texans feeling bitter and powerless. In some cases, this discontent manifested itself in subversive acts of rebellion, and within this setting the first order of the Ku Klux Klan emerged.[11]

Writer Charles C. Alexander in *The Ku Klux Klan in the Southwest*, makes this distinction between the original Klan and subsequent uprisings of the group: "The average citizen does not realize that historically there are not one but three Klans. The first was the Ku Klux Klan of the Reconstruction period—secret, political, often violent, pre-occupied with turning out the Radical Republican state and local governments in the South and with proscribing the recently emancipated Negroes and their white Republican allies." [12]

Bell County certainly had an early order of Klan members and one local historian suggested that the feisty Reverend James Ferguson launched it. This revelation, from a single source, is certainly questionable. There is little in the way of local recorded history to validate or repudiate specific Klan affiliation, a fact not surprising given the secret nature of the organization and the dissociation that became common after people understood the extent of its evils. While Tyler's work, as well as that of other writers of early local history, contains references to local Klan activity, they are silent in attaching names to Klan members. That silence likely confirms the kind of intimidation the Klan's presence imposed.[13]

Tyler described the mission of the early local Klan in a way that seemed to mirror Charles Alexander's description: "It was to protect society, to put the carpet-bagger and the scalawags out of business, to restore the negro to his sober common sense and to readjust the country to normal social conditions."[14]

Most Southerners saw Union efforts such as the Freemen's Bureau as over-corrections to the plight of recently freed slaves. While Tyler's account may seem like an endorsement of the group's mission, in fairness to him, it is necessary to add that he later expressed this opinion about the Klan that later reemerged: "There is not even an imaginary necessity in this day and time for the existence of such an organization in our country, North or South."[15] The original version of the Klan was relatively short-lived. It began in 1867, but by 1870 was disbanded through an order of the commander, Grand Wizard Nathan B. Forrest, a former Confederate War general. Though the ill-conceived, vigilante-style concept of order lay dormant for several decades, unfortunately when it returned, it did so with a vengeance.

Whether or not the Reverend Ferguson led or otherwise participated in the fleeting efforts of that early Klan activity, one point is clear. Timidity would not have been a reason for the reverend's detachment from this or any other controversial activity. By all accounts, the good reverend was no stranger to controversy and was never afraid to speak his mind. Parson Ferguson was a fiery character, described as a man of distinction who also displayed tendencies for impulsiveness and rashness. Even though he was blessed with large doses of physical strength and was a man of God, his staunch political opinions at times so provoked his listeners that they challenged him to physical fights. It seems that the spirited reverend's pontificating sometimes tested the boundaries of his listeners' tolerance for criticism and conflicting opinion. Of necessity, Ferguson, like other circuit-riding ministers of the day, carried a Bible in one hand and a six-shooter in the other. It was dangerous work that paid little and too often left the minister's family alone and vulnerable. [16]

In 1871, the year of Jim's birth, Parson Ferguson had the rare experience of reading his own glowing obituary in a newspaper. Written by a friend who had fought alongside him in the Civil War, the article lamented the recent death of the reverend, a tragedy that rendered the writer "grieved beyond the power of expression." The friend further extolled the virtues of the reverend along with his shock in learning that the wound that had at first been declared survivable, had proved fatal. In truth, the first story had been correct; the ball, from a navy six-shooter, had entered Ferguson's face below the eye and lodged near his tongue but had been successfully removed. By the time the reverend read his obituary, he was mending nicely. A retraction of the death announcement appeared the following day and some five weeks later an open letter of thanks appeared from the reverend. In that letter, Ferguson expressed his sentiment saying, "Yet I am published as dead, and have before me two sketches of my life, evidently written by warm hearted friends… My generous friends embalm my memory with a recital of my supposed excellencies [*sic*], and open wide their mantel of charity to hide my faults."[17]

Death came to the reverend in earnest, so to speak, some four years later when he rapidly developed a lethal case of pneumonia while attending a conference in Waco. His funeral, a Masonic ceremony, was well-attended. Many years later the Fergusons' daughter, Ouida Ferguson Nalle, described in detail her grandfather's home-made coffin and the impact the death had on her father who was a child of four at the time. At the time of his demise, James Eldridge Ferguson was fifty-one, his widow just thirty-six. The couple's surviving children were Alvah, age sixteen, Kate thirteen, Joe Lee ten, Jim four, and Alex one.[18]

With the death of the elder Ferguson, a difficult existence became even more so for Fannie and her young brood. Fannie soon (and often) petitioned the court for permission to sell off small parcels of land, requests she made with this expressed need: "in support of my minor children." The labor of her children was critical to the family's survival throughout Jim's childhood. Years later Jim expressed distaste for the sport of hunting because he saw it as a painful reminder of a desperate time when hunting was a necessity. When Jim was eleven, another element rocked the stability of his surroundings when his doting sister

Kate married and moved to distant Haskell County with her husband, Frances M. Morton. [19]

The personality of the rough-and-tumble willful child named Jim revealed itself early in his life. He was competitive, outspoken, often got into physical fights with other boys, and relished any opportunity to express his opinion. Sam Sparks, Jim Ferguson's enemy-turned-friend, turned-enemy again, told one story about the boyhood antics of fifteen-year-old Jim. Sparks, the son of the sheriff of Bell County and later the sheriff of that county himself, attended the same Salado school as Jim in 1886. Many years later, he told a story about his first day at school when Jim, without provocation, challenged him to a fight. Per Sparks, he bested Jim in the fight but apparently no grudge resulted because soon after, the two became friends. They remained friends from that time until 1913 when their political ambitions collided. [20]

Many children in rural families of that day received sporadic educations due to the need for their labor on the family farm, often working the fields alongside former slaves. Bell County records for the year 1900 show the average amount of time spent at school was just over four months. Though the Salado area, with its emphasis on education, offered a good environment and opportunity for a quality education at its fine school, the private school was not without cost. It took a sacrifice on the part of the family to send a child to the popular institution on the hill, forgoing his labor at home. Young Jim was fortunate that his widowed mother Fannie made such a sacrifice for her children. Fannie knew well the importance of education; her Uncle Benjamin Fitzpatrick had twice been the governor of Alabama and had also been a state senator. While Jim's younger brother, Alex, was able to obtain an education sufficient to enable him to complete his education at Texas A & M University where he later also taught, it seems that Jim was not inclined to muster the same level of self-discipline. [21]

In fact, an overabundance of pride ended Jim's formal education. His good fortune related to his educational opportunities included his living quarters during his years at the esteemed Salado school. He boarded at the historic James Anderson house in Salado, an impressive home built on the edge of a former Indian encampment within easy walking distance of the school. But when Jim was sixteen this ideal situation ended abruptly with his expulsion for disobedience. When a teacher asked Jim and other boys to cut and bring in firewood for the school, Jim's resolve not to do so apparently outweighed his scholastic ambition, and he boldly refused. This defiance provides an early glimpse at Jim's temperament, but his waived opportunity to remain in school with a simple apology speaks volumes. Jim Ferguson made no apologies. [22]

By the time of his expulsion in 1887, Jim's three oldest siblings were married. This left Fannie to run the farm and mill with thirteen-year-old Alex and, at most, a few hired hands. The free time that was then available to Jim afforded him an opportunity to assist his mother in running the family business, but the restless and curious adolescent chose instead to embark on an adventure. His mother's scorn for his expulsion may also have contributed to Jim's imprudent decision to take up traveling, but more likely Jim found the prospect of chopping wood at home no less appealing than it had been at school. Considering the sacrifices Fannie made to send her son to school, she probably expressed her disappointment in the petty argument that ended his education. Whatever the cause, the young teen headed west on a prolonged journey, eventually making his way all the way to California and back, where he no doubt learned a multitude of lessons in the school of hard knocks. Years later, Ouida Ferguson Nalle described her father's exploit in this way: "The pioneer urge was pushing Jim Ferguson to move on; the West was calling. He had lived all of sixteen years in Bell County, Texas! It was time to make a change, so, without imparting his thoughts and ideas to any of his family, he disappeared. For almost two years, neither family nor friends had the remotest idea where he was." [23]

Interestingly, years later, in 1914, Jim spoke of his westward adventure in his first political speech in Blum, Texas, saying, "I bid farewell to my Mother and . . ." [24] This seemingly innocuous statement is thought-provoking. Assuming his daughter's account of events was true, for two years Jim's widowed mother suffered the uncertainty of not knowing her son's fate or whereabouts. The modification of the story Jim crafted in his 1914 speech cleverly altered that critical point. A more mature Jim likely realized the implication of his actions, but rather than admit to his juvenile insensitivity, James Ferguson simply retold a sanitized version of the tale.

On this westward exploit, which included a stint in Washington State, a variety of unskilled jobs including work in a mine, a vineyard, a barbed wire fence factory, a restaurant as a waiter, and as a bellman at a hotel, barely sustained the adolescent Jim. He returned to Bell County with little more than a satisfied curiosity about western states and bragging rights about his great adventure, which he may have embellished. [25]

Once he was back in Bell County, Jim went to work as a bridge builder for the railroad, a job he held for several years before returning to work the family farm in 1895. Suddenly struck with the notion that being a lawyer was a good idea, Jim approached boyhood friend John D. Robinson, who was attending law school, and asked him to pass along his lecture notes. It was the beginning of a self-education in law that eventually afforded Jim an opportunity to become a lawyer while bypassing law school. He studied law books at night, but as Jim himself admitted, it was not a comprehensive study; he later described it as "simply a study of the basic fundamentals of law." [26]

Jim Ferguson's prospects may have seemed bleak to an observer, but his inability to see those limitations allowed him an optimism that served him well as a young man. His actions support the notion that he was confident, tenacious, and unafraid to try the seemingly impossible. Armed with only an elementary command of the law, he was admitted to the bar, but even this accomplishment, while noble, was not without controversy. Obtaining admission to the bar during the nineteenth century was quite easy, but even the relaxed standards of the day were compromised in Jim's case. Jim confessed that the committee of three lawyers whose task it was to give him an oral exam for admittance to the bar, did not ask him a single question. Instead, they passed him with a toast of whiskey on the strength of their friendships with his long-deceased father. While the oral testing method was appropriate in the 1890s, doing so without a legitimate exam certainly was not. The gentlemen did society in general and young Jim Ferguson in particular, no favor in passing him without an earnest test. A traditional education in law certainly would have rendered him more successful at practicing law, and it might have sent Jim in a different direction entirely. He later said of the legal profession, "It did not exactly suit me." [27] The responsibility for the oral examination clearly fell to the lawyers appointed to that duty, but Jim's comment on his question-free licensing is interesting. "A green lawyer can't do anybody much harm. If he doesn't work and gain an adequate knowledge of the law, nobody will hire him. If he is to make a living, he must know something about the law… There is no efficacy in working youngsters to death making them learn the answers to questions that the boys or the professors who asked them can't answer three weeks later. Just turn 'um lose, and if they are lawyers, it will soon show up in their success." [28]

Perhaps Jim's best show of persistence was in his pursuit of neighbor Miriam Wallace as a wife. The Joseph Wallace family consisted of six children, including the two Ferguson daughters that Eliza brought to the family unit. Two Wallace sons, Warner and William, were born in 1871 and 1873 respectively. Miriam was born on June 13, 1875, the third child but Joseph's first natural daughter. In 1877, the arrival of Miriam's sister, Susan Priscilla, blessed the family. Susan Priscilla, tagged "John" at an early age, found the nickname inescapable. Two other Wallace children died young, but the remaining four girls (including the two Ferguson stepdaughters) and two boys enjoyed the stability and benefits of a loving and flourishing, God-fearing home. Miriam's half-sister Annie Ferguson married and left the Wallace household in 1873, two years before Miriam was born, and Mary Ferguson married in 1883. Their initial homestead was a log cabin that Joseph built on the banks of the Little River a few miles northeast of Salado. When the children were still young, Joseph relocated the family some six miles to the northwest to a large holding of rich prairie-like farmland where he built a grand new home.

The major distinction that defined the Wallace family was prosperity. Miriam's father, Joseph, was a frugal man, dedicated to his family and farm; his years of hard work and good judgment had allowed him to accumulate a fortune and a somewhat privileged existence for his family. In addition to other accomplishments, the family had secured a good education for all of the children, even the daughters.

Joseph Wallace was a pioneer in every respect but was particularly progressive in fence building, tick eradication, and well digging. His spring-fed well produced such an abundance of clear water that he invited neighboring families to use it, an act of generosity that brought the Wallace family a degree of social prominence. So popular was Joseph that neighboring children dubbed him "Uncle Joe." Clean, cool water was a precious commodity in the Texas heat and the plentiful supply made it possible for the creative Mr. Wallace to set up a unique bath house with several tubs, complete with running water. Neighbors enjoyed these novelties by the wagonload when in search of a quick and easy bath, a rare treat for most. [29]

Post-Civil War Texas inadvertently offered an opportunity that benefited anyone smart and energetic enough to capitalize on it. This opportunity stemmed from a surplus of cattle in Texas, a condition in stark contrast to a depleted source of beef in the northern states due to the war. Joe Wallace was both smart and energetic and was among the ranks of those who made sizable profits in raising and transporting cattle by cattle drive or rail to Kansas City and beyond. In addition to the success that the Wallace family enjoyed from raising cattle, they benefited from a farm that was largely self-sustaining. Native pecan trees and an orchard produced a bounty of food and seeds, and cotton, the cash crop in Texas, also flourished.

However, in early February of 1899, the solidity and welfare of the Wallace family was forever altered by the sudden death of their patriarch. An obituary in the newspaper in the nearby city of Temple announced the passing of Joseph Wallace and expressed the opinion that Wallace was, "one of our most influential citizens." The cause of death was pneumonia.[30]

This void left Eliza, Miriam's mother, with the oversight of the large fortune in land, livestock, and cash she inherited. Ouida Ferguson would later characterize her grandfather Joseph Wallace's estate with these words: "Miriam's mother turned away from her husband's grave to find that he had left $50,000 in cash, a sizable fortune for that day, several thousand acres of rich farm land, a couple of cotton gins, and a good block of stock in a Belton Bank." [31]

Bell County probate records offered a more specific inventory and valuation of the Wallace assets. The acreage left to Eliza Wallace totaled 2,582. The value of those acres of timbered land and prairie farmland was placed at approximately $70,500 on April 3, 1899. The estate also included a half interest in three gins, about $5,000's worth of livestock, and about $7,000 in cash and notes receivable. The "good block of bank stock" consisted of four shares in the Belton National Bank valued at one hundred dollars per share. The words that Joseph Wallace chose in drawing his will reflected his strong faith and his abiding love of family. He bequeathed "the estate with which it has pleased God to bless me," to his "beloved wife." A life insurance policy valued at $4,548.00 proved further that Joseph Wallace's plans included taking every precaution to protect his family. The total value of the estate was $87,494.06, indeed a large sum for that day. [32]

Unlike Jim's mother, Fannie, the widowed Eliza was well-supplied with hired hands and other assets needed to facilitate the operation of the family farm, but in matters of business she was less supported. According to recollections later expressed by Ouida Ferguson Nalle, Jim Ferguson was eager to assist Eliza in managing her financial holdings. His visits to the family farm increased, as did his attention to Miriam. Before long, the smooth-talking Jim had managed to obtain a diamond ring for himself, a gift from his grateful Aunt Eliza, but the ambitious young scout had his eye on a larger prize. He was determined to marry Miriam. [33]

Miriam was very well-educated by the standard of the day. The nearby prestigious Baylor College for Women in Belton offered the perfect complement to her earlier education. This expansive, Christian university eventually became coeducational and changed its name to the University of Mary Hardin-Baylor. Miriam and her sister "John" attended the college for two terms beginning in the 1893–1894 term when they studied a general curriculum as well as piano. With her good education and secure home, Miriam had no need to marry to raise her station in life. Family lore held that it was Jim's power of persuasion applied in liberal doses that compelled the complacent Miriam Wallace to agree to marriage. Young Jim, who had successfully campaigned for the position of Belton's city attorney shortly before the couple became engaged, likely impressed young Miriam with this and other displays of ambition. Their wedding took place on the last day of the century,

December 31, 1899, in the parlor of the beautiful Wallace home, where County Judge D. R. Pendleton officiated. [34]

Newlyweds Jim and Miriam enjoyed the benefit of Miriam's prosperous family from the beginning of their union. The widowed Eliza was generous, building the young couple a house on a prominent corner that Jim purchased on May 14, 1900, in nearby Belton. Here they lived happily for the first seven years of their marriage during which time two significant events occurred: the births of two daughters, Ouida (pronounced Wee-da) in 1901, and Ruby Dorrace, who was always called Dorrace, in 1903. [35]

Jim successfully ran a second campaign for Belton city attorney and his boyhood schoolmate and friend, Sam Sparks, ran a successful campaign for sheriff. From the beginning, Jim spared no advantage to his bride Miriam and her comfort. The household employed a maid and a yardman early on, and later when the babies arrived, Jim sent for his mother, Fannie, who came and assisted. Jim's belief that he had married "up" set a tone of respect and admiration in his marriage, and this veneration, which never waned, extended to his daughters. The female members of the Ferguson family responded in kind and except for of some sibling rivalry, the family unit was extremely strong.

Life was good and a bright and prosperous future seemed almost certain for the young Ferguson family. But Jim's restless nature, so dominant that it had prompted him to take an impulsive trip west, and the disregard he exhibited toward his family's feelings in his decision to do so, were pervasive characteristics that continued to exist in Jim Ferguson. Several years of peaceful life lay ahead for the family, but Jim's impulsiveness and willfulness would eventually manifest themselves into a journey of a different kind, a journey that would dominate the rest of their lives.

Form 618   Maverick-Clarke Litho. Co., Stationers, Printers, Lithographers, San Antonio. 198   55

MARRIAGE RECORD.

THE STATE OF TEXAS,

County of _Bell_

To any Regularly Licensed or Ordained Minister of the Gospel, Jewish Rabbi, Judge of the District or County Court, or any Justice of the Peace, in and for _Bell_ County—GREETING:

You Are Hereby Authorized to Solemnize the Rites of Matrimony Between

Mr. _James E. Ferguson_ and Miss _Miriam A. Wallace_

and make due return to the Clerk of the County Court of said County within sixty days thereafter, certifying your action under this License.

Witness my official signature and seal of office, at office in _Belton_

the _30th_ day of _Dec_ 1899

Ben D Lee Clerk

of County Court, _Bell_ County.

By _A. M. Lee_ Deputy.

I, _D R Pendleton_, hereby certify that on the _31st_ day of _December_ 1899 I united in Marriage _James E Ferguson_ and _Mrs Miriam Wallace_ the parties above named.

Witness my hand this _8th_ day of _Jany_ 1900

D R Pendleton County Judge Bell Co Texas

Returned and filed for record the _8_ day of _Jany_ 1900, and recorded the _24_ day of _Feby_ 1900

Ben D Lee County Clerk.

By _R H Turner_ Deputy.

THE STATE OF TEXAS,

County of _Bell_

To any Regularly Licensed or Ordained Minister of the Gospel, Jewish Rabbi, Judge of the District or County Court, or any Justice of the Peace, in and for _Bell_ County—GREETING:

You Are Hereby Authorized to Solemnize the Rites of Matrimony Between

Mr. _J W Thompson_ and Miss _Nettie Bailey_

and make due return to the Clerk of the County Court of said County within sixty days thereafter, certifying your action under this License.

Witness my official signature and seal of office, at office in _Belton_

the _30th_ day of _Dec_ 1899

Ben D Lee Clerk

of County Court, _Bell_ County.

By _A. M. Lee_ Deputy.

I, _R M Dunlap_, hereby certify that on the _31_ day of _December_ 1899 I united in Marriage _J Thompson_ and _Nettie Brasley_ the parties above named.

Witness my hand this _31st_ day of _Dec_ 1899,

R M Dunlap Minister of the Gospel

Returned and filed for record the _9_ day of _Jany_ 1900, and recorded the _24_ day of _Feby_ 1900

Ben D Lee County Clerk.

By _R H Turner_ Deputy.

1899 Marriage Record for James E. and Miriam A. Ferguson

13

Chapter 2
Life Unencumbered

The opportunistic and impetuous aspects of Jim Ferguson's character presented themselves early in his life, but nowhere were they more prevalent than in his choices of business ventures. From the beginning, he was speculative, spreading his business interests in a variety of directions and frequently jumping from one venture to another, all in areas where he was not well-versed, perhaps a testament to his self-confidence. During the first years of his marriage, Jim dabbled in various undertakings including a second term as Belton city attorney, which he won in 1902. In May 1901 he and other investors chartered the Gusher Oil Company in an attempt to capitalize on the oil boom that was sweeping the state. In January of that year, the salt dome Spindletop oil field had struck vast supplies of the fuel, rousing, almost overnight, hordes of "wildcat" speculators most of which, like Ferguson, were unsuccessful. In 1902 Ferguson was among five who chartered the Central Company of Belton, an endeavor meant to establish and maintain a hotel. After his stint as city attorney, Jim engaged in a short-lived law practice with John D. Robinson, the friend who had graciously shared his notes from law school. That relationship apparently ended amicably, with Ferguson moving into a private law practice in a space he shared with two other attorneys. Robinson was successful; he eventually became a district judge and a hearty supporter of Jim Ferguson's first political campaign in 1914. In January of 1904, Jim, with two associates, D. R. Pendleton and E. C. Clabaugh, chartered the Belton Trust and Loan Company, an establishment whose primary purpose was that of lending money to farmers.[1]

The newly chartered Belton Trust and Loan Company, as well as Jim's law practice, ended abruptly between the hours of ten and eleven p.m. on the frigid night of February 18, 1905, when a fire destroyed the space that each occupied as well as an opera house on the floor above. The details of the calamity, as reported by three newspapers, were somewhat inconsistent. What is certain about that

February night is the complete loss of the opera house structure, which occupied the upper level of the building, and the loss of at least three other businesses located below. Only the efforts of a bucket brigade saved a number of nearby residences from a similar fate that windy night. All accounts agreed that the office space shared by lawyers D. R. Pendleton, John B. Durrett, and James E. Ferguson were included in the loss. One version of events held that a feed store, located below the opera house, had also been destroyed. The greatest contradictions came in reports of estimated property value and the amount of insurance coverage that existed, though all accounts agreed that the opera building was underinsured and the contents of the law offices, as well as the contents of the loan company, were entirely uninsured. [2]

Jim Ferguson had much to lose in that mid-winter catastrophe because the loss represented a triple threat to his business interests. In addition to his investment in the loan company and his law practice, he was among five investors who owned the opera-house portion, which was by far the largest part of the lost building. This group, among whom was Ferguson's lawyer friend D. R. Pendleton, had acquired the opera house in March of 1903 for a sum of $12,800. Pendleton alone had purchased separately the three storefronts under the opera house for $2,500 in September of the same year. In Ouida's account of the story, the loss of Jim's investment in the underinsured opera building, together with the destruction of his legal library, resulted in a heavy financial loss to the family. However, as a basis for this calculation she placed the value of her father's legal library at $6,000, twice the value that newspapers reported at the time of the fire, and twelve times the $500 value that Pendleton placed on his law library. She further claimed that her father was compensated with a cash total of $2,000 for his loss. [3]

The damage to the structure was extensive; daylight revealed little more than a blackened lot. In view of the devastation and formidable task of rebuilding, four of the opera house owners, including Jim, chose to sell out their interest in the establishment to the fifth owner rather than rebuild. Likewise Jim and associates Pendleton and Clabaugh agreed not to reopen the loan company and Jim used the opportunity to discontinue his private law practice. Perhaps it had occurred to Jim by that time, as he later confessed, that the law profession did not suit him.

The one-year life of the Belton Trust and Loan Company may have been a stormy one for its owners. In 1914, when Jim Ferguson ran for governor, former associates Pendleton and Clabaugh strongly supported his opponent. When, that same year, the trust company was accused of having charged usurious rates, Jim Ferguson diminished his role saying, "If there was any crime about that, I want it to be remembered that I was only the secretary-treasurer of the company." [4]

Judging from his future business pursuits, Ferguson had decided that another venture in banking was more to his liking. In September of 1905 he joined forces with two new Belton associates, Columbus Jackson and C. W. Shannon, and chartered a new bank, the Farmer's State Bank of Belton, which opened on October 1. Ferguson was the president of the establishment, but not for long. In September of 1906 J. Z. Miller, president of the First National Bank of Belton bought controlling interest in the establishment and closed its doors, ending the one-year life of the Farmer's State Bank of Belton. [5]

Soon after his exit from the Farmer's State Bank of Belton, Ferguson set his sights on the fast growing nearby sister-city of Temple, which was expanding rapidly due to the growth-producing activity of major rail lines. As one old-timer put it, "After a few years of mud-bound infancy, Temple began to grow like Johnson grass." By 1900, Temple's population had risen to over 7,000, greatly surpassing Belton's population of 3,700. By 1907, Temple's population had reached over 12,000 and she boasted of the construction of 300 new residences in 1906 alone. The Gulf, Colorado & Santa Fe and the Missouri-Kansas-Texas (nicknamed the Katy) rail lines spurred much of the growth. They established a fine depot while providing employment and increased commerce via the flow of incoming and outgoing goods. The city also boasted a fine Y. M. C. A., a large hospital operated by the Santa Fe railroad and an array of other businesses and public buildings. Temple was so prosperous that a plan for relocating the county seat from Belton had once been launched. Although that plan never materialized, it did nothing to diminish the outlook of the booming town. Indeed, at the turn of the century, the city of Temple was certainly considered a rising star among towns in Central Texas, so much so that her popularity generated this saying: "If you want to play, go to Temple; if you want to do some business, go to Temple; and if you are sick, by all means go to Temple."[6]

Temple began the year 1906 with three banks, the First National Bank, chartered in 1884, the Temple National Bank, chartered in 1887, and City National Bank, chartered in 1902. Newspapers reported that a healthy sum of two million dollars was held collectively by these prosperous banks as 1906 began. But early in that year the Temple National closed, leaving not only an opportunity to capture its portion of the market, but a vacant space specifically suited for a bank. Ferguson seized the opportunity, chartered a new bank, and moved into the vacated space. On May 1, 1906, the Temple State Bank, after some delays, opened under the leadership of J. E. Ferguson, president, with a beginning capital of $50,000. Ferguson's initial percentage of ownership was not disclosed, but in 1915, his ownership in the bank amounted to a little over one-fourth.[7]

The operation of the Temple State bank offered a level of stabilization to the career of its young president but the eight-mile trolley commute from Belton to Temple proved inconvenient, an annoyance for which Jim soon concocted a remedy. The obvious solution was a move to the flourishing town of Temple. On March 22, 1907, Jim purchased a residential double lot from James and M. A. Stanton at a cost of $4,250 on the prestigious north side of Temple. The price suggests and another source indicates that a home already existed on the property when Ferguson purchased it. The Stanton house was likely moved to the farthest corner of the lot and converted to maid's quarters. The location, only a few blocks from the bank, was ideal for the family and Jim soon contracted the construction of a new two-story Victorian-style mansion for his young family. The mansion included every modern convenience of the day, including sleeping porches, indoor plumbing, and three fireplaces. The structure also boasted expansive wrap-around porches on two levels, rich woodwork, two staircases, a stylish portico, and a detached carriage house and servants' quarters. However, according to Ouida, the plan lacked one critical aspect: an endorsement by Mrs. Ferguson.[8]

If his wife's approval was an obstacle in fulfilling his plan to move, it proved a small hurdle. Jim Ferguson apparently obtained a concession, and the family made the move to Temple. The family's cook and gardener relocated with the Fergusons, and the household added the services of a chauffeur to their staff because the prestigious Ferguson family also boasted ownership of another modern extravagance, an automobile.

The young Ferguson family was well set because Eliza Wallace, Miriam's widowed mother, generously divided and distributed most of her fortune to her children in 1907. On November 29, 1907, Eliza conveyed for the consideration of "love and affection" and one dollar, tracts of land to each of her and Joseph's four children. Miriam and her brother William received 832 acres of prairie land while siblings Priscilla (aka John) and Warner each received 470 acres of forested property. The estate Eliza had inherited in early 1899 included, in addition to that land, a considerable amount of personal property, a large amount of livestock, and life insurance totaling over $87,000, enough for each of the children to receive a sizable inheritance. Eliza would live the balance of her life with her time divided between her adult children to whom she had been most generous. It appears that she held back very little of the fortune she and Joseph had accumulated; when she died in 1915, the value of the assets she had retained was a mere $5,000. [9]

Remembering that Jim was Eliza's financial advisor adds an interesting element to the story. Miriam's part of the inheritance included the Wallace homestead, a substantial asset. Located about twelve miles south of Temple near a community called Sparks, the property was generally referred to by the family as the Sparks farm. This inheritance added a nice cushion of financial security to the promising future of the Ferguson family.

When the 1907 move to Temple occurred, Ouida was six years old and Dorrace three. It was, by Ouida's admission, a very happy time. Though their personalities were vastly dissimilar, Jim and Miriam had, by all accounts, a loving relationship built on mutual respect and a shared devotion to their daughters. Jim was gregarious and keenly interested in politics. He craved social interaction, but found it difficult to work with others because he was highly competitive and domineering. Miriam was quite the opposite. She was largely apolitical and generally avoided social contact with the exception of church. She was fiercely protective of her family and though not particularly demonstrative, was a doting mother. Though her good education, urban setting, and relative leisure made her a good candidate for the emerging movement that saw increased social involvement by women, her personality did not. She consistently declined invitations to join women's clubs and other secular groups. She was a Christian, but her faith was not shared by her husband. Miriam often lamented that Jim's religious views were not in harmony with her own, but claimed that he had put aside his feelings and attended church with the family as a "spectator." Jim also made references to his lack of faith from time to time. In one early political speech he said, "In my time I have neither preached nor prayed but little." Though he frequently clashed with religious leaders in his life, and demonstrated little in the way of faith, this stark difference in religious philosophy seemed somehow to have been reconcilable between husband and wife in the Ferguson household.[10]

Interestingly, the temperaments of the Ferguson daughters mirrored their parents' with startling similarity, Ouida having the outgoing and spontaneous traits of her father. As children, Ouida was mischievous and outspoken, much to the chagrin of her mother and sister, while Dorrace was a docile and obedient child, a sensitive soul who shied away from the spotlight at every opportunity. The Ferguson sisters, with their polar personalities, both admitted that the stormy nature of their relationship lingered into adulthood. Ouida seemed never to outgrow the belief that her mother preferred Dorrace to her, saying: "Next to Dorrace, Mama loved flowers more than anything else."[11]

Ouida Ferguson's perceptions and remembrances were sometimes short of accurate. She described the life of the Ferguson family during those early days in Temple as typical of small-town America. In reality, the typical 1907 Texas family lived on a farm and was far less advantaged. Her description of the Temple home, which was the envy of those who watched its construction, was thus: "It was a mansion for Temple in those days, but it never, by the wildest stretch of the imagination, could have been called beautiful." Her Uncle Alex would have disagreed. So enamored with the home was he that he built an identical home in Howe, Texas, for his family. The Fergusons enjoyed the prestige of being one of the more prominent families in town, and they lived a privileged life in almost every respect. Ouida and Dorrace enjoyed an array of luxuries beginning with their well-appointed home. Also included in their good fortune were private schools, music lessons, custom-made clothing, a household free of financial concerns, and evenings spent at the local opera house where the girls watched stage productions with their parents. Routinely, the family delighted in drives in the country in the family's automobile, another extravagance. These trips saw Miriam or the family chauffeur at the wheel because Jim never learned to drive.[12]

Politics was always a topic open for discussion in the Ferguson home and the privilege of expressing one's opinion was not limited to the adults. An eavesdropper to those early conversations about women's suffrage would have witnessed a decided opposition to the notion by Jim. He certainly feared, quite legitimately, that the female vote would usher in prohibition. Miriam's sentiment leaned more towards indifference, not an uncommon view given her inclination to follow Victorian principles. The social climate of her day had many women holding a view that business and voting were burdens that were simply better left to their male counterparts. But the enfranchisement of women in the territories of Utah and Wyoming and the state of Washington, followed by California, Oregon, Kansas and Arizona, had by 1912 brought renewed confidence to suffragists. Even those in the more reluctant southern states believed that the female vote was obtainable.

On the subject of alcohol, there was no ambiguity in Miriam's view; she was against it in every respect while Jim's view was harder to characterize. Without question, he was an ardent anti-prohibitionist but his opposition to prohibition was rooted in his conservative view that local governing bodies should make such decisions without interference from higher authorities. He was active in local campaigns against prohibition but claimed that he rarely drank. His bar tab at one local establishment suggested otherwise. In later years Ferguson's tab at a Temple saloon called the Brass Rail was not only notable because it belonged to the well-known Ferguson, but also because it went unpaid.[13]

Certainly the family finances of the day were the domain of the male head of household, and so it was with the Ferguson family. Jim was generous, perhaps to a fault. With an ample supply of money and the generous nature of the keeper of the family purse, the young ladies of the Ferguson household could go to the local shops and buy what they wanted, even treating their friends with the words,

"Please charge this to Daddy." Ouida admitted that, as children, she and sister Dorrace never learned the value of a dollar.[14]

From the choice location on Main Street, the Temple State Bank operated in apparent prosperity for five years in a rented space. By early March of 1911, however, Jim Ferguson was ready to make a bold, strategic business move. Temple had proudly announced that in the planning stages was the erection of a new post office meant to occupy a large space adjacent to the city's town square. In anticipation of this key business facility, the attractiveness and value of the property surrounding the square immediately increased. The site was only two blocks north of the Temple State Bank's existing location but Jim, with much fanfare, purchased a large lot on the northeast corner facing the square where he announced his intention to build an imposing new complex for the Temple State Bank. He proudly published the $25,000 purchase price of the property, which contained two homes, one of which belonged to a Mr. Greathouse's family. Ferguson would move the Greathouse home to 8th Street and would demolish the other home. Ferguson promised not only a lavish new bank building, but many additional "business houses" meant to eventually cover the entire north side of the square. He predicted completion of that project within a two-year period at which time he planned to begin a second project, an expansion that would include new business spaces that would extend a block up Main Street.[15]

The following December, with construction of the new bank building well under way, Ferguson made another grandiose announcement in the local newspaper. A lengthy article containing a large picture of the young Jim carried a headline announcing a proposed trust company with anticipated capital stock of a half-million dollars. It dominated the page. The article, promising "Big Things from a Big Brain," outlined Ferguson's plan to bring new business to Temple. Under his leadership, the Temple State Bank was to transform itself into a large trust company with the sale of new capital stock, stock which Ferguson assured readers was "rapidly being taken up." The bank building under construction boasted of a basement, "blasted from the rock," and a foundation and walls of heavy construction that could accommodate additional stories to form a skyscraper, if desired. The young banker invited potential shareholders to submit their applications for stock purchases and predicted that the venture would be "marvelously profitable to the stockholders."[16]

Tucked neatly within the sentences announcing Ferguson's ambitious plan, a hint of friction between Ferguson and his competition, or perhaps city leaders, had a subtle presence. Ferguson extolled the advantages of the new location, with this additional comment, "and bring new business to Temple, rather than indulge in bitter strife for supremacy in the home territory." Another clue that tension surrounded Ferguson's relationships with other Temple leaders was evident in a July 1915 article that stated that Ferguson's judgment and foresight had been "vindicated" (an odd choice of words) with the success of his bank. [17]

In 1912 construction of the new building was complete and the Temple State Bank relocated. In this new location, the bank offered modern rentable office space in the upper floor and basement, with five storefronts at ground level. Lawyer and doctor offices, as well as a barber shop and other businesses shared the northeast corner of the town square with the bank. The new post office located directly across the street further enhanced the location. However, no further mention of the trust company or of other proposed businesses that were to complete the north side of the square was ever made. Ferguson's call for investors had apparently been answered by several who may not have gotten what they expected. A new trust company never materialized but the capital stock of the existing Temple State Bank jumped from $50,000 to $250,000 shortly before it moved to its new location. [18]

Later that year, Jim Ferguson made another grand gesture meant to add to the prosperity of Temple. He proposed to erect a new theater and auditorium at a cost of $50,000. This was meant to replace an opera house in Temple that fire had destroyed early in December of 1911. Although the directors of the Chamber of Commerce initially agreed to Ferguson's request for a guarantee of 2,000 tickets at $5 each for the first ten attractions, the guarantee was later rescinded and the object of the plan never materialized. [19]

Jim's most passionate investment interest was in ownership of farmland. He added adjoining tracts to enlarge the holding that Miriam had inherited near Sparks. The couple's holding in that area eventually encompassed over 2,200 acres of farm land. [20]

Jim continued to buy and sell shares in other businesses including two investment companies, a creamery, a life insurance company, as well as stock in banks in Moody and Belton. For a period of two years, Ferguson held a small amount of stock in the local power company, until mid-1912 when Texas Power and Light purchased the franchise. Ferguson sat on TP & L's board for two years but also retained stock in the Temple Electric Company, an electrical supply company. By 1916, only one of the banks and the stock in the electrical supply company remained as assets on his personal financial statements, but Ferguson added new investments to his holdings including stock in a drug store, a cotton gin, and a furniture store. His investments included small holdings of stock in two additional small-town banks of Heidenheimer and Pendleton and a half interest in the Lignite Coal Company in Bastrop. All of his undertakings had a common theme: they were small operations incorporated for personal protection and included other investors who shared the entities' risks.[21]

Jim also purchased several large tracts of land totaling 7,350 acres in nearby Bosque County. Near the town of Meridian, Texas, about sixty miles to the northwest of Temple, this property included a pleasant red farmhouse with many of the same conveniences that graced the Fergusons' city home. The impressive property also boasted large numbers of beef cattle, dairy cows, hogs, sheep, mules, and horses, as well as plentiful fencing and barns. The farm became an important retreat for the family during its darkest hours, but it also indirectly contributed to the eventual downfall of James Ferguson. Maintaining the Bell-Bosque Stock Farm required a great deal of capital, apparently much more than it was generating.

As a businessman active in civic affairs, Jim enjoyed the friendship of other prominent men such as Alexander Dienst. Dienst's father, a German immigrant who was both a doctor and dentist, certainly set a high standard for his son. Alex was only slightly less accomplished; he became a doctor of dentistry but not a medical doctor. After completing studies at Philadelphia Dental College, he moved to Temple from Missouri in 1889. A bright and enthusiastic man, Dienst indulged himself in a lifelong hobby that later had great significance to Texas history. One self-proclaimed local historian and old-timer from Temple referred to Dienst as a "tooth dentist" (as if there was any other kind!), and a "history nut" who was "better known for his historical collections of Indian relics than he is for his teeth doctoring." A man of his day with a severe toothache might have disagreed. This characterization, by anyone's standard, is a gross understatement. Dienst spent forty-plus years amassing a vast and priceless collection of rare books, relics, and historical documents, including a collection of documents related to Ferguson. A substantial portion of his collection is today housed at the Dolph Briscoe Center for American History at the University of Texas in Austin, and a smaller collection of items of local interest is housed at Temple's Railroad and Heritage Museum. Dienst also became a renowned lecturer and contributor to historical publications, and an authority on many aspects of Texas history. [22]

The friendship between Jim Ferguson and Alex Dienst was a curious one considering Dienst was an avid prohibitionist and a very religious man, while Ferguson was neither. The prohibition issue, in particular, was so heated that it often rendered friendships with persons with opposing views unsustainable. Somehow Dienst and Ferguson were able to overcome their differences on these divisive and sensitive issues and they remained loyal to their convictions and their friendship. During Jim Ferguson's first political campaign, Dienst would offer, to the shock of his fellow prohibitionists, a rousing public endorsement of Jim Ferguson.[23]

Another Ferguson friend and business associate was Frank L. Denison, a neighbor and sometime business partner. Denison owned a prosperous Temple bridle and buggy store in partnership with a man named Thomas Laramey. With the advent of the automobile, the Denison and Laramey store gradually made the transition from buggy to auto, but their business morphed still further into something of a hardware store by virtue of its sales of tires, tubes, harnesses, and farm implements. Frank Denison would play a decided role in Jim Ferguson's political future. [24]

In reviewing the life story of the Fergusons, three very distinct sections emerge, the first being a happy, unencumbered time before politics forever altered the course of their existence. Jim's decision to enter politics launched a second phase of life that brought the temporary joy of fame but the permanent loss of anonymity. His eventual fall from grace cast a cloud over the family that was thereafter inescapable. Growing up under the scrutiny of this political spotlight would later bring unique reactions from each daughter. Ever outspoken, Ouida reveled in the spotlight and participated in peripheral politics to a great degree all of her life. In contrast, Dorrace found the lack of privacy and unsolicited attention burdensome.

The growing neighborhood on North 7th Street was a safe and happy place for the Ferguson family in 1907. But, by 1913 this unsuspecting family that believed itself typical, was about to meet an atypical lifestyle head-on. Jim Ferguson had found the practice of law unsuitable; likewise his ambitious yet impulsive nature did not find sufficient fulfillment in the routine business of banking—a discontent that changed everything.

Chapter 3
Political Plunge

While the Ferguson household enjoyed a degree of status and privilege, Jim busied himself with promoting the interests of the bank. In February of 1912, he spoke before a group of about one hundred at the Fourth District Bankers' Association in Waco on the subject of overdrafts. The following day, the *Dallas Morning News* published this statement in its report on Ferguson's remarks, "He could sympathize with and appreciate the position of the man who was sometimes forced to take this step, but declared the promiscuous over drafter was as much a parasite as the proverbial chinch bug."[1]

Always passionately opinionated and vocal, Jim spoke out against banking reforms that he believed gave the government too much sway in the private sector. His exhaustive work in keeping Bell County free of local-option prohibition further confirmed his interest in politics and his (then) conservative leanings. In 1902 he acted successfully as county campaign manager for Congressman Robert L. Henry of Waco. He took part in the campaign of Robert Davidson for governor in 1910, worked toward Oscar Colquitt's re-election as governor in 1912, and supported Champ Clark's bid for the nomination for US President in 1912, all early hints at his own developing political aspirations. [2]

Jim was never content to relegate himself to the passive role in life except, perhaps—as Miriam suggested—at church. Whatever forces compelled him to take the leap, by late 1913 Jim Ferguson moved from the periphery squarely into the middle of the political arena. Once committed to enter the political fray, Ferguson, unlike most newcomers, was brash enough to start at the top, setting his sights on the governorship.

Sharing his political interest and involvement in campaigns was friend and associate, John G. McKay, a man who harbored his own political ambitions. The two men had worked together in support of Colquitt's first campaign, among others, while McKay lobbied in hope of securing the position of Texas Secretary of State. Colquitt gave that choice appointment to another, but offered McKay the position of state purchasing agent, a job he accepted in January of 1911 and held for two years. [3]

John McKay, like Ferguson, was born and reared in Bell County and had similar leanings toward diverse business interests and an escalating ambition for political attachment. Between 1896 and 1912, he had been a postmaster, druggist, deputy, district clerk, railroad claims agent, and state purchasing agent. On March 23, 1912, he tendered his resignation as purchasing agent to manage a newly formed dry goods establishment called the Texas Store. His partner and financier in that endeavor was James Ferguson. However by 1913, perhaps anticipating a second chance at the position of Secretary of State, McKay was ready to make another move, that of campaign manager for his friend Jim. There was another compelling reason that may have occasioned McKay's career change: the store the men co-owned, and of which he was president, was not making money. [4]

It was a stormy time in the Texas political arena when Ferguson and McKay joined forces to attempt the near-impossible. The harsh memory of Reconstruction, which held a strong association with the Republican Party, had cast the Lone Star State into an unshakable position of allegiance to the Democratic Party. Famed writer O. Henry, while working as a Texas newspaperman in the 1890s, offered this amusing comment, "We have only two or three laws [in Texas], such as murder before witnesses and being caught stealing horses, and voting the Republican ticket." With this attitude, the Democratic Party had long dominated Texas politics, with a few notable exceptions, but it did not follow that this condition brought harmony to the state's political atmosphere. [5]

The changing landscape of Texas and other factors such as labor unrest, dissatisfied farmers, and the issues of suffrage and prohibition were at the heart of heated political differences that created factions within the party. Since the passage of the Terrell Election Law in 1905, voters selected state, county, and district candidates through primary elections. Primary elections in Democratically dominated Texas often appeared similar to two-party elections with the exception that both candidates were Democrats. Absent a candidate receiving a plurality (later changed to a majority) in the primary, the top two candidates would face a runoff election soon after. Once selected, either absent a Republican or third-party contender or unthreatened by their existence, the Democratic nominee generally anticipated the win with confidence. [6]

A candidate looking for a group of malcontents who might bring him a large number of votes did not need to look far. Those individuals in the rural community, which comprised about two-thirds of the population of Texas in 1913, were particularly dissatisfied with the political climate and welcomed the chance for firm representation in Austin. At a time when the state was moving from rural to urban settings at a rapid pace, they generally distrusted the government and believed that their unique needs for stable cotton prices and easy credit were not being addressed. In some respects, the changing demographics of the state created a "them against us" mentality between city and rural communities, and Jim had no qualms about capitalizing on that friction. In particular, the unstable price of cotton left farmers begging state and national legislators for help. Ferguson's predecessor, Colquitt, had some success in temporarily raising cotton prices with the use of surplus warehousing and reduced production, but unpredictable economic factors still left farmers vulnerable and at the mercy of the price of cotton.[7]

The plight of the state's many tenant farmers was an even more pressing issue. It was a vital social concern that too often perpetuated a cycle of poverty for struggling families who represented the poorest of the poor. This group felt virtually powerless despite a small degree of hidden power that rested in its large numbers. These tenant farmers, who owned no land, represented over half of Texas farmers in 1910. These tenant farmers owned no land. Each rented a plot, often paying for the privilege of farming it with such a large percentage of the yield that the tenant and his family barely survived. They depended, to a great extent, on credit, and were often exploited in that pursuit as well. Defenseless tenants found themselves at the mercy of land owners who often increased their take by entering into exploitative oral agreements with tenants who had few, if any, options. [8]

Jim Ferguson certainly did not originate the idea of addressing the plight of tenants. With limited success, the Renters Union, among others, had attempted to improve the tenants' predicament. But newcomer Jim Ferguson promised tenants a legal remedy in the form of a law that would limit the land owner's percentage of the harvest, a promise that, coming from a gubernatorial candidate, sounded encouraging. Early critics saw Ferguson's message as an exaggerated tactic meant "to woo the partiality of the farmers by exciting their prejudices." While tenant concerns were important and had the ability to secure a large block of votes, no campaign was viable without a stance on other, more litigious issues, and Jim knew he had to lay a careful plan to address them. [9]

Prohibition was, without question, the hot topic of the day. The Texas local-option provision, a law that was part of the Texas Constitution of 1876, had not held the moral argument at bay. The "dry" faction continuously pushed for a statewide and, later, a national ban on alcohol. They watched the number of dry counties increase under local-option law and took that trend as a sign that a majority of Texans agreed with their conclusion that alcohol was the root of many social ills. By 1901, in response to continued pressure for a ban, the Texas Brewers Association formed an organization to represent the interest of the liquor manufacturers and sellers. Prohibitionists pushed back. They upped the ante by merging, in 1908, two major prohibition groups: the Anti-Saloon League and the Texas Local Option Association. Another prohibition vote in 1911 failed by a narrow margin, a sign the dry faction took to mean that sentiment was growing in their favor, but they knew that Texas brewers were spending and would continue to spend millions to block prohibition. In gearing up for the next election in late 1913 and early 1914, neither side could afford to rest. [10]

A candidate who could defuse the passion associated with the alcohol issue to any degree, thereby slightly tipping the scale in the near-even divide between prohibitionists and anti-prohibitionists, would obtain an immediate advantage. But it seemed an impossible task on a topic that seemed to have no middle ground.[11]

Intertwined with the alcohol issue was the dispute over women's suffrage. This connection came via women's tendency to favor prohibition, and though neither side embraced their cause in 1915, suffragists were squarely on the "dry" side of the liquor argument.

Governor Oscar Colquitt was an anti-prohibitionist and prohibition Democrats were eager for the expiration of his term. They sought a candidate strong enough to carry their agenda to Austin and, at the very least, protect it. Eventually, after much haggling, they settled on Thomas Ball of Houston. Like Ferguson, Ball's father was a Methodist minister, and had died when Tom was very young. Ball had overcome that unfortunate event as well as the death of his mother when he was only seven. In 1914, Ball was a fifty-five-year-old attorney who specialized in helping corporations and railroads, and a seasoned politician who had served in Congress for six years. He had also chaired the statewide prohibition forces in the 1911 amendment campaign. The anti-prohibitionists needed a tough but appealing candidate of their own, but the novice Jim Ferguson initially received little notice. The group considered better-known options such as Speaker of the House Chester Terrell, Clarence Ousley, and Ferguson's childhood friend Sam Sparks, among others. Sparks had done well since his early days as Bell County's sheriff; in 1906 voters had elected him State Treasurer, a position he retained for six years. [12]

Though the choices for a "wet" candidate who would challenge Thomas Ball were plentiful, no single potential candidate stood out as ideal. In view of that problem, the anti-prohibitionists settled on the idea of holding a convention in which they would summarily eliminate candidates. This tactic mirrored the elimination convention that prohibitionists had held earlier in the year, a process that resulted in Ball's selection. Ferguson would certainly have been a victim of the elimination process at that early stage so, mimicking a tactic from Walter Lane, a prohibitionist candidate who refused to participate in his group's elimination convention, Jim declined to take part in the process. Without the threat of elimination, Ferguson gained some much-needed time. He was well aware that his status as a newcomer kept him from being viewed as a contender in the minds of most anti-prohibitionists, so he launched a plan to quickly put himself on the political radar. His first order of business was that of securing the name recognition that was essential to his chance for nomination. Every day was critical to the advancement of his plan as he set in motion a two-part strategy to minimize the prohibition question and rally the rural community. [13]

Ferguson's most ardent opponents soon recognized that he had a gift. His farm-boy vernacular became legendary, beginning with the first speech he delivered in a light snowfall in Blum, Texas, on March 12, 1914. Combining his power of persuasion and likability with an innate ability to size up his listeners and play to their vulnerabilities, Jim Ferguson captured the support of his audience. Because his primary target was the rural voter, his good ol' boy delivery and down-home style were messages in themselves; Jim Ferguson was one of them.

That original speech, written in his own hand and composed in the parlor of the Temple home in a Blue Jay school tablet, was significant because it marked Jim's earnest ascent into politics. The somewhat crude, penciled document shared the pages of the tablet with his children's math problems and a crayon drawing of a Christmas tree. Jim read and re-read the speech many times before his greatest supporters, Miriam, Ouida, and Dorrace, who were united by contagious enthusiasm and pride. Apart from its immense political significance, the tablet represented a time when a critical change in the Ferguson family was taking place: a change with consequences so broad that they were surely beyond the family's grasp at that time. [14]

As Jim stood on a platform draped with traditional political bunting that cold March day in Blum, the farmers gathered at that rally did not know the pretext to his presence there. Their soon-to-be champion, quickly tagged "Farmer Jim," was a bit of a trickster who had launched his political career with the benefit of that craftiness. Instead of initially claiming his intentions outright, the unknown Ferguson had made his entry by publicly suggesting that another man, Tom Henderson of Cameron, seek the nomination. Knowing full well that he had no desire to run for office, Ferguson wrote a letter to Henderson suggesting that he seek office because, according to Jim, the most promising prospect for a Texas governor was a farmer/rancher with a business background. It was, of course, an exact description of himself. He sent the letter to Henderson, but also sent copies to the local newspaper. He achieved the anticipated and well-staged result when Henderson declined the offer and suggested instead that Ferguson seek the office. This subtle approach to his political entrance was the kick-off to a future wrought with much political posturing and maneuvering but its success likely confirmed its necessity and legitimacy in the mind of Jim Ferguson. [15]

The message that Ferguson relayed was far more important to his audience than any shenanigans he had employed to put himself in a position to deliver it. But even his platform, studied with the advantage of retrospect, seemed custom-made to showcase Ferguson as the only viable candidate. He promised to protect the tenant farmer and promote rural education because he had rural roots. He claimed that he would diminish the weary argument related to alcohol by skirting it because, as a relative unknown, he could get away with it. He railed against traditional politicians because he was not yet considered one and he insisted that the government be run on a business basis because he was a businessman.

The reaction of the rural community was immediate. Within a few days, word of the force that was gathering behind Ferguson compelled the "dry" faction to take notice and reconsider its options. It seemed that everyone was talking about Jim Ferguson. He capitalized on the free press by giving a lengthy interview to the *Dallas Morning News*, in which he announced that he had $30,000 to spend on his campaign. While that statement seemed reasonable, the rest of the story was less so. Jim told the reporter he had saved the money for a family trip overseas but had decided to use the savings to run for governor instead. Even Ouida admitted to the ridiculous nature of the story, which she said made "good copy," an implication that the reporter had concocted the story. Ferguson's reason for creating such a narrative became apparent in later years when the subject of his initial campaign funds involved a heated disagreement that ended in a lawsuit.[16]

Although the sum was less than sufficient to cover all of Jim Ferguson's campaign expenses in 1914, that certainly should not have been the case. A law passed some five years later limited Texas campaign expenses to $10,000, and while the law was written and interpreted too loosely for it to have been very effective, it nevertheless offers a context with which to evaluate the $30,000-plus campaign expenditure. [17]

By the end of March, Chester Terrell, Clarence Ousley, and a reluctant and angry Sam Sparks had withdrawn from the governor's race. Once the anti-prohibition faction had declared Jim their decided choice he began an aggressive campaign against Thomas Ball. Both Sparks and Ousley supported Ball even though they were "wets": a testament to their resentment toward Ferguson. Sam Sparks' relationship with his childhood friend never recovered from the effects of the ill will created by Jim's tricky political maneuvering. Ferguson's refusal to participate in the elimination process, as well as his aggressive early campaigning, had undercut Sparks' efforts to obtain a fair shot at the nomination. Ferguson's old law partner, John Robinson, a district judge, supported Ferguson as did former Governor Oscar Colquitt, but his former business associates, Clabaugh and Pendleton, from the Belton Trust and Loan Company, did not.[18]

Jim wasted no time engaging in negative campaigning against Ball, exploiting any scrap of bad press that he could find and exaggerate. Rumors of marital problems, according to Jim, grew into stories of gross infidelity and communicable diseases. Even though he had vowed to make alcohol a non-issue, Ferguson obsessed about his opponent's position on the subject. He seized upon the fact that Thomas Ball was a member of the Houston Club, a men's club that served alcoholic drinks and allowed card games. Although Ball tried to ward off any criticism of that membership by admitting to it early in the campaign, Jim made it a point to visit the club and then proclaim that, by virtue of his membership, Ball was a hypocrite. Even the town of Tomball, named for his opponent but having no connection to the governor's race, became part of a negative campaign. There were five saloons in the small town; pictures taken and circulated gave the impression that Thomas Ball was in some way responsible for or connected to the establishments. In addition to his attacks on Ball, Ferguson pushed hard to promote his own agenda, which included prison reform and the establishment of state-bonded warehouses for storing surplus crops.[19]

Governor Thomas Campbell's administration (1907–1911) had touched on many of the issues that Ferguson promised to fix or improve. It had completely restructured the prison system and abolished the practice of leasing prisoners as laborers to outside parties. However, serious problems remained, and financial issues related to the prison system also constituted a major concern. Campbell's administration created the Texas Department of Agriculture to assist farmers and the Texas Department of Insurance and Banking. The legislature during Campbell's terms also improved education by lengthening the school year from four to six months, raising teachers' salaries, and passing the uniform schoolbook law. But rural schools had not been progressing at the same rate as city schools and it was Jim who made it his mission to remedy that situation.[20]

James Ferguson knew that prohibition had created a dichotomy that he could not ignore, but he also knew that the declaration of a firm position on the topic would immediately alienate almost half of the voting public. Though he attempted to minimize the issue with his promise of "no action" on the subject, he could not, in earnest, pretend that he was less than an ardent anti-prohibitionist. The heavy concentration of German-American and Mexican-American populations in South Texas were reliable supporters of the "wet" sentiment but in North, Northeast, and West Texas, support was weak. Texas brewers and other groups that had a financial interest in keeping alcohol legal could not openly support Ferguson financially since the passage of a law in 1907 forbade the use of corporate money in state politics. Joined in purpose, brewing interests and the Texas Business Men's Association, the Farmer's Union, and the German-American Alliance launched a covert campaign disguised as non-partisan and pro-farmer to further their "wet" initiative. R. L. Autry, owner of the Houston Ice and Brewing Company, was chief among those pushing the anti-prohibition agenda. Their scheme included convincing rural voters who favored prohibition that the issues facing farmers took precedence over the wet/dry issue. This gave a decided behind-the-scene boost to Ferguson's campaign. Somewhat less obvious was the association's stance on another continuous issue of the day, a stance that was decidedly against women's suffrage. [21]

Thomas Ball certainly had his backers, chiefly prohibitionists. He also won the support of many national politicians due to his firm support for President Woodrow Wilson. Many religious leaders held a high degree of admiration for Ball, a veneration surpassed only by their loathing of Jim Ferguson. Ferguson's estrangement from organized religion was further strained as many church leaders campaigned bitterly against him. They leveled criticism at him for his lack of education, but their true agenda was primarily about alcohol. In early July, speakers at a Dallas religious rally bitterly assailed Ferguson. The comments of Reverend Robert P. Shuler of Austin, formerly of Temple, were particularly harsh. He asserted that Ferguson was ignorant and alleged that the candidate could not pass an examination for a second-grade teaching certificate on history or make a grade of forty-five in English grammar. This early assault on Ferguson's lack of education may have contributed to his sensitivity on the subject and almost certainly aggravated his disdain for those with college degrees. [22]

Two days after Shuler's verbal assault, Ferguson's ex-law partner, Judge John D. Robinson, defended Ferguson in a speech in support of his candidacy. He claimed that Ferguson hadn't had the advantages of a higher education, a remark that was a half-truth. Robinson also asserted that although Jim, "was a member of no church, in sympathy he was a Methodist." [23]

Locally, Ferguson had the support of the anti-prohibitionists, but he had also received a hardy endorsement from his "dry" friend Alexander Dienst, a testimonial that raised some eyebrows. In early July, the Temple newspaper carried a lengthy article penned by Dr. Dienst, extolling the virtues of his candidate friend, Jim Ferguson. Characterizing his friend as one who was at times "hasty in speech" and "impulsive to demonstrate his friendship and re- sent wrong," Dienst stated his belief that Ferguson was a worthy political op- ponent by virtue of his philanthropy. The article continued with a lengthy list of contributions that Ferguson had presumably made to charities and churches. But Elijah Shettles, a Houston minister and friend of Dienst, was highly critical of the Ferguson endorsement, not only because he disagreed with Ferguson's political planks, but because he believed that the claims of philanthropy were untrue or at least unproven. Shettles based his contention on the fact that the contributions for which Ferguson had been given credit represented pledges that had not yet been paid and might never be paid. [24]

The hint of another issue existed within the columns of the Dienst endorse- ment. Dr. Dienst insisted that Jim Ferguson had paid his taxes, a defensive comment that raised the obvious question: "Who said he hadn't?"

Ferguson's property tax renditions were of interest to at least one news- paper in Texas for another reason entirely. *The Huntsville Item* gained access to the 1913 and 1914 Ferguson property tax renditions and reported that at the beginning of each of those years Ferguson had claimed that he had "not one red cent" in cash. The paper followed that statement with the obvious question as to how Ferguson had amassed a $30,000 savings by November of 1914. [25]

Attacks from the Ball camp did little to dissuade those who found favor with Ferguson. Slowly the tide began to turn as he gained impetus through a widespread speaking schedule. Ball made speeches too, but his message did not have the force to draw large crowds and create momentum. Jim benefited from the strong focus and unity of the Farmers Union and the brewing interests, the significance of which cannot be overstated. In contrast, the prohibition- ists became somewhat distracted from politics on the state level in their quest for a national referendum. By June, it was clear that Ferguson was leading in popularity and Ball supporters began to fear that the over-confidence they had enjoyed in the early weeks of the race might cost them the election. In a last desperate attempt to pull support back to their side, they sought and received a belated endorsement from President Woodrow Wilson. Wilson's delayed backing did not save Thomas Ball; in late July, Ferguson handily won the primary, assuring him the governorship in the November general election.

The *Fort Worth Star Telegram* carried a large picture of Miriam and the Ferguson girls six days later. The daughters, who were fourteen and eleven, sported large hair bows, crisp cotton dresses, and faint smiles. Below the picture, in a brief article, Jim credited the trio with abiding support and his subsequent win. [26]

Jim Ferguson surely had more than his family to thank for his success. The expected rural vote, the backing of the South Texas concentration of Mexican- and German-Americans, and an unanticipated support from North Texas cities, combined to facilitate his victory. These forces had certainly been stimulated by the diligent efforts of brewing interests and earned for Jim a further distinction: he had garnered the highest number of gubernatorial votes that a governor had ever received. Ferguson carried not only his own home county but also Ball's own Harris County. Bemused and dejected prohibitionists had lost more than the gubernatorial election; voters had also rejected by a large margin, a bill for submission of an amendment for prohibition.[27]

Another victory, of sorts, blessed James Ferguson a month after his win in the primaries. The State Democratic Convention, held in El Paso in August of 1914, showcased the new would-be governor, but the spotlight also revealed detractors. Former US Congressman and Senator Joseph Weldon Bailey, a highly influential man in Texas politics, was a staunch supporter of Thomas Ball. Even though he was a vehement anti-prohibitionist and anti-suffragist like Ferguson, he sought to upstage and embarrass Ferguson at the convention by pushing through his planks. A 1906 anti-trust scandal clouded Bailey's reputation, but he was Jim's equal—if not superior—in his ability to deliver an inspiring speech. Bailey tested the limits of that talent at the El Paso convention with a rousing debate that challenged Ferguson, insisting that his "no-action" plan on prohibition was too timid. With the advantage of speaking second, Jim delivered a thoughtful reply in which he carefully diffused Bailey's points and established himself as a contender in such debates. When Bailey's planks were solidly defeated, James Ferguson was left with a renewed confidence and optimism toward his new role and an increased level of respect from many who had witnessed his calmness under fire.[28]

In early December, at the invitation of Governor and Mrs. Colquitt, Jim and Miriam visited the Governor's Mansion in Austin where they enjoyed lunch and a tour of the grand house that they would soon call home. The wives socialized with other ladies whom Mrs. Colquitt had invited to meet the next First Lady of the state, while the men visited various offices in the State Capitol. [29]

James Ferguson was in high spirits in late 1914 as he prepared to move to Austin and take his place as governor. Sadly, long before he left his home in Temple, seeds of destruction were already sprouting beneath the surface. Carefully concealed debt, coupled with a serious cash-flow problem, were slowly rendering the Fergusons' personal financial situation unmanageable. A small annual salary of $4,000 plus increased expenses associated with the governorship would only exacerbate this fragile situation. However, in 1914 Miriam and the Ferguson daughters were unsuspecting, believing always in Jim's ability as their provider. Miriam often described Jim as the smartest man that she had ever known. She would pay a heavy price for that faith.

Jim's confidence soared. Armed with little more than marked determination and a gift of persuasion, he had overcome a somewhat disadvantaged childhood to become a lawyer and businessman; he had pursued and won the hand and heart of Miriam Wallace; and now, without experience, he had secured the title of the twenty-sixth governor of the state of Texas. In light of these successes, he may have wondered if there were any limits on his ambitions.

Indeed there were, as he would soon discover.

Chapter 4
Keeping Secrets

With the governorship secured in early November 1914, James Ferguson began making preparations to move to Austin where he and his family would have the honor of living in the fifty-nine-year-old Governor's Mansion. His first and most urgent order of business was obtaining a replacement for himself as president of Temple State Bank.

In early January of 1915 at the Temple bank, Ferguson met with his choice of replacement, Mr. H. C. Poe. Certainly both men were optimistic, each looking to launch a promising new career in which a reciprocal spirit of cooperation and support was essential. The meeting, which was in no way spontaneous, amounted to the changing-of-the-guard at Temple State Bank. Governor-elect Ferguson was turning over the reins of the bank, now eight-and-a-half years old, to Poe, a man with considerable experience considering his age of thirty-three.[1]

James Ferguson was a name that probably had little significance to Poe prior to the 1914 governor's race except, perhaps, in banking circles. The young banker was likely flattered at the prospect of replacing the governor-elect and was undoubtedly eager to prove that he was capable of the task. At the time, Poe was living in Eastland, Texas, where he had been a teacher and an elected county clerk before taking employment at the City National Bank of Eastland, where he had risen to the position of president. Poe and his wife, Leonora "Nora," had one child, a six-year-old daughter who was called by her middle name, Gertrude.[2]

Poe immediately liked the smooth-talking and personable Jim Ferguson, who reciprocated the feeling. The parties struck a deal and agreed that Poe would vest his interest in the bank by buying a small block of stock. He would begin his duties on or about January 16 and would draw a salary set at $200 per month with an additional perk: Poe would be allowed to lease the prestigious Ferguson mansion for a term of four years. Apparently the governor's plans already included a traditional second term.[3]

Chief among the purposes of that January exit meeting was a transfer of knowledge from old guard to new regarding any items of an unusual nature. The two bankers discussed outstanding loans, including Ferguson's existing obligations, and Ferguson set forth his periodic need to borrow money to finance his many business ventures, primarily his Bell-Bosque Stock Farm. The bank's paid-in capital, initially $50,000 at its incorporation, had increased to $250,000 in 1912, but had very recently been reduced by half with a payment of $125,000 to stockholders. With that hefty payout, Ferguson, the majority stockholder, had acquired some cash for his personal use but left the bank in a much weakened position. If the men discussed the wisdom of that act, it was by then a moot point. Whatever the rationale for doing so, the board had reduced the bank's capital in advance of Poe's arrival, leaving him to make the best of the situation.[4]

The discussions completed, the two men parted, each believing that he had an understanding that was mutual and would serve him well in future encounters. In reality, subsequent events would show that each man failed to have the slightest understanding of the other's goals, motives, character, and capabilities, a situation that was a precursor to a tumultuous relationship that would later wreak havoc with the careers of both men.[5]

On January 17, a day of freezing temperatures, the state's new chief executive and his family traveled to Austin on a private rail car provided by J. K. Hull, an old friend of Jim's who was by then the superintendent of the Temple division of the Santa Fe Railroad. Hull later became a vice-president and director at the Temple State Bank. Hull and Ferguson had worked together some twenty-five years prior on a bridge gang along the Katy Railroad. A bevy of well-wishers met the Ferguson family at the Austin station, one of whom was Dr. W. J. Battle, president of the University of Texas, a man who would play a decided role in the governor's future. Greeters whisked the new First Family to the Driskill Hotel where they awaited the imminent departure of the outgoing Governor Colquitt from the Governor's Mansion.[6]

For Poe and the Temple State Bank, trouble began almost immediately. Soon after Ferguson's departure for Austin, on a day when Poe hoped to meet and greet bank customers, he was instead confronted by a group of angry men, creditors of a mercantile called the Texas Store. Poe was certainly familiar with the establishment; it occupied a large space in the southwestern section of the building that housed the bank, but he was not sure why the creditors were on his doorstep. The angry group insisted on the store's closure and liquidation of its assets so that they could receive some long-overdue payments. Poe knew that the bank held a note for the Texas Store in the amount of $21,000, a note collateralized with shares of the business's stock. He was soon surprised to learn that James Ferguson and his friend John McKay owned the faltering establishment.[7]

Poe was familiar with the McKay name. McKay, he knew, was both friend and campaign manager to Ferguson and was more recently the recipient of an appointment to the office of Secretary of State. Ferguson and McKay had incorporated and opened the mercantile in 1912, borrowing start-up money from the bank to facilitate the undertaking. So keen was John McKay on the new operation that he had given up, in March 1912, the coveted appointment of state purchasing agent he had received under Governor Colquitt. But the store had been a financial failure from the beginning, and McKay had abandoned his position there in late 1913 in order to run Ferguson's gubernatorial campaign.[8]

Poe explained to the anxious creditors his commitment to a trip to Austin the following day where he planned to attend the inaugural ceremonies. His promise that he would work to resolve the group's problem when he returned seemed to pacify them, and a crisis was temporarily averted. As chief executive of the bank, Poe had an obvious stake in the success of a store that owed money to the bank and occupied a large rentable space. As a banker and former county clerk he had the ability to assess and manage the unanticipated task but the very need of it left him with an uneasy feeling. In the exit meeting, Jim Ferguson had been entirely silent on the subject.

As promised, Poe tackled the task of evaluating the financial status of the store, but quickly realized that the establishment had little hope for redemption and absolutely no hope for success. He estimated the value of the store's inventory at $14,000 and received from liquidators a disappointing estimated liquidation value of thirty-five cents on the dollar. To his further dismay, he learned that the value shown for notes and accounts receivable as listed on the company's books exceeded by four times their collectible value of $1,600. Even more troubling was the total debt of the establishment that exceeded $26,000.[9]

The creditors, not anxious to settle for cents on the dollar, pinned their hopes on Poe agreeing to allow the store to operate under his guidance as trustee. This futile measure prolonged the life of the struggling store for another nine months until the suppliers and creditors lost patience and filed a legal petition. This motion put the establishment into bankruptcy, an action that imposed a $16,000 loss on the bank and additional losses on the creditors. With that unpleasantness behind him, Poe immediately turned over to the bank the trustee's fee he had received for his services and concentrated on new challenges that had emerged. The most troubling aspect of the Texas Store debacle had been the careless way in which the governor had responded to it. When notified of the store's trouble, Ferguson had been evasive and dismissive, saying that it was a matter that he had simply forgotten. To Poe, it was a major and possibly deliberate omission, a sign that Jim Ferguson had breached an essential trust. The governor's cavalier attitude disturbed him well beyond the uneasiness of a damaged expectation. It served as an ominous warning that Ferguson and the conservative Mr. Poe were not, by a large margin, of the same business philosophy.[10]

Although the trouble with the Texas Store had been an immediate and shocking initiation into Poe's presidency at the Temple State Bank, Poe soon realized that it was the mere starting point of his troubles. A shortage of cash seemed never to enter into Ferguson's decision to initiate business ventures. In May he invested in two additional oil companies. Poe realized that Ferguson's endless need to borrow money, coupled with his refusal to sufficiently relinquish control over the decision-making at the bank, were and would remain immensely problematic.

When the Ferguson move to Austin was undertaken, the Ferguson couple had a joint debt of $42,000 at the Temple State Bank consisting of a $30,000 note that Jim owed personally, and an additional $12,000 debt attributable to Mrs. Ferguson. (Debt secured by the inherited property in Sparks was in Miriam's name.) Within two days of Ferguson's departure from Temple, two additional Ferguson notes, totaling $50,000, appeared on the books of the Temple State Bank, one for Ferguson personally and the other for the Bell-Bosque farm. These notes represented the second major sign of trouble for the Ferguson-Poe relationship.[11]

The issuance of those January loans was significant on several fronts. Laws governing state banks imposed a limit of 30 percent of the institution's paid-in-capital in regard to its maximum allowable loans to any individual or corporation. In the case of the Temple State Bank, that obligatory limit amounted to $37,500. The issuance of another note to Governor Ferguson in the amount of $25,000 had immediately created a violation of the statute. But Poe later revealed a more disturbing element about those transactions. Poe later swore under oath that Ferguson had drawn up the notes before he left for Austin, without his (Poe's) consent or knowledge. Poe asserted that the notes were forward-dated to appear as if he had approved them when, in fact, he had not. It was a claim Ferguson denied, but the dates on both instruments were January 19, the day of Ferguson's inauguration, a day when Poe was also in Austin.[12]

More trouble loomed. The loan proceeds credited to the Ferguson bank accounts seemed to evaporate overnight and soon Ferguson was acquiring credit on his Bell-Bosque farm account by another means, namely overdrafts. Poe continued to honor the overdrafts for a time; certainly he expected Governor Ferguson to make good on the deficiencies. In August of 1915, Poe authorized an additional $30,000 loan for the Bell-Bosque farm in an effort to convert the sizable overdraft to an interest-bearing instrument, but doing so pushed the violation of the legal loan limit to a new high. That statute violation was not Poe's only concern. Ferguson's excessive loans and overdrafts further constricted the limited resources he needed to make investments and earn income for the bank. But by far, the most exasperating element of Poe's dilemma was the reckless nature that Ferguson exhibited. Even as Poe pleaded for a reduction of the governor's debt, on August 23, 1915, Jim Ferguson purchased an additional 210 acres of land near Sparks at a cost of $26,250.[13]

The anxiety imposed upon Poe by the governor seemed limitless. A letter written to Poe and dated December 24, 1915, demonstrates this problem:

> Dear Poe,
>
> John Robinson was in to see me today and wants to borrow $1000. I wish you would let him have it as a loan to the bank and if he does not pay it, I will hold the bank harmless. You understand why I would like to have him owe the bank and not me direct.
>
> I also enclose you three notices being two from the John Hancock Life Insurance Company, aggregating $2,452.50 for interest on loans which I owe them; also notice from the Texas Farm Mortgage Company for $3,674.50 which under my contract with Will Wallace I have to pay. These payments have to be paid promptly on the first of the month and I wish you would pay them for me. Just as soon as I get a breathing spell I will come up and arrange it.
>
> I have been head over heels since my return and have not had much time to pay attention to my business affairs.[14]
>
> Yours Truly,
>
> Jas. E. Ferguson

This represented a new tactic on Ferguson's part. Instead of pleading for more loan proceeds or risking a rejected overdraft, the governor implored Poe to pay his notes even though he had no funds. Any means Poe chose to facilitate the payments would put the bank at further risk and put the onus for that risk on Poe. Ferguson, who seemed to possess at most a cautious faith in Mr. Robinson's ability to repay a loan, had no qualms in asking Poe and the other stockholders of the bank, to take on the dubious liability. Ferguson's offer to hold the bank harmless was certainly of no comfort to Poe.

This correspondence also revealed another troubling truth: Ferguson's debt was by no means confined to the Temple State Bank. His obligations to other parties also included a note that Ferguson had assumed for Will Wallace, his brother-in-law, an odd circumstance.

Another letter from Ferguson, dated December 28, 1915, further demonstrates Poe's dilemma:

> Dear Poe,
> I have a note for $4500 and interest, given to G. W. Cole Jr., due January 1st and it is payable at the Temple State Bank. I wish you would write Mr. Cole that the note will be paid promptly. He might put it in the hands of an attorney for collection if he saw a chance to do so. I hope to have a remittance to cover this note before maturity, but in case I do not, do not let the note go to protest on me.[15]
> Yours Truly,
> Jas. Ferguson

In this letter Ferguson again saddled Poe with the burden of finding the means to extinguish his personal debt. If Ferguson was unable to secure the money with which to pay it as he suggested in the last sentence, Poe could only take care of it by granting the governor more credit through his bank. The relationship between Ferguson and Cole was a curious one. The governor showed a degree of paranoia in anticipating Mr. Cole's *anxiousness* to obtain an attorney.

Poe's frustrations continued to compound and each new discovery seemed more menacing than the last. In contacting four local note holders in an attempt to collect on their notes, Poe met resistance, sometimes hostile. In each case, the party on the note assured Mr. Poe that he was not liable for the debt in question. All claimed that the true debtor was James Ferguson and assured Poe that if he would simply contact the governor, they were sure that he could explain. Frustration turned to anger as Poe tried to run the bank according to his conservative nature, but too often found that debtors would resort to a plea for leniency based on a connection with the governor—and those relationships were not always positive ones.[16]

By early April 1916, Poe had mustered his courage and written the governor a letter about his debt. Choosing his words carefully, he tried to diffuse the obvious awkwardness of the situation by addressing it head on. "It is a little embarrassing to write you," he wrote, and gently reminded the governor that the bank was "beyond the accommodation permitted by the statutes." He closed with a timid request for "a good remittance at an early date."[17]

The letter produced a response from Ferguson in the form of a plan to move some of his debt to the Houston National Exchange Bank, but the plan was awkward, requiring Poe to make and maintain a balance with the Houston bank in the name of the Temple State Bank as support. Not a true remedy for Poe due to its drain on bank assets, Poe nevertheless agreed to the plan. The move would at least reduce Ferguson's loans at his bank. That would-be remedy also failed; Poe made the required deposits with the Houston bank but Ferguson failed to obtain a loan. [18]

With blatant disregard for Poe's requests for his debt reduction, the governor continued to seek loans from the Temple bank without success. The persistent Ferguson even enlisted the aid of a friend in a deceitful attempt to secure more cash. Judge Floyd M. Spann, a Temple native aged thirty-six, had been the recipient of a district judgeship under Ferguson's appointment in early 1916. The offices of Spann's private legal practices had been in the Temple State Bank building before he received his judgeship. In mid-1916 Spann submitted a loan request to the Temple State Bank using as collateral bonds issued by the Lignite Coal Company, a company in which Ferguson held half-interest. Spann made little pretense of his intentions, asking that the $20,000 proceeds of the loan be deposited to Ferguson's account. Poe promptly returned the bonds and denied the loan, but the audacity of the act left him seething. [19]

In a letter dated July 27, 1916, Poe significantly accelerated the pressure on Jim Ferguson with these words:

> Honorable James E. Ferguson, Austin, Texas
> Dear Governor:
> The election is over and you have won, and we are all feeling good over the results, especially in view of the fight that has been made. I have to go to Sherman to a bond sale, but hope that I can see you first part of next week. Your overdraft and excessive line must have immediate attention. Some of the best men on our board are going to quit us if your line is not cared for, and besides it is dangerous to permit practice of this kind.
>
> Now since we have cared for these matters and permitted your past due paper and overdraft to run as it has and the election is over, I certainly hope you will take care of this as you must do without causing us further embarrassment.

We have never permitted Mr. Jarrell, Mr. Hull or Mr. Maresh to know about this situation, feeling that it was not best to permit even all of the Directors to know the condition which you have been allowing your account to run.

I hate to write you this letter, but we must have a reduction in this without further delay. [20]

Yours very truly,

H. C. Poe, President

This letter, too, generated no payment.

While it was true that Ferguson had just won the governorship for a second term, the victory had been hard-fought and he had not won with the wide margin he had anticipated. The governor had not been the victor in his home cities of Belton and Temple. Ferguson's opponent, Charles Morris, had put up a robust fight and that fight had included some interesting accusations. Morris reminded voters that although Ferguson could boast of substantial increases in appropriations to schools, the funding had come at the expense of taxpayers paying a higher ad valorem tax. His criticism included more serious allegations that the governor had misappropriated state funds in purchasing groceries with state money, and Morris extended the condemnation to Ferguson's family as well, calling them spendthrifts. His criticism of Miriam included references to her flamboyant wardrobe and her personal secretary. Morris also accused the governor of cronyism and made a more sinister accusation that the he had inappropriately deposited a sum of $100,000 of state money into the Temple State Bank, an act from which he allegedly profited.

In the context of hard-fought political campaigns, these charges had not been sufficient to cause any serious damage to Ferguson's bid, but they had planted seeds of doubt in the minds of some regarding his ethics. Ferguson was largely undaunted by the negative publicity.

Desperate but fearful of a confrontation with Ferguson, Poe continued writing letters that alternated between attempts to salvage an increasingly fragile relationship and blunt demands for payment. He knew well that the governor was confrontational, crafty, elusive, and quick-tempered when provoked, but his own temper also flared under the weight of the situation. Certainly the more conservative Poe realized that James Ferguson possessed traits that made him ill-fitted to manage a bank where the temptation to borrow recklessly and extend credit to his friends was entirely too enticing. Ferguson's business ventures seemed to lack the kind of planning and follow-through necessary to make them successful, and his stubbornness and arrogance made it impossible for anyone to advise him. Caught in a web of deceit and secrets, Poe dared not expose the reason that his own professional future was in peril: that he had attached his aspirations to those of a careless and inept businessman who also happened to be the governor.

Perhaps most troubling was the realization that Texans had elected Jim Ferguson to the highest state office based largely on a lie. In his first campaign speech in Blum, he had proclaimed, "It is the height of ignorance to expect that a man who has never shown any ability in his own business affairs can ever manage with any degree of success, the business affairs of Texas which spends over 15 million dollars every two years in support of its government." [21]

A 1914 newspaper article paraphrased Ferguson's stated intentions as governor. He would, it claimed, "apply to the State government the same business principles he has followed successfully in banking, farming and ranching." The implication was clear; Ferguson's contention was that, as an astute manager of his own assets, he was well qualified to oversee the assets of the state of Texas. [22]

In desperation, Poe began to weigh his options. James Ferguson was not only a powerful man; he was the kind of man who demanded loyalty under all circumstances. There was an unspoken understanding that those entrusted with Ferguson secrets were duty-bound to closely guard those confidences. But a conflicting responsibility for following the fiduciary statutes fell squarely on Poe's shoulders, and this put him in a delicate and perilous position. He knew that if he contacted the Insurance and Banking Commission he would be taking a calculated risk. The commissioner of the agency, John Patterson, was a long-time friend and an appointee of Ferguson's.

Poe's nerves were quickly unraveling. His attempts to talk to some of Ferguson's friends had yielded no result, yet he felt that he was harboring a secret too important to keep. Ferguson had an insatiable need for cash but too few financial earnings from his business interests to support that need. His judgment was entire lacking. His solution to a struggling business with angry creditors had been to leave town without a word and his staggering debt and mounting interest seemed of little consequence to him.

Poe needed a plan. Perhaps he was noble, as he would later claim, in deciding that he had kept the governor's secret's long enough. On the other hand, the move that Poe eventually undertook was more likely an attempt to escape a situation that, for him, had simply become unsustainable. Certainly anger, frustration, and fear drove him as he wrestled with his options. He had risked much when he left a secure job in Eastland and moved his wife and young daughter to Temple to head Ferguson's bank. Whatever course of action he contemplated, Poe knew that extreme caution was necessary because H. C. Poe was not without some secrets of his own.

Chapter 5
Guilty Knowledge

Hosea Calvin Poe was named after a paternal uncle but must not have liked his given name. Even though the tradition of using men's initials, particularly in matters of business, was widely used in his day, Mr. Poe's adherence to the custom was unusually far-reaching. He went solely by his initials, H. C., and even his tombstone is so inscribed.

Born in 1881 in rural Arkansas, young Hosea and his family moved from Magnolia, Arkansas, to Eastland County, Texas, when Poe was barely a teen. He grew up on a farm with four younger siblings in a family that must have been keen on education. Of the three sons, two became teachers and the other a dentist. For Poe, teaching was a temporary career choice, followed by an elected position as county clerk and a subsequent career in banking. [1]

While 1915 had proved an eye-opening year for the new president of the Temple State Bank, his dealing with Governor Ferguson in 1916 repeatedly confirmed his worst fears and suspicions. Poe realized that he had made a poor choice in accepting the position as head of the Temple bank but was committed to salvaging his relationship with James Ferguson if possible.

A magazine article featuring Poe in April of 1915 had characterized the young executive as "a jolly, liberal and energetic businessman." By late 1916, with his enthusiasm tempered, Poe labored to mask his anxiety and maintain a cheerful public persona. He continued his duties as president of the Fourth District Banker's Association and vice-president for the state section of the American Banker's Association. He also remained aggressive in his pursuit of new methods to promote the bank. In particular, he was active in heading programs in support of farmers and young prospective farmers. Among those endeavors was a program that loaned money to young men for the purpose of acquiring, raising, and later selling hogs, a plan meant to teach young would-be agriculturists lessons in both husbandry and finance. Another promotion aimed at youngsters included a gift of a single gold coin to youngsters as an incentive to open their own bank accounts. By far, Poe's most important contribution to the growth and prosperity of the bank was the establishment of a bond department that allowed the bank to issue city, county, and precinct bonds. Apparently Poe's efforts made him popular in the community; Temple's leading men had assigned him, by popular vote, the considerable honor of being toastmaster at Temple's 1916 annual Stag Party. [2]

But these successes on Poe's part did nothing to lessen Ferguson's unauthorized involvement in the bank's activity. On February 13, 1916, the governor wrote, in part:

> Dear Poe,
>
> Your favor of the 2nd in reference to Jake Reynolds' application of a $1,200 loan is received. You acted entirely right. He has been owing me this money for two or three years and has been collecting dividends off of the stock and not paying me the interest on his note. I told him when I was in Temple that he must get busy and pay me. I never dreamed that he would undertake to unload the loan on the bank. Confidentially, I am trying to sell out the Square Drug Store so that the bank can get its money out of it. [3]

Ferguson had conceived the idea for the Square Drug Store for the same purpose as the Texas Store: it paid the bank seventy-five dollars per month in rent. Ferguson and two friends, Ed Love and Jake Reynolds, had organized and incorporated the establishment, initially contributing $1,000 each toward the business's capital. Love and Ferguson also borrowed additional start-up capital of $3,000 from the Temple State Bank, a loan that assigned equal liability to each. Ferguson later attempted to disavow any obligation under the loan, forcing Ed Love to produce, in court, the note bearing Ferguson's signature. [4]

Jake Reynolds had also borrowed his thousand-dollar investment in the Square Drug Store from the Temple State Bank, a debt he failed to repay. Even with that old debt unpaid, he approached Poe in 1916 for another loan, a request that Poe denied. Ferguson's choice of words, "owing ME this money," revealed an important point. Jim Ferguson had a blurred perception when it came to distinguishing bank assets (in this case a note receivable), from his own assets. Poe must have been taken aback by the entire scenario. Certainly he wondered why Ferguson had allowed the payment of dividends when the stockholders, including Ferguson, had made no attempts to reduce their debt. It seemed a near certainty the store was unprofitable since Ferguson was trying to quietly unload it. If that were the case, paying dividends was a very bad business decision. [5]

A letter dated May 22, 1916, written by Ferguson's secretary, Mr. Davis, was among many that created anxiety for Poe.

> Gentlemen,
> Enclosed herewith find note for $100 representing money advanced to J. C. House, a tenant on Governor Ferguson's farm, to make crop for 1916. You will note that same has been transferred to you by the Governor, and he asks that you have Mr. House execute the note and handle the transaction. In other words he wants you to advance the money.[6]

Poe's authority as bank president had again been undermined. Ferguson's instructions, sent through his secretary, Mr. Davis, directed Poe to make the loan in which he, Ferguson, was the beneficiary. If the farm tenant was successful, Jim Ferguson would get paid; if not, the bank would be left holding the note. The degree of risk could scarcely have been higher, a fact Ferguson knew well. The very core of his campaign platform had been based on the abject poverty of tenants.

There were many similar loans made by Ferguson prior to Poe's arrival as bank president in January of 1915, loans that proved uncollectible. Jim Ferguson further forbade Poe's writing off the bad loans, a fact that added to his frustration and embarrassment when the situation caught the attention of a bank examiner. Poe could hardly defend his inaction by blaming the governor; doing so would have required a confession that he as bank president had allowed Ferguson to intimidate him into employing unsound business practices. [7]

By June of 1916, Ferguson's personal account was experiencing the same kind of perpetual overdrafts that had long plagued his Bell-Bosque farm account. However, Poe was not the only one struggling with Ferguson's antics to secure cash. The Union National Bank of Houston ostensibly had no qualms in declining the governor's request for a loan of $30,000 in the spring of 1916. They had the freedom that Poe did not: freedom to anger James Ferguson without the fear of immediate and personal reprisal.

Although the personal financial statements that accompanied Ferguson's loan request showed a net worth of $388,575, even a casual glance at those statements certainly raised a multitude of concerns with the lending officers of the Houston bank. The statements were undated. The listing of assets, comprised primarily of land and livestock, had no accompanying notes to explain the basis used in their valuation. The liabilities section of the statement showed indebtedness to four life insurance companies, nine banks, and four individuals, totaling $317,275. Absent was any potential tax liability or accrued interest, amounts that would have been substantial due to the common interest rates of the period that stood in the range of 9 percent. Other financial statement omissions would have been less discernible to potential lenders in 1916. The statement showed no cash and failed to disclose Ferguson's sizable liability from overdrafts at the Temple State Bank. These red flags were apparently not lost on the prudent loan officers at the Union National Bank of Houston, who declined Ferguson's request for a loan with a gentle letter of rejection. They returned with that letter of rejection, bonds issued by the Lignite Coal Company that Ferguson had offered as collateral.[8]

Ferguson's letter of response reflected his surprise and disappointment at the rejection. "As is well known, I have never speculated, and have always confined my operations to established lines of business," he wrote. He also assured the bank that he did not need the money. "To be sure, I am not even pressed for the money, and it will cause me no inconvenience by your not accepting the loan, but since the loan seems to have been declined upon the grounds of insufficiency, I feel it in justice to myself to make this explanation."[9]

Poe's dilemma in dealing with the governor was multi-layered. By late 1916, he feared that Ferguson simply did not have the prospects to which he often referred, prospects that would allow him to pay off even a portion of his mounting debt. Denying further credit to the governor did not stop the accumulation of his indebtedness. Often Ferguson, unable to pay even the interest on a maturing note, added the accrued interest to the balance before renewing the instrument. Poe was desperate to remedy the illegality of the excessive loans, or at least to acknowledge them to someone in authority, but to do so risked exposing some major problems for himself. Poe had been at the bank's helm when Ferguson's debt had gone over the legal limit and, worse, Poe had not been entirely honest with some of the bank's board members about the Ferguson debt problem.

Poe was no innocent. Although he had been angry when he discovered Ferguson's $50,000 notes in January of 1915, he had later agreed to the renewal of those notes. He had put his signature of approval on Ferguson-generated overdrafts that reached a high of over $48,000. Poe also knew that large sums of state money were periodically deposited in the Temple State Bank, a practice that had begun within a few months of the governor taking office. Although Poe was not responsible for the legitimacy of the practice, the implications were unthinkable. During times of insufficient reserves, it meant that state money funded new loans. His silence on that matter surely rendered him culpable to some degree but he had no basis with which to make that judgment. The temporary nature of the state deposits, which were periodically transferred to the state treasury, only added to the precariousness of their benefit. [10]

There were other offenses. The struggling bank had, in early 1916, sought new investors. Certainly an understanding that the establishment was sound and prosperous was, at the very least, implied, a pseudo-assurance Poe achieved largely through a lie of omission. In courting prospective investors, Poe had simply withheld the information regarding the daunting issues that threatened the bank. An article in the July 1916 edition of the *Texas Bankers Journal*, boasted that deposits at the Temple State Bank had increased by 85 percent in 1915. There was, of course, no mention of the state money that comprised much, if not all of that increase. Once Poe had secured additional stockholders he found it necessary to keep up the charade that all was well. Poe would later testify to that circumstance saying: "Mr. Jarrell and Mr. Hull were elected at the January meeting and, that is, the February meeting of 1916 and we had invited them to take stock in the bank and become members of the board of directors, and we felt like if they really knew the real situation there that they would consider it too large, and we felt like from the governor's promises that we would soon have his account straightened out and they never would know about it, but the further it went, the worse it got, instead of getting better." [11]

Poe was living with this and other guilty knowledge and escalating anger for the man at the center of his grief. He drank at times, sometimes to excess, and other times he acted somewhat irrationally. Poe later admitted that he had also, when he felt it was warranted, lied to the citizens of Temple about the condition of the bank. He explained, "Whenever you are trying to keep a bank going and to keep down public sentiment against you, you have to defend it and say things that you know in a way are not absolutely true. . . When fellows up there are scrapping the bank and the Governor and would come around and try to peck information out of me to knock the bank with I would tell them most anything to get rid of them."[12]

Poe had also signed the annual bank report in 1916 swearing to the "good" status of the bank's notes based on little more than another in a series of Ferguson promises. Once Poe had confessed his transgression to the bank board members he had misled and deceived, he could hardly turn to them for support.

Not every problem stemming from the failed Ferguson-Poe relationship was directly related to the bank. During the second campaign in 1916, Charles E. Maedgen, a former vice president of the Temple State Bank and a Ferguson enemy, made the mistake of divulging a Ferguson secret. Before a large Temple crowd at a political rally for Ferguson's opponent, Charles Morris, Maedgen informed the group that during Ferguson's 1914 campaign, while he (Maedgen) was a vice president at the Temple State Bank, Ferguson had received $30,000 in cash for his campaign, donations that Maedgen claimed came from Texas brewers. The detailed story, as Maedgen told it, seemed plausible; the first and second exchanges, paid in $10,000 cash, had taken place in a Fort Worth Hotel room and the final $10,000 had been in the form of a check from the Houston Ice and Brewing Company. It was a serious allegation. Taking money from brewers was a breach of a 1907 law prohibiting corporate sponsorship of a politician. If true, it not only carried the implication that Ferguson's influence had been for sale from the beginning of his campaign, but also proved that he had misrepresented himself to voters. [13]

Maedgen's story cast new light on a long-forgotten newspaper interview with Ferguson that had taken place soon after he had entered the race for governor. In that article, Jim had gone to great lengths to explain a sum of $30,000 he claimed he had saved for a trip overseas, savings he had decided to convert to campaign funds. A rather defensive statement had followed that declaration: "I won't allow any person of interest to contribute to my campaign." In light of Maedgen's statement, that precautionary stance suddenly made sense. Ferguson had probably hoped to head off any questions that might have arisen about the source of his large campaign fund. [14]

Poe had quickly gone public in Ferguson's defense with a declaration to the press that he had examined the 1914 records of the bank and found no such deposits. This and other displays of support for Ferguson now became problematic for Poe. In joining forces with the Ferguson camp, which always included persecution of Ferguson enemies, Poe had alienated some powerful people. He was sure that an investigation would expose any questionable actions he had taken on Ferguson's behalf. Further, he feared a reversal of allegiance would be difficult, leaving parties on both sides of the aisle angry at him. These were valid assumptions. [15]

In the fall of 1916 Ferguson sued Maedgen and H. C. Glenn as well as the Temple Publishing Company, owner of the local newspaper, for printing negative information about him in that paper. Though the offenders were in Bell County where the offense had taken place, Jim filed his suit in Brenham, Texas, in Washington County. This would become a favorite Ferguson tactic, filing lawsuits in a jurisdiction that was Ferguson-friendly. In the Maedgen case he sought from each source the sum of $50,000 but dropped the suit in February of the following year in exchange for public apologies from Maedgen and Glenn. There were apparently other acts of retaliation meted out to Maedgen. Poe would later testify that he had warned Ferguson about one of the bank's board members who wanted to sell his stock and sever his connections with the bank: "I believe he is selling on account of our attacking Mr. Maedgen as severely as we did in the campaign just closed." The letter went on to say that "He [the board member] suggested two or three times that we would have some damage suits on our hands if we did not quit it and [he] did not seem to like the way we burned Mr. Maedgen up on account of his slanderous lies." [16]

Poe had clearly been party to these kinds of alliances and attacks on Ferguson's enemies, attacks so malicious that perhaps they had caused at least one bank stockholder to put some distance between himself and the group of Ferguson allies.

Mr. Poe had enjoyed certain perks as he piggybacked on the fame of the governor. Among other things, Poe was chosen as one of five men given the privilege of going to Washington D. C. with the governor in December of 1915 to lobby for Dallas as the location for the next national Democratic convention. Quitting his job outright was one of the obvious options for getting out from under his dilemma, but even with all of its problems, he was loath to give up his job. His relationship with the governor had taken on characteristics that often made it seem like a pact with the Devil. Getting out of such a pact would not be easy. Poe knew firsthand the reprisal that would await him once he publicly denounced the governor, and he even had logistical problems. He was not only living in Governor Ferguson's hometown, working in the governor's bank with a nest of Ferguson loyalists, but he and his family lived in the Fergusons' own residence.

By late-1916 the situation had become entirely unsustainable. The bank simply had no chance to prosper under the strain of the limited working capital it held under Ferguson's influence. While Poe was laboring under impossible conditions to make money for the bank, Ferguson added a new layer of insult. He began to blame Poe for the bank's poor performance and groused at the lack of dividend payments. The bank's condition was so dire that Poe would later make this testimony: "Candidly, if I had not gotten those bond deals, the Temple State Bank would have had to close its doors in 1916; that is the absolute truth, gentlemen."[17]

Poe finally made the decision to contact the state Commission of Insurance and Banking. He spoke with C. O. Austin, the chief clerk of the department because, as he later testified, the commissioner, John Patterson, would not schedule an appointment to receive him.[18]

It was not likely that, had Commissioner Patterson agreed to meet with Poe, he would have offered the exasperated banker any assistance. John S. Patterson was a successful lawyer practicing in Waco, Texas, when he met James Ferguson in 1910, well before Jim entered politics. The two men had joined in at least one business venture together, part ownership of a bank in Moody, Texas. When Jim announced his intentions for the candidacy for governor in 1913, Patterson supported him and, once he was elected, Jim appointed Patterson to the position of Commissioner of Insurance and Banking.[19]

In 1916, a troubled bank in Teague, Texas, the Farmers and Merchants State Bank, was the focus of a state investigation. The Insurance and Banking Commission found the bank's reserves seriously inadequate, a situation sufficiently serious to warrant the closing of the bank. In late August, Patterson accompanied bank examiner Eldred McKinnon to Teague to facilitate that closing. T. R. Watson, who owned the troubled bank that also employed his two sons, begged for concessions that Patterson refused. Watson exploded. In a rage he pulled a handgun and shot Patterson at point-blank range, a wound that proved fatal. Though one of Watson's sons fired three shots at bank examiner McKinnon, the frightened bank examiner managed to escape unharmed. Patterson died on August 30, 1916, and on September 1, James Ferguson appointed C. O. Austin, the commission's chief clerk, to replace Patterson. [20]

Poe's cautious exchange with then-Chief Clerk Austin had gained nothing in the way of relief. The young bank president was further discouraged with Austin's assessment of the situation, a discussion that amounted to a scolding. Austin offered Poe a small measure of sympathy for his dilemma but assured Poe that the responsibility for the loan limits rested entirely with him. [21]

Letters between Poe and the governor during 1916 showed the downward spiral of their relationship. As late as November, Poe, attempting to prop up the precarious relationship, signed with this closing, "With regards to you and your family, I am Your Friend...."

A letter dated December 18, 1916, reflected a friendship lost.

> Honorable James E. Ferguson, Austin, Texas
> We have declined payment on your check of one thousand dollars.
> Your total indebtedness including the note of Mrs. Ferguson is more than
> One Hundred Seventy Thousand Dollars and we positively will not pay
> your checks any longer.[22]
> H. C. Poe, President

Though his message was curt, it fell short of showing the level of anger that continued to build in Poe. In a matter of three weeks his unbridled rage would spill out in a letter that he would regret writing for the rest of his life. The "jolly, liberal and energetic businessman" would be pushed to the breaking point by the antics of James Ferguson.

Poe may have wondered if his voice alone was strong enough to initiate the kind of scrutiny necessary to prompt an investigation of the governor's activities. After all, the governor had committed no crime; he merely teetered on the edge of legality, usually dodging any responsibility for his questionable acts. If Poe believed that it was necessary for Ferguson to alienate other, more powerful forces before any action might be taken to investigate his conduct, he relished the opportunity to join those forces.

H. C. Poe may not have been aware of the magnitude of it, but by the end of 1916, those very winds of change were beginning to blow.

Chapter 6
It Is Good to Be King

J im Ferguson began his first term with a bounty of enthusiasm. A retrospective look at his career could scarcely christen 1915 anything less
than his finest hour. At the January 19 inauguration, he appeared
confident and capable showcasing his talent for pleasing an audience.
Like a consummate wordsmith, he delivered an uplifting and well-received inaugural speech in which he emphasized and re-emphasized a sense of profound
responsibility and a need for co-operation in securing those things that represented
the people's will. "You and I upon whose shoulders has fallen the mantle of the
Democratic Fathers, must wear the insignia of power, with credit to ourselves and
with honor to the age in which we live," he told the group. Lieutenant Governor
William Hobby followed with his own compelling words of optimism. The two
leaders were similarly positioned on key issues. With a relationship that was entirely amicable, they launched an administration filled with promise.[1]

The momentum of his victory gave Governor Ferguson a great boost to his
early days in office; he reveled in the popularity and the power that were his. A
decline in popularity of his predecessor, Colquitt, at the end of his term served to
further bolster Ferguson's appeal. The prohibitionists knew that on the state level
they were, for a short while at least, stalled except for opportunities to push for local
option elections in the hope of a "dry" vote. The farmers looked to their new savior
in Austin with hope, and the governor knew that he could ill afford to forsake the
force that had elected him.[2]

Governor Ferguson used his power of appointment liberally, revealing early
a discernible pattern of reward and punishment for those who were Ferguson supporters and those who were not. Not surprisingly, campaign manager and friend
John McKay received his long-awaited appointment as Secretary of State. Even
McKay's wife received a seat on the board of the state library and historical commission and the couple's son, Leslie, received a clerkship in the state offices of the

banking division. Dentist Alexander Dienst, considered a dark horse for the position, was the recipient of a federal appointment as Temple's postmaster. An endorsement from Ferguson and Congressman R. L. Henry facilitated Dienst's selection to that post, a contest in which he beat a dozen hopefuls. To fill three open positions on the Board of Regents of the University of Texas, Ferguson selected Dr. George McReynolds of Temple, Dr. S. J. Jones of Salado, and a man he did not know but who came with high recommendations, Rabbi Maurice Faber of Tyler.[3]

Other men in established state positions who had not supported Ferguson's bid for election soon found themselves unemployed. One such unfortunate was an accomplished black educator and administrator named Edward Blackshear. Since 1897, the well-qualified Blackshear had been the principal of Prairie View Normal and Industrial College and the school had flourished under his leadership. A prohibitionist, Blackshear had supported Thomas Ball in the 1914 race, an act that soon cost him his job. In mid-1915, Ferguson's plan to oust Blackshear succeeded despite protests from many who spoke on behalf of his accomplishments and his abiding love for the college. Ferguson facilitated Blackshear's removal by packing the board with men who would do his bidding, and under extreme pressure the distinguished gentleman resigned. Ferguson had no qualms about stating one of his motives for replacing Blackshear. In his argument for removal, Ferguson stated, "A Negro, has no business whatever taking part in the political affairs of the Democratic party, the white man's party." The ease of the displacement of his perceived enemy and the method he used to obtain that goal, likely further bolstered Ferguson's belief that his authority was extensive.[4]

Within a few months of taking office, Ferguson demonstrated repeatedly his predisposition for a flagrant use of "spoils politics." His desire to dismiss Dr. F. S. White, superintendent of San Antonio's Southwestern Insane Asylum, met with heated resistance. In particular, W. C. Rigsby, a member of the board of managers for the asylum, protested the dismissal of Dr. White, a man he felt had done an exemplary job. Seeing no legitimate reason for White's dismissal, many suspected that Governor Ferguson was eager to release him because he had promised the job to someone else. Rigsby, who remained adamant in his protest of the removal of Dr. White, was himself dismissed as a board member by Ferguson and soon after, in early April, Dr. White suffered the same fate. Ferguson then cast the deciding vote in electing Dr. Beverly Young, his early choice, as Dr. White's replacement.[5]

A similarly displaced state official, W. O. Stamps, the commissioner of prisons, refused to take his dismissal quietly. Stamps penned an angry letter to the governor defending his record as commissioner and challenging the governor's motive. "You know that you fought the confirmation of Mr. Bass and myself for no other reason than we were both prohibitionists and supported Ball in the primaries last summer." This display of frustration on Stamps' part may have given him some level of satisfaction but it did not save his job.[6]

The struggle of capable men and women to maintain their positions at the head of various state agencies continued as Ferguson stacked boards with people who would vote in accordance with his wishes. Mrs. John G. McKay was among those placed on the board that directed state libraries, an act that precipitated the ousting of E. W. Winkler from his post as state librarian. [7]

While Governor Ferguson was busy attending to state matters those first months, Miriam and the couple's daughters, now ten and fourteen, were adjusting to the drastic changes that had taken place in their lives. Ouida described inauguration as, "The end of my simple childhood." Life in the Governor's Mansion was a bit of a shock to a family who had lived in relative seclusion and quiet in the small city of Temple, Texas. No doubt, the biggest adjustment was the loss of anonymity that befell the female members of the Ferguson household as they assumed their roles in the state's First Family. Miriam and her daughters certainly embraced one particular aspect of their public personas; they dressed in high fashion, often sporting fur-trimmed garments and other trendy embellishments.[8]

Miriam, who had resisted being socially involved while in Temple, knew that the public expected her to entertain and interact with the community as the First Lady of Texas. The family that had ridden a wave of popularity based on being the epitome of the common man was suddenly required to blend into the upper echelon of Austin society, and it was an awkward fit. Miriam, feeling fully unequipped to manage the social demands of her post, hired a social secretary to assist her, an action that newspapers quickly picked up. This new notion was one that many Texans did not find palatable. It was not particularly surprising that Miriam felt a need for navigational support on Austin's social scene; however, her choice of Mrs. Edwina Snider of San Antonio proved a bit of a blunder. Mrs. Snider was unfamiliar with Austin's elite and the specific social customs of that audience. Mrs. Ferguson's motive in hiring a secretary, no doubt, was to avoid social faux pas, but ironically the very act of hiring a social secretary inadvertently caused a greater stir than might have resulted from any infractions due to imperfect social skills.[9]

Though Ouida would later write that her parents paid the salary of Mrs. Ferguson's social secretary, Governor's Mansion payroll records submitted to an investigating committee in early 1917 show that the State of Texas paid a monthly salary of $50.00 to Mrs. E. C. Snider, Social Secretary. Laura Johnson, the Fergusons' long-time family maid from Temple, was also on the state payroll as a wash woman who drew $15.00 per month. By 1917, Fairy

Ferguson, the daughter of Jim's brother, Alvah, had replaced Mrs. Snider as Mrs. Ferguson's secretary.[10]

Ouida later spoke of those awkward early social encounters with Austin's elite, a group she divided into three distinctive subgroups: "There is the old Austin set that smugly snubs the other two. There is the University group, who bask in their intellectual superiority, but who, for the sake of University appropriations, tolerate, and at times are very sweet to, the political group on Capitol Hill. The third group, the Politicos, arrive in Austin taking themselves very seriously; they have been sent by the people to save the State government from the other two groups, whom they call high-hat snobs."[11]

Only a strong entrenchment in the Ferguson camp could have exempted any elitist from Ouida's categorization in this manner. Her sentiment was very telling; it indicated that the disdain for the upper class was a sentiment in the Ferguson home not limited to Jim. It also demonstrated well the prejudicial elements in Ouida's writing and showed that the negative nature of the Ferguson family's judgment of others was in place well before Jim Ferguson ran afoul of the University of Texas and, ultimately, the Texas legislature.

But Ouida's reflections were not written until 1946. In 1915, the guests at the Governor's Mansion were probably unaware of the bias held against them as they sipped alcohol-free punch, a mandate of Miriam's, endorsed by Jim. Many of those guests certainly held their own prejudices against "Farmer Jim" and his family. [12]

Adding to the melancholy that plagued the Fergusons as they adjusted to their new surroundings in 1915, were the deaths of both grandmothers within a few months of each other. In March, Eliza Wallace died of pneumonia, and in October, Fannie Ferguson, described in her obituary as a saintly woman, was laid to rest in Salado, Texas. The cause of Mrs. Ferguson's death was listed as "a general breakdown and collapse." At the time of her death, Fannie was twice distinguished by being the current Texas governor's mother, and the niece of a former Alabama governor, Benjamin Fitzpatrick. For Miriam, a period of mourning provided a brief respite from the duties of socializing, duties that she never fully embraced.[13]

The Governor's Mansion, built in 1856, had received extensive repairs just prior to the Fergusons' arrival but it was still in need of some modernization. The winter of 1915 was brutally cold and the Fergusons quickly discovered that the heating in the mansion was grossly inadequate. In spite of the generous appropriation sums for mansion improvements in the 1911–13 and 1913–15 biennial budgets that funded a multitude of much-needed repairs, every inadequacy of the stately old home could not be addressed. The major additions and repairs, made during the Colquitt administration, were completed just days before the Fergusons' arrival at the famous home. They included a conservatory, new bedrooms, an entire new kitchen wing, and a basement. Exterior upgrades included removal of most of the outhouses in the rear of the mansion, new street paving and the painting of the tan brick exterior to the bright white that defines the structure today. By the time the Fergusons arrived, the mansion was in the most beautiful condition of its sixty-year history. [14]

Beautiful though it may have been, the home was uncomfortable in the absence of a much-needed steam-heating system, a failing that resulted from the depleted renovation budget. Dependent to a great extent on the home's fireplaces and scarce gas radiators for heat, an impractical solution for such cavernous spaces, the house was so icy cold that guests and family members rarely shed their coats during winter months. However, when the Fergusons were given an allowance for mansion improvements of their choosing, their selections did not include a heating system. Miriam requested a greenhouse and arranged to have her name written in a block of wet cement to solidify her connection to the structure. Though "set in stone," so-to-speak, Mrs. Ferguson's action did not achieve the permanence she sought; Mrs. Hobby, the following First Lady, removed her name, a move that still did not end the story. **Governor** Miriam Ferguson later reinstated her name at the greenhouse entrance in 1925, and no subsequent First Lady dared disturb it, perhaps for fear of her return. Jim's choice of improvements was for screening of the upstairs porches, a request that received approval but initiated the scorn of one professor of Architecture at the University of Texas. S. E. Gideon complained that screened porches did nothing to compliment the architectural style and dignity of the stately building. In so doing, it is fair to surmise that Professor Gideon earned himself a place on the list of elitists that the Fergusons found objectionable. The desperately needed steam heating was finally installed during the following administration of Governor William Hobby. [15]

Ferguson detractors, resigned to making the best of Ferguson's two-year term, re-examined and re-evaluated their options under the new administration. In early January newspapers carried an open letter written to Ferguson from the Women's Suffrage Association, seeking the new governor's support. Annette Finnigan, the writer and president of the organization, reminded Ferguson that twelve states had already granted the ballot to women and five others had similar amendments pending. The governor did not respond. Ferguson's inaction probably did not surprise the women's group, but his next move may have. The governor proved he had an entirely different goal in mind for Texas women when he issued what he called "what I most wish for Texas." In that statement, he encouraged an increase in population which he backed by offering cash rewards to the first set of twins and first set of triplets born in 1915. His wish list also included more immigration, less cotton in favor of more corn production, more hogs, cattle, and sheep, and more railroads and highways. [16]

Ferguson knew the importance of establishing a working relationship with President Woodrow Wilson, and set out to do so even before he began his term as governor. A friendly relationship with the president was not a natural fit since Wilson was a prohibitionist, but, remembering that many of Colquitt's problems were a result of his troubled relationship with federal leaders, Ferguson tried to avoid making the same mistake. Wilson's endorsement for Thomas Ball was apparently forgiven or tabled. Ferguson began with a consolatory letter to Wilson on the death of his wife and progressed to a visit to Washington in October, a visit that included a short conversation with the president. Knowing that federal support in handling border disputes had been a point of consternation for Colquitt, Jim offered his approval of any actions Wilson thought appropriate in dealing with the issues on the Mexican border. In doing this, and with other statements made in support of the national Democratic platform, Jim achieved the amicable relationship with Wilson that he sought. [17]

The border trouble that had plagued Colquitt increased dramatically just as Ferguson took office. Problems stemmed, in part, from the chaos and violence associated with the Mexican Revolution, violence that spilled over the border into South Texas. Colquitt struggled to curb the loss of property and life created when Mexican rebels raided Texas farms, homes, and trains. When he received inadequate help from President Wilson, Colquitt ordered his own Texas Rangers to the border. This group of Rangers was far too small to be very effective and their aggressiveness earned them a reputation for violence. They were often powerless to catch bandits who quickly escaped across the Rio Grande to the safety of Mexican soil. When Colquitt sought permission from President Wilson to enter Mexico in pursuit of the criminals, the president denied the request. Because the US had refused to recognize any of the three revolutionists who sought acknowledgment as the official leader of Mexico in 1914, any serious dialogue between the two countries was impossible, further frustrating Governor Colquitt. [18]

Fear and racial tension reigned in border towns, but the discovery of a bizarre plan called the Plan of San Diego (named for San Diego, Texas) further exacerbated the situation. The details of the plan, discovered in January of 1915 with the arrest of one of the Mexican rebels, Basilio Ramos, were frightening. The document exposed the intent of its drafters to eliminate the white race in several states, beginning with South Texas. The plan further sought to take these areas by force and later annex the border states back to Mexico. This finding placed a renewed urgency on the border situation. [19]

Additional Texas Rangers deployed to the troubled areas with some success but raids on Texas ranches and towns continued and the pillaging and indiscriminate murders left Texans no less frightened. In the summer of 1915, Ferguson took decisive action when he assigned Ranger Captain Henry Ransom to recruit members for a newly formed Company D, whose mission it was to clean up the border mess by whatever means necessary. Ferguson did not mince words, telling Ransom that he wanted the problem cleaned up if he had to "kill every damned man down there." Ferguson further assured Ransom that he had the pardoning power necessary to exonerate the men who carried out the mission. Ferguson's declaration of an anticipated need for pardons seemed to almost invite unscrupulous tactics. [20]

Ransom had a reputation for using unconventional means, means that were unacceptable to most members of law enforcement and they feared the result of his newly acquired power. Their fears were justified. Swift recruitment absent a well-conceived plan and the governor's granting of carte blanche proved disastrous. Within a few months, rumors of abuses by Rangers against Mexicans began to surface. The most common infractions were hasty executions of prisoners without trial, but rumors of torture and cover ups of the atrocities also surfaced. These acts were an unfortunate blight on the reputation of the lawmen and, even though questionable actions by Texas Rangers existed before and after James Ferguson's terms, Ranger misconduct under the Ferguson regime was particularly egregious. The years 1915–1917 proved a dark chapter in the history of the force. [21]

In October of 1915, President Wilson finally recognized Venustiano Carranza as the leader of the Mexican Republic. The following month, Ferguson met with Carranza in Nuevo Laredo where Carranza agreed to curtail the rebels and, for a short while, the violence slowed. Few doubted the temporary nature of the reduced turmoil and violence, however. [22]

By the time Ferguson's term as governor was in full swing, World War I had been raging in Europe for six months. The United States' involvement in the war was neither immediate nor enthusiastic. The fighting Europeans received American sympathy but no immediate intervention as President Wilson tried to maintain an increasingly unrealistic position of neutrality. A warning of future involvement came when Wilson agreed to the formation of a plan called "Preparedness," a plan designed to expand the army in readiness of war. Many Americans opposed the plan, but Ferguson, who still guarded his relationship with Wilson, openly backed the president. It was the initiation of conscription in 1917 that caused Ferguson's support to waver. [23]

In late July of 1915, the Fergusons' hometown of Temple was the scene of two horrific crimes. Five members of the Grimes family were brutally attacked in their sleep and, to the best of Will Grimes's impaired memory, the attacker had been a black man wielding a hammer. The young family lived on a farm just southeast of Temple, where a neighbor who had visited the home hoping to borrow some motor oil discovered the gruesome murder scene. Three of the Grimes children, twins aged seven months and their older brother William Jr., aged seven, were apparently bludgeoned while they slept. Both adults, Will and Annie, were also savagely beaten while asleep, beatings they miraculously survived. The perpetrator had also sexually assaulted Mrs. Grimes. Three other Grimes children, sleeping in an adjacent room, escaped harm.

News of the crime spread quickly through the community and the outrage was broad and intense. When word of the tragic murders reached Governor Ferguson, he offered a reward of $500 for information leading to the capture of the perpetrator, and Bell County Sheriff Hugh Smith offered an additional reward of $200. Law enforcement soon located three suspicious black men in the nearby city of Rogers with the help of local authorities. Two of the men were locals, but the third, Will Stanley, was from Fort Worth, or so he claimed. He had hopped a ride on a train and arrived in the area early that morning. There was compelling evidence against Stanley, who wore two pairs of pants, the outer pair containing the printed name of Will Grimes inside. Stanley claimed he had gotten the pants from the other two men, a claim they denied. Officials detained all three men, but considered Stanley the key suspect.

Law enforcement knew immediately that they had a tough job ahead of them in protecting Will Stanley from the angry public that began gathering in Rogers. As they transported their suspect to Temple, a long stream of cars filled with revenge-seeking members of the community followed them. Once in Temple, the size of the mob and the intensity of their rage swelled as they demanded that Stanley be turned over to them for immediate punishment. Efforts at negotiations between those in authority and mob spokesmen lasted for several hours before the restless mob pushed their way into the jail and took control of the prisoner. The crowd dragged the suspect to the town square and there they burned him in a raging fire while hundreds of spectators, including women and children, watched. In the aftermath, some collected souvenirs from the ashes while others hung his charred remains from a telephone pole where it remained for several hours.

Officials released the other Negro men for their own protection and the pair quickly left the area. Although the anger generated by the murder of the Grimes children was understandable, the crowd's savage reaction was indefensible. The evil was compounded by a complete absence of outrage over the brutal murder of Will Stanley. There were no arrests, no serious investigation, and certainly no punishment for any of the members of the mob who murdered the suspect without a trial. Authorities, who had argued and attempted to negotiate with mob leaders on that fateful evening, clearly knew their identities. Remembering that this same citizenry had over the years dedicated a great deal of effort to fight the ill effects of alcohol and other perceived evils rendered any reconciliation of these conflicting values impossible. Local officials let the matter drop and Governor Ferguson issued a statement saying that he would not order an investigation.[24]

James Ferguson probably held no more or less racial prejudice than the average southern white man of his day. In view of that, Ferguson's failure to take any action to force an investigation against the murderous mob that killed Mr. Stanley is not particularly unusual given its timing. One year later a similar scene played out in Waco, Texas. This lynching and mutilation of a seventeen-year-old Negro boy also went unpunished. The significance of these stories, as they relate to Ferguson, is in their ability to quash any notion that James Ferguson was a man who championed or protected the rights of blacks. His contention that he was a defender of the rights of the less fortunate and his stance against the Ku Klux Klan may have led some to draw the erroneous conclusion that he was a great humanitarian.[25]

In Austin, Governor Ferguson enjoyed a high level of popularity and a relatively harmonious relationship with legislators. His first year in office was a successful one and he was true to his campaign pledges. The legislature was supportive of most of his ideas, and with that support he was able to make some valuable changes for the state. It was early April when Ferguson's "no action" promise was first tested by the legislature. House Bill 385, which passed the legislature without opposition, sought to reduce the tax on certain quantities of alcohol sold by druggists and suggested other restrictions on alcohol. With much fanfare the governor vetoed the bill, citing his campaign promise to do so, before returning it to the Secretary of State.[26]

Governor Ferguson was anything but neutral about the sale of alcohol, a subject that was both political and personal to him. Prior to his governorship, he had fought for many years to keep his home county "wet," and his move to Austin and his declaration that he would make prohibition a "non-issue" had done nothing to minimize his true sentiment. Under so strong an opinion, his publicly stated neutral stance on the subject could not endure. In November of 1915, Ferguson betrayed that pledge when he launched a two-day campaign with powerful speeches in Rogers and Temple, ending on the eve of a Bell County local option vote. In two almost identical speeches before large crowds who endured a drizzling rain to hear him, Ferguson expressed his belief that the county election was a personal attack organized to discredit him. In turn, he attacked local church workers for their efforts in support of a dry vote, and denounced a recent revival that he claimed disparaged his name. For over an hour he railed, veering off subject to remind the audience of his good works as governor and making a veiled threat to farmers that, should they vote for his enemies, the tenant bill might be reversed. [27]

Ferguson received a double blow the following day when Bell County voters chose to ban alcohol. He had lost both battle and war when his impassioned plea could not raise public sentiment in his favor, even with the prestige of his title. For a man whose power of persuasion generally met with success, the loss represented a significant rejection. The impact on Bell County was soon realized; some twenty-two saloons closed on the following Christmas Day in response to the new law. [28]

The anti-prohibitionists soon received another disappointment. Brewing interests, long suspected of infusing large sums of money into elections in an effort to thwart and offset prohibition efforts, became the target of an anti-trust suit by Attorney General B. F. Looney. The suit, filed in January of 1915, took an entire year to come to trial. The result showed that, indeed, brewing interests had spent enormous sums in support of wet candidates over a period of many years. The offending brewers pled guilty and quickly paid their $281,000 fines to quiet the subject. [29]

In spite of Ferguson's efforts to help tenants with a law to regulate rents, the legislation that became law failed to impact the tenant problem to any significant degree. The law, found unconstitutional in 1921, was never well enforced. Legislators passed a compulsory school attendance law and approved generous state funding for rural schools and other schools including the University of Texas. A new law encouraged school districts to pay for public text books with tax money so that even the poorest of children had access to school books. Ferguson was also instrumental in obtaining funding for a large new facility for the insane, and the State Board of Public Accountancy was established under his watch. The failure of the Gibson Bill, designed to relieve some restrictions on out-of-state insurance companies, was a major disappointment to the governor. Though he supported the bill heartily, in his farm-boy vernacular he claimed he was "not sore" when it failed to pass by a slim margin. [30]

The funding for education did not come without a cost to taxpayers. The state ad valorem tax rose from 12.5 to 30 cents, an increase that Jim had to defend during his re-election campaign in 1916. [31]

Jim was entirely correct in his belief that Texas schools needed support and funding. Because Texas was not keeping pace with other states in the area of education, an embarrassingly high illiteracy rate resulted. While his emphasis was on rural schools, he assured the University of Texas that their funding would not suffer as a result of that emphasis. During his first term, he kept that promise—albeit with a large string attached. A pattern began to emerge: when Jim Ferguson used his considerable influence to obtain something for somebody, the recipient was in his debt in all respects. Payment of that debt required absolute loyalty and anyone who misunderstood that unspoken rule quickly incurred the wrath of the governor. [32]

In July 1915, the governor addressed a large group of county school superintendents and teachers at the University of Texas. The acting president of the university, William Battle, introduced him. He encouraged and praised the distinguished group, and in acknowledgement of the large number of women in the audience, said, "I am not afraid to tell you how I stand on the suffrage question. If a woman wants more power, the only thing to do is to give it to her, for she'll get it anyway. A man and his wife never did have a fight but that the man came out second best. If the women want to vote, why I say, let them vote." Ferguson was clearly humoring his audience; his subsequent actions showed that he had no interest in aiding females who sought enfranchisement. [33]

Eight months into his term, a powerful hurricane hit Galveston and the surrounding coastal area with disastrous results. The calamity killed several hundred people and caused $50 million in property damage. The seawall, a structure built after the devastating hurricane of 1900, lessened the impact of the twenty-one-foot waves; even so, flooding was a major problem. Newspapers published Ferguson's public appeal for contributions of money, food, and clothing for the displaced. The appeal ended thus, "I can give the quickest relief with money, but if you haven't money, you can send food or clothing, and I shall undertake to see that it is properly distributed. Remittances and donations can be made to me direct, at Austin, Texas." [34]

Jim Ferguson had a particular interest in Texas prisons and prisoners. For some years, the Texas prison system had attempted to fund itself through a system of leasing convict labor to third parties, a practice abolished in 1910. But state-owned farms also used prisoners for agricultural labor, a plan that Ferguson believed was a better fit. The governor expanded this program, buying substantial amounts of additional prison farm acreage. During 1916–1918, the money generated from state prison farms rendered the system temporarily profitable. Even with this success, the subject of prison reform was not without controversy for Governor Ferguson.[35]

As part of his prison reform strategy, the governor declared that he planned to hear the plea of every one of the 3,800 convicts in the Texas prison system. The declaration, made at the Texas State Fair on opening day, came at a time when there were already one hundred pardons pending as a result of his plan. While his intention of pardoning those lawbreakers who were good candidates for assimilation back into society may have seemed noble, it was certainly controversial, as it stood to undermine the authority of judges and jurors. A prison system that depended on the early release program as a system to reward good behavior was weakened as prisoners shifted their efforts from earning early release through good behavior to sending their families to Austin to appeal to the governor. Even so, Ferguson granted a sizable number of pardons, the first two within his first thirty days in office. When he was highly criticized, Jim defended his actions, saying that pardons helped to right the wrongs of the prejudicial courts. Later, when rumors of sold pardons began to circulate, the buzz overshadowed any positive aspects related to the plethora of concessions that the governor granted during his term. It was a subject that would forever link him, and later Miriam as well, to controversy.[36]

Though Ferguson tried to link his liberal pardon policy and push for prison reform to his humanitarian spirit, his message was not consistent. In his 1914 campaign he had expressed his desire to treat prisoners who behaved well humanely, leaving his listener to wonder what kind of treatment the poorly behaved prisoner might expect. He also made a statement in opposition to reform saying, "This much talked about idea of reformation of criminals does not appeal to me. . . I welcome his reform but when he comes back I want him to go away back and sit down. I want him to evidence his reformation by sincere humility."[37]

The pardon policy was not enough to adversely affect Ferguson's overall reputation during his first term. A prominent feeling of well-being was his to enjoy as cotton prices stabilized after a critical drop and began to increase. Though the increased demand for cotton was due to the war raging in Europe, Texas, like many states, welcomed one of the few fortunate side effects of war, a boost to its economy. Dealings with the federal government remained harmonious. Ferguson's popularity was undeniable, leaving one senator to predict as early as August of 1915 that no man would have the political guts to take on Ferguson, whom he dubbed "the Democratic Moses."[38]

Chapter 7
A Season of Success Begins to Fade

In January of 1916, trouble in Mexico erupted again. Pancho Villa, seeking recognition as the leader of Mexico, was angry that the distinction had gone to Carranza, a fact that left him determined to continue the violence against Americans. Under his leadership, members of Villa's army stopped a train and summarily executed eighteen Americans on January 19, 1916. Two months later, Villa led four hundred men who raided and burned the town of Columbus, New Mexico, killing both private citizens and cavalry troops sent to defend them. In mid-March, in response to these attacks, President Wilson sent American troops under the command of Brigadier General John Pershing into Mexico in pursuit of Villa, an expedition that lasted almost a year. While the pursuers were successful in crippling the band of marauders, they did not kill or capture Villa. But for a time, Texas had the benefit of federal support in its border-war effort.[1]

In June of 1916 President Wilson directed the entire National Guard to the Texas-Mexico border, a show of force that essentially ended the bandit wars, except for minor clashes that continued for another two years. On April 6, 1917, the escalation of World War I diverted the nation's attention from domestic issues when the United States entered the fray. However, in Austin, the legislature was still grappling with the border crisis and ways to avert future trouble. In early May, with Ferguson's backing, members of the legislature passed a bill that provided for the addition of a thousand men to the Texas Ranger force.[2]

Unfortunately, an addition of new members was not the solution to the problem of rogue rangers already within the group's ranks. That remedy would not come until 1919 when an investigation launched by a representative in the legislature, Mr. J. T. Canales of Brownsville, looked into the atrocities that had occurred along the border at the hands of Texas Rangers during the period known as the Bandit Wars. The results of that investigation proved that some bad apples did exist in the Ranger barrel, and ended with a tightening and reduction in the Ranger force.[3]

Jim Ferguson had amassed great power within the Democratic Party and proved he was eager to use it when the 1916 Democratic conventions were held. He not only mended his relationship with Joseph Bailey, but he also partnered with that flamboyant delegate. The two took charge of the state convention in San Antonio in May of 1916, ensuring that they tabled all efforts to promote prohibition and women's suffrage. To cement their intentions, they defined their opposition to suffrage and prohibition as "unalterable" in their platform draft. Their domination at the convention served several purposes, not the least of which was a change in rules that ensured Ferguson a spot as a delegate to the upcoming Democratic National Convention in St. Louis. The two men were successful in achieving their goals when delegates passed their plank by an astounding majority. [4]

At the Democratic National Convention held in June in St. Louis, Missouri, the Ferguson-Bailey pair was not satisfied to simply ignore the thousands of women who came to appeal for suffrage. The pair attempted to publicly humiliate the female force with speeches that included references to "a woman's place." In the end, however, the women who overflowed the galleries of the convention hall turned the tables on Ferguson with a hissing response that was humiliating to the state of Texas in general and to Ferguson in particular. President Wilson, who had not always been in favor of women's suffrage, had by 1916 altered his view and thrown his support to the female cause. Ferguson and Bailey might well have re-examined their own views in light of the rising number of states that were granting women the right to vote. It was a movement whose time had come. Jim Ferguson's much belated acceptance of the female in the voting booth proved a great irony later in his life, but in 1916 he seemed to underestimate the magnitude and imminence of the advancing force. [5]

As Governor Ferguson rode a wave of popularity with the public in 1916, few knew that his private business affairs were in turmoil. In subsequent years, the Fergusons would point to the governor's salary and the expense of the impeachment as a reason for their deplorable financial condition, but in reality, the family's financial situation was in peril well in advance of his governorship. From his first day in office, Jim Ferguson was living on borrowed money, a slippery slope for a man living under the glare of public scrutiny—a man who purported to possess the business sense necessary to run the state. If the governor expected the Bell-Bosque or the Sparks property to generate income sufficient to compensate for his scant salary, it was a critical miscalculation. Both properties were highly leveraged, including both land and stock, and there is no evidence that either was sufficiently profitable to support the Ferguson family. The insubstantial dividends and earnings from his other holdings were likewise inadequate to make up for the deficit. [6]

H. C. Poe was not the only Temple resident suffering a troubled relationship with the governor in 1916. In April, the trustees of Memorial Baptist Church of Temple sent a letter to the governor reminding him of an outstanding pledge in the amount of $375. Their request met with an angry response in which Ferguson accused the Reverend Carroll Smith of having "willfully misrepresented" him during his campaign, and an assurance that no further pledge payments would be forthcoming. [7]

In August, the secretary of the Temple Chamber of Commerce, John Land, wrote Ferguson asking him to assist his hometown in securing a coveted federal farm loan bank. Temple was one of several cities under consideration for the project. In addition to asking for Ferguson's participation on the committee that would work toward securing the bank for Temple, Mr. Land sought advice and suggestions from the governor. Ferguson's reply that he would rather see the bank go to one of the other cities must have shocked Mr. Land. "As I have so many good, true and loyal friends in these towns, and as I appear to have so few friends in the Temple Chamber of Commerce, I do not feel that I ought to take any active interest in this contest. The activities of your officers have made my further connection with the Temple Chamber of Commerce wholly distasteful." [8]

In October, a local hospital sought to collect, by letter, a pledge that Mrs. Ferguson had made in the amount of $212. Ferguson rebuffed the request with this message, "There is no contract or obligation of Mrs. Ferguson or anybody else to pay this money… It was further understood at the time that your association would at least divide its bank account in Temple …."[9] It seemed evident that the source of Ferguson's anger and the reason he did not intend to honor Mrs. Ferguson's pledge, was the exclusion of the Temple State Bank from those that were recipients of the association's deposits.

The governor wasn't the only Ferguson experiencing financial difficulties in 1916. Jim Ferguson's oldest brother Alvah, father of ten, was struggling. In the same manner that he had used his political connections to secure a position of postmaster for his friends Fred Guffy and later Alexander Dienst, Jim worked to get Alvah a postmaster position. His efforts included a telegram sent to Postmaster General A. S. Burleson in Washington in late August. Even though Jim had, in a personal letter to a friend, referred to Charles Culberson as "a lunatic" the month before, he implored the ageing Senator to aid him in securing a postmaster position for Alvah. Culberson obtained confirmation in early September. When Jim wrote Alvah with the good news, he included a lecture about personal finances, admonishing his brother to be "economical" and save some of his earnings. "This is about your last chance," the governor wrote. "Explain the matter to your family, and above all things, do not become extravagant because of being appointed to the office." [10]

As Ferguson's first term drew to a close at the end of 1916, he began to succumb to Poe's pressure. Knowing that Poe would like nothing more than to have him out of reach of any authority in the bank, he approached Poe with the proposition that he sell his entire block of bank stock to him. The two were never able to agree on a price, but Ferguson wrote to Poe in November of 1916: "You are missing a chance of a lifetime if you do not buy this stock. I would like to see you have it; but feel there is a $50,000 intangible asset by virtue of the going business and the location of our bank. Please let me know at once if you would be interested as I have some notes maturing soon, secured by the stock, which I will have to renew."[11]

By Ferguson's own admission, debt encumbered his stock. Selling it to Poe or anyone else would not have raised enough cash to pay off Ferguson's debts. Poe had balked at the price Ferguson asked for the stock and he was not alone. When Poe approached the bank's board with the possibility of buying back Ferguson's shares, they agreed that Ferguson sought an inflated price. While the cost of the building may or may not have reflected an undervaluation, there were other intangible liabilities that offset that appraisal. The reputation of the bank was fragile; the revelation of its secrets could have thrown it into serious trouble at any time. Keeping solvent renters in the bank's open storefronts and offices was never guaranteed, a realization that Poe had faced in relation to the problems with the defunct Texas Store. This surely left Poe and the members of the board to doubt that they were "missing the chance of a lifetime" in their decision not to buy the stock. In the end, Ferguson retained the stock and his financial problems continued. However, his financial dilemma, though serious, would soon take a backseat to other, more pressing and public issues. [12]

In the summer of 1916, Governor Ferguson busied himself with a campaign for re-election. Charles H. Morris, a banker from Houston, challenged Ferguson for the nomination, and in doing so made some interesting allegations against the governor. Among them was a charge related to the misappropriation of state funds.

The courts had decided a similar case against Governor Oscar Colquitt, Ferguson's predecessor, for the misuse of state money appropriated for lights, fuel, and ice. Colquitt explained that the money in question, an amount less than $200, had been used to pay for chicken salad, chips, olives, and punch served at an official reception. These kinds of functions, he contended, were an expected part of the governor's duties. In light of Colquitt's explanation and the small amount of money involved, the infringement did not seem particularly egregious. But the case had forced a clarification in the interpretation of the law. The court ruled that the governor's groceries were *not* an expense of the state regardless of their purpose. The subject seemed closed once Colquitt reimbursed the state for the expenses in question. Charles Morris accused Ferguson of the same infraction, an accusation that initially received little attention but laid the groundwork for future scrutiny. Likewise, other charges made by Morris, including the accusation that $30,000 in campaign funds from Texas brewers had financed Ferguson's 1914 campaign, aroused little interest. The harmony Governor Ferguson had enjoyed with the legislature and his resulting popularity were waning slightly but were apparently strong enough to overshadow the allegations against him for a large number of voters. Ferguson defeated Morris but not with the sweeping margin he expected. [13]

In December 1916, Secretary of State McKay announced his resignation from the position for which he had lobbied, citing insufficient remuneration as the reason. He immediately took up another position with the state, that of manager of a large state-owned prison farm. The 6,000-acre prison farm in Madison County produced large amounts of cotton with the use of convict labor. McKay would oversee the operation. [14]

Ferguson's second term, beginning in 1917, was not particularly productive. Greater appropriations led to greater ad valorem taxes, which reached a record high of thirty-five cents. The administration was successful in establishing the State Highway Commission during that time, but little else. A major distraction was brewing that would take legislators completely off course. The catalyst that would set that catastrophic chain of events in motion was a minor difference of opinion between the governor and the acting president of the University of Texas that had begun in 1915. This friction, which later precipitated an intervention by Will Hogg and other heavy-hitters, would leave a deep scar on Texas history. Ironically, the name of the man who became Jim Ferguson's nemesis in this history-making battle with the University of Texas was William J. Battle.

Chapter 8
A Falling Out and a Fall from Grace

Though harmonious on most fronts, the governor's first term was not without hitches, the most serious of which was a festering dislike for some of the staff members of the University of Texas. If the governor's early popularity left him looking for a chance to flex his gubernatorial muscle as well as a chance to indulge his grudge against the elite "university crowd," as he often described them, he found such an opportunity early in his term when the two-year university budget reached his desk toward the beginning of 1915.

In 1914, the president of the University of Texas, Sidney Mezes, resigned to take a position as president of the City College of New York. The Board of Regents, the nine-member board that held the authority to do so, chose as a temporary replacement a classics professor and the dean of the faculty, Dr. William J. Battle. The pairing of Ferguson and Battle, even briefly for a single purpose, produced a colossal clash of cultures. Battle had distinguished himself in the study of Greek, Latin, and classical studies, and was the son of a former president of the University of North Carolina. He had earned his Ph.D. at Harvard University. By contrast, Jim Ferguson characterized his own education as a sixth-grade equivalent. Ironically, the two men met with the shared goal of supporting and advancing higher education for Texas but no subject more perfectly represented the great divide that existed between them.[1]

Their duties intersected in the spring of 1915 when Governor Ferguson summoned Battle to his office to discuss the university budget that awaited his approval. Interim-President Battle was at a slight disadvantage because the budget that he had presented on behalf of the university was not of his own making. He had taken the budget that his capable predecessor had prepared, reviewed it, obtained approval from the regents, and submitted it. Certainly Dr. Battle did not expect trouble. Governor Ferguson had initiated the request for a generous appropriation for the institution, a move that seemed to represent his full support. Legislators had granted that request and had also approved the associated budget. But the meeting quickly became uncomfortable for Dr. Battle as Governor Ferguson sternly questioned certain budgeted items. Battle addressed the questions to the best of his ability but was unable to diffuse the governor's attitude of distrust and agitation.[2]

Though Ferguson eventually signed the budget, his subsequent actions proved that he had no intention of letting the matter drop. He persisted with condemnation of the university's budget process and pushed for a rule that would require future itemized budgets. Battle pushed back; he found itemization impractical and unnecessary. The governor expanded his rant, denouncing Battle to the board and declaring him unfit for the job. The board, chaired by Will Hogg, took no immediate action against Dr. Battle, a fact that further angered the governor.

William C. Hogg was the oldest son of Governor James Hogg, a fact that might have endeared him to Jim Ferguson, but for some reason, did not. "Will" Hogg was an accomplished businessman and an avid supporter of the arts, a commitment he proved throughout his life with innumerable quiet acts of philanthropy. Above all else, Hogg was an advocate for higher education. In particular he supported and championed the University of Texas from which he had obtained a law degree in 1897, founding the institution's Ex-Students Association. But Hogg's support for education was by no means limited to Austin. He established student loan funds at colleges throughout the state and left in his will large sums of money for that purpose.[3]

Will Hogg was aware of the governor's propensity for unprovoked acrimony. A mild dispute between Mr. Hogg and James Ferguson had arisen very soon after Ferguson had taken office in 1915. Hogg's view on the subject of a single board for the state's two largest universities seemed to anger Ferguson from the beginning of the discussion. By September of 1915, when Ferguson's anger seemed interminable, Hogg felt compelled to write a letter requesting a meeting of reconciliation. Hoping to establish a tone that would encourage cooperation, Hogg wrote, "There are orderly, non-frictional ways of settling points of differences between fair-minded men if they will banish anger." With Hogg's term as a regent set to end in 1916, these differences between the two men in late 1915 seemed relatively inconsequential, and compared to later events, they certainly were.[4]

Hoping to act as peace-maker, Will Hogg responded to Ferguson's accusations against Dr. Battle with an offer of intervention that met with an immediate rejection by Ferguson. His request for a meeting with the governor elicited this response: "If it is your purpose to have a conference with a view of retaining Dr.

Battle as President of the University, no good purpose can be subserved [*sic*] by talking about that question."[5]

By the time the governor did finally meet with Will Hogg and other regents, his anger had advanced to a stage that would not be placated with anything less than the immediate dismissal of Dr. Battle. He had no qualms about stating his intentions, telling the board, "the longer you keep Dr. Battle, the harder I am going to make it on the University." When the group again asked Ferguson about his reasons, he responded, "I don't have to give any reasons. I am Governor of the State of Texas."[6]

As the board continued its search for a permanent university president, in October of 1915, Dr. Battle withdrew his name from consideration citing "the positive ill-will of Governor Ferguson" as an obstacle to the necessary co-operation of the administration he would require to properly perform his duties. The committee of four charged with making a recommendation to the board for a new president asked Dr. Battle to continue in that capacity until they could secure a replacement, a request he graciously accommodated. In April of 1916, Battle stepped down in favor of the newly elected president, Robert E. Vinson. Jim Ferguson's tirade would not be quieted with this change, however. In fact, the board's election of Dr. Vinson, absent a request for approval from Governor Ferguson, only antagonized him further.[7]

The forty-year-old Dr. Vinson came from a position as president of the Presbyterian Theological Seminary in Austin, a distinction he had held for eight years. He had received his education from Austin College at Sherman, Union Theological Seminary in Virginia, and the University of Chicago. Afterward he had taught for fourteen years at the seminary in Austin where he had risen to the position of president. Jim Ferguson was not impressed.[8]

When Vinson called on the governor in June 1916, he asked the chief executive for two things: the governor's cooperation, and an assurance that the governor would make frequent speeches on the university's behalf. If the latter appeal was an attempt to appease and flatter the governor who loved nothing more than public speaking, Ferguson's reaction was true to his nature. He readily agreed to make frequent speeches, but let Vinson know that very little, if any, cooperation would be forthcoming. The governor made no pretense of his animosity toward the new university president, informing Vinson that he believed him unqualified for his job. He further railed against certain faculty and staff members, Battle among them, whom he wished to see removed from their positions, demanding that Vinson oust them. A startled Vinson responded with a request for specific charges against the accused men, but Ferguson remained vague about his grievances. Ferguson's final statement was a threat;

if Vinson did not terminate the objectionable faculty and staff members, he would make things very difficult for the school. The governor promised Vinson that, absent his cooperation in removing the targeted employees, he was in for "the biggest bear fight of his life."[9]

If Vinson doubted the degree of the governor's antagonism toward him, he was soon confronted with another example of the depth of the chief executive's ire. Vinson planned and executed a large dinner party at which the governor was to be the guest of honor. Not only did Ferguson fail to attend, he also failed to extend the courtesy of a response to the invitation.[10]

A series of letters that passed between the two men best demonstrates their subsequent communications. On September 5, 1916, Vinson wrote to Ferguson asking for specific charges against the offending faculty so that the board could undertake an investigation. No doubt Vinson carefully chose his words as he wrote:

> The Honorable James Ferguson, Governor of Texas, Austin, Texas
> Dear Governor Ferguson:
> The next meeting of the Board of Regents of the University of Texas will be held on the fourth Tuesday of October, next being the twenty fourth . . . Sometime during the month of June, in a conversation which I had with you in your office, you indicated to me that there were certain charges which you desired to make with reference to certain members of the present faculty of the University. In order that I may have some basis on which to work in this matter, I am taking this opportunity to ask you if you will not be kind enough to have the material in your possession upon this point in such shape that I may make immediate investigation and have time enough to ascertain the facts, so as to be able to make a suitable report to the Board of Regents. I am leaving for El Paso tonight, and expect to return one week from today, after which time I shall call upon you in your office and go into this matter as thoroughly as you may desire.
>
> Very cordially yours,
> Robert E. Vinson, President [11]

The letter infuriated Ferguson. Vinson's reference to the material in his possession amounted to a calling of his bluff. Ferguson had intimated to Vinson in the June meeting that he had evidence against the men in question, evidence that he intended to deliver when he felt the time was appropriate.[12]

The governor replied to Vinson's letter four days later with this writing:

Dr. Robert E. Vinson,

President, State University, Austin, Texas.

Dear Sir:

Your favor of September 5 is received. In the first place, I emphatically deny that I ever indicated or intimated that I wanted to make any charges against anybody; and I told you then and there the names of the members of the faculty whom I thought objectionable, and I have not changed my mind.

I think for the future it will be better for us to remain in our respective jurisdictions, and no good purpose can be subserved [*sic*] by any further relations between us.

I shall deal with the Board of Regents, and you can do likewise; and you can rest assured that I shall promptly and surely meet the issue which it is apparent from your letter that you intend to force upon me.

Very Truly,

James E. Ferguson, Governor[13]

After returning from El Paso, Vinson made an additional lengthy reply in a letter dated September 16. In that document he suggested that the governor had misunderstood his motives in writing the first letter and assured him that he was trying to do what was proper and in the best interests of the university. He quoted the bylaws that required the president of the university to "be prepared to give the board information regarding the competence and loyalty of officers, teachers and employees." Vinson made every attempt to appease the governor; his letter was sincere and respectful, and he offered his full cooperation and the assurance that he had an open mind to discuss the issue further.[14]

Ferguson, not waiting for a reply from Vinson, began to draw support for his "bear fight" where he could. He crafted a letter to Dr. Maurice Faber, the rabbi he had appointed to the university's Board of Regents during his first month in office on the advice of friends. The letter was a blatant and reckless effort to secure Faber's support without further discussion or clarification as to Ferguson's accusations against the faculty, thinly veiled as an appeal for co-operation. The letter, dated September 11, 1916, read:

Dr. M. Faber, Tyler, Texas

Dearest Doctor: it appears from recent developments that certain members of the Board of Regents are conspiring with certain members of the faculty, including the President of the University to perpetrate certain members of the faculty who, in my opinion contrary to every principle of right and decency [*sic*].

It is quite apparent that the issue is going to be decidedly drawn. I am, therefore, writing you to say that unless I may be assured of your full and complete co-operation, I will much appreciate your [*sic*] sending to me at once your resignation as a member of the Board of Regents under my appointment.

You can rest assured that I have nothing against you personally, but the time has come when I must know who is for me and who is against me.

Yours Truly,

JAS E. Ferguson, Governor [15]

Ferguson's prediction that the issue would be "decidedly drawn" proved to be a gross understatement. Dr. Faber's reply on September 20 stated in part,

My Dear Governor:

When, at the solicitation of my friends, you saw fit to confer upon me the distinction and honor of appointing me one of the Regents of the University of Texas, I took the oath of office to serve the State in that capacity, to the best of my ability and according to the dictates of my own conscience. I never dreamed that such an appointment has any significance; nor that is the appointee expected to be a mere marionette to move and act as and when the chief executive pushes the buttons or pulls the string. . . I am not aware of any development that certain members of the Board of Regents are conspiring with certain members of the faculty, and while I hold no brief to defend them, I must say, as far as I know, such an accusation is without foundation. They are men of integrity, highest moral character, who have earned their golden spurs in the arena of public service and in the republic of letters.

I cannot give you an assurance of my "full and complete cooperation" with your avowed plans concerning the affairs of the University of Texas without a thorough investigation into the merits of each individual case. I cannot pledge myself to follow the arbitrary will of any person, no matter how high and exalted, without being convinced of the justice of his demands. In my humble opinion, such action would disorganize and disrupt the University, the just pride of the people of Texas. . . With all due respect to you, my dear Governor, I do not concede to you the right or authority to interfere in the internal management of the University of Texas: that is the sole business of the Board of Regents, and for that purpose they are created. I would by far rather return to my honorable obscurity than to stand in the limelight of public glamour purchased at the cost of manhood and conscience. [16]

Dr. Faber made good on his offer to return to relative obscurity when he resigned the following month, November of 1916. The governor promptly replaced him with a long-time Ferguson supporter, Sherman banker W. R. Brents, a choice that would later prove a disappointing one to the governor. Brents found no objection to Dr. Vinson as the university's president. Ferguson's removal of Dr. Jones from the board angered Brents, and he refused to vote to confirm Ferguson's selected replacement. He thereafter, like Faber before him, suffered the governor's wrath. [17]

On October 10 Vinson had called a special session of the Board of Regents in an effort to placate Governor Ferguson. In that meeting the regents pressed the governor again for specific allegations against the accused men, a request that only further provoked him. He condemned the board, saying, "I will tell you now if you undertake to put these men over me I am going to exercise my constitutional authority to remove every member of this board that undertakes to vote to keep them."[18] The governor's moves were well calculated. He was keenly aware of the additional power he would gain at the end of the year with the expiration of three regents' terms.

No one was taking the row between these two powerful forces lightly. In response to the concerns of many legislators and the public, two separate investigations of the questionable employees were undertaken, the first by the regents and the second by the legislature. Both inquiries reached the same conclusion: only minor expense report violations existed. Based on those results, the regents and legislators shared the opinion that dismissal of the accused men was entirely unwarranted.

Those who anxiously awaited the results of the investigation by the Board of Regents faced a daunting task in sifting through the contents of a report that was both complex and lengthy. In an effort to condense the information for readers, Roy Bedichek, city editor for the *San Antonio Express*, studied and summarized the 172-page regents' report titled, *Investigation by the Board of Regents of the University of Texas Concerning the Conduct of Certain Members of the Faculty*. When major newspapers published Bedichek's summary, Ferguson went on the defensive with criticism of the conclusion as well as Bedichek's summation. The governor accused Bedichek of being biased by virtue of the fact that he was "connected with the university crowd." He characterized the journalist's summary report as "garbled," and attempted to draw on what he perceived as his safety net when he invoked the name of "the people," suggesting that Texans would side with him if they ignored the summary and read the report verbatim.[19]

Indeed, Mr. Bedichek was not impartial. He was himself a University of Texas graduate and his very good friend, John Lomax, was among the university employees that Ferguson targeted for discharge. As a student in 1899, the young Bedichek had worked in the registrar's office under Lomax, and the two had forged a close friendship that had survived many years and an abundance of changes in their respective lives. A passion for the written word in many forms bound Lomax, Bedichek, and a small group of others at the University who were similarly inspired. The members of this group enjoyed lifelong friendships, rooted in heightened appreciations for Victorian literature, poetry, nature, and in Lomax's case, Texas folklore. All dedicated themselves to the furtherance of the awareness of exceptional writing and distinguished themselves with their own publications.[20]

Certainly Ferguson's attack on Lomax rendered Bedichek querulous on the subject. But Ferguson's remarks that called into question his journalistic integrity struck a raw nerve. Particularly offensive was the use of the word "garbled." A gifted writer, Bedichek fashioned a rebuttal in a brilliant open letter to the governor that hit newspapers the following week.

Bedichek laid bare the facts, declaring that the crime of the accused faculty members was, in his opinion, "the heinous offense of opposing you [Ferguson] politically" and that the objects of Ferguson's "vituperative rage" were almost anyone who disagreed with him. Bedichek expressed his personal frustration in being embroiled in an argument with a man of power, saying,

But the unhappy accident of such a man's occupying the exalted position of governor of this state gives any rabid utterance which he chooses to make currency far beyond the circle of people in which he is personally known… I wish to make it entirely clear in this preface that I would consider it unnecessary to waste good newspaper space denying any charge that you might make, provided that you had no wider audience than the one you would get as a private citizen. But, with the megaphone of the Executive Office in your hands, you reach people who do not know you, and so I feel compelled to answer your slur upon my character, and descend, with a grimace of disgust, to the language that you can understand. A reputation for accuracy, so far as reporting news is concerned, is the most valuable asset that a reporter can have, and since you seek to take that away from me, I rise to a point of personal privilege, so to speak… When the people of this state finally have it brought home to them that their governor stood up before the Board of Regents of the University of Texas (when they) met in executive session and tried to bull-doze and browbeat them into dismissing in disgrace men from the faculty of the institution who have given the best years of their lives to its service, and that without a chance to be heard in their own defense, the people of the whole state will repudiate you… We, the people, believe in giving the humblest a hearing when charged with a crime. [21]

One additional sinister point revealed itself in the details of Bedichek's rebuttal. Governor Ferguson had, at the last minute, added to the list of those being investigated, the name of one state employee named Lochridge. Ferguson had done this, Bedichek asserted, merely because Lochridge was the enemy of Ferguson's private secretary, Mr. H. A. Wroe. This assertion had also been made by George Littlefield when the item was first introduced in the investigation. Bedichek's response to Ferguson was thus: "The inference is irresistible: you are using in this manner the great power of the Governor's office not only to persecute men against whom you yourself had conceived a dislike, but you prostitute this power still further by indulging the whims of your private secretary, Mr. Wroe." [22]

As the calendar turned to 1917, the ongoing rift with the university sparked new life in the allegations that Charles Morris had made against the governor during the last campaign. Rumors of banking violations had reached the ears of the legislators from another source as well, a letter from H. C. Poe. Poe, who had been forced out of his position at the Temple State Bank, had finally made the firm decision to expose the governor's secrets. In response to derogatory remarks that Ferguson made against him in the senate chamber in mid-February, Poe issued and circulated a lengthy "tell-all" letter of refutation that he invited newsmen to print. Newspapers eagerly accommodated the request. The information contained very specific details of Ferguson's antics as they related to the Temple State Bank and his personal finances. Soon thereafter papers carried an open letter from the directors of Temple State Bank countering Poe's exposé and assuring the public of their faith in the governor. The damning information compelled members of the House to take action and on March 5, they voted in favor of an investigation of the governor's financial dealings and drew up charges against him.[23]

Hearings would begin on March 7, 1917. The ten charges leveled against the governor included several related to misappropriations of public funds, as well as various violations in connection with the Temple State Bank. The final charge regarded Charles Austin, the Commissioner of Insurance and Banking. That charge alleged that Mr. Austin was aware of the governor's violation of the civil and criminal banking laws at the Temple State Bank, and had taken no steps to enforce the law. [24]

The strong-willed Ferguson had certainly strained the limits of his authority and pushed the argument with the university toward a dangerous showdown. Even Ouida expressed this sentiment: "Had Daddy controlled his temper in the beginning of the University controversy as perfectly as he did in his final plea for exoneration, things would have been different." [25]

The impending investigation was a warning sign that Ferguson's authority was not supreme, that other powerful forces, if pushed too far, could take action to restrict or remove it. Jim Ferguson would later give testimony that confirmed what many suspected; Ferguson's true grievance with the men he targeted was his belief that they had not been supportive of his candidacy. Attempting to use the power of his office as a tool to punish those dissenters, he failed to predict that some of those men had, and would employ, their own influential connections. A host of powerful men, like Will Hogg, would not sit idle as the governor waged war against university staff and faculty who fell short of absolute allegiance to Ferguson's philosophies.

As evidenced in the opportunity he bypassed as a boy in 1887 to return to school with a simple apology, no inclination towards concession seemed to exist in Jim Ferguson. Had the governor heeded the warning signs in 1917 and reined in his will to punish those who opposed him, the magnitude of such an act might well have precipitated a substantial change in Texas history.

Instead, on March 3, 1917, the Texas Senate met to hear the reading of the Johnson resolution, a document drafted by Senator W. A. Johnson, a future lieutenant governor from Hall County. The resolution outlined the ten specific charges against the governor. As Representative H. P. Davis read the charges, Governor Ferguson entered the chamber and quietly took a seat in the back of the room.

"Shall the resolution be adopted?" The question echoed through the chamber.

Senator William Bledsoe moved that the governor be allowed to address the House, a motion that prevailed without objection. Ferguson approached the podium where he did the worst possible thing that he could have done under the circumstances. Launching into a tirade of unbridled rage, Jim Ferguson demonstrated before the distinguished gentlemen gathered there to assess his behavior, the depth of his anger and the extent of his inability to control it. The target of his wrath was Senator Johnson, whom he called "A Nigger lover from the North." Still speaking of Johnson, he continued his venomous rant saying, "You look like a Nigger and you are a Nigger." [26]

A number of outraged members jolted from their chairs in vigorous protest and demanded an apology. As cooler heads prevailed, the governor regained his composure and made a declaration that he wished to retract his statement. The stunned audience adjourned until the following Monday, a day the Chair scheduled to resume the discussion. But no slated break was sufficient to diminish the memory of the shocking scene the men had witnessed. Even firm Ferguson friends must have been re-evaluating their allegiance. If Ferguson's egregious breach of professional conduct and lack of decorum embarrassed him, he recovered quickly. His behavior seemed not to have left him with any lingering feeling of embarrassment or regret, because his next action before the committee would also lack any sign of compunction.

Chapter 9
An Investigation

The Speaker of the House selected a committee of seven gentlemen for the purpose of examining the charges leveled against Governor Ferguson and set the hearings to begin on March 7, 1917.

The distinguished attorneys opposing each other in the investigation before the Texas House of Representatives' Investigating Committee were well matched. Both were well-known, accomplished, highly respected lawyers who maintained a private practice in Texas. Martin M. Crane served as chief counsel for the state. A former state senator, lieutenant governor, and attorney general, Crane was often referred to in court as "General." He had distinguished himself in public service and as an able attorney in a number of high-profile cases.[1]

The chief defense counsel representing Governor Ferguson was William A. Hanger, an attorney in private practice in Fort Worth. He was a former state senator, a seasoned trial lawyer, and a friend of Jim Ferguson's. As such, Hanger was an excellent and obvious choice to defend the governor against the charges. Since Texans regarded both litigators as skilled debaters, many anticipated with interest the sparring of these two great legal minds.[2]

EXHIBIT "A"

A copy of the lengthy letter Poe had penned and circulated some three weeks earlier became Exhibit A. One House member read the document aloud to the full House of Representatives. As part of the record, Poe explained that he had recently resigned his position as president of the bank in order to be "fair to the stockholders and other parties with an interest in the bank." In reality, Poe's separation was not quite so noble; he had resigned under the threat of an impending dismissal at Ferguson's insistence. Ferguson's version of Poe's separation as bank president came in later testimony when he stated that he had given an ultimatum to board members who then voted to dismiss Poe. It was "a question of whether it was me or Poe," the governor explained. Soon after, Poe "retired."[3]

In the written statement read before House members, Poe explained his disappointment and the difficulties he had experienced dealing with the governor during his tenure at the Temple State Bank. He alleged that Ferguson had misled him from the beginning as to the extent of his debt and claimed that Ferguson had secured additional loans almost immediately without his consent or consult. Poe further relayed his surprise at later finding that additional liens were held on property that he believed had only a first lien, and that some debts in other parties's names were actually Ferguson's concealed obligations. He spoke of his distress with Ferguson promises, broken repeatedly, and his desperate attempts to reduce Ferguson's debt. Poe described how he had finally enlisted the help of the bank board whose attempts at a remedy had also failed.

Poe's statement contained quotes from minutes taken from the December 1916, bank board meeting. According to those minutes, the board had not only demanded an end to extending credit to Ferguson, but they had also discussed the possibility of filing suit to collect on Ferguson's existing notes. When that news reached Ferguson he was so enraged that he drove to Temple and confronted board members, scolding them for their threats to obtain legal action against him. Intimidated board members immediately backed down.

In the letter marked Exhibit A, Poe denied that he had asked the legislature to investigate the governor, a statement that challenged a recent newspaper report. Near the end of the statement Poe offered an expression of regret that it had been necessary for him to make the information public, and he assured readers that he had done so because he thought the public had a right to know the truth.[4]

However, the "truth," as Poe told it, was not entirely comprehensive. As if to head off questions he anticipated about his 1916 statements against Mr. Maedgen, Poe had written, "These are matters in which I am not interested, as those transactions are charged to have taken place before I had any connection with the bank." Poe conveniently omitted his part in the controversy. In response to Maedgen's 1916 claim that Ferguson had received $30,000 in campaign money from Texas brewing interests, Poe had assured the press that he had examined the bank records and found no such deposits. It was a subject Poe now wished to avoid.[5]

The morning of the first day of the investigation was somewhat chaotic. Martin Crane expressed his dismay at having arrived in Austin after six o'clock the preceding day. He claimed that, although he had stayed up until midnight reviewing evidence, he felt ill prepared to begin the proceedings. In a plea for a postponement that would allow him to make better use of the committee's time, he respectfully requested a delay until the following morning. In the midst of discussions between the attorneys, Mr. Hanger announced that the governor wished to make a brief statement to the committee, a request that the group was quick to accommodate.[6]

Ferguson's requested "brief statement" proved anything but brief. It was a repetitive, verbose, and rambling argument that contained seven references to unfairness, two references to persecution, five statements in opposition to any delay, and two references to the Cattlemen's Convention the following week, a function he was loath to miss. The following excerpt, taken from the transcripts, represents a fair sample of Ferguson's rant:

> It is going all around town here, all sorts of stories being told about how the Governor has swindled the State. The record is here, the witnesses are here, the lawyer is here, and simply because they have employed a lawyer who says he don't know anything about the case certainly is no affair of mine or of this Committee. If these matters are of the gravity claimed and can be so easily proven and so clearly proven, I think, gentlemen, in justice to all of us, we ought to go into it. Next week the Cattlemen's Convention will meet at Fort Worth and I have arranged to be there, and I want to be there, and to let Mr. Crane and Mr. Davis take up the time of the usual lawyer's delay here is certainly not fair to me.[7]

This display of impertinence on the part of the governor was significant on several levels. He had, before a single witness had been called, taken the floor and made demands of his accusers, a bold move that seemed entirely void of forethought or any degree of restraint. His behavior showed disrespect for the investigative process and served to confirm his unappeasable need to indulge himself by having his opinions known. With that defensive stance, Ferguson seemed only to reaffirm the root of the problems that precipitated the investigation, that is, his insolence and utter refusal to rein in his need to dominate.

Perhaps the most troublesome element of the governor's ill-conceived rant was its timing. Only three days had passed since his last embarrassing outburst, an eruption that had reached a level so offensive it had subsequently drawn a retraction, the sincerity of which was now likely called into question.

Almost certainly his statement was a test to gauge his ability to hold sway over the proceedings that lay ahead. Customarily Ferguson was in a position of leadership and did not like situations where he lacked control. He was well aware of the fact that he was the highest ranking man in the room. The chairman faced a decision that would set the tone for the proceedings. He could proceed under the pressure brought to bear with the governor's remarks, or adjourn as an accommodation to Mr. Crane.

The chairman spoke loudly and clearly. He granted the delay and the committee stood adjourned for the day. [8]

The following morning, March 8, 1917, the first witness appeared before the committee. He was State Comptroller H. B. Terrell, called to testify about the circumstances surrounding allegations of asset misappropriation leveled against the governor. The charge stemmed from information indicating that the governor had paid for groceries and other inappropriate personal items using the state fund appropriated for water, lights, fuel, ice, and incidentals. The category in question, referred to by the state comptroller's office as Y-14, would probably be labeled "utilities" in today's vernacular.

For Comptroller Terrell the controversy represented "round-two" in the debate about allowable mansion expenses. He had, in early 1915, been the subject of court action in the case of *Middleton vs. Terrell*, a case that stemmed from charges made by Representative W. C. Middleton of Rains County regarding similar expenditures made by Governor Colquitt. The Thirty-third Legislature, in evaluating a reasonable appropriation for the next year, had used as a basis the itemized expenditures of the past administration's Y-14 expenses. While reviewing those outlays, legislators noticed that two of the bills were for food and punch that had been consumed at a state reception under the Colquitt administration. Middleton maintained that expenses for food were not allowable. The case, which became known as "the Chicken Salad case," included an injunction that prevented Terrell from paying for any additional bills of that nature. A court decision affirmed Middleton's assertion that groceries were not an allowable state expense under any circumstance. Terrell appealed the decision, but on June 14, 1916, the Court of Civil Appeals upheld the finding of the lower court. The Texas Supreme Court denied a rehearing thirteen days later, an action meant to render the decision final. [9]

Chief Justice William Seat Fly of the Fourth Court of Civil Appeals believed that the actions of the drafters of the Texas Constitution represented a deliberate intent to promote economy in state affairs. In keeping with that sentiment, he ruled that a strict interpretation of the wording used to describe the mansion appropriation was in order. The absence of a mention about groceries was seen as a deliberate directive to exclude them.[10]

There was one additional element involved in the Colquitt case. Because the appropriation for mansion expenses had already been depleted, a deficiency warrant, similar to an overdraft, had resulted. Though advised by Attorney General Benjamin F. Looney that it was inappropriate to do so, the then-newly inaugurated Ferguson had signed off on the bill authorizing the deficiencies. Colquitt had eventually repaid the state for the charges, putting an end to the dispute at least as it related to him.

Evidence gathered prior to the start of the state's investigation indicated that Governor Ferguson had continued the practice of charging groceries to the same mansion appropriation, and that he too had spent well beyond the appropriation, creating deficiency warrants. There was no conjecture regarding grocery expenditures charged to the Y-14 category. Martin Crane entered into evidence a substantial number of paid vouchers showing clearly that the Y-14 appropriation for 1915 and 1916 included expenses for various kinds of groceries, stock feed, stationery, car repairs, laundry expense, tires, blankets, a typewriter, and a ukulele. The total questionable grocery and personal expenses amounted to about $4,600. (Not all were found to be in violation.) Also entered into evidence were a handful of invoices from previous administrations showing small mansion expenditures that might have been challengeable under the same level of scrutiny. Even so, in view of the high court's decision, it seemed there was no ambiguity and little reason for further debate. In view of the ultimate resolution of the Colquitt case, it seemed that a concession from Ferguson in the form of an immediate reimbursement was all that was necessary to put the issue to rest.

Mr. Terrell's testimony, however, revealed an interesting twist to the story of Governor Ferguson's use of the funds in question. Terrell disclosed the details of a meeting that Governor Ferguson had requested with him in the latter part of 1915. In that meeting, Ferguson had told Terrell that he intended to enter into a contract with a man named W. A. Achilles who was the proprietor of a grocery store. This contract, the governor had explained to Terrell, would save time and paperwork by giving Achilles the responsibility for paying all of the governor's water, lights, fuel, and ice charges during the year. To accommodate the plan, it was necessary to advance the entire appropriation in that category to Achilles when the parties signed the contract. [11]

Terrell, probably sensitive to any further problems that might involve court action, tried to dissuade Ferguson by informing the governor that the transaction would represent a payment for future services, an arrangement that was not allowed. Despite his warning, Terrell testified, soon after the meeting a warrant (check request) made payable to Achilles for the entire balance of the appropriation came to his office for payment. Terrell, anticipating this action, had warned his chief clerk to refuse any such warrant, and the instrument was not honored.

During Mr. Achilles' testimony, he confirmed that he owned a grocery store where he also sold stock feed, and he acknowledged the terms of the contract that he and the governor had agreed to execute. His understanding of the agreement was that he would pay all of the utilities and other incidentals at the governor's request using the funds advanced to him. Achilles added a footnote to the discussion telling the committee that there was a verbal side agreement to the contract. That agreement, he explained, was intended to act as a hedge on inflation for the governor. Ferguson, anticipating rapid inflation as a result of the war in Europe, extracted a promise from the grocer that, as grocery prices rose, the prices charged him would remain stable.[12]

Because the deal with Achilles was not consummated due to the refusal of the warrant, any further discussion of the contract was extraneous. The larger question became the seriousness of the deceitful nature of the governor's intentions, his disregard for Comptroller Terrell's advice and his disobedience and disregard for the court's ruling in the Chicken Salad case. Without a contract, the governor continued to buy groceries and stock-feed from Achilles but he lost the ability to conceal the itemization of those expenses from the comptroller's office or other prying eyes.

In view of the low salary paid to Texas governors, it was an obvious hardship for any governor, including Governor Ferguson, to entertain and host state functions without the benefit of an allowance for food. For this reason, the infraction may have seemed trite to some members of the committee. To counter that sentiment, Martin Crane, chief counsel for the state, called former Governor Joseph Sayers (1899–1903), who testified that he had understood and honored the law and never purchased groceries without using his own personal funds. [13]

Early in the process, one potential witness for the state had asked council to excuse him. That witness was Mr. Charles Maedgen, the former vice president of the Temple State Bank, a man whose history with Jim Ferguson was stormy. Maedgen's reluctance to testify was understandable on several fronts. He had been the target of a Ferguson lawsuit the previous year for remarks he had made about the source of Ferguson's campaign money in 1914, a suit that ended with his public apology and retraction. Ferguson had rallied his bank employees to his defense, all swearing that no money had flowed through the Temple bank as Maedgen had insisted. This left Maedgen, who was by then the vice president of Temple's Farmers State Bank, at an extreme disadvantage. With no access to Temple's bank records he could not prove his accusations and with a bevy of witnesses against him, he had virtually no chance of beating the powerful governor in court. He chose instead to make an apology in exchange for Ferguson dropping the suit against him. He certainly did not want to revisit that drama.[14]

Charles Maedgen, for unknown reasons, was excused from testimony but his story had already been told the year before in an ad he had purchased in Temple's newspaper. Maedgen's July 1916 dispute with Governor Ferguson had escalated far beyond his initial accusation that Ferguson had received money for his campaign from Texas brewers. The two men had engaged in a war of words that escalated into vicious verbal assaults from both sides. Ferguson stated that Maedgen had been an incompetent when he was an employee of the Temple State Bank, a comment that unleashed Maedgen's fury.[15]

In a full-page ad in the local paper the following day, July 20, 1916, Charles Maedgen had written an open challenge to the governor, who was in the final days of his second campaign. In that challenge Maedgen spelled out the details about the brewery-supplied campaign money in minute detail. He charged that Ferguson had begun to experience overdrafts due to his expenditures early in his campaign. He alleged that Ferguson had gone to Fort Worth, where he arranged some financial assistance. Ferguson had summoned by telegraph Mr. C. A. Hughes, the bank's cashier, to the Westbrook Hotel in Fort Worth where Ferguson gave him $10,000 in cash to transport back to Temple, the ad stated. Maedgen claimed that he had met Hughes' train at the Santa Fe station in the middle of the night before the two men carried the briefcase full of cash to the bank. A second transaction had happened in the same manner soon after, Maedgen claimed. The third $10,000 contribution had come in the form of a check from the Houston Ice and Brewing Company, a check that Maedgen maintained Ferguson had deposited in the account of one of his closely held corporations. [16]

In response to Ferguson's allegations that he was incompetent, Maedgen challenged the governor's memory, saying that in December 1913 Ferguson had visited him at his home and offered him a job at the bank. This he had done, Maedgen asserted, because he was unhappy with one of the bank's vice presidents "who caused you trouble because you were continually unloading your obligations on the bank." Maedgen asserted that it was on Ferguson's recommendation that the directors had elected him vice president. Maedgen claimed that he had begun to sell off his $13,750 worth of stock in early 1915 and offered this challenge in bold capital letters: "Governor Ferguson, you know the reason why I tried to get rid of my stock in your institution. Tell the public why. I insist you be a man for just one time and do it."[17]

As part of his challenge, Maedgen had furnished a long list of signatures from local citizens in support of his statements and his good character. But Ferguson had enjoyed the last laugh with a lawsuit that elicited an apology and retraction from Maedgen. That retraction put Maedgen again in an impossible position. Though he avoided testimony, the tormented banker must have hoped that someone else would have better luck in exposing the governor's misconduct.

In anticipation of the next witness, Mr. Crane made two rather odd declarations. He advised the court that he did not know the next witness personally and stated further that it was his understanding that the issue with the Temple State Bank was a "badly contested affair." Crane's sense of foreboding set a negative tone for the next witness well before that gentleman entered the room. Whether Crane's opinion was based upon his own interaction with the witness, or came from other sources, his comments suggested that he expected some level of instability in his next witness and gave the distinct impression that he wished to distance himself from that anticipated controversy.[18]

That potentially explosive witness was none other than Mr. H. C. Poe.

Chapter 10
Testimony Most Telling

His nerves spent from two years of chaos, the unemployed ex-bank president H. C. Poe finally arrived at the hour he could openly share the secrets he had harbored, secrets that had short-circuited his career and turned his life upside down. Unfortunately for him, his own secrets were so intertwined with those of the governor that any sense of relief was tempered by feelings of fear and regret. If there was any joy to be had in publicly exposing the governor's misdeeds and shortcomings, Poe's hushed tone did not betray that emotion.

Poe, still a young man of thirty-six, spoke so softly that committee members could scarcely hear his testimony and repeatedly requested that he speak more loudly. Under Crane's direct questioning, Poe established that he had taken over the presidency of the Temple State Bank in January of 1915, and that the bank's reduced capital, which Ferguson and other board members decreased by half shortly before his taking charge, had imposed critical limits on the bank's lending ability. [1]

When prompted by Crane, Poe told the court about the difficulty he encountered in his efforts to collect certain loans at the bank when the responsible party was not clearly defined. He elaborated on the unique characteristic of each circumstance explaining that the common thread was Ferguson's masked debt. One such note in the amount of $6,500 bore the name of John Spires (sometimes spelled Spryors and Spyers in the transcripts), a Ferguson friend. Poe explained that when he contacted Mr. Spires for collection, he became angry, denying that the debt was his. A similar situation occurred with a note carried in the name of Ferguson's friend and campaign manager, John McKay. Poe was unsure of the exact amount, but to his best recollection, the McKay note had been $9,000. McKay had become so angry when contacted for payment that he had written Poe a heated letter, a letter that Poe had never actually seen. McKay apparently regretted the letter soon after he mailed it and enlisted one of the cashiers at the bank to intercept it.

Another dubious note carried by the bank, Poe explained, bore the name of Will Wallace, Jim Ferguson's brother-in-law. This debt, acquired when Ferguson entered into an agreement to lease Wallace's land, was particularly perplexing. Ferguson paid Wallace $20,000, using bank funds, but registered the note in Wallace's name. Ferguson later testified that the lease contract between himself and his brother-in-law also included an additional obligation on his (Ferguson's) part to pay off an existing Wallace note of $8,500 to another lender.

Poe continued, explaining the next note in question in the amount of $2,000, which bore the name of the local newspaper. When John McKay had taken funds from the bank to pay the Temple newspaper for advertising expenses related to Ferguson's 1914 campaign, Ferguson had recorded the debt in the name of the newspaper. Another note in the amount of $8,500 from the Whitley Cotton Company resulted from a loan that Whitley Cotton Company made to Jim Ferguson personally. When Ferguson could not repay the company himself, he paid them with bank funds, but recorded the note in the name of the Whitley Cotton Company. Poe told the court that he found the governor's cavalier attitude toward his concerns about the instruments unsettling. Ferguson had claimed that he had simply forgotten to mention them to Poe but promised to take care of them himself.

Still under direct questioning from Crane, Poe spoke of his failed attempts to help the governor reduce his debt with a demeanor that mimicked that of a reluctant witness. He claimed that he regretted the necessity of having to relay damning stories against a man who had once been his friend, stating that he would rather go to jail than go into details about the governor's account. In response, Crane pressed forward, assuring Poe that he was doing the right thing because the committee needed to know the full story. The distraction incensed Mr. Hanger, the chief opposing counsel. He interrupted the testimony, accusing Poe of feigning his reluctance to testify as a ploy to add drama to the proceedings.

Hanger's accusations were probably valid. It was no secret that any affection Poe had held for the governor had long since dissipated under the weight of his frustration and anger. Poe certainly wanted the governor's misconduct exposed. He had in the past weeks denounced him on several occasions and had written the open letter outlining Ferguson's wrongdoing. But fear and intimidation probably played a part in Poe's reluctance to embrace the full measure of his opportunity to expose Ferguson. Jim Ferguson was still a powerful man.

The underlying dread of having his own secrets exposed also concerned Poe. He knew that as a key witness Mr. Hanger would attack his creditability and character, and he knew the instrument of assault that would be used to accomplish that goal. The knowledge of a particularly heated letter that he had written to the governor on January 4, 1917, produced in him a great anxiety. The letter, he knew, would certainly be entered into evidence and its content would not reflect well on the young witness. His timidity, whether theatrical or real, may have been an attempt to soften his image in anticipation of the exposure of that dreaded document.

Poe told of meeting the governor in November of 1916 at the Houston Democratic Convention where Ferguson anticipated receiving a large amount of money from a source he did not name. Poe knew only that the funds never materialized. Soon after, Ferguson acknowledged the need to liquidate some of his assets and offered to sell his bank stock to Poe. He stated that he had an initial interest in buying the stock, but backed down when Ferguson later raised the price.

Poe relayed another story that exemplified the strained relationship between him and the governor. In late November 1916, in his absence, the governor had gone to the Temple bank and secured two additional loans. Poe testified that after he informed Ferguson that he would be in New York for ten days, Ferguson had taken advantage of the opportunity and gone to Temple and secured two additional $25,000 notes at the Temple bank. Ferguson had not only overridden his authority as bank president, but had deliberately waited until he (Poe) was out of town, knowing that the bank clerk would be too intimidated to refuse him the loans, Poe asserted.

Continuing his testimony, Poe explained his attempts to enlist the support of the bank's board members in resolving the problems relating to Governor Ferguson. The board established a committee of men who went to Austin and met with the governor, but their efforts were ultimately futile. His voice still low, Poe elaborated on his dilemma in 1916 as he struggled to make money for the bank with limited working capital. He spoke specifically of trying to bid against other banks for bonds. "[W]e could not pay the interest on our indebtedness. At that time the drafts of the bank were being declined by our correspondent banks in Chicago, New York, Galveston, Dallas and at Waco, and I threw away these commissions, that is we threw the commission in on the price of the bonds provided the money would come back and be deposited in the bank in order to get money in the bank to pay off our indebtedness."[2]

Next, Poe told of learning that Ferguson had additional mortgages against land he had used as collateral for loans at Temple State Bank. Poe insisted that Ferguson had asked him not to record the liens and that he had honored that request in good faith, never suspecting that Ferguson would use the same collateral at other banks. Poe claimed that Ferguson was very specific in naming the reason that the liens go unrecorded: he did not want his enemies to have access to information about his debt through public records.

Crane continued his questioning, asking Poe if he had with him copies of his correspondence with the governor during the months in question. Poe's response was at first vague. He had retained copies of the letters, he said, but had not brought them to the hearing. When pressed for a reason he replied, "Well, I don't think this Committee has any right to the personal correspondence between Governor Ferguson and myself."[3]

The members of the committee bristled. One member suggested that Poe be given instructions as to his obligations and further suggested that he be held in contempt if he did not comply. In response, Poe's attitude improved slightly, but Crane's questions showed that he was less than pleased with the witness. He extracted a promise from Poe that the correspondence he held would be brought to the committee the following day. The stalling tactics Poe exhibited before the distinguished members of the committee did nothing to increase his likeability or his creditability and likely only heightened the curiosity of the committee members as to the content of the documents.[4]

His first round of direct questioning complete, Crane made a remark to the chairman that would ensure that the committee knew Poe was not the only defiant character when it came to producing records. Crane requested aloud that a subpoena be issued to Insurance and Banking Commissioner C. O. Austin because, Crane claimed, Austin had refused his request to see the commission's files of correspondence with Temple State Bank.[5]

Poe's shifting demeanor and the significance it had on the State's case were not lost on Ferguson's attorney, William Hanger. He began his cross-examination with questions that focused on Poe's behavior, specifically his earlier reluctance to testify against Ferguson. Hanger challenged Poe to explain his sorrowful manner in light of the accusatory letter he had released for public consumption. The question was a rhetorical one, of course, meant only to emphasize a point. Crane continued to interrogate the witness, directing his next questions in a way that reminded the committee that Ferguson's loans and overdrafts had accumulated under Poe's watch. Hanger shrewdly crafted his line of questioning in a manner meant to remind the audience that Poe had not been truthful with certain members of the bank board at times, and that he had routinely signed the annual reports attesting that the bank's loans were secure.[6]

With little transition, Hanger asked questions related to Poe's personal conduct, suggesting that Poe was guilty of public intoxication. The inference of a drinking problem on Poe's part brought an immediate objection from Crane based on relevancy, and the subject was temporarily closed. Next, Hanger asked Poe about his contact with Mr. Austin, the head of the Insurance and Banking Commission, stating that Austin had accused Poe of threatening to destroy the

Temple State Bank and ruin the governor if Ferguson fired him. Poe denied having made any such statements.

On the following day of testimony, March 10, it appeared that Poe had been advised by someone to adjust his attitude before the committee. He had with him the copies of correspondence that the committee had requested—including the letter he was disinclined to produce the preceding day—and he answered all questions in a straightforward manner.

Mr. Hanger was probably eager to inject the controversial letter, but Mr. Crane refused him the pleasure by introducing it himself. The act precipitating the letter began with a telegraph from Ferguson to one of the Temple State Bank's bond brokers in Toledo, Ohio, in December of 1916. The bond broker, Sidney Spitzer, frequently worked with Poe to secure bonds for Temple State Bank. After Poe and Ferguson's relationship had become strained beyond repair, Ferguson telegraphed Spitzer directly without Poe's knowledge, insinuating that Poe was dishonest and requesting that future bond commissions be sent directly to him in Austin.[7]

Spitzer, unaware of the antagonism between Poe and Ferguson, expressed his surprise to the governor by return mail, adding that he had always had the very best impression of Mr. Poe. Spitzer sent his reply to the bank in Temple rather than to Ferguson in Austin and, whether intentional or not, Poe read it. The level of Poe's anger was near hysteria, and on January 6, 1917, he allowed that anger to spill out in print.

> Dear Sir:
>
> I am inclosing [*sic*] [for] you herewith [a] letter addressed to you from Sidney Spitzer And Company of Toledo, Ohio. I do not know whether or not the envelope in which this letter arrived was addressed to me or addressed to you or that my stenographer opened it in error. I notice the letter is addressed to Jas Ferguson, Temple, Texas and not Austin, Texas.
>
> It makes no difference, however, with reference to this letter falling into my possession, as Mr. Spitzer had sent me copy of [a] telegram you sent the firm, and also copy of his reply with full explanation of the entire matter . . .
>
> You felt in writing Mr. Spitzer that you would give me a knock and that I would never be the wiser. You acted the part of a damnable cur in doing this and I have the nerve to say this to you over my signature, that you can know that I have the nerve and courage to put my signature to the above statement. You did not have the honor about you, I am sure, to say to Mr. Spitzer that you owed this bank extremely heavy lines and that the past six or eight months, several different times you have promised in various ways to reduce this heavy indebtedness and that instead of you

reducing this and clearing up, as you have promised on several different occasions, that on the second night after [I left] for New York on my recent trip you came to the bank to the cashier in my absence, and the cashier not having the nerve and courage to decline, you put additional notes of $25,000 each into our work, which you knew was rotten cowardly [*sic*] trick in you taking this advantage of me in my absence and instead of being honorable in doing what you had promised and reducing your lines and put the above notes in, as I stated.

Mr. Spitzer's statements with reference to my expense account and brokerage due and our entire connection in every respect confirms my statement to you in the presence of the board of directors, and I am glad that he wired you without consulting me in the slightest, because of the fact I have been absolutely honorable and square and told the truth in every particular and he has confirmed my statement from one end of the transaction to the other.

I understand from a source that I consider thoroughly reliable, that you have undertaken to give me a knock with two reserve city banks in which I have personal friends, by writing them letters casting insinuating slurs at me, as you have in the telegram to Mr. Spitzer.

You may have a few days in which to furnish these gentlemen with apologies for your dirty cowardly act, and in the event you have not, I have my stenographer now making up copies of the letters and telegrams which I have sent you with reference to your excessive lines and the checks on which you have refused payments, and I am going to send to these banks copies of these letters and telegrams that they may fully understand the entire situation and who is right and who is wrong.

The fact that you are Governor of Texas in no way bluffs or scares me, and a man that will mortgage real estate as you have to this bank and ask that the mortgage not be recorded and then go out and mortgage the same real estate for $70,450.00 additional money, is either in desperate financial condition, or you are either absolutely void of the slightest conception of what honor and integrity means.

... I certainly hope that you will pay us in the amount as you promised by the date you have agreed and that it will not be necessary for us to have any further trouble over this account.[8]

By the standards of his day, Poe's letter had the ability to greatly humiliate him and further damage his value as a witness. Innuendos about public drunkenness at a time when passions ran high on the subject cast more negative light on the key witness. Certainly the governor was guilty of misconduct that had negatively impacted Poe's life. But ironically, it was in large part his own conduct, both past and present, that kept Poe from making a rational and plausible witness.

However, the behavior of Mr. Poe was not the central issue before the committee. Their task was to examine all of the evidence and make a judgment as to the degree of the governor's culpability on specific legal violations, and to recommend a suitable action. To that end, they would weigh the evidence from Poe against other evidence yet unexamined, not the least of which was the governor's own version of the events in question.

Chapter 11
In His Own Words

nyone with the slightest understanding of his personality traits knew that James Ferguson was impatient to have his turn to testify. As a man who not only enjoyed the spotlight, but felt particularly confident in his persuasive skills, he was likely convinced that he could rather easily answer the charges to the committee's satisfaction. Ferguson's attorney, W. A. Hanger, conducted the opening questioning in a way that allowed the governor some latitude in answering the specific charges that Terrell, Achilles, and Poe had made against him in earlier testimony. He also allowed the governor to ramble off topic and soon the committee was hearing about the profitable prison system and other Ferguson accomplishments. [1]

Mr. Hanger returned to the subject of alleged misappropriations. Ferguson did not refute the charge, admitting freely that he had approved the documents in evidence that represented payments for groceries and other personal items under the lights, fuel, and ice appropriation. He told the committee that he believed that a motion for a rehearing of the issue before the State Supreme Court had not been ruled upon. He stated that he awaited that ruling and would abide by that decision. He did not mention, however, his immediate plan to write the judges of the Texas Supreme Court in an effort to influence their decision on the matter. [2]

When asked about the failed contract with Achilles, the governor explained the concept as a measure meant to bring expediency to the payment process. It would have allowed the Comptroller's Office to avoid the need for the issuance of multiple small vouchers, he explained. He explained the purchase of other inappropriate items, including a ukulele and jewelry, as simple errors.

The questioning advanced to the subject of the Temple State Bank and the governor's debt at that institution. Hanger made reference to Poe's earlier testimony regarding the double and triple liens on Ferguson property, a subject that drew an immediate and adamant response from the governor. "That is absolutely untrue and deliberately false," he asserted. [3]

The governor admitted that after securing a loan from the Temple bank using a portion of his property as collateral, he had later obtained a loan from another source, namely the American National Insurance Company of Galveston, using the same collateral. But Ferguson swore that he had not asked the Temple bank to withhold the recording of its lien. As if to minimize the importance of recording the lien, Ferguson declared that the value of the land far exceeded the amount of the combined loans against it. General Crane objected to Ferguson's assessment of the value on the grounds that his appraisal of the property's value was not admissible testimony. The objection angered Ferguson who retorted, "All right, I say on my oath, before high heaven, General Crane and all his crowd, that that property is worth $100,000 and when I got that second mortgage on there, there was no intention to impair and injure and no injury was in fact done to the Temple State Bank. It did not make their loan one five cents less valuable, and did not make their loan one five cents better. There was enough to pay everybody and two times over." [4]

A second, similar loan from the Temple bank held a lien marked "second" on its face but was in fact a third lien due to the same circumstance. Ferguson's defense was the same, that the collateral was sufficient, in his opinion, to satisfy all parties in the event of foreclosure.

The most complex questioning related to the Ferguson obligations recorded in the names of other parties. The testimony, meant to explain or clarify the circumstances surrounding the transactions, seemed to further complicate things in most cases. Every explanation seemed to further highlight the clandestine nature of the governor's personal business relationships and make one fact perfectly clear: the governor was a master manipulator. Like the misappropriated assets, the solid evidence made denial impossible; the governor chose instead a defense strategy that simply minimized the importance of his acts.

Ferguson's explanation of the Wallace note for $20,000 was rambling and disjointed. "[I]t was figured out that a reasonable trade would be that I should have a lease on his land for nine years in consideration of which I was to pay off his loan, that is, it was agreed that he and his wife should join in the lease to me for nine years upon his tract of land and in consideration of which I was to pay his $8,500 loan to the loan company, put his raw land in a state of good cultivation, and return the land to him at the end of nine years in as good condition as when I received it, less wear and tear." [5]

The rambling continued with little clarity. Ferguson claimed that

Will Wallace subsequently borrowed $20,000 from the Temple bank and immediately gave half of that sum to him because he had completed the terms of the lease early. He failed to explain the details of that odd transaction.

Ferguson's account of the circumstances surrounding the Spires note, though easier to understand, was no less troubling. Ferguson began with a lengthy description of Mr. Spires' fine character and credit worthiness, adding that he was a good friend. "On the occasion this matter came up," explained Ferguson, "something came up one day that I needed five or six thousand dollars, and the directors' meeting would probably be some time off; I forgot now just how long it was off, but it was when it was not possible for me to get the consent of the board of directors for the bank to loan me the money, but the bank being amply supplied with funds to loan I told John Spryor's [sic] about it… I took his note to the Temple State Bank and the money was placed to my credit and I gave him my note…."[6]

The governor did not elaborate on whether or not the board had knowledge of the facts surrounding the Spires note, if it was collateralized, or why he failed to have the note put in his own name at a later date.

The McKay note, Ferguson explained, resulted from a shortfall of his 1914 campaign expenses. The governor told the committee that McKay had spent six or seven thousand dollars beyond his allotted campaign allowance of $30,000. He did not explain why the note to cover the deficiency was in the amount of $9,000, nor did he explain who had received the excess loan proceeds. McKay, according to Ferguson's testimony, had approached him asking for more money soon after the election was over. Ferguson testified to his specific response to McKay. "I said, John, I haven't got any money, and I don't know what you are going to do about this matter. I want you to straighten this matter up some way until I can get a breathing spell to pay this. And to settle the matter, Mr. McKay executed his note to the Temple State Bank and Mr. McKay paid the Temple State Bank and I paid Mr. McKay and that's all there is to that proposition." [7]

The number of questionable notes seemed endless. Ferguson explained away two more problematic notes for two and three thousand dollars. The final instrument discussed was the largest note in question. Poe referred to the $15,000 note as the Whitley Cotton Company note. Ferguson explained that the company, located next door to his bank, had approached him for advice when they had excess cash that they wanted to invest. Ferguson accepted the funds but instead of investing the money through the bank, he took the money, giving the Whitley Cotton Company his own note. He told the committee that Whitley Cotton later conveyed his note to the Temple State Bank without his knowledge or consent. He offered no explanation as to how Whitley Cotton could have conveyed the note to the bank where he was president, without his knowledge, why the bank paid off his obligation, or why the Whitley payout was then listed as a loan in Whitley Cotton's name rather than his own.

Ferguson recounted the details of his first official meeting with Poe and their mutual understanding about the governor's need to borrow money to run his many business interests. He offered no explanation as to why he had not informed Poe about the potential problems related to the questionable loans. He admitted that his debt had grown exponentially, but claimed that Poe had been cognizant of every cent. He used the occasion to express his disappointment in Poe's performance as president of the bank, adding that the bank had not been able to pay a dividend under his (Poe's) leadership. The governor tried again to ease into a discussion of Poe's "bad habits," an action that was quickly thwarted by an objection from Martin Crane.

Crane's success in blocking the discussion of Poe's alleged public drunkenness did not endure, however. After protracted debate among committee members about the appropriateness and admissibility of the information, the derogatory testimony was finally allowed. Mr. Hughes, the head cashier at Temple State Bank, testified that he had been with Poe on two separate occasions when Poe was drunk in public, so drunk in fact that he needed help in getting home. After further discussions among lawyers and committee members, Crane challenged the relevancy of the information in this manner: "[S]uppose that Poe did get drunk, and suppose that Poe was unfit for the presidency of the bank, does that authorize Governor Ferguson carrying a loan equal to the capital stock and the surplus of the bank? That is the issue here, and it is plain to me that it [Poe's behavior] is irrelevant." [8]

After more debate between the members of the committee and the attorneys, Ferguson continued his testimony. Speaking about Poe, he said, "I noticed in the early part of 1916 that when he would come to Austin he continually had a pint or a half pint of whiskey in his pocket, and he always had an automatic pistol in his possession, and that he continually carried this pistol every time he was in Austin." [9]

The governor next told of hearing the news from Mr. Hughes, the bank cashier, that the bank's board was considering filing suit against him in late December of 1916 because of his overdue notes and overdrafts. The governor's reaction was so heated and extensive that the retelling of the account encompassed seven pages of testimony. He had been furious. By his own admission, he traveled to Temple on the day of the next board meeting, stormed into the meeting and immediately took the floor, leveling his fury at the astonished board members.

"There is not a man around this table but what owes his connection and his position with this bank to my influence and desires, and of course, naturally, I am surprised, I am hurt, I am chagrined that you gentlemen, after years of our relations, that you would do me an injustice, irrespective of what I may have been to you and that you feel called upon to pass a resolution to bring suit against me without ever giving me any notice that you intend any such action, without giving me a chance to ask why you are passing such resolution. ..." [10]

The governor relayed his memory of the details of his rant in statements that were repetitive and filled with references to his wealth, his connections, and his reminders to board members of their ingratitude. He explained at length his perception of the value of his various holdings of land and livestock, saying that he could sell them at a moment's notice if the bank needed the money.

"Gentlemen," he continued, "it might occur to you that that is a large amount of money to owe, and I will admit it is, if it was invested in suburban property or property that doesn't earn any revenue; I would quite agree with you if that was the case, that there might be some question about it, but, I said, I want to call your attention to the fact that of this $425,000 that I owe, $260,000 of the amount is in actual bank stock, which you know about, and which I can put on the market tomorrow."[11]

The personal financial statements dated December 1, 1916, that he supplied to the committee showed only $50,950 in bank stock.[12]

He continued, saying, "I think Mr. Poe said something about violating the Criminal Statutes, and I said to Mr. Poe, I have got a little knowledge about the law, I don't pretend to know and understand a great deal about it; but, I said, there is no penalty attached to it, and there is no bank in this town but what has violated that law time and again and under some circumstances, it might be a technical violation but there was no penalty attached." [13]

Ferguson seemed to take particular pride in telling the committee how he had intimidated and bullied members of the bank's board that evening: "Gentlemen, you never saw a lot of men turn and face front in your life the way they did and begin to run." [14]

It is difficult to imagine that Ferguson believed his testimony would help him. His admission that he did not know or understand much about the law and his ignorance about the bank statutes were certainly no defense for a man in his position. For two years, Ferguson had been unable to reduce his debts in response to Poe's pleading. Ferguson had, under the imminent threat of an investigation, paid off the McKay and Love notes by the time the hearings took place. The Spires note was also paid but not by Ferguson. When John

Spires paid the note at the Temple State Bank, he told the cashier that Jim Ferguson had given him the money with which to pay the debt. It was an obvious attempt on Ferguson's part to keep the secret he had kept from the bank board that John Spires had never been responsible for that debt. No one inquired about the source of those funds. Other interesting points had emerged from the testimony, namely Ferguson's admission that as early as 1914, he had no money. [15]

Under his own attorney's questioning, Ferguson had enjoyed a level of freedom. He would enjoy no such liberty under Mr. Crane's interrogation. But another important witness was in the wings awaiting his turn to testify. Commissioner of Insurance and Banking, Mr. Charles Austin, also had a story to tell.

Chapter 12
The Crane Swoops In

T here was no question that Charles Austin and H. C. Poe had met on a few occasions in the previous year to discuss the trouble that plagued the Temple State Bank. Neither was sure of the exact number of times they had met. Poe testified first and Charles Austin was anxious to refute portions of his testimony. Austin had more than a casual interest in Poe's version of events as they pertained to those meetings because he was the subject of one of the ten charges. The charge alleged that Austin knew of the banking violations at the Temple State Bank and was remiss for not taking any action against the institution. The two men had last met in late 1916 while Austin was still the chief clerk at the Insurance and Banking Commission; he was later appointed commissioner by Governor Ferguson after the death of his superior, John Patterson. The meetings, all initiated by Poe, had been amiable though not particularly productive. Poe sought a remedy that Austin was unable to supply because Austin's boss at that time, Commissioner Patterson, was part of the problem, at least according to Poe's version of events. Poe held that Austin had shared a confidence with him in their last meeting, that Commissioner Patterson kept the records of the Temple State Bank under lock and key. The commissioner had done this, Poe asserted, in an attempt to conceal the fact that the "Temple State Bank was in the most serious condition of any state bank in Texas."[1]

Poe also told the committee that Austin had asked him to delay drawing up the bank's annual report in late 1916. Poe claimed that he had asked Austin by letter to put that request in writing, an appeal that was never acknowledged. A copy of Poe's letter asking Austin to confirm his request in writing remained in his office in Temple, Poe explained, and he promised that he would produce it the following day.

When Mr. Austin took the stand, his testimony could scarcely have been more contradictory. He denied having told Poe that Commissioner Patterson kept any records locked away and claimed that he knew of no such practice. He vehemently denied having requested a delay of the banking reports and further stated that he had received no letter from Poe on the subject. Austin's chief remembrance from his last meeting with Poe was of the banker's agitation, which included threats that he intended to lock up the bank, go to the District Court with his story, and have the governor unseated if Ferguson fired him from his position at the bank.[2]

The only point upon which the two gentlemen agreed was that Austin had advised Poe that a remedy to the excessive loan issue was ultimately his (Poe's) responsibility. Poe had also voiced concerns to Austin about a large number of bad loans that Ferguson had forbidden him to write off. But, aside from the bank examiner's notes that mentioned the bad loans, no support had been forthcoming from the commission. Austin explained in his testimony that the bank examiner's authority was limited. An examiner could only suggest that notes be written off; the final determination as to the collectability of loans fell to the officers and board members of the bank. And so, without saying so directly, Austin intimated that the disagreement between Ferguson and Poe regarding bad loans was an issue that the two men needed to work out between themselves, a conflict that did not require intervention from the commission. The excess loans being a separate issue, Austin addressed that point in greater depth, but not surprisingly, the gist of his interpretation of the situation put the onus on Poe and held the commission blameless for their inaction.

The process surrounding enforcement against violations of the excess loan statute appeared amazingly lax, at least as Austin described it. He admitted that it was a rather common violation, generally handled through a written report that served to advise the officers of the bank to take care of the problem. Routinely, banking authorities did little else, he said. Most surprisingly, Austin claimed that there was no penalty for the violation, a statement that drew an immediate request for clarification from General Crane.

Crane: "What if they didn't do it?" [Take care of the problem].

Austin: "In the course of time if they don't do that we demand the removal of the officers of the bank. You see that is all we can do. There is no penalty attached to the banking laws, except the general penalty in the discretion of the Commissioner to close the bank up and forfeit its charter. We never think of closing a bank up because they have violated the excessive loan law, which is violated by banks both State and National every day of the world all over the United States."[3]

Soon thereafter, Mr. Austin must have been somewhat embarrassed when Crane produced and read aloud this provision in the banking law: "Any officer, director or employee of any State bank or trust company who willfully or knowingly failed to perform any duty imposed on him by law, could be convicted of a misdemeanor and punished by a fine, by time in the county jail, or both."[4]

Crane extracted one additional fact from Mr. Austin before he allowed the witness to step down. On the day of Austin's last meeting with Mr. Poe, a date that Austin believed was January 4, 1917, someone had apparently tipped off the governor. Austin testified that Ferguson came into his office looking for Poe but he was too late. Poe had already gone.

The governor returned to the stand and the anticipated cross examination by Martin Crane began. The tired subject of the appropriations was revisited but the state's attorney got right to the point asking the governor why he had continued to defend his actions regarding the grocery expenditures in view of the court decision against him. Ferguson argued that a final decision rested with the State Supreme Court. Crane corrected the governor saying, "they did decide it against you and you are asking them to reconsider it." [5]

In a subsequent exchange Ferguson expressed his opinion of the judicial system:

Crane: "The District Judge so ruled and also the Court of Appeals, at San Antonio, also ruled on that question, but that did not alter your course. You must have had a pretty firm conviction as against all those courts."

Ferguson: "Absolutely, I will be frank with you; I think the courts are all wrong."[6]

The topic moved to that of Mr. Craddock, Ferguson's "consultant." The point of contention was somewhat minor: that Ferguson charged Craddock's salary to the appropriation for law enforcement. Ferguson, who under direct questioning had made a weak case for the appropriateness of the practice, made no apologies and defended his actions, saying he believed that his discretion in deciding how to spend the fund was almost limitless.

Crane: "And you can employ as many men as you see fit within the limitation of that appropriation and at such salaries as you may think they are entitled to?"

Ferguson: "Yes, as long as that discretion is not abused, my decision is absolute."[7]

Crane asked the governor about his loans in excess of the statutes. Because the evidence proved without question that the statute had been violated, Ferguson could do little to defend himself. Again he referenced his judgment and his belief that his ability to repay the loan was the underlying factor in deciding its legitimacy.

Crane: "Your theory is if the loan is good, if the man is good, the law doesn't apply to him?"

Ferguson: "As a practical application of the banking business, a banking

proposition, not that the law don't apply to him but it is a lame statute."
Crane: "Why do you make any distinction between the law which puts a limit on that and any other law?"
Ferguson: "As a practical business proposition, evidently that was true because the law don't put any penalty there for not obeying it."[8]
Again General Crane read the statute, reiterating the existence of a penalty. Ferguson was not swayed and continued his argument that the statute was impractical.

Crane next pressed Ferguson on the issue of the multiple liens, asking him about Poe's assertion that the Temple State Bank's liens were withheld from the filing process at his (Ferguson's) request. Jim denied the accusation. His defense remained as before, that there was more than enough value in the land to cover all of the notes. When asked why he had not told the American National Bank that their lien was a third lien, Ferguson responded, "Well they never inquired about it, never asked me about it; and I entirely forgot; I never thought about it. If they had asked me, I would have told them all about it."[9]

Ferguson denied that Poe had pressed him to pay his debts even though several letters in evidence showed otherwise. It seemed a ridiculous argument. Poe's knowledge of the debt and his success or failure to collect it, did not alter Ferguson's culpability.

Again counsel raised the question of loans that lacked a clearly defined debtor, and introduced into evidence an additional note in the name of George McGee. Jim explained that McGee had borrowed $14,000 to pay him for an investment in half ownership of his cattle on the Bell-Bosque farm. McGee later changed his mind and the full ownership of the cattle reverted back to Jim, but the note remained unpaid.[10]

Ed Love, the Ferguson friend and business associate who had joined Ferguson and Jake Reynolds in opening the Square Drug Store, testified about his joint note with Ferguson. In earlier testimony Ferguson had sworn the entire $3,000-debt was solely Mr. Love's obligation. Mr. Love, anxious to set the record straight, did so by presenting the note signed by Jim Ferguson proving joint liability. Over a period of three years, Ferguson had renewed the note several times but made no payments. Recently, however, under the scrutiny of the investigation, Ferguson had paid the entire amount.[11]

In an attempt to minimize the damage inflicted upon Poe's character in earlier testimony, Crane suggested to Ferguson, in the form of a question, that perhaps Poe had carried a pistol to protect himself from an unstable man in Temple who had threatened him. Poe had also been deputized, which accounted for his habit of carrying a gun, Crane theorized. Ferguson denied knowledge of either circumstance.[12]

Poe returned to the stand and under Crane's questioning responded to the allegations against him. Poe explained, as Crane had suggested, that he carried a gun to protect himself after an unstable Temple man had made threats against him. He explained that he had fired the gun in question only five times, shots made on an isolated country road in order to test the weapon. He also confirmed that Sheriff Hugh Smith had deputized him, an action that gave him the authority to carry a firearm. In response to allegations about his drinking habits, Poe admitted that he drank alcohol but stopped short of admitting public drunkenness or any problems related to its use.[13]

Ferguson had publicly accused Poe of being a weak and ineffective bank president, a point to which Poe was particularly sensitive, he told the committee. The governor's debts had created for him a condition of insufficient working capital for the bank, a condition he felt powerless to resolve. His pleas for help from the bank board and Mr. Austin at the banking commission brought no remedy, he said. The most he ever received from his pleas for help was a low level of ineffectual sympathy. Poe testified, "He [Mr. Austin] would say that... [the bank] was in bad condition, that it ought to have attention, but he would say, 'You will have to be very diplomatic in handling the Governor; you have got to be mighty careful with him in things like that.' But he never did write us a letter and never did say we had to charge out that bad paper."[14]

Poe presented a copy of the letter that he had referred to in earlier testimony regarding Austin's alleged request to delay the bank report in late 1916. The letter, dated Dec. 26, 1916, read: "Dear Mr. Austin: Since my letter of the 23rd, if you really think best that the Directors not make up the annual report, if you will advise me over your signature to this effect it will put me in the clear and I will comply with your request. Thank you for your kindness shown."[15]

Unfortunately for Poe there was one serious problem with his copy of the letter. He had been unable to find the actual copy and his stenographer had duplicated the letter from notes, which Poe readily admitted. That fact, coupled with Mr. Austin's denial that he had ever received such a letter, certainly cast suspicion on its legitimacy.

Routine examinations of the Temple State Bank in 1916 and copies of the reports from those reviews were in evidence, but Eli Marks, the bank examiner who conducted the examinations, was not called to testify. His reports were consistent: each addressed the bank's excess loans. The mid-year report, dated June 5, 1916, and filed with the commission three days later, contained these statements regarding the bank's condition:

> The violations under which this institution is laboring are those
> of excessive lines of Hon. Jas. E. Ferguson and Bell-Bosque Farm

of $81,165.65 and $46,140.25 respectively, $48,505.94 of which is represented by overdrafts. It is my opinion that the above situation is of material seriousness and the reduction of same to comply with the requirements of the state banking law is imperative. It is entirely possible that a continuation of such condition would lead to much embarrassment for all concerned and careful consideration of same, as well as lengthy discussion with officers, forces me to make [the] above recommendations.

I consider the management of this bank efficient and honest, as well as fairly conservative, conducting their affairs in a safe and satisfactory manner, other than the above, and trust that you approve my conclusion in this examination, on which I have spent three days. [16]

The August report included these observations from auditor Marks: "Little change is noted in the condition of this bank since last examination. They are still operating under violation of section 173, through indebtedness of Mr. Jas. E. Ferguson of $89,974.65 and Bell-Bosque Stock Farm of $46,140.25, both of which remain unchanged approximately." [17]

By the time the December examination occurred, the bank's board had advised Mr. Marks, the state auditor, that a plan was in place to reduce the excess indebtedness:

In violation of Section 89 (Cureton & Harris Digest of the State Banking Law) this bank is carrying lines of Jas. E. Ferguson in the sum of $73,000, as well as that of the Bell-Bosque Stock Farm of $58,000.... At a meeting held by Directors on December 25, 1916, an agreement was entered into between officers and Directors of the Temple State Bank and Jas. E. Ferguson, by which a reduction in the lines of Mr. Jas. E. Ferguson and the Bell-Bosque Stock Farm will be brought about.[18]

There was, however, a major problem with the plan. Ferguson needed to reduce $150,000 of debt in the Temple bank and his plan to do so would essentially move half of the liability, on paper, to others who were not in a position to secure it. Ferguson intended to redistribute $150,000 of his debt by obtaining four new loans in the amount of $37,500 each. Ferguson planned to divide the four loans into notes in his own name, his brother's name, the name of the separately incorporated Bell-Bosque Farm, and in the name of Ferguson's secretary, Mr. James H. Davis. Ferguson's plan to personally guarantee each note rendered the solution totally ineffective. Why the bank examiner had accepted such a plan as a solution to the problem is a mystery.

Mr. Austin, during his testimony, reminded the audience of a key point: that he had not been the commissioner during most of 1916 when the examinations had been undertaken and therefore he had no knowledge of them at that time. He had assumed the position after Mr. Patterson's death in September of 1916.

Five days of testimony had passed when the governor again approached the committee with a request to attend the cattlemen's convention the following day. When the committee chairman asked if the investigation could continue in his absence, a seemingly unconcerned Ferguson responded, "Yes Sir, just go right ahead." [19]

The investigation was nearing its end, but Crane had another important question to ask the governor. The question was in regard to the source and disposition of an amount of $100,000 in insurance money that had been in the governor's possession. Ferguson deposited most of the money in the Temple State Bank shortly after he had taken office. Ferguson confirmed that he had placed the bulk of the money in his Temple bank but assured Crane he had subsequently paid out the entire fund for its specific purpose, the rebuilding of a school that had burned. That simple explanation seemed to satisfy the committee.

The following day March 12, 1917, in Fort Worth, Texas, James Ferguson approached the podium to speak to the Cattle Raiser's Association. The crowd greeted him with a rousing standing ovation. The necessity of his hand held upright to quiet the crowd so that he could speak confirmed their loyalty. He declared that he had managed to "break away" from the proceedings and "return to the herd." Expressing a sentiment that he favored a dipping vat for politicians to clean them of their muckraking, he also told the members of the crowd that he expected that they, like him, had borrowed money. "Men that [sic] borrow money, improve their country and fought the battles of their country," he said. The statement made little sense but did nothing to diminish the crowd's enthusiasm. The audience seemed to understand Jim's blurred message: that they, like him, might be victimized without his intervention in state government on their behalf. [20]

While Ferguson was receiving a fresh supply of ego-boosting support in Fort Worth, the committee members deliberating in Austin faced a sobering responsibility. They certainly knew the significance of their decision and their leanings were likely toward giving the governor the benefit of the doubt. Without further probing they would make their decision. What they almost certainly did not know as they reviewed the evidence before them was that they had barely scratched the surface of the questionable conduct of James Ferguson.

Chapter 13
The Ruling and the Aftermath

In its report, the committee opined that the governor had misused the mansion appropriation but the group conceded that a creeping encroachment upon the interpretation of allowable mansion expenses had taken place over several years. The evidence showed that other governors, to a much lesser extent, had taken similar liberties and, since no serious question had ever arisen in regard to those expenditures until the Colquitt administration, a loose interpretation of the fund had become something of a custom. [1]

The committee found that transactions between Governor Ferguson and the Temple State Bank were "deserving the severest criticism and condemnation," adding that, as governor of the state, Ferguson was responsible for the enforcement of all laws. Though he was found to have knowingly encouraged the officers of the bank to violate the banking law, the report stated further that the committee did not believe Ferguson exhibited willful or criminal intent to defraud the bank or its depositors. The committee understood that Ferguson had paid the debts at Temple State Bank except for a single note in the amount of $36,500 owed by the Bosque stock farm, an amount within the legal limit. The fact that Ferguson had settled his debts seemed to have pleased the committee, and they did not inquire as to the source of the funds that had materialized after having been out of his grasp during the previous two years. The committee concluded that while the governor's conduct was "unjustified and wholly unwarranted," it did not in their view, merit the "severe pains and penalties of impeachment."

Governor James Ferguson was merely censured. He received a reprimand and an admonishment that he must reimburse the state for groceries and other personal expenses paid with state money, including the deficiency warrants. Of the ten counts against him, the committee pronounced him guilty of seven. The first three counts and count five were very similar, dealing with the expenditures: he was found guilty on all four. The fourth charge pertained to the hiring of the adviser/consultant, Mr. Craddock, using funds designated for enforcement of law, a charge for which he was found not guilty. Counts six and seven were for violation of state banking laws, and both received guilty verdicts. On count eight, the alleged violation of multiple mortgage liens, he was found not guilty.

Charge nine asserted that Ferguson was guilty of approving a plan to change the Temple State Bank from a bond bank to a guaranty bank in order to save the bondsmen in case of a bank failure. The committee made no finding on count nine. The final count alleged that Charles Austin, the Commissioner of Insurance and Banking, was aware of Ferguson's violation of the banking laws but made no effort to enforce those laws. The report stated that while Mr. Austin claimed that he did not know of the condition of the excessive loans before January 1917, they believed that his failure to ascertain those facts represented an absence of reasonable diligence. While the committee found Ferguson guilty of negligence, they believed that no collusion or conspiracy existed between the governor and the banking commissioner. Mr. Austin retained his job, as did the governor.

The motives for the committee's generosity toward James Ferguson in arriving at his punishment were known only to them. Respect for his office and the embarrassment of unseating a governor may have been factors that influenced their decisions but, given the evidence, it is clear that they made every concession in favor of the governor. Food purchased to feed the family and staff at the Governor's Mansion and groceries purchased for state parties, even though clearly in violation of the statutes, were far less egregious than other charges made to the mansion appropriation. Over a period of eleven months beginning in September 1915, "Farmer Jim" had used state funds to pay for hundreds of pounds of cow feed, oats, alfalfa, and hay. His failed agreement with Mr. Achilles was evidence that his decision to do so was both deliberate and calculated. [2]

On March 13, 1917, the ordeal behind him, James Ferguson was once again in the business of being governor. He received approval for the three appointees whom he had placed on the Board of Regents of the University of Texas before the hearings began. The outcome of the investigation buoyed Ferguson's self-confidence, which created a fresh sense of bravado and, unfortunately, renewed trouble.

The war that was raging in Europe and the involvement of the United States in that war offered a distraction from the friction that Ferguson faced with the University of Texas. He might have channeled his attention in that direction, letting go of the animosity that he harbored for the university staff, but he did not. Governor Ferguson had dodged an investigation that could have resulted very differently. He had convinced the committee that he had extinguished his debt at the Temple State Bank in April. In truth, he had done no such thing. [3]

Poe had vacated the Ferguson home after his separation from the bank, initially moving just two doors down to 610 North 7th. Lawrence Heard, the son of the new president of the bank, himself a new employee, moved into the mansion. Efforts to run the Temple State Bank had been difficult before the investigation, but the officers and members of the bank board soon found that difficulty compounded after the institution's problems were laid bare before the investigating committee. In announcing Poe's "retirement" the month prior to the investigation, the officers and board members offered the public their assurance that the Temple State Bank was not only stable but prosperous. The accompanying comments related to Mr. Poe's retirement were inconsistent. T. H. Heard, Poe's successor, offered thanks and wishes of success to the displaced ex-bank president but refuted, in the same document, the "slanders and malicious statements against Governor Ferguson." Mr. Heard expressed "confidence in his [Ferguson's] integrity." But, without Poe as a buffer, and under increased public scrutiny, Poe's successor would last less than two years at the bank's helm before he too would "retire." [4]

If Mr. Poe believed that the entire distasteful experience was behind him, he was sorely mistaken. With Ferguson's power restored and his anger stimulated, it was a particularly bad time to be a Ferguson enemy.

This headline hit newspapers on Friday, April 27, 1917: "H. C. POE IS TAKEN INTO CUSTODY."

The article read,

Mystery today surrounds the taking into custody by the Dallas police last night of Mr. H. C. Poe, former President of the Temple State Bank and chief witness against James E. Ferguson at the investigation conducted by the Davis House Committee. A long distance call to Temple brought from Sheriff Hugh Smith of Bell County the statement that he held a warrant against Poe made out on an affidavit by William Blum yesterday charging Poe with embezzlement in a real estate deal. The Sheriff said the total amount of money involved totaled $3,000. [5]

The above reference to a real estate transaction appears to be an error. Court records detailing the charges made no mention of a real estate transaction. Poe was immediately at a distinct disadvantage because the judge in the case was none other than F. M. Spann. Spann was the Ferguson appointee and friend whose attempt to secure a loan for Jim at the Temple State Bank had failed a year earlier over Poe's objection. [6]

The complaints lodged against Poe under the charge of embezzlement involved activities at the Temple State Bank that had occurred while he was the bank's president. The first allegation stated that Poe had, in January 1917, asked H. F. Blum, the bank's assistant cashier, to draw up a note in the name of Spitzer and Company in the amount of $5,000. An implication followed that Poe had taken the money in question. The additional three charges alleged that Poe had taken three shares of bank stock, specifically numbers 96, 97, and 98, without paying for them. Poe produced records showing that he had deposited the $5,000 in question to an Austin bank in the name of the Temple State Bank shortly after he drew up the note. He also produced two appropriately dated cancelled checks showing his personal payment for the stock certificates in question.

The District Attorney, M. M. White, after examining the evidence, placed this opinion into the record: "The State has been unable to procure or produce any testimony whatever that would or could authorize the Court to submit to the jury any issuable fact which, if decided adversely to the defendant and in favor of the State, could support a conviction. That in the opinion of the District Attorney it is not only useless, but would serve no good purpose besides it would incur foolish and useless expense and improvident expenditures to the County and State to even make a show of a trial of the defendant in either of these cases." [7]

The headline for which Poe had long awaited appeared on March 1, 1918.

"H. C. POE IS FOUND NOT GUILTY OF CHARGE"

Belton, TX, March 1, The case of the State of Texas vs. H. C. Poe, former President of the Temple State Bank, who was charged by indictment in three counts to wit: embezzlement, misapplying funds and fraudulently becoming indebted to the Temple State Bank, came to a close this afternoon. When all evidence had been introduced and both sides had rested, counsel for the defendant made a motion for the court to instruct the jury to return a verdict of not guilty, which the court did. This motion was made and granted on the grounds of insufficient evidence to convict. Earlier in the trial counsel for the defendant made a similar motion which was overruled and taking of testimony was completed.

There were a number of witnesses examined today, among them being several prominent Temple men, who testified as to the good character and reputation of Mr. Poe. The defendant took the stand this morning and much of the testimony introduced involved technical banking matters. [8]

The young Poe never regained his professional footing, at least not in banking. He had announced shortly after the investigation's end that he would open a new bank in Temple. That vision was lost under the weight of the embezzlement charges that consumed a year of his life. Poe may also have lost his personal stability. He moved with his wife and young daughter to Kansas City, Missouri, where he turned his professional efforts to oil speculation. It appears that soon after, Poe and his wife may have separated; census records show daughter Gertrude residing with Mrs. Poe in St. Louis and later Columbus City, Missouri, while Hosea lived in rooming houses. In December of 1918, someone filed a complaint of embezzlement against former State Treasurer Sam Sparks in relation to funds held in trust by Sparks in an oil lease. The charges were quickly dismissed, and the judge expressed his opinion that the complaint was entirely baseless. Sparks' accuser was H. C. Poe. [9]

Although Poe's plight has been largely ignored by writers of Texas history, his story belongs in even moderately comprehensive accounts of the Ferguson saga because it personifies in great detail, the deceitful nature and the modus operandi of Jim Ferguson. Ferguson succeeded in his 1917 efforts to deflect attention away from his own wrongdoing by disparaging Poe's reputation as a banker. Uncontested, that character assassination has survived the ages. Banking associates such as Mr. Spitzer and the state bank examiner had found Poe competent and conservative. In Miriam's biography, the authors branded Poe a "weak [bank] president" and belittled him further labeling him a "lightweight little bank clerk," characterizations that are entirely unfair in view of the evidence. While Poe was no hero, the destruction of his career (and probably the ruin of his life) seems more than sufficient punishment for any culpability that might be assigned to him. [10]

After several years of poor health, forty-five-year-old Hosea Poe died on June 1, 1927, in Kansas City. His death certificate listed meningitis as the cause. In death he was returned to the state that had offered him much promise before he placed his aspiration in the hands of James Ferguson. He rests near his wife, Leonora, daughter Lavinia Gertrude Poe Sutton, and his parents in an Eastland County cemetery. [11]

Poe may not have been the only one subject to the governor's punishment. On April 5, less than a month after the close of the investigation, the governor vetoed slated raises for Texas judges with a lengthy list of reasons. Among other reasons he offered for his veto, Ferguson took specific aim at Supreme Court judges with this comment: "The higher courts of this State have given their approval to the proposition that the Governor of the State must be restricted to a salary of $4,000.00 and no more; and it does occur to me that if the dignity of the Governor's office is to be thus restricted by the decree of the higher courts to $4,000.00 a year, they, themselves, ought to be satisfied with their present salaries, which are as much or more than the Governor's salary."[12]

In May of 1917, Ferguson had sitting on his desk the two-year appropriations budget for the University of Texas in the amount of $1.8 million. It had passed the legislature in special session and awaited his signature. It was a case of *déjà vu*, the destiny of the document that meant so much to so many, resting in his powerful hands. Approval was critical to the future of the university, and with that importance, it represented Ferguson's leverage in the unfinished business that seemed his obsession. As such, that budget was a powder keg on the verge of detonation.

Jim Ferguson's impending actions would prove that he had no intention of putting the university dispute to rest—short of obtaining his goals. He wired the members of the Board of Regents, announcing a meeting that he intended to hold three days hence, saying only that it was for the purpose of dealing with matters of the utmost importance to the university. With his three new appointees, the governor likely had sufficient support to follow through with his plan to remove those faculty and staff members he found objectionable. This sweep would surely include Dr. Vinson, who had earned a place on the governor's list of offenders by virtue of his defense of the others. But the support of the board members was an essential first step to fulfilling the plan. As word spread about the important meeting called by the governor, a meeting meant to dispatch old issues related to the university, fears resurfaced among faculty, staff, students, and alumni.

At eleven a.m. on the appointed day, May 28, 1917, six of the nine regents met with Ferguson to hear his prepared statement. The governor had scarcely begun when an interruption occurred that would halt the meeting but accelerate Ferguson's determination to punish his detractors. Rumors of the meeting had spread and a large group of students, ex-students, and other individuals supporting the university had formed a march of protest. The crowd, including a marching band, paraded from the campus to the Capitol in support of the faculty and staff. Members of the group, including a few women and some young men dressed in military uniform, carried banners with such phrases as "we oppose one man rule." Marching to the tune of "The Eyes of Texas," the group made its way toward to the Capitol.[13]

Advised by an assistant that a protest was underway, Ferguson went to the window and opened it as he and the regents watched the group approach. His first instinct was to bolt outside and physically confront the leaders of the assembly but several board members advised him not to do so. Averting the possibility of a more serious physical confrontation by staying inside, Ferguson nevertheless engaged in banter with the crowd from his window perch. The demonstrators made their presence and intentions known while Ferguson advised them that he was not intimidated. The governor would later testify that he believed that Vinson and certain faculty members had sanctioned the demonstration. Nothing more serious than an exchange of words occurred that day but the demonstration greatly raised the level of awareness about the university dispute.

An injunction filed on behalf of John Lomax, an administrative staff member and secretary of the Ex-Students' Association, who was among those targeted, tied the hands of the board to remove any employees when they met again on May 30 in Galveston. The following day Ferguson removed two regents who were not strongly in his corner and, on June 2, he declared that he would veto the university's appropriations. Extending the time allotted for him to take the decision to its maximum, Ferguson arranged a conference between Regents Littlefield and Allan, and university staff members Vinson and Lomax. In the meeting, the regents put forward a Ferguson-backed solution for the pair's consideration. If Lomax and Vinson would resign, the governor would approve the appropriation. Vinson, who took some time to make his decision, refused the deal, and Lomax concurred. Ferguson made good on his promise on June 7 when he vetoed all but a very small portion of the appropriation. In a written veto message, the governor expressed his belief that rich men's sons ran the university and had set up an "educational aristocracy" through their fraternities. In a speech in Haskell the following week, the governor declared that the University of Texas appropriations "had been vetoed and would stay vetoed" and that "any talk of it not being vetoed was all clap-trap."[14]

Ferguson's veto of the university budget had ostensibly been made over objections to its content. The deal offered to Vinson and Lomax was curious in light of that fact because it seemed to prove that Ferguson's concerns about the budget were either disingenuous or minor. The ousting of Vinson and Lomax would have done nothing to change the details of a budget that Ferguson was willing to trade for two resignations.

In early July the court dismissed the lawsuit filed to temporarily protect staff member John Lomax and on July 12 and 13 the Board of Regents met in Galveston and discharged the seven men in question. Vinson remained. The governor, still not satisfied with the release of the offending faculty, knew that most Texans were uneasy with the unrest between the governor and the university. In an effort to deflect criticism, he toured the state railing against the university and attempting to garner support for his veto. In the minds of many, the future of the university seemed to hang in the balance, at least figuratively. The school would most likely have operated on deficiency warrants had it been a necessity, and other plans of contingency brewed. Nevertheless, the subject of the vetoed budget was no less unsettling.[15]

The impact of the firings on the lives of the men at the center of the controversy is well demonstrated in the story of John A. Lomax. A sensitive man with a wife and three young children, Lomax was frantic and genuinely shocked when he learned that his name was among those on the Ferguson list of objectionable employees. Lomax would later write of the crushing fear associated with the dilemma he characterized as that of the "salaried man" whose "very selfhood was at risk" when a precarious relationship existed with an employer. He made numerous attempts to find other employment well before his actual release, but each failed effort only heightened his anxiety. Nolan Porterfield, Lomax's biographer, chronicled the two-year ordeal in a chapter appropriately titled, "Hell in Texas—1915–1917."[16]

If the governor felt that his foes were conspiring to remove him from office, he was entirely correct. Ferguson had overstepped the boundaries of his power in the eyes of too many opposing forces. The groups pulled together tightly and formed their own power base. The university's ex-students placed newspaper ads asking for the governor's removal while other opponents, such as the prohibitionists and the suffragists, took advantage of the tide of negative publicity that rolled over him. They heavily circulated negative literature about the governor. The most tireless opponent, Will Hogg, the former regent and member of the central committee of the Ex-Students' Association, staunchly defended the university. Hogg, in cooperation with many like-minded men and women, stirred the pot of anti-Ferguson sentiment, printing and offering for sale at a low price, copies of the transcripts from the earlier investigation. Will Hogg facilitated the public's grasp of Ferguson's transgressions by printing the most egregious Ferguson quotes in the front of the publication. In response, Hogg received an avalanche of letters of support as well as letters accusing him of passing premature judgment on Ferguson. He responded to most pro-Ferguson letters with a diplomatic reply and a copy of the transcripts from the investigation, inviting the reader to learn the facts. Hogg and former Ferguson friend Sam Sparks, along with other powerful and determined men like them, became too vocal for Ferguson to silence.[17]

The seriousness of the situation reached a new level when a Travis County grand jury began a new investigation of the governor's financial dealings. Ferguson testified privately under the protection of the grand jury, but publicly denied any wrongdoing.

Another dispute, one unrelated to the University of Texas controversy, was brewing. Governor Ferguson and Texas Speaker of the House Frank Fuller were at odds in a quarrel that grew so strong that it became a catalyst for increased efforts for the impeachment process. The friction related to a duty that the men shared with three others as a committee to select a site for a West Texas location of Texas A & M University, a designation coveted by several cities. In June of 1917 the group was ready to make its decision. The committee members voted by written ballot and Ferguson pronounced Abilene the winner, but soon thereafter three committee members revealed the disturbing fact that they had not voted for Abilene. In view of that claim, Fuller maintained that he met with Ferguson and asked the governor to re-examine the vote. Fuller claimed that the governor refused to do so and asked him to drop the matter.[18]

On July 23, Speaker Fuller called a special session of the legislature to consider new impeachment charges against Ferguson. Few knew that the additional implication regarding the A & M vote played a critical part in Fuller's actions. The called session by the speaker was not entirely kosher; only the governor actually possessed the power to call such sessions. Fuller hoped that a required minimum of ninety-five house members would show up for the session and create a quorum, but he and others eager to bring the Ferguson issue to a head knew that there was no assurance of that.

Upon hearing that the grand jury had indicted him, Ferguson made a two-hour speech in Walnut Springs on July 29, labeling the charges a frame-up and a political conspiracy. One newspaper's review of the speech claimed that Ferguson used very emphatic language in several instances when referring to the grand jury, language that they refused to print. The report stated further that Ferguson made references to the high life and high rollers associated with the university, particularly fraternity members. And, as if to prove himself unfettered by the latest developments, Ferguson announced his intent to pursue a third term as governor.[19]

On the night of July 30, the governor, hoping to take control of the situation, called his own session. In doing so he announced his purpose, which was to re-evaluate the university's appropriation. He scheduled the session for the same day that Fuller had chosen, August 1, intending to take immediate command of the floor and avoid entirely the topic of impeachment. But the governor's call proved too late to achieve its goal, because, between the announcement of the Fuller and Ferguson calls, two significant developments occurred that weakened Ferguson's position significantly. The first development was a release by the Travis County grand jury of an indictment against him (and others) on nine counts, and the second was the arrival of a very large number of legislators in Austin in response to Fuller's call.

Hopeful that having called his own special session would give him the ability to control its purpose and content, Jim Ferguson did not suspect that the action would result in a situation that was the equivalent of bringing a rope to his own hanging.

Chapter 14
Let's Try This Again

O n August 1, 1917, the special session met with 118 members of the House of Representatives in attendance. Speaker of the House Frank Fuller wasted no time in taking the floor where he began to read the thirteen charges he had drawn against Governor Ferguson. It was soon apparent that the pro-impeachment forces were in control even though Ferguson loyalists attempted to stall them.

Within a few days, Fuller, working with other like-minded representatives, had established a Committee of the Whole to investigate the evidence against the governor. The impeachment process would be a two-part undertaking beginning with an investigation by the House, a critical first step that could abruptly end their course of action. Based on its findings, the House would decide whether or not to submit a bill of impeachment to the Senate. To the dismay of those who were anxious to move forward with a trial, serious issues with the first step of the impeachment process soon emerged, issues so significant that they had the potential of jeopardizing the entire process.

Speaker Fuller, the champion of the pro-impeachment force, soon became a detriment and an obstacle in the path of the group seeking a bill of impeachment. Among the thirteen charges Fuller drafted against the governor, two related to the voting dispute for the Texas A & M, West Texas location. It was apparent that Fuller had motives beyond exposing any financial dealings and abuse of power that might render Governor Ferguson the subject of impeachment. Fuller had broadened his charges to include bribery based on his accusation that the governor had given him a low-interest loan in an attempt to persuade him to drop his request for a re-examination of the suspected voting irregularity. While Fuller's version of events unsurprisingly differed from Governor Ferguson's, it also differed from that of other witnesses. In short, Fuller's testimony in the initial phase was disastrous, with Fuller appearing contradictory and dishonest. This testimony, which came in the middle of the two-week investigation, significantly weakened the case for an impeachment true bill. [1]

If the pro-impeachment force had serious doubts as to the chances for obtaining their goal, they were soon relieved when the pendulum of evidence swung back in their favor. Ferguson's own testimony produced this result when he mentioned in a casual manner that he had borrowed $156,000 from "friends" to pay off his debts and avoid bankruptcy. The disclosure of the loan was not particularly alarming, but Jim Ferguson's refusal to name the lender or the terms of the loan was. When pressed by the court to reveal the names of the friends in question, the governor held firm. This act of insolence was so disturbing that it served to offset the problematic effects of Frank Fuller's testimony, restoring momentum to the movement looking to secure a bill of impeachment. With his unsolicited admission and his impertinence, Jim Ferguson had shot himself in the proverbial foot at close range. [2]

The investigation by the House lasted more than three weeks, ending with a vote of 81 to 52 in favor of a bill of impeachment. Due to the perilous nature of some of the issues that Fuller had included in the initial list of charges, the committee redrew the articles to exclude Fuller's contentious charges. Even with those omissions, the list grew to twenty-one accusations as the Texas Senate readied itself to act as a High Court of Impeachment. During the two-day interval between the vote and the Senate's adoption of the bill, Ferguson, conducting his duties as usual, granted twenty pardons on his last day in power. Between July 26 and August 24 the governor had issued a total of 141 pardons to a wide variety of offenders. On the morning of August 24, Lieutenant Governor William Hobby took what he believed was temporary control of the governor's office. The trial, set to begin on August 29, experienced a delay of one day and began August 30, 1917. [3]

At the end of the March investigation, Martin Crane had, almost as an afterthought, asked the governor about a sum of over $100,000 that represented insurance proceeds for the rebuilding of the Canyon City Normal School, which had burned. Ferguson had assured the committee that he had fully disbursed the money in question, an explanation that seemed to satisfy them. A closer examination of bank records, however, showed that Governor Ferguson handled the funds in an unusual manner. Colquitt, who had custody of the funds before Ferguson, had placed the funds in an account where they had drawn interest. Ferguson, on the other hand, divided the funds, depositing them in various banks where he had a financial interest. The Temple State Bank and the Heidenheimer Bank, both banks where Ferguson was a stockholder, were recipients of deposits. The American National Bank in Austin and the Union National Bank of Houston also received deposits, and soon afterwards, Ferguson approached each for a loan. None of the banks paid interest to the state for the deposits. Far more alarming was the discovery that someone had paid $5,600 to the First National Bank of Temple in August of 1915 to satisfy a personal loan payment due from James Ferguson from those state funds. Also damaging to Ferguson's defense was testimony that revealed that the distribution of the funds for rebuilding the school happened at a painfully slow pace that caused unnecessary delays for the contractor. Because no one had discovered the erroneous personal loan payment until the investigation, further probing was necessary to ascertain how Ferguson had been able to disburse the correct sum with a shortage of $5,600 in the account. The answer to that question gave rise to another. Ferguson had diverted money from the State Adjutant General's fund to cover the shortage in the Canyon City account, money he later repaid.[4]

The findings of the initial investigation in March had resulted in a reprimand with some essential points, one of which required the governor to pay back the money spent for groceries and other disallowed expenditures, as well as the related deficiency warrants. This the governor had failed to do. These yet unreimbursed expenses, amounting to about $2,400, represented the bulk of Ferguson's punishment from the initial investigation, and his failure to pay them likely cast an impression of ingratitude for the leniency that had been shown him. It was true that Ferguson, who was already severely cash-poor, still drew a meager salary and had the additional burden of lawyers' expenses heaped upon him. However, when questioned by Prosecutor Crane, Ferguson mentioned none of these defenses to explain his failed promise to reimburse the state. Instead, he again challenged Crane about the validity of the assessment against him and stated that he would pay the amount only if the legislature ordered him to do so. They promptly did so. Finally, on August 25, Ferguson paid the assessment under protest.[5]

New revelations involving the Temple State Bank were also forthcoming, revelations that carried implications that were far-reaching. The Temple State Bank, as testified by H. C. Poe, was in a position in 1915–1917 where the institution's working capital was dangerously low. Jim Ferguson, it seems, had come up with a remedy, albeit a temporary and unprincipled one. He had arranged for the deposit of large sums of state funds into the Temple bank beginning in early 1915, a practice that continued through 1917. Ferguson had no direct control over department funds; it had been necessary for him to enlist the cooperation of others to channel state funds to Temple. One such collaborator was then Secretary of State, John G. McKay. The usual custom for handling the Secretary of State's funds, which came primarily from franchise taxes, involved monthly deposits into an Austin bank where checks were cleared. Once that clearing process was complete, the funds went into the state treasury. Shortly after John McKay took office, he began transferring large amounts of his department's receipts to the Temple bank where they were held until the end of the quarter before being transferred to the state treasury. Ferguson freely admitted that he had suggested this practice to McKay, that he believed that quarterly deposits to the state treasury were sufficient and that he had hoped for the largest deposits possible. "All bankers seek deposits," he explained.[6]

Under the theory that "all bankers seek deposits," Ferguson had apparently arranged to share the luxury of holding state funds on deposit with two other banks. The two institutions that had received portions of the Canyon City insurance fund shortly before each was approached for a loan also received, at separate times, deposits from the state penitentiary funds.[7]

Martin Crane had done his homework. Reading from the statutes, he informed the court that article 3840 required that the fees collected by the Secretary of State "shall be by him paid into the State Treasury monthly."[8]

John Patterson, Governor Ferguson's friend and appointee to the position of Commissioner of Insurance and Banking, had made similar, smaller deposits of his department's funds to the Temple State Bank before his death, beginning in July of 1915. When C. O. Austin took the office after Patterson's murder, he opened an account at the Temple bank and continued the custom, but discontinued the practice when the initial investigation began in March of 1917. Testimony also revealed that Ferguson had suggested that the state highway funds be deposited in the Temple bank, an action that was not taken.[9]

Ferguson answered each charge. Regarding the Canyon City School Fund, he made no excuse for putting the money in the bank where he was the majority stockholder, simply saying that he had put the money where it was easily accessible. He claimed the payment of his personal loan, paid out of the fund in error, had come as a surprise to him when he learned of it in July of 1917 as a result of the evidence-gathering process. He argued that state money placed in the bank where he held stock was not illegal. He claimed to have done it to "make a showing," but insisted that he did not benefit from its use. During testimony, Crane required the bank clerk, Mr. Blum, to tabulate the total state funds that had flowed through Ferguson's Temple bank. The amount exceeded $760,000.[10]

Ferguson solved the problem of the excess loan amounts at the Temple bank when he paid most of that debt beginning in April, not long after the first investigation. However, the circumstances surrounding those transactions uncovered a larger issue for the embattled governor. Although he acknowledged he had received a sizable loan from friends, he remained adamant that he would not disclose the specifics, vehemently defending his perceived right to withhold any information about the loan. If Martin Crane believed that asking the obvious question outright was futile, Senator Jeff Strickland of Palestine apparently did not. As required, Senator Strickland wrote his question down and passed the note to the chairman for a reading before the court. Strickland's question, read aloud, was direct: "Governor was any of this money obtained directly or indirectly from anyone connected in any way with a brewery or liquor interest?" The governor replied, "I borrowed that money from personal friends." He added a comment meant to halt any further inquiries when he told members of the court that they would not be allowed to deduce the name of the lenders though the process of elimination. This insolence brought bitter discussions and disagreements within the Senate as to the severity of his disobedience. It also heightened the skeptical nature of the entire transaction. What friend would insist on anonymity in his efforts to help another friend unless something sinister was in the details?[11]

The senators wrestled with finding an appropriate response to the governor's defiance. They put the question to a vote that carried, requiring him to answer the question or face contempt charges, but Ferguson did not budge.

One month before Ferguson had secured this "secret" loan, at the end of the initial investigation in March, he had assured the House Investigating Committee that he had arranged for the Houston National Exchange Bank to assume two of his four notes at the Temple bank in the amount of $37,500 each. This arrangement had been necessary to alleviate the problem of excess loan amounts at the Temple bank. Since that time, however, information had come to light that Ferguson had sent the notes to the bank in Houston for a period of only a few days—enough time to testify truthfully that the loans were no longer in Temple. It was a deliberate ruse. Mr. Fox with the Houston National Exchange Bank testified that Mr. Heard, president of the Temple State Bank, had asked him to take the loans for a period of fifteen to twenty days. [12]

The subject of the university dispute also took up much of the testimony and Dr. Vinson made a competent witness against Ferguson, answering with confidence even the most technical questions regarding cost per student and faculty hours. His polish and command of emotion rendered his testimony an asset to Mr. Crane's prosecutorial efforts.[13]

The university's Board of Regents did not wait for the results of the trial to take action. On September 15, they met and reinstated six of the seven previously dismissed faculty members. John Lomax had secured another job as a bond salesman in Chicago and, feeling an obligation to stay with his new employer, he chose not to return to Texas immediately.[14]

As the governor's personal affairs were laid bare, another troubling tale surfaced. While the story had only slight relevance to the charges against him, it spoke to the governor's character and his custodial ability, or lack thereof. In 1912, James Ferguson in partnership with others had sold some 3,200 acres of heavily wooded land to a lumber company in Liberty County, Texas. During the sales transaction a title search showed that the title to some 1,700 acres of the land was in question. The sale was completed with a stipulation and a written contract calling for the establishment of an escrow account that would temporarily hold the revenue generated from the sale of lumber on the land with questionable title. The revenue was to remain in escrow until clear title could be rendered. Ferguson volunteered his Temple bank as the repository for the escrow funds, an offer the parties accepted.[15]

By mid-1917, the title had long been cleared and one of the partners, Mr. H. P. Mansfield, approached the governor to obtain his portion of the settlement. Mansfield testified that Ferguson stalled, ignoring and finally threatening him when he pressed for a disbursement. Ferguson warned Mansfield that, if pressed further, he would issue invoices against the escrow representing fees for his services, fees that would wipe out Mansfield's share of the fund. Mansfield retained an attorney, but he too received Ferguson's rebuke when he asked for a statement of the activity and balance of the escrow account. At the time of the impeachment, bank records revealed that the account that had initially totaled $24,000, held a balance of only $50. Jim Ferguson had spent the money entrusted to his care.[16]

Another uncomplimentary aspect of the land transaction came to light under the scrutiny of the testimony. Judge A. G. Brooks, the judge who had ruled on the lumber company case, had rendered a verdict that was not pleasing to Governor Ferguson. When that judge later wrote to Ferguson for a general reference as to his satisfactory service on the bench, Ferguson had refused the request and made a reckless admission, citing his dissatisfaction with the judge's ruling on that specific case as his reason.[17]

At the conclusion of almost three weeks of testimony from a lengthy string of witnesses, everyone anticipated closing arguments. Prosecutor Crane expressed his willingness to forgo closing arguments, but the defendant did not agree. Each side readied itself for summation. Ferguson made an impassioned two-hour plea for exoneration, a plea that Ouida Ferguson later characterized as being free of bitterness and delivered with a controlled dignity. Her interpretation of the mood on the Senate floor, however, was thus: "The very air of that Senate Chamber breathed 'Hang him!'"[18]

There had been much discussion among the senators regarding certain elements of the unprecedented procedure that rested in their hands. They were at first uncertain as to the nature of the proceeding, that is, whether it was a civil or criminal trial. Ferguson capitalized on that uncertainty in his closing comments, suggesting that he had not received a fair hearing. "The laws of this State," he said, "have provided that for every citizen of the land, except the Governor, on trial for his official position, the form of the verdict shall be 'guilty' or 'not guilty'...." This comment was in response to the Senate's decision to vote "aye" or "nay" to the validity of each charge at the end of the trial, and had no bearing on Ferguson's guilt or innocence. [19]

During his plea, the governor often rambled until the point he was trying to make was entirely lost. "I realize the condition and you realize the condition under which this accusation has been brought against me, and you understand, and I know you understand and I want you to know I understand just as much as you, and I understand the conditions." [20]

The crux of Ferguson's message centered on the dispute with the university and he indulged himself with an additional jab at the institution's staff and faculty. "[T]he only way in which they could get the money to continue their unholy spree of educational hierarchy out there was to rend in twain the Governor of this state and to bring his fair name and the name of his family, articles of impeachment...." He expressed his objection to Vinson as president of the university based on his (Vinson's) lack of "educational attainments" saying, "he had graduated in a preacher's school up here somewhere." Though Ferguson had admitted earlier that he, the governor, had not been past the sixth grade, the irony of those comparisons seemed to have escaped him entirely. [21]

After the governor's speech, Martin Crane offered several key points to a solemn audience. The Canyon City Normal School fund, a portion of which had, probably in error, gone to pay a large private debt owed by Ferguson, was a fund entrusted to the care of the governor. Yet the error had gone undetected in spite of a large red flag, that is, the premature depletion of the fund. Even so, not until the grand jury brought it to the governor's attention was the error detected. Crane suggested that this, at a minimum, proved the governor was an unfit trustee of public funds. Hammering away at the governor's repeated refusals to abide by the court's decisions regarding expenditures for groceries, Crane accused Ferguson of thinking himself above the law. He reminded the senators that Ferguson had indeed benefited from the use of the state's money when the combined capital of the bank was insufficient to run its operations and when Ferguson's loans exceeded the entire sum of the bank's capital. Finally, Crane used a befitting analogy as he appealed to the businessmen in the room saying, "If you had furnished a ranch, hired a man for $4,000 a year, and no more, and had given him the use of the ranch property to live in, and then he would use your money that you had given him for other purposes to handle your estate, to buy groceries, you might not send him to the penitentiary, but you would do with him what we are trying to do with Governor Ferguson now— you would leave him out of that job; yes, he would not be that manager anymore." [22]

Crane raised a final point: If the senators excused the actions of this governor, what might they expect in the future? He demanded that Texas "extract from her officers, obedience to [the] law." [23]

The trial ended on September 26, 1917. Ten charges were upheld and eleven dismissed. Three of the eleven charges carried a majority but failed to carry the two-thirds margin needed to uphold them. Testimony related to the struggle between Ferguson and the university resulted in three of the charges against him being upheld. He was found guilty of attempting to influence the Board of Regents to gratify his wishes, guilty of removing regents without cause, and guilty of a more specific charge of trying to influence one regent by remanding a bail bond to him in exchange for his cooperation. Among the other charges upheld were five related to misuse of state funds, one regarding violation of the excess loan statute, and one for official misconduct in refusing to divulge the source of the mystery loan.

Of the eleven articles that failed to carry, four related to dishonesty in Ferguson's March testimony before the House Investigating Committee. The article concerning the grocery expenditure reimbursement was not upheld, that debt having been satisfied in late August. One charge accused the governor of libel against university faculty and staff members when he publicly referred to them as grafters and liars. This charge was not upheld, nor was a charge that he had failed to uphold the constitution with his veto of the university appropriation.

Four Ferguson allies had voted "nay" on every charge, among them Archie Parr of Duval County. These and others who favored leniency fought to block a majority vote that would bar the ex-governor from holding any future state office. Ferguson devised an attempt to thwart the ban. Just three days earlier, Ferguson's response to rumors of a possible resignation had been an emphatic, "not a chance on earth." However, in the face of imminent impeachment, the governor drafted a letter dated September 24, tendering his resignation. He submitted the document to Secretary of State Churchill Bartlett in an attempt to dodge the inevitable. [24]

In his letter, an unrepentant Ferguson stated his desire to devote time to the preparation of his candidacy for a third term as governor. He explained, "I take this action only because I have been reliably informed that the Senate of the State of Texas is attempting to pass some pretended and illegal order or judgment for the purpose of preventing the people of Texas from electing me governor for a third time and to prevent my holding said office by virtue of their election." Secretary of State Bartlett announced his resignation on the same day. [25]

The age-old tactic of "you can't fire me—I quit" did not work. The ploy failed to protect Ferguson from the associated stigma or to preserve his right to hold a future state office. He immediately began his bid for public sympathy and support, choosing not to acknowledge his punishment by referring to it as his "attempted impeachment." The former governor seemed to take great comfort in the fact that eleven counts in the indictment had not received sufficient votes to carry, a fact that provided him a starting point from which to launch his cries of "foul."

The Senate body was weary. The ordeal had been very public, very technical, and very time-consuming, but above all it had been significant to the future of the

State of Texas and the senators bore the weight of that responsibility. One senator expressed his sentiment in these terms: "In the closing hours of this unfortunate impeachment trial, which I hope to get off of my mind and my nerves and forget as far as I can. . ." [26]

Some senators were disappointed in Ferguson's unwillingness to accept his punishment like a gentleman. In view of their efforts to grant the governor every concession, three senators publicly voiced their displeasure at Ferguson's unprofessional comments and actions, saying they regretted their earlier attempts to defend him against the lifelong disqualification penalty. Senator Hudspeth in particular had pleaded fervently in Ferguson's behalf and was irate that the ex-governor was so disrespectful of the high court, apparently believing he could vindicate himself from its judgment. [27]

Chief among those fixed on Ferguson's innocence was fifty-eight-year-old Senator Archer (Archie) Parr of Duval County. Parr had no objections to Ferguson's post-impeachment comments. Parr, who had voted "nay" on every charge and had spoken in support of Ferguson throughout the initial investigation and the impeachment trial, had narrowly escaped conviction himself in 1914 on charges of theft of public funds. Archie Parr, and later his son George, were known as the Dukes of Duval County due to their stranglehold on every aspect of politics within a nest of South Texas counties where the Parrs and their powerful friends held sway. Rumor held that the Parrs maintained political influence in every county west and south of Corpus Christi for many years. With their clouded reputations and consummate power, it would seem that the only thing worse than having them for a friend, would have been having the Parrs as enemies.[28]

After being elected county commissioner in 1898 and again in 1900, Archie Parr had risen in popularity and power within the predominantly Hispanic population of Duval County. In 1907, someone murdered the politically powerful County Tax Collector John Cleary, a murder that was never solved. Parr quickly stepped in to assume Cleary's role among locals. This burgeoning power allowed Parr to control elections, give and take jobs, and help himself to county funds. In 1914, allegations of misuse of county funds brought by two local Republicans triggered a long-overdue audit of county records. Though the examination found plenty in the way of convincing evidence that theft had occurred, it was never completed due to a mysterious fire that destroyed the county courthouse and records on August 11, 1914. Officials indicted Parr and several other county officials, but the loss of the records and the failure of witnesses to show up on the day the trial began ended the matter with a dismissal of the charges. [29]

It was many years after the death of Archie Parr that the full extent of the Parr influence was understood and made public. Following an investigation in the 1970s into the corruption that thrived under the leadership of Archie's son, County Judge George Parr, former Chief United States Judge and former Director of the Federal Bureau of Investigation William Sessions said, "It was clear that the population and resources of an entire county had been subverted through corruption for decades to the personal exploitation of one powerful man—the Duke of Duval— and the handful of accomplices through whom he ruled." One author, writing about the boss rule that dominated certain Texas counties, described Archie Parr as "one of the most notorious corruptionists in the history of the state." The Parr name became synonymous with voter fraud as the pair used blatant acts of voter manipulation, intimidation, and fraud to secure offices for themselves and to fill local elected positions with those who would do their bidding. In state elections, they traded voting blocks for political favors and cash and became increasingly brazen and confident in their ability to deliver the requested vote. [30]

The Parr-Ferguson relationship was a solid one as evidenced by Archie Parr's unwavering support of his embattled colleague. This friendship certainly had roots in previous shared political maneuvering and time would see those strategies re-employed. [31]

Elder Ferguson daughter, Ouida, forbidden by her father to attend the trial, had done so nevertheless with the escort of her suitor and future husband, George Nalle. Miriam and Dorrace, ever the less rebellious members of the family, had honored Jim's wishes and stayed away from the proceedings. All stood by their patriarch as they had always done, and they shared his sentiment that nothing more than a conspiracy by Ferguson enemies had caused the ordeal. The family united in a quest for vindication, a quest that largely consumed all with the possible exception of Dorrace.

The media focus that had enveloped the Ferguson saga through the better part of 1917, faded quickly amid speculation that Ferguson's political career and influence were things of the past. One member of the House wrote this opinion to Will Hogg on October 3: "The papers have entirely ceased to mention Governor Ferguson. One of the newspaper men told me that he was on the front page of the dailies for the last time unless he killed somebody."[32]

By September 28, the Ferguson family was headed back to their Temple home. Miriam and Dorrace returned by train. Ouida and Jim, along with Cousin Fairy Ferguson, an employee on the governor's staff, came by car. Jim, who had never learned to drive, was not in the driver's seat. Likewise, he was no longer in the driver's seat for the State of Texas. In a manner of speaking, the state had revoked his license and had confiscated his keys.

This would not be an obstacle to the plans of Farmer Jim, however. He rested in the knowledge that, indeed, his devoted wife, Miriam, could drive for him.

Chapter 15
Seeking Redemption

T he dispute with the university is generally cited as the reason for Jim Ferguson's impeachment; however, only three of the ten charges that were upheld against him related to the university matter. Indeed Ferguson's financial dealings, and perhaps more importantly, his refusal to provide information about the mystery loan, in addition to the exposure of his efforts to stack the university board, ultimately led to his undoing. The university dispute, without question, served as a catalyst that united efforts to bring charges against him and spurred deeper examinations of his financial foibles. Those examinations could not pass the obvious evidence of misconduct and taken together with his misconduct surrounding the university, led to the governor's unseating.

By the end of September 1917, Jim Ferguson was out of office and out of Austin but was by no means out of the woods when it came to trouble. The criminal indictment issued against him in July by a Travis County Grand Jury remained open. Five others had also been indicted as a result of information that came to light in the impeachment trial. The charges were as follows: Commissioner of Labor, C. W. Woodman, eight counts; Secretary of State C. J. Bartlett, four counts; Commissioner of Banking and Insurance, C. O. Austin, four counts; State Superintendent of Buildings and Grounds, C. L. Stowe, one count; and former Secretary of State McKay, two counts.[1]

The glare of public scrutiny generated by the impeachment made returning to Temple difficult for the Fergusons. Many of Temple's citizens subjected the former first family to their own harsh judgment and were unsympathetic to the family's financial problems. Mr. T. H. Heard remained president of the Temple State Bank, which continued to struggle. Ouida Ferguson was not happy at the prospect of being "incarcerated in the camp of my enemies" when her parents counseled her to stay in Austin long enough to finish the term at Whitis private school. To her delight, a snub by the school in the form of a prompt removal of the Ferguson name as references in the school prospectus sufficiently angered her parents into re-evaluating the benefit of the institution. She was quickly enrolled at Temple High School.[2]

In a 1922 newspaper interview, Miriam told of the harsh treatment the family sometimes received. "People pass us on the street and say 'There go the Fergusons.' Children who have been reared with mine have cast slurs upon them." A Ferguson friend told of an incident that described the kind of castigation that befell Jim Ferguson. During a celebration and parade in downtown Temple the ex-governor stood on the sidewalk where not a single person acknowledged him. There was a time when his presence might have been the reason for a parade, the friend remarked, but in late 1917 Temple citizens shunned the former governor.[3]

The family retreated often to the seclusion of the Bell-Bosque Farm. The Bosque property offered greater privacy than the city of Temple, but the citizens of nearby Meridian, Texas, also had their eyes on the famous family. The family car, a flashy one driven by a chauffeur, rendered any pretense of anonymity a farce. A cook and yardman were part of the staff not sacrificed by the financially strapped Fergusons, and these extravagances also raised eyebrows.[4]

Jim, who had declared after his expulsion that he was returning to "stock and hog" was unable to find solace in the relative quiet of farming and ranching. To a man with Jim Ferguson's personality, it is fair to surmise that the humiliation was not the worst element of his punishment. Being out of the public eye, feeling isolated, powerless, and irrelevant, *not being heard*—these were the unbearable constraints that private life imposed on James Ferguson.[5]

Jim suspected that he still had a base of supporters in the rural community. Tapping that resource might allow him to duplicate his early political success, but communication with his constituency was imperative for testing and further stimulating that resource. His next move would give him a vehicle with which to make that connection as well as a means of expressing the opinions he was so eager to share.

Though duplicitous in motive, *The Ferguson Forum* was exactly the kind of vehicle that Jim needed to restart his political engine. It became the Ferguson bullhorn, a voice that roused his political lifeblood: rural voters. He had long enjoyed a good debate, but *The Ferguson Forum* offered him the opportunity for a consistent, unfiltered, one-sided discussion and, more importantly, allowed him to vent his frustrations against his persecutors. His political opinions were neatly placed among doses of agricultural advice. The *Forum*'s letterhead described the enterprise as a "Texas newspaper for Texas people" and proclaimed, "The Truth Always." It was, of course, Jim Ferguson's version of the truth. The telephone number of the establishment in 1917 was 185.[6]

On November 8, 1917, the first edition of the oversized, four-page weekly rolled off the press in the basement of the Temple State Bank building. A large clip-able ad invited readers to subscribe to the *Forum* at a cost of one dollar per year. Meant to draw in rural readers, the first and largest headline asked, "Is Cotton a Slacker Crop?" Beneath it, a lengthy "statement to the citizens of Texas" appeared; it was a mission statement of sorts. The article railed against traditional state newspapers and promised to "give battle to the newspaper submarine menace." The article promised a steady stream of wisdom for producing better livestock and crops, and warned that the *Forum* would "get into politics when it wants to." Editor James E. Ferguson wasted no time in demonstrating this intention. In the first edition Ferguson wrote, "There are too many gourd heads in the Texas Legislature." In the second issue he announced that he intended to run for governor for the 1919–20 term. "The bear fight has just begun," he prophesied. Dorrace Ferguson, a teenager, went to work as a part-time employee in the office of the *Forum* press. [7]

In December of 1917, Travis County officials dropped the indictments for embezzlement, diverting a special fund, and misapplication of public funds for all of the accused, including Ferguson. The district attorney had, in the initial announcement, failed to explain beyond a simple statement, the reasons for the dropped charges. Officials had announced that the indictments were insufficient to warrant or sustain convictions, a much-abbreviated explanation in the minds of many. Jim used the scant explanation as a basis for public comment in support of his contention that the indictments had been groundless. William Hogg, angered by Ferguson's distortion of the facts, pleaded with Judge Hamilton to make a public statement to counter Ferguson's claims. In June 1918, Judge James Hamilton and District Attorney John Shelton finally issued a public statement in response to pleas from both Hogg and the public, but the explanation was not easily understandable, except perhaps by lawyers. While the answer was a complicated one, the judge assured concerned citizens that the dismissal did not mean the court held Ferguson not guilty. Issues with jurisdiction complicated matters because the accused had deposited the public money in question in Bell, not Travis County. Shelton further explained the complex wording in the law that created an obstacle for a legal indictment since Ferguson was technically not the receiver or depository of the public funds in question. [8]

In early February of 1918, Ouida married George Nalle in the Christ Episcopal Church in Temple, just a few blocks from the Ferguson home. She was a mere seventeen years old and the groom was twenty. The church yard, crowded with uninvited guests, created some difficulty for the bride who later recalled the experience saying, "More people had come to gape at us than to wish us well…" Maid of Honor Dorrace resented being abandoned by her sibling, blaming the family's tarnished name and lack of money for her sister's early marriage, an act she described as an escape from the embarrassment of being a Ferguson. [9]

William Hobby, a mild conservative, had hardly warmed the governor's chair when the prohibitionists began applying extreme pressure for a statewide ban on alcohol. The passion associated with the war effort gave rise to a sentiment by the dry faction that a moral duty existed to protect the large numbers of American soldiers in Texas training camps from the effects of intoxicants. They pushed for a special session to address the issue. They viewed such a ban as a compromise to the full ban they wanted, but even so, the measure represented an extensive restriction on the sale of alcohol. Hobby, who feared the prospect of facing a strong prohibitionist candidate in the next election, tried to appease the group by any means short of calling the special session they sought. [10]

The new governor initially resisted and stalled, but by February of 1918 succumbed to the pressure for a special session to address the alcohol issue. The session struck serious blows to conservative Democrats when it passed, not only a stern law prohibiting the sale of alcohol within ten miles of training camps, but also ratified the national prohibition amendment. Prohibitionists were elated as were suffragists. The session also granted Texas women the right to vote in primary elections. This softening by Hobby and many legislators was not spawned by sympathies for suffragists as much as by a fear that Jim Ferguson might regain power. [11]

As Hobby's gubernatorial term came to a close in 1918, he prepared to run for the next term. If he ever doubted that Ferguson was a serious candidate due to his disqualification, those doubts soon lifted. Jim's declaration that he would seek a third term was no bluff and the Senate's ruling that he could not hold a state office had no effect on his decision to push forward. A bevy of those faithful to Ferguson worked successfully to put his name on the Democratic primary ballot.

Beginning with a well-received speech before the Cattlemen's Association in March, Ferguson drew large crowds at his campaign speeches. Doing his best to turn the past controversy to his advantage, Ferguson used the issues with the University of Texas as a tool to fan the flames of distrust that rural voters held for the business and political communities. He indulged his need to denigrate perceived enemies often, referring to the Texas Senate as a kangaroo senate and his impeachment as an illegal act. Of course, Ferguson's opponent, Hobby, received a liberal dose of Ferguson's criticism as well. Among other things, Jim labeled Hobby a "sissy." [12]

As part of his campaign tactics, Ferguson, who had always been nothing less than a passionate anti-suffragist, had little choice but to publicly soften his stance against the female vote. In a July 25 speech in Palestine, Texas, Ferguson made a tepid appeal to the women in the audience saying he had always been in favor of "letting them vote if they wanted to." He had made a similar plea in Athens, Texas, the day before. [13]

One point may have seemed conspicuously absent in Jim Ferguson's campaign speeches: there was no hint of apology or admission of guilt for the disgraced ex-governor's misdeeds. One Dallas editor wrote this of Ferguson's absence of shame:

> Mr. Ferguson is mistaken if he imagines that his lack of shame proves him innocent. What it proves is that his sense of shame is too dull to make him a safe repository of public authority. The people can have no greater warranty that public servants will prove faithful than a lively sense of shame. It is men who would be wounded to the quick by even the charge of wrong-doing, much less the proof of it, who may be depended on to discharge a public trust faithfully. It is not necessary to put such men under bond or oath. Their sense of self respect, their jealous regard for their good name, is a better warranty than both.... It is for this reason that the candidacy of Mr. Ferguson is a challenge to the moral sense of the State. [14]

Though other Democrats encouraged Hobby to challenge the validity of Jim's name on the ballot, he chose not to do so. Instead he embraced and capitalized on the negative publicity surrounding Ferguson, emphasizing his own clean record. Even John McKay, a longtime Ferguson friend and past recipient of Ferguson appointments and favors, publicly announced his support of Dan Moody. [15]

America's entry into World War I had created a vehement anti-German sentiment in some Texans. Hobby forces capitalized on those misplaced feelings of distrust and attempted to link them with the unresolved issue of the $156,000 Ferguson loan. This they did through insinuations that the money had come from the Kaiser, a ridiculous notion. Ferguson, who had vowed not to disclose the source of the loan, was left to defend the allegation with little more than a protest. This was an exploitive tactic on the part of the Hobby camp but probably had little to do with the outcome of the race. When Ferguson was solidly defeated in the primaries, his short-lived softening on the issue of the female vote quickly dissipated. Not only did articles appealing to women in the *Forum* cease after the election, by June of 1919 the tone on the subject had taken a severe turn. One *Forum* column stated, "It has been shown by an emphatic majority that the qualified and legal voters of the state do not want woman [*sic*] suffrage, and its attendant train of social equality with Negros, feminism, domination of elections by hypocritical political preachers and union of church and state in an unholy alliance." [16]

The votes of Texas women in the state primaries proved influential not only in the election of Hobby but in the victory of the first female to obtain a state office by election. Annie Webb Blanton, an accomplished teacher and former president of the Texas State Teachers Association, won the office of superintendent of public instruction. [17]

During the campaign against Hobby, Jim admitted often that he was broke, blaming the impeachment and his enemies for his fate. With this latest defeat,

Ferguson might have been sufficiently embarrassed, humbled and impoverished to give up politics, but he had no such intention. Because he had the ability to extract great joy and encouragement from small victories, the 200,000-plus votes he had received against Hobby with virtually no campaign money, pleased him. It was, at least, enough inspiration to keep him in the game. [18]

In early August of 1918, however, Ferguson's enthusiasm was about to experience a severe setback. An investigation by the U.S. Department of Justice had resulted in indictments against three San Antonio brewers accused of taking income tax deductions related to expenses incurred in pursuit of political influence. A Galveston brewer testified that he and other Texas brewers, as well as the San Antonio Brewers Association, had contributed to a loan fund for Governor Ferguson beginning in late 1916. The witness disclosed the details of the documents supporting the transaction as three $50,000 notes, paid in cash, payable on maturity and carrying a 5 percent rate of interest. The president of the Lone Star Brewing Association confirmed the information under oath, admitting to his part of the contribution. Lawyers asked potential jurors in the trial if they knew a man named Q. U. Watson, an attorney and former state senator, who acted as an agent between the brewers and the governor in the execution of the loan. The significance of that question came to light a few weeks later. [19]

The 1917 mystery loan from "friends" was no longer a mystery. Ferguson had testified before the Court of Impeachment that the lenders had not been anyone in need of his political influence, a bold lie. Even in the face of the new indisputable evidence, Ferguson at first denied any knowledge of the transactions. A few days later, on August 8, Ferguson made a brief public statement defending the loan. His defense: that other politicians, who remained nameless, had been similarly obligated. [20]

On October 17, 1918, a *Dallas Morning News* article appeared with this headline: "James E. Ferguson Transfers Land to a former State Senator, Q. U. Watson." A deed had been conveyed for eight tracts of land in cancellation of three promissory notes, the article stated. Two of the three $50,000 notes had been drawn in April of 1917 and the third bore a February 1917 date. Each note carried an interest rate of 5 percent. The land was conveyed by James and Miriam Ferguson to Watson, an attorney representing certain Texas brewers. [21]

The land that secured the brewers' loans had come to the Ferguson family as a result of the generosity and trust of Miriam's mother, Eliza, in 1907. [22]

Chapter 16
Optimistic Defeat

The man who had succeeded H. C. Poe as the Temple State Bank's chief executive early in 1917, T. H. Heard, resigned that position in December of 1918. Heard, the former president of the Heidenheimer Bank, had experienced his own challenges with Jim Ferguson. In late December of 1916 insufficient funds had forced him to turn down a large check that Ferguson had written on an account at the Heidenheimer bank. This had angered Ferguson who, in open court, accused Heard of being full of "Poe poison." In August of 1917, as the new president of the Temple State Bank, Heard was called before Judge William Masterson of the Fifty-fifth District Court to explain why he could not turn over the sum of escrow money that Jim Ferguson was presumably holding in the Temple bank in the land sale. There was little Heard could say since Ferguson had spent the money in question.[1]

Jim reclaimed the presidency of the Temple State Bank but the position had long lost any semblance of prestige. The Fergusons' personal financial situation remained perilous, but Jim continued to use a sort of "scatter" business approach, investing in a variety of ventures hoping one or more would take hold and flourish. None did. In addition to his newspaper, *The Ferguson Forum*, Jim owned (or co-owned) a creamery in Bosque County and held stock in a meat market and a produce market, both in Temple. Probably his greatest hope rested in his renewed endeavor: oil speculation. He made several attempts, drilling in Liberty and Eastland Counties, starting his own Money Oil Company, Chance to Lose Oil Company, and Kokernot Oil Company in the process. In January of 1919, Jim announced his intention to drill for oil on his Bosque County property, an ambitious task requiring expensive equipment that would require a large amount of start-up capital. His enthusiasm and boldness were evident in the sizable ads he placed in the *Forum* and other newspapers in an attempt to raise funds. The ads varied slightly but all pitched to potential investors the possibility of making large sums of money very quickly and boasted of "economical management of the business." Ferguson placed one ad with the express hope that 600 speculators would join the enterprise by sending an investment of $100 each.[2]

In September of 1919, Ferguson sold his share of Lignite Coal Company stock to friend and co-owner Frank W. Denison of Bastrop, Texas. Frank W. was the son of Jim's Temple neighbor/friend Frank L. Denison. Jim's half interest in Lignite Coal had played a small role in the initial investigation in March 1917 in support of Jim's contention that he was a worthy credit risk by virtue of his large holding of valuable assets including Lignite Coal. Ferguson had offered Temple State Bank's worried board members assurance that he had a net worth sufficient to cover his debts. That assurance came in part, Ferguson asserted, from eight million dollars' worth of un-mined coal that belonged to the Lignite Coal Company.[3]

On at least two occasions while governor Ferguson had tried and failed to borrow money from banks using bonds issued by Lignite as collateral. Potential lenders were apparently not impressed with the company's financial statements with the possible exception of two brewing company executives who invested heavily in Lignite Coal Company's bonds. The $175,000 cash infusion must have evaporated rather quickly; the financial statements for 1916 were not impressive. The company listed cash in the amount of $58.70 (in the Temple State Bank) and inventory valued at $5,410.66. A footnote to the balance sheet stated, "While the mine is carried on the books for only $150,000 . . . as shown by the report of the state mining inspector, there is over eight hundred million tons of coal yet un-mined which by the smallest estimate would make the value of the mine $200,000." It seems that Ferguson may have confused dollars and tons of coal in his estimates of the company's value, but neither projection had a foot in reality. Jim sold his half interest in the company for $35,000.[4]

In the summer of 1917, while embroiled in the University of Texas-Ferguson dispute, Will Hogg had received an interesting letter regarding the Lignite Coal Company. A gentleman named W. C. Silliman wrote to Hogg suggesting that as part of his investigation into the possible misconduct of Governor Ferguson, he might wish to speak with the State Purchasing Agent, George Levy. Silliman claimed that, in response to a bid he had submitted in hopes of receiving a contract to supply the state's lignite needs, Levy had advised him that the contract had already been let. The recipient of the contract was Frank L. Denison, Ferguson's friend, agent, father of Ferguson's business partner in the Lignite Coal Company, and Ferguson appointee to the State Mining Board. In early December of 1917 Levy testified as part of an overall investigation of state agencies mandated by the legislature. When questioned about the lignite contract, Levy confirmed he had awarded the contract to Denison but claimed that he did not know that Denison was a member of the State Mining Board.[5]

Suing newspapers that printed disparaging comments about the ex-governor became one means of supplementing the Ferguson household income. There was an added benefit to this cash-generating endeavor since newspapers, hoping to avoid future lawsuits, might steer clear of printing negative information about the ousted governor—or at least think twice before doing so. Certainly the case against some offenses had merit, but probably no more than the slanderous remarks that Ferguson frequently leveled against his political opponents. The material in question did not have to be patently false to render the publisher the target of such a lawsuit; it needed only be an unverifiable allegation for Ferguson to challenge newspapers in court. And challenge them he did. Jim sued the *San Antonio Sun* and received a settlement of $75,000. In April of 1919 he filed five separate suits against the *Houston Post*, asking for judgments of $100,000 each, for remarks they had printed during his gubernatorial campaign against Hobby. Some of the suits were eventually dismissed, while others ended with jury awards or settlements well below Ferguson's requested damages. Though the money generated by these lawsuits was much-needed, it was in all cases quickly absorbed by Ferguson debts and the family's financial situation remained dire.[6]

In November of 1919, Ouida gave birth to the first Ferguson grandchild. The boy was initially named Ernest for his paternal grandfather, but some five years later his parents changed his name to George, Jr. This they did to avoid confusion after another Nalle family member named their son Ernest.[7]

World War I ended in November of 1918; during and after the war some significant changes took place in America, due at least in part to the nation's war effort. Under Hobby's governorship and Wilson's presidency, the conservative principles that Ferguson had closely guarded had all but disappeared. Hobby's administration had been successful in obtaining the female vote in primary elections, after which a federal amendment fully enfranchised women in Texas. If this were not enough proof in the minds of strict conservatives that states' rights were evaporating, in January of 1920 national prohibition became law. Even though Texas had enacted its own statewide prohibition law in advance of the national statute, Texas conservatives were no less displeased with the increased level of federal control. Jim Ferguson and others with similar leanings, such as Joseph Bailey and T. H. McGregor, railed against what they saw as a weakened Democratic Party in Texas. Bailey and Ferguson united briefly under their shared desire to "save the Democratic party," but the two strong-willed men could not work out their differences and soon went their separate ways politically. Both hoped that disgruntled ultra-conservative Democrats would break away from the party, and each was ready to lead any such organized offshoot.

Ferguson's frustrations, coupled with his anger at the state's Democratic Senate that had impeached him, manifested into a drastic political conversion, at least in appearance. Hoping to draw from a pool of discontented Democrats for support, Ferguson made a bold move when he founded his own party, the American Party, and began a campaign to rally supporters. In April of 1920 he declared his candidacy for the office of President of the United States. Such an imposing goal was easily explainable. As part of his punishment, Ferguson was barred from putting his name on the state's primary ballot—but the ruling left open the option of seeking federal office. There seemed little confidence on anyone's part that this—to put it mildly—*ambitious* goal would do more than create publicity for Ferguson and his newly formed American Party, but for a man meticulously plotting a comeback as Ferguson certainly was in 1920, it was a sufficient goal.[8]

In response to his opening campaign speech in Dallas, a mere eighty-five people gathered. Ferguson refused to speak to the embarrassingly small group, leaving his fellow American Party gubernatorial candidate, T. H. McGregor, to go it alone.[9]

The American Party platform was circulated on broadsides that proudly spelled out the party's views. "Which do you want," the heading asked, "The Republican party of Europe, The Democratic Party of Africa or the American Party of the United States?" The party demanded liberal pensions for veterans and their families, denounced women's suffrage and national prohibition, and demanded that labor receive its "just reward." The broadside was signed, James E. Ferguson, National Committeeman. Ferguson's categorization of the Democratic Party as one "of Africa" is telling. It points to the real source of fear that he and many of his contemporaries had with the female vote. The Democratic Party had long excluded blacks from voting in its primaries by writing rules that excluded them and using intimidation to ensure that the rules were not tested by blacks. They feared that once the primary was open to women, it would encourage blacks to demand their constitutional right to vote.[10]

After the disappointing launch of his presidential campaign, Ferguson gained a small measure of traction, but the presidential race was never a realistic endeavor for the ex-governor. At the August state convention of the newly formed American Party, 262 delegates appeared. The previous day Ferguson had publicly predicted a showing of one thousand. A rousing round of "Hail, Hail, the Gang's All Here" did little to muster enthusiasm among the crowd that one journalist characterized as being comprised of "distinctly agricultural" types with a "preponderance of old men." By October, in a speech before a group of about two thousand gathered in Waxahachie, Jim admitted that defeat was inevitable, but tempered the admission with the prediction of a future victory saying, "four years from now as sure as there is a God in heaven... the fellows who want post offices better start coming around."

James E. Ferguson

Ex-Governor of Texas, 49 years old, Ranchman, Farmer, Business Man, and Editor is a

CANDIDATE FOR

PRESIDENT

Has more real friends and more mean enemies than any man that ever lived in the Lone Star State.

Read What He is For
And What He is Against

He has issued

A PLATFORM.

Yielding to no irresistible pressure, moved by no appeal from a great concourse of friends, urged by no special interest, controlled by no clique or clan, boosted by no hired newspaper, but with an unfaltering faith in the things which I shall propose, with the courage of conviction which God has given me, I, Jas. E. Ferguson, announce myself a candidate for the high office of President of these United States of America.

Broadside promoting James E. Ferguson for President. Courtesy of the University of Houston Library, Special Collections

The November presidential ballot contained the names of eight presidential hopefuls, and the victory belonged to Warren G. Harding, a Republican. [11]

The gubernatorial race of 1920 saw Joseph Bailey in a runoff with staunch Baptist Pat M. Neff who, not surprisingly, was an ultra-dry. Neff prevailed by a large margin and as governor immediately launched a predictable crusade against law breakers, particularly bootleggers. His harsh stance against the criminal element of Texas society, which included his own strict pardon policy, was meant to offset the leniency of the pardon policies of his predecessors William Hobby and James Ferguson. An uncooperative legislature prevented Neff from making sweeping changes that would have tightened many aspects of law enforcement.

In February of 1921, courts declared Ferguson's tenant land law of 1915 unconstitutional. A second test of its constitutionality later upheld that opinion. In May of the same year, State Commissioner of Insurance and Banking Ed Hall closed the troubled Temple State Bank. Ferguson, in an attempt to save the struggling institution, had approached other banks in Temple who agreed to loan his bank $45,000 even though Temple State Bank was already $85,000 in debt to other banks. When Mr. Downs, president of the First National Bank of Temple, sought permission from Commissioner Hall to make the loan, the permission was denied. Soon thereafter, the long-distressed Temple State Bank found itself in the hands of the State Commission. Ferguson cited "heavy withdrawal of deposits" as the reason for the bank's low capital, and he railed against the State Banking Commission for not allowing the additional loans he believed might have saved it. [12]

In his admonishment of the commission, Ferguson failed to mention that though he believed a $45,000 loan might have rendered the bank sufficient operating capital to continue, he had again amassed debt at the institution totaling $79,491.15. This sum included debts of $5,816.07 to his oil companies, $5,100 to the *Forum*, and even a debt of $81.66, in the form of an overdraft, to the long-departed American Party. [13]

In July of 1921, Ferguson took great comfort in learning that the state Senate had voted to include his portrait with the others in a gallery of Texas governors that hung in the rotunda of the State Capitol. Though the decision spawned two hours of debate regarding an appropriate inscription for Ferguson's portrait, senators finally reached a decision. A suggestion that the caption include a reference to Ferguson's impeachment did not carry, and in the end the inscription bore only his years of service. The controversy surrounding the inscription did not dilute Jim's euphoria; he later declared that legislators had forgiven him and referenced the inclusion of his picture in the gallery as evidence of that clemency. [14]

In January of 1922, Ferguson, without fanfare, dissolved the American Party and five days later announced his intention to run for the United States Senate.

That move did, of course, require a return to the Democratic Party and a lot of backpedaling.

A serious campaign in 1922 necessitated something akin to an apology, something quite foreign to Jim Ferguson. Jim had consistently disparaged the Democratic Party during his absence from its ranks referring to it, among other things, as "the infernal Democratic Party" in the *Forum*. While name calling may have seemed a frivolous offense to top Democrats, they found other actions less excusable. In an October issue of the *Forum*, Jim had issued this headline: "REPUBLICAN BRETHREN: LET US DWELL TOGETHER." In that column, Ferguson proclaimed, "The Texas politicians, all democrats, have not the pride of a jackass or the decency of a skunk. . . they stand for nothing and they are nothing." Though he failed to do so, Ferguson tried earnestly to ensure that Texas would not have a Democratic victory in 1920. Understandably other proud and loyal Democrats were not eager to welcome the wayward and fickle Ferguson back into the fold. [15]

Beginning in Atlanta in 1915, the Ku Klux Klan had resurfaced and began to spread its ill-conceived brand of social justice across southern states. By 1920 the Klan had made its way to Texas where its membership experienced a period of rapid growth. This new attraction to Klan affiliation grew largely from a public dissatisfaction with the enforcement of the moral standards of the day, but the group's efforts suffered from an unclear mission and rules that were not uniformly administered. While the Klan initially appeared to represent a lodge of like-minded individuals whose main goal was to support patriotism and morality, its exclusionary aspects dominated the enterprise and quickly came to define it. Only white, American-born Protestants were eligible for membership, and all others were subject to the scrutiny of the Klan's strict morality code. This scrutiny included harsh punishment for those guilty of legal and moral infractions such as infidelity, gambling, bootlegging, abortion, and inter-racial mingling.[16]

This growing membership created problems when local Klan groups began to swell in numbers that allowed them to dominate some city and county governments. As members of law enforcement, politicians, judges, civic leaders, and clergy joined its ranks the Klan's vigilante justice often went unprosecuted and unpunished. In this manner, domination and intimidation contributed to the group's power. In 1922 the Klan hoped to greatly expand its presence in politics with the election of many Klan-affiliated members. Against this growing force, a protest and counterattack emerged. Some who challenged the Klan faced coercion and very real danger while others employed counter measures that were as impractical as the Klan's own primitive tactics. Martin Crane, the attorney for the State of Texas during Ferguson's impeachment trial, was among those who stood up publicly in opposition to the Klan. He chaired the Dallas County

Citizens' League in an effort to bring awareness to the unlawful nature of Klan activity. [17]

In this contentious political climate Jim pushed forward with the next step of his redemption-seeking plan: the taking of a US Senate seat. He not only used the negative aspects of the Klan controversy to his advantage but embraced them so thoroughly that for many years they were the instrument of his attack on all foes. No matter how far-fetched the charge, Ferguson began to attach the stigma of Klan sympathies to those who opposed him. During the 1924 race, the Klan controversy may have been the perfect kind of polarizing issue that gave substance to campaigning but it was certainly not Jim's only focus. Highest on Ferguson's list of goals was the kind of legitimate re-entry into politics that required a sanction from voters in the form of a political win. Also high on his agenda was passage of an amendment that would allow the sale of beer and wine, as was an increase in support for labor unions. Ferguson's initial barrier was cast by a group of Democratic leaders who worked diligently to keep his name off the ballot. His name was finally included on the ballot after much haggling but not before Jim had concocted a secondary plan. Miriam had also filed as a candidate but promptly requested the removal of her name once Jim secured the placement of his name. [18]

During campaigning, Ferguson vacillated between bravado, his usual fervent attacks on opponents, and appeals to his audience for sympathy. He spoke with emotion about the support of his friends and begged for a chance to tell his wife that they were free from the stigma of the impeachment and its punishment. Incorporating his family into his appeals proved an effective tactic. So impassioned were his pleas at times that his audiences were moved to tears. [19]

While Ferguson appealed intensely for compassion for himself and his family, he extended none to his political opponents. Charles Culberson, the incumbent seeking his fifth term, seemed at first to represent Ferguson's clear competition. Long forgotten seemed the favor Culberson had done for Jim in 1916 when he had helped secure Jim's brother a postmaster position. The elderly senator's age and fragile health rendered him an easy target for denunciation, and Ferguson had no qualms about capitalizing on those weaknesses. Ferguson goaded Culberson, challenging the seasoned statesman to appearances and debates that Culberson's weakened physical condition could not withstand. [20]

There were a total of six candidates vying for the nomination for the Senate seat, two of whom boasted Klan sympathies. A third Klan candidate, Sterling Strong, dropped out of the race at an early date. One of the Klan candidates was Robert L. Henry of Waco. Jim had once been a staunch supporter of Henry, acting as his campaign manager in Henry's successful bid for Congress in 1902. The other Klan candidate, Earle Mayfield of Bosque County, also a Ferguson friend, took first place in the primary. Surprisingly Ferguson had enough votes to place second with Culberson third. Without a clear majority, this left Mayfield and Ferguson to battle it out in the runoff.

Stunned voters found themselves with a painful choice going into the runoff, a choice between the Klan and an impeached governor. Some men, like Barry Miller, who had championed Culberson's bid as a campaign manager, made the painful decision quickly in support of Ferguson. For others, like Culberson himself, the choice was so distasteful that the elder statesman chose not to endorse either candidate. A disgusted Martin Crane declared that he would not vote in the Senate race, while others supported Mayfield in spite of his Klan affiliation because he was a prohibitionist. During campaigning for the runoff election, the candidates engaged in bitter character assassinations of each other. Mayfield beat Ferguson by a margin of more than 52,000 votes and looked to the general election with confidence, unafraid of the Republican candidate who would challenge him. [21]

Other plans were brewing. An anti-Klan group calling themselves Independent Democrats was so troubled by the prospect of Mayfield's impending victory that they refused to sit idly by and let the inevitable play out. They quickly assembled for the purpose of finding a suitable candidate to challenge Mayfield and landed upon the name of George Peddy, a thirty-year-old assistant district attorney from Harris County. Texas Republicans dreaded Mayfield's certain victory so acutely that they joined forces with the Independent Democrats. Their determination was so keen in fact, that they even persuaded their candidate, E. P. Wilmot, to withdraw himself from the race in an effort to boost Peddy's chances to block Mayfield. [22]

Although Ferguson was out of the running he was eager to support anyone who had the slightest chance of beating Mayfield; however, the group's choice of candidates created an interesting dilemma for the ex-governor. George Peddy, who was staunchly opposed to the Klan, had vehemently supported Jim Ferguson when he faced Mayfield. But five years earlier, a young George Peddy had been front and center in the protest parade that had angered Ferguson at the University of Texas following Jim's veto of the school's budget appropriation. Ferguson, who always referred to the marchers as a mob, was particularly incensed at Peddy who was wearing his army officer-candidate uniform on that fateful day. Only five years earlier, Ferguson had railed against Peddy and accused him of the most flagrant disrespect. Ferguson now, without apology, threw his full support behind Peddy, but not without the raised eyebrows of many who found it hard to stomach Ferguson's swift and complete about-face. Petty took his share of criticism for the dubious alliance with Ferguson as well. So incensed were the members of Petty's First Methodist church that they asked him to step down as the teacher of a Men's Bible class. He promptly complied and pushed forward with his campaign. [23]

But Ferguson's endorsement was the least of George Peddy's election concerns. Getting his name on the ballet without a clear party affiliation was a task so formidable that, in the end, he was left relying heavily on write-in votes. The effort proved futile; Mayfield prevailed comfortably in the general election.

Also futile were further efforts of the anti-Mayfield forces who bitterly contested his win, a battle that was finally decided by the US Senate in Mayfield's favor. Mayfield's victory was a significant one for the Klan, and Jim, even with his loss, felt that he had made significant inroads toward a political comeback. He had also established himself squarely on the "anti" side of the Klan issue, an issue that would remain a source of divide for some time.

Governor Neff won the nomination for his second term with a clear majority despite criticism that he had been far too timid in denouncing the Klan during his first term. He had disappointed and angered men like Martin Crane who expected a firm stance specifically directed at the Klan.

During his campaign and subsequent support for George Peddy, Jim had been in close contact with one of his campaign managers, Dallas attorney Pat Short. In December, Short and his law partner, W. W. Nelms, also a Ferguson advocate, announced the impending addition of James Ferguson as a partner in their Dallas-based law firm. Ferguson had not practiced law in twenty years, but as if to thwart criticism, the announcement acknowledged his long absence from the legal profession, stating that Ferguson would not only act as a publicist for the firm but would also actively participate in trials. The article assured readers that Jim would not forsake his other business interests. Ferguson would continue to publish the *Forum*, which would necessitate a move to Dallas, and he would retain his stock farm. [24]

Absent from the news release, however, was any mention of the oil business.

Chapter 17
The Accidental Governer

In early 1923 Jim Ferguson was living in Dallas where he resumed publication of the *Forum*, but as always he courted the possibilities of other business pursuits. It seems, however, that one particular endeavor did not materialize or was short-lived; there was no further mention of his proposed partnership in the Dallas law firm that precipitated his move. But Jim was soon engrossed in a new business prospect. In January he drew up and submitted a proposition to the State Senate and House of Representatives in which he proposed to lease the entire state prison system for a period of ten years in exchange for the state's appropriation for prison expenses. Presumably, Ferguson believed he could run the prison system with such efficiency that the resulting profit would benefit all parties. Under the terms of the proposal, Ferguson and his associates would pay the state $260,000 per year for the lease, establishing a bond to secure the payment. Interestingly, the terms of the proposed agreement also allowed for a liberal pardon policy, but legislators rejected the proposal and summarily returned it to the former governor after a vote in the House of Representatives failed to approve it.[1]

In February 1923 Ferguson friends in the Senate attempted to play a brazen trick upon their fellow senators through the rapid adoption of an unexpected resolution exonerating the impeached governor. Ferguson's friend, Senator Archie Parr, requested and received temporary permission to preside over the Senate body in the brief absence of Lieutenant Governor T. W. Davidson. Davidson had simply stepped out to his office in another building when Parr and his collaborators sprang into action, launching a well-orchestrated plan so quickly that it was almost incomprehensible to those who witnessed it. Within a few minutes the conspirators read aloud and adopted a resolution for exoneration, an action that was immediately followed by a declaration of adjournment by Senator Burkett. Even elder Ferguson daughter, Ouida, was in on the plot, having offered her presence in the Senate that day to evoke sympathy on her father's behalf and hasten an affirmative vote. The scheme did not, however, go uncorrected. Upon his return to the chair, Lieutenant Governor Davidson rescinded the action and expunged it from the record. The following May, a legitimate resolution asking to set aside Ferguson's punishment failed to pass the Senate by a vote of 16 to 6.[2]

Jim had barely set up shop in Dallas when he came into conflict with some of his fellow Dallas businessmen. In securing advertisements for the *Forum*, Jim attempted to barter with a number of Jewish merchants and became angry when he perceived a trade imbalance that was not in his favor. He believed that business alliances existed between certain high-ranking Klan members and these Jewish merchants, a situation that angered him. His agitation spilled out on the pages of the next edition of the *Forum* with alarming inappropriateness. "Me and my friends are getting damned tired of these Jews running to us and asking us to defend their liberties and then running to the Ku Klux to sell them dry goods," he wrote. The fate of his proposed partnership in the Dallas law firm was never made public, but by July of 1923 Jim had abandoned his Dallas-based endeavors and retreated to Temple, leaving the city of Dallas and a host of new enemies behind him.[3]

The *Ferguson Forum* was promptly moved back to the city of its origin. Jim had for some time been using the newspaper to fan the flames of a growing revolt against the Klan in anticipation of future political moves. He teased readers with hints of his future plans; in the January 3, 1924, edition he proclaimed, "The most momentous political year in the history of Texas in now upon us." This was a precursor to an announcement that he would seek the governor's chair in the 1924 race. Three weeks later, he confirmed his intention to the surprise of very few.

Jim used the *Forum* to every advantage, admitting that it was his "weapon" of choice against his foes. He continuously begged for readers to renew and solicit additional subscriptions from their friends. By the February 28 edition, he boldly asked for donations, initially suggesting a modest fifty cents. By July the suggested donation had reached the $100 mark. He manipulated the subscription price beginning with an increase to $2.00 per year in January of 1924, citing the high cost of production as the reason for the higher rate. However, as the primary election approached, he temporarily lowered the price again. It seemed that candidate Ferguson had decided that he needed readers who would ostensibly become voters in his favor even more than he needed the money that subscriptions generated.[4]

Behind the scenes Ferguson was also working to broaden his support base for the 1924 race. The wrangling of several hopefuls for the Democratic nomination for the presidency offered him such an opportunity. Initially Jim supported inventor and auto maker Henry Ford but Ford soon dropped from the list of aspirants. Another of the early contenders was Oscar Underwood, a senator from Alabama who appealed to Jim due to his anti-prohibition and anti-Klan stances. When Underwood's team spoke with Ferguson about an endorsement however, they quickly learned that the former governor's influence was a commodity for barter. Ferguson agreed to endorse Underwood under the condition that Underwood's team would support him in the next governor's race. Underwood rejected the deal, much to the irritation of Jim Ferguson. He thereafter endorsed potential candidates with views on prohibition that differed from his own to avoid giving Underwood any backing. He did, however, remain true to his Klan opposition.[5]

Ferguson announced his intentions in January of 1924 for a place on a ballot that would quickly become crowded. Nine names completed the roster of gubernatorial hopefuls in the July primary. In January, those candidates were not yet a direct threat to Jim's aspirations, but the Democrats who doubled their efforts to keep Jim's name off of the ballot certainly were. Jim believed that the moment he announced his intentions forces within the Democratic Party would take action to block him, a belief that was entirely correct. In anticipation of this resistance he attempted to stave off objections with an announcement that the 1917 trial action against him was invalid. Therefore, he theorized, there was no legal barrier to his taking office. He betrayed any real confidence for success using that logic when he announced an alternate plan—the candidacy of his wife, Miriam. This, he stated, would happen in the event that "partisanship" prevented the inclusion of his name on the ballot.[6]

The anticipated fight for placement on the ballot advanced to the Texas Supreme Court where a June 12 decision upheld the 1917 impeachment and its judgment. Though Jim Ferguson's name was not permitted on the ballot, the Ferguson machine continued to hum. Just as Jim had promised, Miriam filed and obtained the placement her husband coveted. The change required only a minor modification to Jim's campaign, which was already in full swing.

Squabbles within the Klan rendered the group's initial efforts for seating a governor anything but unified. Criminal District Judge Felix Robertson, a prohibitionist, was the favored Klan candidate, but two others who had solid Klan connections refused to set aside their own aspirations and entered the race. Interestingly, Felix Robertson had supported Jim in his 1914 bid for the governorship. Vying for the anti-Klan vote, along with Mrs. Ferguson, were two individuals who shared a colossal handicap: they had the same last name: Davidson. Putting aside that hindrance, T. Whitfield Davidson, the lieutenant governor under Governor Neff, and Lynch Davidson, another former lieutenant governor, entered the race with equal determination and optimism. It appeared from their campaign strategies that they saw Mrs. Ferguson as no threat, at least initially, since each concentrated the bulk of his campaign energy against his namesake.[7]

Within a few days of filing, Miriam made a lengthy statement regarding her candidacy. She acknowledged the criticism that she anticipated and the difficulties she expected to undertake as a novice running for governor. She spoke candidly, expressing her love of home and family over politics, and appealed to voters to help her reclaim pride for her family name. "If any wrong has been done, God in heaven knows we have suffered enough. Though we have lost most of our earthly possessions in these years of trouble, we shall not complain if the people will keep us from losing our family name which we want to leave to our children." Miriam could not resist indulging herself with an assault on the senators who had impeached her husband seven years earlier, expressing her belief that his punishment was excessive, saying, "he is conscious of no wrong." She admitted that Jim's failure to become a Christian was a source of sorrow for her. "Men of his type need Christ in their hearts at all times more than men of milder natures," she lamented. Miriam also began filling the columns of the *Ferguson Forum* with her political messages, messages that were decidedly lenient compared to Jim's fiery editorials.[8]

By June 18, Jim had carefully mapped out a schedule of speaking engagements for the Ferguson campaign, an ambitious agenda that included fifteen speeches in eleven days. In almost every appearance, Jim spoke on behalf of—and often in the absence of—his wife. The crowds that gathered to hear him speak seemed satisfied with the arrangement; they assembled in increasing numbers, and frequently offered standing ovations and cheers of support. The Ferguson platform included a self-sustaining prison system, reduced taxes, reduced government spending, generous appropriations to rural schools, and above all, laws to curtail the power of the Ku Klux Klan. He assured listeners that his wife was a lifelong prohibitionist, and that as such, she would ensure the enforcement of prohibition laws. Never absent from Jim Ferguson's speeches were references to his own accomplishments as governor and his opinion that his ousting represented a miscarriage of justice.

A record number of Texans turned out to vote in the hotly contested primary of July 26, and, predictably, the top spot went to Felix Robertson due to his solid Klan backing. Equally predictable was the effect of the vote splitting that the Davidson candidates created. The other Klan-affiliated candidates received so few votes that their presence on the ballot was inconsequential, but this was not the case for the anti-Klan entrants. Both Davidsons received a substantial vote, each making a showing close to that of Mrs. Ferguson. Lynch Davidson in particular pulled so many votes that a decision regarding the second place spot was in limbo throughout much of the tabulation process. His lead began to diminish after the second day when the results from some of the more remote counties were tabulated. Mrs. Ferguson edged past Davidson, winning with a margin of about five thousand votes.[9]

Certainly the Fergusons had fate to thank for the second place slot that Miriam obtained. In the absence of either Davidson candidate, the other would almost certainly have secured the anti-Klan, anti-Ferguson votes that were instead split between them, eliminating Mrs. Ferguson. But other more covert acts from a most unlikely source also helped advance Miriam into the runoff election. Robertson's campaign manager later admitted that he had helped to promote Miriam in the final days leading up to the primary. This seemingly odd gesture was part of a calculated plan to eliminate the candidate that, in his judgment, had the greatest chance to beat Robertson in the primary. That candidate was Lynch Davidson. Robertson forces, who perceived Miriam as a far less formidable opponent than Lynch Davidson, quietly abetted the Ferguson campaign.[10]

In 1924, the candidacy of a woman for the office of governor was big news worldwide, so much so that it offered the Fergusons an abundance of free publicity. The Ferguson camp enjoyed immediate benefits as a result. "Campaign donations rolled in like a gulf tide as soon as it was certain that Mama was to be in the runoff with Felix Robertson," Ouida later wrote. She described it as a rags to riches story, saying "Mamma and Daddy no longer had to travel together to save hotel bills. Thanks to the need for conferences along the way, they moved from chair cars to drawing rooms, and from cheap hotels to suites."[11]

The accompanying frenzy pushed Miriam from the relative privacy of home and family as persistent reporters and well-wishers descended upon the Ferguson house. Amid the flurry and in Jim's absence, Miriam had to make some quick decisions, some of which had regrettable, lasting repercussions. In allowing reporters to photograph her in poses suggesting a lifestyle that did not represent reality, Miriam created an image that she could never shake. Wearing a tattered and dirty bonnet, a symbol that would come to represent her campaign, she posed in front of two mules on the family farm as though she were in the middle of a day's farm labor. A shot of the candidate peeling peaches gave the impression that she was the perfect complement to "Farmer Jim" and would thus champion his agenda in support of the rural community. There were however, limits to her tolerance. Although besieged with requests to pose for pictures depicting her domesticity, she flatly refused to allow photographers to take pictures of her milking a cow and later admitted that she was, in fact, afraid of most cows.[12]

By far the most significant and enduring by-product of the campaign was the moniker that Miriam soon acquired. A clever nickname, "MA,"—crafted from her initials to save newspaper space—was soon her identifier, and it followed that Jim was quickly tagged "PA." As the "MA" tag became associated with Mrs. Ferguson, so too did the bonnet, and soon catchy songs and slogans capitalized on both. "Me for MA" and "Two governors for the price of one" were among the most popular catchphrases and "Put on Your Old Grey Bonnet" became her theme song. Much to her chagrin in later years, Miriam found it impossible to cast off these characterizations that seemed imbedded in the minds of Texans. During a later campaign, a fan shouting, "Hi, MA," received this stern rebuff from Miriam: "I'm not your mother." [13]

Not unlike the Senate race of 1922 when many Democrats faced a similar conundrum caused by an unsettling choice of candidates in the primary, the 1924 choice between Ferguson and Robertson gave most voters pause. Some tried to recruit Will Hogg to run as an independent, but a disinclined Hogg avoided all attempts to draft him.

So pervasive was the Klan issue in the 1924 race that the candidate names might have seemed almost inconsequential except for the stigma that had attached itself to the Ferguson name beginning in 1917. Otherwise, the Klan issue seemed a divide that would render either a victory or a defeat for the future of the Klan, period. But that was not entirely the case; even with national prohibition in place, the topic of alcohol never failed to be a consideration to many voters. The Ferguson team was split on that tissue; one wet, one dry. Because of that, a host of potential Ferguson supporters speculated on which Ferguson would dominate if Miriam should win.

Many who would be considered the most unlikely of Ferguson backers reluctantly yielded to the cause of Klan annihilation in support of Mrs. Ferguson. In view of their own fervent denouncements of the Klan, the eliminated Davidson candidates had little choice but to throw their support to her. A strong anti-Klan sentiment compelled Martin Crane to favor Mrs. Ferguson and some state newspapers who had been harsh critics of Jim Ferguson, rallied behind the anti-Klan Ferguson force.

So controversial was the subject that at least one group concealed its support from the glare of public judgment. In 1932, Martin Crane admitted publicly the extent of an agreement that "a group of [top] Democrats" had made with Miriam Ferguson in 1924 in exchange for their assistance in helping her get elected. Knowing well that Jim would be the governor behind the governor, the group specifically addressed that concern calling for Mrs. Ferguson to "refrain from doing the things that had made her husband's administration objectionable." The terms of the agreement also set forth an understanding that her election would not serve as a vindication of her husband, and specifically required that she would not offer for re-election at the end of one term.[14]

With his past actions, Jim had supplied the Robertson campaign with ample ammunition against the Ferguson name. The Robertson camp reminded voters of the $156,500 loan from Texas brewers, Jim's abandonment of the Democratic Party, and his more recent rant against Jews. Jim countered with stories that Robertson was a heavy drinker who only pretended to oppose alcohol. Both sides campaigned with vigor, but Jim and Miriam were able to cover more territory by separating their efforts into two appearance-making teams. Dorrace, who worked in her mother's campaign headquarters, often accompanied Miriam in her travels, and Ouida and husband George Nalle and grandson, Ernest (soon thereafter renamed George Jr.), age four, were also included on many campaign trips.

Both sides continuously looked for weaknesses in the other that they could exploit and in early August Jim Ferguson found such an opportunity. The Grand Wizard Hiram Evans was involved in an incident that was somewhat sensational given his Klan affiliation. Evans had in his employ the services of a large black man who acted as his helper and bodyguard. During an overnight train trip Evans had been accused of causing a stir when he allowed the employee to sleep in the Pullman car with the rest of his entourage, a car that was designated for whites only. Evans defended his actions saying that the man had simply entered the car in order to speak with him but some of the other passengers had been outraged and complained bitterly. One newspaper reported the story under the caption "Whites Object to Negro in Pullman." Jim Ferguson was far less civilized in the rant he expressed in the columns of the *Forum*. Using an abundance of the most offensive racial slurs at his disposal Ferguson fanned the flames of prejudice in an insidious attempt to enlarge the offense in the minds of voters. [15]

The Republicans waited in the wings and watched the runoff campaigns with interest as they formulated their own strategy for the general election. The degree of fervor surrounding the campaign posed the possibility that a Republican might benefit when voters found the victorious Democratic choice distasteful. However, their candidate, Thomas Lee, seemed to lack any optimism about a Republican advantage, a position that caused him to make a critical error. He wired a letter of encouragement to Jim Ferguson expressing his hope that Mrs. Ferguson would prevail in the runoff election. Lee apparently went entirely too far with his words of encouragement in the minds of fellow Republicans, when he further stated that if such were the case, it would render his own nomination an "empty honor." It was a most unusual act meant to reflect Lee's anti-Klan sentiment and one that Ferguson quickly publicized to the detriment of candidate Lee. Many Republicans took issue with Lee's message to Ferguson, believing his hearty words of support were akin to an all-out endorsement of Mrs. Ferguson. [16]

Voter turnout for the August 23 runoff set another record for Texas elections. The breakdown of statewide votes cast in favor of Mrs. Ferguson by more than 97,000, sparked some interesting questions. The heavily concentrated and staunchly "wet" German counties of North Texas that had always supported Jim Ferguson, remained faithful to the Ferguson name, this in spite of Miriam's hearty endorsement of prohibition. That result likely reflected one of two possibilities: Klan opposition overshadowed the liquor question for the group, or voters in German counties were confident that Jim, who remained adamantly pro-alcohol, would make the decisions as governor. Another interesting statistic came from Duval County where Ferguson prevailed by only five votes. [17]

While capturing the nomination was generally tantamount to winning the election, given the passion associated with the 1924 race, it was not safe to assume anything. However, with the greatest part of campaign tension lifted, the Fergusons indulged themselves in the belief that their victory was imminent. In the August 28 issue of *Ferguson Forum*, Jim wrote, "For seven years I have walked in the woods.... Often I have been tempted to give up the struggle.... The dearest thought and the happiest feeling that comes to me in this hour of victory is that the honor has been given to my good wife and myself [*sic*] afterward." [18]

The Ferguson runoff victory produced an enthusiasm that was far-reaching. At the state Democratic convention, held within a few days of the runoff election, the Klan received considerable censure. It was clear that regardless of the outcome of the upcoming election, Klan power would continue to erode. [19]

Republican candidate Thomas Lee's blunder had cast suspicion on his ability to represent his party successfully. Under pressure, he withdrew as the Republican nominee. The dean of the University of Texas Law School, Dr. George Butte, soon replaced Lee as the new Republican candidate. Surprised at the prospect of his nomination and distracted by a recent trip overseas, Dr. Butte had little time to craft and launch a viable campaign. He resigned his position at the university in an effort to concentrate on the election and began his official campaign on October 1. Butte attempted to create momentum by embarking on an ambitious speaking tour using a strategy that included a minimization of the significance of party affiliation. In an attempt to open the eyes of Democrats to the possibility of voting outside their party, he proclaimed that, though his name was on the Republican ticket, he was running as a Texan and as an American. He had the robust support of some Democratic heavy hitters such as Thomas Love who had resigned his position as Democratic National Committeeman from Texas in response to Mrs. Ferguson's win. Butte's critics found him too timid and his platform too vague, small handicaps compared to the one his party affiliation imposed. [20]

While Butte vigorously campaigned, Miriam and Jim rested in their Temple home. Miriam, who suffered from allergy attacks, found the transition from home life to a very public life strenuous. She soon discovered that newspaper reporters did not rest or honor a request for privacy. Despite her declaration that she was on an "armchair vacation," reporters pursued her. Escape was near impossible: the Bosque Ranch, long used as the family retreat, had become a casualty of foreclosure by mortgage holder Dan Japhet for non-payment of a $75,000 mortgage. The family later made arrangements to rent the property until they could again secure financing to repurchase it. [21]

By late October, Jim, who had joined Miriam in the "armchair vacation," grew restless and apprehensive. On October 23 at Hillsboro, he took the podium before a large crowd and began to attack his latest nemesis. Ferguson referred to the Republican ticket as the Republican Ku Klux ticket, an association that was entirely false. Within a larger context, he referred to Dr. Butte as "a poor ignorant professor" and claimed, "I think they say he has four college degrees and diplomas, he has never been able, even to this hour, to promise or suggest one governmental reform that might benefit the people." [22]

In early November, the Fergusons, buoyed with confidence that Miriam would likely be the next governor of Texas, were ready for a hometown rally that would allow them to gauge the backing of local constituents. The response from Bell County residents was overwhelming. The audience held nothing back, showing their enthusiastic support through their large numbers and frequent, robust cheers. The theater that housed the rally swelled with people, every seat and aisle filled to capacity. Many would-be attendees were turned away for want of space. Jim Ferguson did the vast majority of talking, denouncing the Klan and defending his decision to first leave and then to return to the Democratic Party, and reminding listeners of his past accomplishments as governor. Then he unleashed his fury. "All of you newly rich roughnecks in Temple have it in for me because I have licked you here every time in the last eight years." He groused, "I have kept you from putting it over me. You are not against my wife or the platform, but you are mad at me. In spite of you, I am going to make Temple a big city. I put Temple on the map." [23]

Still they cheered.

Little that either candidate said was sufficient to offset the impact of the dominance of the Democratic Party in the state in 1924. Had George Butte held the same philosophy that James Ferguson had during his last two races, the fine showing he made with the November 4 election would have pleased him. He had attracted over 300,000 votes, by far the most of any Republican gubernatorial candidate in Texas history. No similarly positioned candidate had ever received even 100,000 votes. However, because Dr. Butte did not prevail, and because he was not running to support future political aspirations, his valiant showing was of little consequence to him. For two weeks, quibbling persisted over a correct counting of write-in votes, but in the end Butte conceded that a spread of over 120,000 votes rendered Miriam Ferguson the clear victor.[24]

There was much celebrating in Fergusonville. The entire world seemed ready to join the excitement sparked by the novelty of a woman governor. Ferguson friend Will Rogers soon affectionately dubbed Jim the "Governor by Marriage." As Ouida explained, "Mamma's foreign mail was now heavy." So famous was the Temple mansion that a letter from Rome with the sparse address: "M. A. Ferguson, U.S.A.," promptly made its way to the governor-elect. Though Mrs. Ferguson had not carried Temple or Belton, she had carried Bell County. Those tallies were of little consequence as the Fergusons prepared to leave Temple in a whirlwind of reacquired fame. They were satisfied that they had been vindicated and had reclaimed the coveted driver's seat that had been taken from them in 1917. With the City of Temple in their rear-view mirror in late 1924 Jim, Dorrace, and governor-elect Miriam Ferguson headed south. They would never again call the Temple mansion home.[25]

Chapter 18
Shadow Governer

The inauguration of the state's first female governor was set for January 20, 1925, but Jim Ferguson did not wait for his wife's swearing-in to parlay his new connections into a lucrative contract. On January 3, he announced that he had entered into an agreement as general counsel and advisor to W. T. Eldridge, owner of the Sugarland Railroad and three other railroad lines. Though not illegal, the arrangement constituted a serious conflict of interest because, as he had stated throughout his wife's campaign, Jim intended to act as an advisor to the new governor. It was an early hint that Governor Miriam Ferguson might not honor the agreement between certain top-ranking Democrats and herself, an agreement that she would insure that her husband refrained from behavior that could be seen as objectionable. [1]

If the inauguration ceremony was any indication of the collective optimism felt by a large number of Texas' five million, it was truly a day to celebrate. "Ten thousand cheering admirers of their 'Farmer Jim' idol made the hills of Austin resound with acclaim," wrote the *Dallas Morning News*. On that day it seemed as if even the doubters had cast aside their skepticism in favor of hope that the woman at the podium might provide the glue necessary to bind great political divides. Texans had, it seemed, embraced the new governor's gender and she assured the audience that the significance of that fact was not lost on her, saying, "We women have been recognized and admitted into all the rights and privileges of citizenship. Let us give our state the best that is in us, not so much because we are women, but because we are citizens who are now to stand side by side with men upon the foundation of equal rights and equal justice." She encouraged teamwork and assured listeners that she entered upon her duties, "With love for all and malice towards none." Later, in the privacy of the governor's office, Jim Ferguson proved far less cordial than his wife. In response to the Bible verse left open on his wife's desk by Governor Neff, Jim declared that Sunday school was dismissed and the governor's office was open for business. This he said as he tossed the single white rose Neff had left for Mrs. Ferguson on a nearby window sill. [2]

Mrs. Ferguson was only slightly behind her husband in using her newly acquired fame to generate cash. The first week of February she announced that she had hired a personal secretary who would attend to her personal business from an office in the Governor's Mansion. In reality, the new employee, Clare Ogden Davis, was a well-known newspaper woman who was employed to ghostwrite a series of articles under the governor's name. The arrangement, which included selling the articles to newspapers, lasted only one year. Jim's contribution to exchanging information for money came in the form of some poorly conceived offers to sell interviews and other time consuming gubernatorial courtesies. A writer for *Collier's Weekly* magazine alleged that in response to his requests for an interview with the first female governor of Texas, Jim had informed him that an interview and picture taking session would take time and, for that reason, it was not free. Other journalists from eastern states made similar complaints. [3]

The hallways of power echoed with rumblings of a future Senate resolution to absolve the impeachment charges against Jim; this too made its debut well in advance of Miriam's swearing-in ceremony. Larry Mills, the former campaign manager for Felix Robertson who had surreptitiously assisted Miriam in the primary election, was among the first to publicly proclaim his support for an amnesty bill. The bill, meant to restore Jim to a status of full citizenship with all its privileges, would also allow him to again hold a state office. Certainly there were those who felt that the suggestion was premature, that Jim Ferguson's future conduct as advisor to the governor would go a long way in determining his worthiness for such an award of civic redemption. [4]

The initial exposure to the breadth of the governor's responsibilities might have shocked the new Governor Ferguson had she not had the benefit of the ex-Governor Ferguson's forewarning. The appointment process began early. Initial appointments, announced on January 6, included the first woman Secretary of State, Mrs. S. W. Meharg, and C. O. Austin as Banking Commissioner. [5]

Those seeking pardons swarmed the lobby of the governor's office, as did job seekers; an estimated 900 applicants sought 50 state jobs. A concession constituted Governor Ferguson's first official act. She extended the parole of a father of eight so that he could earn income for his large family. The man in question had murdered his abusive brother-in-law. On January 24, a task of signing approximately 150 official documents further initiated the new governor. [6]

Governor Pat Neff, who preceded Mrs. Ferguson, had taken a strict stance on pardoning state prisoners due to his disapproval of the liberal pardoning policies of both Governor Hobby and Jim Ferguson before him. He cited weakened laws and a lack of enforcement as his reasons for curtailing the pardoning practice. Neff had granted a mere 92 pardons and 107 conditional pardons during his four years in the state's highest office, compared to 2,253 pardons by Jim Ferguson in the three years he held the office. Governor William Hobby, also a liberal pardoner, issued 1,518 concessions during a three-and-one-half year period. Although the number of parole seekers annoyed him, Jim Ferguson had, by his past actions, certainly encouraged those in pursuit of pardons and other favors to line up outside the governor's office. Many would be rewarded for their trouble. [7]

Seventy-five members of the House, exactly half of that body's numbers, were new members, a result of the sacking of many Klan-affiliated members in the past election. Lee Satterwhite of Carson County won the Speakership. Lieutenant Governor Barry Miller led the mostly seasoned members of the Senate. The unifying effects of the inauguration seemed to linger and the first weeks of activity between the new governor and the legislature proved particularly harmonious. Miriam's recommendations for state appointments were quickly accepted. On the sensitive subject of appointments to the university's Board of Regents and in the face of seven appointment opportunities, the Fergusons wisely enlisted the advice of the Ex-Students' Association. The appointments satisfied most parties. [8]

On March 9, 1925, the governor signed the (Luke) Mankin anti-mask law in fulfillment of her chief campaign promise, an act surrounded by much publicity and a great deal of joy on her part. The new law made it illegal for any secret society to allow its members to wear masks or disguises in public.

The following day a personal distraction came to the state's First Family when Jim's only sister, Kate Morton, died at age sixty-two after a brief illness. Kate had shouldered much of the responsibility for the care of her baby brother, Jim, before she married and left home in 1882. She had since lived in Grayson County with her husband, Frances M. Morton, a well-known and successful cattleman and businessman. Mr. Morton had preceded his wife in death by less than two years, leaving her a sizable estate of about $300,000. While the couple had no natural children, they had a foster son and were particularly close to a niece, Annie Kate Ferguson, the daughter of Joe Lee Ferguson. Her brother's impeachment had embarrassed Kate, a sentiment she openly expressed to family members in 1917. Mrs. Morton's husband had likely loaned money to Jim at a time when he was under extreme scrutiny in the March 1917 investigation. Whether or not these factors entered into Kate Morton's decision to slight two of her four brothers in her will remains a mystery, but some notion compelled her to do just that. [9]

The circumstances surrounding Mrs. Morton's will were unusual, even though the hand-drawn document included specifics indicating that she had prepared it with much thought. She specified that $50,000 be used to build a hospital in Haskell, Texas, in memory of her late husband. She left a sum of $5,000 to the couple's foster son, $1,000 to her sister-in-law, and 640 acres of land to niece Annie Kate, who had lived with the couple in their later years. To James and Alvah Ferguson, she bequeathed a mere $100 each and specified that the remainder of the estate be divided between her other brothers, Joe Lee and Alexander. [10]

The most unusual aspect of the will, drawn in Kate's handwriting, was its timing. Created on the eve of a trip to an undisclosed location, the document included this curious statement: "I am going on a journey and I may never come back alive so I make this will, but I expect to make changes if I live." The destination and perilous nature of that trip remain a mystery, but the fact that Mrs. Morton survived the trip is certain. Her subsequent failure to amend her will created a loophole for Jim and his brother Alvah to contest the document's validity. This they did on the grounds that the document was conditional and no longer valid after their sister returned home. In so doing, the brothers embarked on a six-year wait as the case made its way through the Texas court system. Despite bitter feelings within the family, Jim remained steadfast in his pursuit of a larger share of his sister's inheritance as the case slowly advanced through three levels of court decisions, stalling settlement. Jim would not see resolution until late 1931, and Alvah, who died one month prior to the State Supreme Court's judgment, never knew that he and Jim failed in their attempts to invalidate their sister's will. For his efforts Jim had gained nothing except the enmity of many of his family members.

On March 31, parties favoring Jim's amnesty managed to put bill #252 on the governor's desk and a beaming Mrs. Ferguson signed it with a gold pen given to her by friends from Temple. Her exuberance, however, belied her knowledge of the controversy surrounding the subject and the tenuous nature of its validity. Early on in the process, with the drawing of the Woodward bill for amnesty, Attorney General Dan Moody warned those who would listen that the legislature was overstepping its legal authority in passing such a bill. He predicted that the amnesty, if tested in court, would not be legally binding. Jim Ferguson could hardly contain his rage at Moody's comment, "The war is on and I do not know where it will end," he declared. Demonstrating the depth of his belief that his wife's election entitled him to a bill of amnesty, he continued, "Dan Moody and his crowd, all aligned against us, and they are attempting to deny us and the people the rights we have won and are entitled to." [11]

Despite Moody's warnings, the bill moved through the process and, for a time, Jim Ferguson basked in the knowledge that he could again hold a state office. (The bill would stand unchallenged until its repeal in 1927.) This initial disagreement and subsequent war-of-words that passed between Jim Ferguson and Dan Moody marked an early end to any hope for an amicable relationship between the governor's husband and her administration's attorney general.

Mrs. Ferguson's pet project was the fulfillment of a campaign promise to cut state spending as a remedy for an anticipated sizeable revenue shortfall. To accomplish this goal she recommended deep spending cuts, a tax on vehicles as well as a gasoline tax, and a tax on certain tobacco products. Legislators honored her requests for spending cuts but the tax proposals met with resistance, particularly from lobbyists. Many legislators balked at passing any new laws, fearing that government was growing too large, and in the end, legislators failed to pass any new tax bills. Mrs. Ferguson's appropriation reductions to various state departments totaled $767,338. An appropriation for an assistant to Attorney General Moody was among the financial casualties. Also on the chopping block were the Department of Journalism, the Department of Music, and the School of Library Science at the University of Texas. [12]

With the axing of the Department of Journalism at the University of Texas came the displacement of Will H. Mayes, dean of the department, an action that held particular significance due to Jim Ferguson's long-standing dislike for him. Mayes had been among those faculty members that Ferguson found objectionable in the 1917 clash with the university, and the reason had nothing to do with his performance as a teacher. A former lieutenant governor, Mayes had also briefly sought the nomination for governor along with Jim in 1914, but it was his subsequent actions as a newspaper publisher that incited Ferguson's scorn. During a Ferguson campaign, a Brownwood newspaper that Mayes edited and partially owned had published articles that were uncomplimentary to Ferguson. The governor had, during the impeachment proceedings, freely admitted that those articles were the reason for his antipathy toward Mayes. It may have been a mere coincidence that Miriam Ferguson's expense-cutting measures cost Mr. Mayes his job. The possibility also existed that the new Governor Ferguson intended to subscribe to the same reward and punishment system that the ex-Governor Ferguson had used so liberally.[13]

Among the many scrutinizing the Fergusons' conduct was Attorney General Dan Moody. Young and popular were the best adjectives to describe the thirty-two-year-old attorney general in 1925. After completing law school at the University of Texas, he had practiced law for a short time before joining the Texas National Guard to aid the World War I effort. The red-headed young man gained fame in Texas in 1923 as the county attorney in Williamson County when, against great odds and at risk to his own personal safety, he sought and secured the prosecution of Klan members, most notably, a man named Murray Jackson. This occurred at a time when both prosecutors and jury members greatly feared Klan retaliation in cases against Klan members. Jackson was one of several Klan members who had been party to a severe flogging of a traveling salesman named Robert Burleson on Easter Sunday of 1923 near the community of Jonah. In addition to the beating that almost killed him, the victim suffered the horrible effects of tarring. He was left naked, chained to a tree in the town square in Taylor. His alleged crime was adultery.[14]

After obtaining a guilty verdict and a five-year sentence for Jackson, Moody continued to prosecute other Klan members with success. The notoriety associated with these prosecutions brought suggestions that the young lawyer run for the position of attorney general for the '25–'26 term. With the momentum of the same anti-Klan sentiment that helped elect Miriam Ferguson, Dan Moody managed a successful campaign. Moody's goal of putting the Klan out of business was in perfect harmony with the Fergusons during the campaign, but both parties soon realized that a desire to rid the state of the Klan was largely the extent of their common ground.

Governor Miriam Ferguson had expressed her intent to administer a liberal pardon policy, but in practice the staggering number of concessions she granted strained the tolerance of many judges and law enforcement officers. They saw the action as an over-ride of their judgment and authority as did many private citizens. Jim and Miriam, and later daughter Ouida, defended this practice with vigor, equating the pardons with mercy for those that could ill afford attorneys to defend them. A reasonable number of pardons may have passed the mercy test, but to most Texans the numbers transcended reasonableness and the gestures were too often illogical. In May, the governor pardoned a man convicted of selling intoxicants before his case, which was on appeal, made its way through the courts. Other lawbreakers' pardons happened so hastily that the subjects never made it to the prisons meant to confine them.[15]

Though the sheer number of pardons was troubling, the governor's deflection of the criticism was equally agitating, particularly to newspaper reporters. In response to media condemnation of Miriam's pardon policy, she announced on April 25, through her private secretary Ghent Sanderford, a ban by the Secretary of State's office on the release of information to newsmen regarding pardons. Two days later the governor denied, again through Sanderford, that she had initiated such a ban. Reporters, however, confirmed that the day following the announced ban they had been denied access to the pardon records. Sinister rumors circulated alleging that the reason for plentiful pardons had less to do with mercy than their ability to line the Fergusons' pockets with cash. If the governor was aware of the extent of the buzz, it did nothing to impede her generosity in granting more pardons. By the end of her first year in office, she had granted over 1,200 concessions, an incredible number considering the total population of Texas inmates at that time was about 3,700. [16]

Jim Ferguson responded to the criticism of numerous pardons when he spoke before the Texas Bar Association in early July. He quickly shifted the blame by chastising his audience of Texas lawyers, asking them to conduct themselves in a way that brought dignity and confidence to the profession. He also stated that Governor Ferguson was proposing the offer of a reward for the conviction of violators of the liquor laws, an offer that only applied to offenders who were worth over $5,000. The specifics of the reward may have seemed strange to those who might not have understood that it was aimed at specific Ferguson enemies whom they considered well-known if not flagrant drinkers. The chief executive made good on her threat and used her position and the states' coffers to target her personal enemies later that year with an offer of a $500 reward.[17]

The *Ferguson Forum* enjoyed a substantial increase in circulation immediately after Miriam's election along with a decided change in format and content. The agricultural weekly quickly morphed into a paper of advertisements, the ads placed by a bevy of businesses that had little or nothing to do with agriculture. So busy was the advertising section of the *Ferguson Forum* office that the paper added a full-time ad salesman, Joseph Furst, to its staff. His job was to visit pre-selected contractors, utilities, and government suppliers with a smile and a letter from Jim Ferguson petitioning their support in a special feature of the *Forum* titled the "better roads" program. Furst later admitted that it took no marketing skills to sell ads to the targeted businesses who were almost entirely firms that would benefit from the creation of goodwill with the governor's husband. So large and plentiful were the ads, in fact, that the *Forum* produced two large special editions to accommodate them. Furst estimated the value of the "special edition" ads at $17,000.[18]

This activity later led to an investigation that revealed details of the scheme. Investigators heard the testimony of a long stream of men, sixteen on one particular day, who testified to their participation in the ad-buying arrangement. One of these was Dave T. Austin, a Houston contractor. Mr. Austin's story was thus: Joseph Furst had approached him in November of 1924 with the suggestion that he buy an expensive ad in the *Ferguson Forum*. Furst informed Austin that he was aware that he (Austin) had not voted for Mrs. Ferguson and suggested that he redeem himself by placing a goodwill ad in the *Forum*. Austin, who balked at the price, negotiated with Furst until the two finally settled on a price of $250, which Austin agreed to send to the *Forum* office. But Furst continued to press Austin, insisting that he pay immediately because, he said, Jim Ferguson was in a financial condition so dire that he had recently been forced to sleep on the floor of a hotel because he could not afford a bed. Austin relented and gave Furst a check made payable to James

Ferguson. Austin stated that the drama did not end there. He later received by mail another solicitation for an $800 ad, which he ignored. In support of his testimony, Austin presented the $250 cancelled check endorsed by Ferguson to investigators. [19]

Advertising was not the only newly lucrative component of the *Forum* after the Fergusons took office. State employees received pressure to subscribe to the *Forum*, pressure so intense that one who refused to subscribe, W. B. Shoe, claimed that he had subsequently been asked to resign. A former state employee, John Ward of Austin, testified about the pressure that his boss applied to him regarding the *Forum*: "It was understood in the office that if you didn't subscribe for the *Forum*, your head went off." Ward testified that his superior called him and other members of the staff individually asking if they subscribed to the *Forum*. The implication existed that the supervisor expected either a reply of "yes" or the immediate procurement of a subscription. [20]

Many of the largest ads in the *Forum* were from road contractors. The structure of the State Highway Commission was such that the control of its budgeted twenty million dollars rested almost entirely in the hands of three appointed commissioners. Soon after taking office, the new Governor Ferguson filled two commissioner positions by appointing Frank V. Lanham and Joe Burkett to join the third commissioner already in place under an appointment by Governor Neff. Frank Lanham, the son of former Governor Samuel W. T. Lanham (1903–1907), was made commission chairman but Jim Ferguson attended every meeting, essentially commandeering the process. Ferguson closed the doors of meetings that had once been open to outsiders. The absence of the Neff appointee whose illness rendered him unable to attend most department meetings, added to the ease with which Ferguson dominated the commission's activity. Journalist/humorist Don Biggers made this amusing observation related to Ferguson's involvement: "He [Ferguson] had no more right to 'sit in' at highway board meetings and boss things around than any other private citizen had." [21]

Rumors of wrongdoing continued to circulate. Complaints filtered out that unqualified companies, Ferguson friends, and contractors who advertised in the *Ferguson Forum* received the bulk of road maintenance contracts. Others alleged that contracts were routinely let without bids or were given to contractors who had not submitted the lowest bid.

In mid-1925, Louis Kemp, executive secretary of the Texas Highway and Municipal Contractors Association, was asked to investigate suspicions that a private road contractor was using a piece of state-owned road paving equipment for jobs that were not under state contract. Kemp's probing found that, indeed, a Houston contractor had possession and use of a large piece of state equipment that was being used for private contract paving. Hoping to resolve the matter, Kemp paid a visit to Jim Ferguson but received a cool reception. Ferguson became angry and demanded to know if Kemp was a member of the Klan or if he supported Mrs. Ferguson's administration, questions that were both irrelevant and inappropriate. Kemp responded that his organization was not affiliated with either party, a response that only further angered Ferguson. Having obtained no remedy from the governor's advisor, Kemp immediately notified Attorney General Dan Moody of his findings and the details of his visit to the ex-governor. Moody launched his own investigation and, finding that Kemp was correct, promptly filed an injunction against the Houston contractor to prevent any further payments to them under the state contract.[22]

Kemp, not convinced that the inappropriate use of state equipment was an isolated incident, continued his research into the State Highway Commission's ac-tivities. He also began to publish his findings in the Texas Highways and Municipal Contractors Association's newsletter. The association, which initially supported Kemp's efforts, withdrew its backing after Kemp met with Lanham and openly challenged the cost of many of the state's road contracts. Under pressure from some undisclosed person or parties, the association demanded that Kemp cease including charges of corruption in the newsletter, a demand that Kemp refused to honor. This refusal cost Louis Kemp his job but did not stop his investigative work, performed largely at his own risk and expense. He continued publishing his findings in a se-ries of letters he circulated titled "Goat Bleats." Most major newspapers, fearing Ferguson's reprisal, were unwilling to print Kent's discoveries. The following month, mid-September of 1925, when Kemp attempted to examine the minutes of the State Highway Commission meetings, Chairman Frank Lanham turned him away. [23]

On September 29 in Amarillo, Texas, Kemp spoke before the Association of County Judges and Highway Commissioners about the investigation that had become his obsession. In particular he wanted to share his most distressing find-ings. The American Road Company, a Dallas-based company, was formed in New York on March 27, 1925, incorporated one day later under Delaware law, and had opened an office in Dallas one week later. Within three days the company secured two million dollars in Texas road contracts, a figure that soon grew to five mil-lion. They had secured the coveted contracts without bids and the State of Texas was the company's only client. So great were the company's profits that dividends totaling $319,000 had already been declared and paid to company stockholders. Company assets included an asphalt plant that the company had purchased from Frank Lanham's Texas Road Company.[24]

Moody's investigation of the Houston contractor had unearthed more than unauthorized use of state paving equipment. An examination of the company's records revealed that a check for $3,500, made payable to cash, was a curious part of the project expense. Auditors testified that when they inquired about the transaction, the contractor told them that the company used the cash to pay promotional expenses, one of which was a contribution to the Ferguson campaign fund.[25]

Moody broadened his investigation. In mid-October he advised Frank Lanham that his findings led him to believe that several existing state highway contracts were questionable and suggested that Lanham have them voided. Lanham was not appreciative of the advice. He rebuffed Moody's assistance indirectly through newspapers complaining that Moody was "Giving an opinion dictating the policy of the Highway Commission which was not requested." A few days later Governor Ferguson offered her support to the Highway Commission, giving her opinion that existing contracts should be honored.[26]

Kemp's legwork proved invaluable to Dan Moody. In late October Moody announced that he had recovered a sum of $436,861.26 from a Kansas City bank on behalf of the state as a result of his investigation. The American Road Company had agreed to return the money to the Texas treasury after Moody's examination of what he called, "Grossly improvident contracts let at an unconscionable price." The recovery of the money was only the starting point. A suit filed soon after ended on November 20 with a total recovery from American Road Company of $600,000, cancellation of all American Road contracts and the forfeiture of the company's permit to do business in Texas. Lanham and Burkett resigned from their jobs with the highway commission soon after the ruling. By mid-December testimony in a similarly charged case against the Hoffman Construction Company was being heard in anticipation of cancelled contracts. A third suit against the Houston company Sherman-Youmans was also pending. Authorities took this action in spite of Governor Ferguson's attempts to help the Highway Commission block it using lawyers paid with state funds. [27]

On December 14, the Fergusons and members of the State Highway Commission traveled to Temple to witness the grand opening of a new road between their two former hometowns of Belton and Temple. Amid a whirl of publicity, the Fergusons were given the privilege of being the first to travel the new and experimental "invisible track." In view of the controversy that was hovering over their administration regarding road maintenance, their joy may have been tempered with fear of another investigation into the details of the new road. If they were not worried, they should have been. This project too was riddled with graft, the details of which would soon be disclosed. [28]

Attorney General Moody's court actions and subsequent recovery of substantial amounts of state money were proof positive to many observers that, at the very least, questions of incompetence and dereliction of duty were valid charges against the governor's administration. Legislators had hoped for a called session to address the issues with road contracts but some legislators had another goal: to use a session to call for an investigation aimed at impeaching a second Ferguson. Miriam, fearing their intent, refused to appease them. So intense was the argument for a special session that Speaker of the House Lee Satterwhite, a Ferguson friend, severed his friendship with the ex-governor when the two men became embroiled in a bitter argument. Satterwhite declared that Jim Ferguson was "mad with power" and warned him that he would call for a special session himself if Mrs. Ferguson failed to do so. Forty-five members of the legislature signed a petition advising the governor that if she did not call for a session by December 10, they would meet and proceed on their own. With talk of a forced session circulating, the governor openly admitted to her fear that history would repeat itself with a special session ending in impeachment charges. [29]

However, threats of a forced session ended without action. With the first year of Mrs. Ferguson's term almost spent, thoughts turned to the next campaign that would soon begin. Top Democrats who had extracted a promise from Mrs. Ferguson that she would not seek a second term in exchange for their support, certainly hoped to hold her to that promise. Others wishing to rid themselves of the Fergusons and the turmoil that seemed to always accompany them, attached their hopes to removing the couple from the governor's office the old fashioned way. They were determined to see to it that team Ferguson was soundly defeated in the next election.

Miriam's childhood Home. Courtesy Bell County Museum, Belton, Texas

A young Miriam Wallace (1896). Courtesy Bell County Museum, Belton, Texas

A young James Ferguson. Courtesy Bell County Museum, Belton, Texas

Inside Wallace Home—Jim and Miriam's wedding gifts (1899). Courtesy Bell County Museum, Belton, Texas

Interior of Belton National Bank (circa 1900). Courtesy Bell County Museum, Belton, Texas (Author believes that second man in line at far right is Jim Ferguson)

The Temple Mansion. Courtesy Bell County Museum, Belton, Texas

Bell County Court House, Belton, Texas (circa 1904). Courtesy Bell County Museum, Belton, Texas (Building in right background is the opera house which housed Ferguson's law office in space at street level)

Temple State Bank's Original Location (circa 1910). Courtesy Dolph Briscoe Center for American History, University of Texas at Austin

Temple State Bank's second location and the Texas Store. Courtesy Bell County Museum, Belton, Texas

Miriam, Dorrace (left) and Ouida (right). Courtesy Dolph Briscoe Center for American History, University of Texas at Austin

Ouida Ferguson. Courtesy Bell County Museum, Belton, Texas

Dorrace Ferguson. Courtesy Bell County Museum, Belton, Texas

Young Ferguson fan. Courtesy Bell County Museum, Belton, Texas

Jim Campaigning (circa 1914). Courtesy Bell County Museum, Belton, Texas

Miriam Ferguson (circa 1924). Courtesy Bell County Museum, Belton, Texas

"PA" and "MA." Courtesy Bell County Museum, Belton, Texas

"MA"

SON

MAURER
PHOTO

Governor Miriam Ferguson (1925). Courtesy Bell County Museum, Belton, Texas

The Greenhouse at the Governor's Mansion. Courtesy Bell County Museum, Belton, Texas

Jim Ferguson with foreman Joe Miller and stock. Courtesy Bell County Museum, Belton, Texas

Ferguson Austin
Home (1928).
Courtesy Bell
County Museum,
Belton, Texas

Ferguson Austin Home. Courtesy Bell County Museum, Belton, Texas

Thanksgiving at Governor's Mansion, 1934. Courtesy Bell County Museum, Belton, Texas

Jim, Dorrace, and Dorrace's son James Watt (1941). Courtesy Bell County Museum, Belton, Texas

Miriam's Eightieth Birthday Party (1956). Courtesy Bell County Museum, Belton, Texas

Ouida, George Nalle Jr., Miriam, James Watt, and Dorrace. Courtesy Bell County Museum, Belton, Texas

Coke Stevenson.
Courtesy Bell
County Museum,
Belton, Texas

Chapter 19
See Ma Run (Again)

T he first gubernatorial candidate to announce his intentions was none other than Lynch Davidson, whose declaration came early. He expressed his intentions in the fall of 1925 and celebrated the fact that no other office seeker with the name Davidson would challenge him. Davidson had sufficient reason for not fearing Miriam Ferguson as an opponent, but he was pressing his luck in hoping that the popular attorney general, Dan Moody, would not seek the nomination.

Miriam Ferguson had, during her first campaign, made a private promise, and later a public one, that she would not seek a second term. In late February of 1926 she announced otherwise. Attempting to offset the anticipated backlash from those who expected to hold her to her word, she took a defensive posture, saying, "There are those impelled by their own personal ambitions who want to deny me the right to again appeal to the people and say that I have received vindication, and in the same breath they say that the amnesty bill [exonerating Jim] is unconstitutional. It therefore does not lie in their mouths to say that I have received vindication and should not for that reason run again."[1]

Amid rumors that Dan Moody would run for governor, Governor Ferguson's comments were undoubtedly directed at him. She reasoned that his lack of faith in the amnesty bill gave her the right to continue her quest for vindication through a second term. It was, of course, double talk. If the amnesty bill was the only true path to vindication, valid or not, there was nothing she could do in a subsequent term that would change it.

Dan Moody's popularity had grown with his successes in recovering money on abusive state highway contracts and this made him the obvious choice to challenge Mrs. Ferguson for the '27–'28 term. Moody, however, was slow to commit to such an undertaking. He had no personal finances with which to support a campaign, but with the assurance that supporters would help him raise the needed money, he finally announced his candidacy in early March of 1926. Moody backers hoped to capitalize on an association between "honesty in government" and the Moody name. Among the six candidates who filed for the office were three women, including Governor Ferguson. Lynch Davidson's campaign was again a wild card in a race for the nomination that seemed destined to produce a Moody-Ferguson showdown. [2]

Early in 1926 a problem erupted that made the need for a special session of the legislature increasingly critical. The US Supreme Court had agreed to hear a case involving some controversial road improvement bonds that authorities in Archer County, Texas, had issued. The case needed to be addressed because of the great significance it held to the legitimacy of all bonds of its type in the state. Taxing authorities had assessed taxes on certain property owners in Archer County based on the issuance of road bonds that the citizens had not approved. The group claimed that the bond issue was illegal and further protested the use of the bond proceeds that they believed had been used to make improvements to roads outside their area of benefit. The group complained that they tried to present their objection to authorities who denied them a hearing. In early 1926, the US Supreme Court issued its opinion that the property owners were correct, a decision that immediately rendered the questionable bonds invalid. The possibility of repercussions for similar bond issues in other counties resulted in increased pressure for a special legislative session to address the problem. But Mrs. Ferguson stalled, hoping to postpone that inevitable meeting for reasons that were entirely personal. Her inaction frustrated and angered many legislators who knew that she was waiting for the election to pass before she called a session. [3]

The case against the Hoffman Construction Company continued in January 1926. Resolution of the case did not come until the end of the year but reports of the testimony in January and subsequent months shed further light on the inner workings of the highway commission while Jim Ferguson sat, somewhat indiscernibly, at its helm. W. T. Montgomery, a San Antonio contractor, and H. S. Wilder, a Houston contractor, testified before the House investigating committee that they had approached Frank Lanham in 1925 anticipating an opportunity to bid on road contracts. Both men swore that Lanham had advised them that their efforts would be futile because the contracts had already been let to the American Road Company. The contractors also testified that Lanham had revealed to them that, although he was the chairman of the commission, he had no say in the matter. According to Montgomery and Wilder's testimony, when asked who had awarded the contracts, Lanham had named Jim Ferguson. When questioned under oath, Lanham denied the conversation entirely. [4]

In February of 1926 Jim and Miriam jointly sued Reverend Atticus Webb and the American Printing Company, publisher of the *Austin American Statesman.* The suit was filed in Bell County. The couple sought damages in the amount $100,000, half of which was to compensate Miriam Ferguson for the mental anguish, distress, and humiliation she had suffered at the hands of the newspaper when they printed details of an interview with Atticus Webb that were uncomplimentary to her. In part, the paper attributed this quote to Webb: "If she [Mrs. Ferguson] really wants to catch the rich bootleggers, I suggest that she employ Captain Frank Hamer and B. C. Baldwin whom she dismissed from the ranger force for pestering rich bootleggers in South Texas."[5]

Webb's comment stemmed from a troubled relationship that the Texas Rangers had experienced with both Fergusons. Mrs. Ferguson had, immediately upon taking office, reduced the Ranger force from fifty-one to twenty-eight, abolishing Captain Baldwin's entire company. This she had done as part of her cost-cutting efforts, but that move, coupled with severe limitations placed on the Rangers' missions and Mrs. Ferguson's liberal pardoning policy, disgusted Frank Hamer so thoroughly that he resigned his position in June of 1925. After attorneys from both sides agreed to do so, the court dismissed the lawsuit against the newspaper and Webb in October 1929. [6]

In the background of the Ferguson drama that seemed to play out continually, was the looming election. In May, Mrs. Ferguson made a daring, if not ridiculous move that reflected a high degree of confidence in her ability to prevail in the primaries—a confidence that later proved misplaced. Governor Ferguson offered an unusual and ill-conceived challenge to Dan Moody in her opening speech in May. Her current term as governor would expire on January 24, 1927, but she promised Moody her immediate resignation after the July 1926 primary if he beat her by so much as a single vote. To validate the offer, Moody had to agree that he would immediately resign his job as attorney general if she led him by no fewer than 25,000 votes.[7]

Moody accepted the challenge, a move that a number of his supporters condemned. They saw his acceptance as a gesture that lent dignity to the absurd proposition. Candidate Lynch Davidson took full advantage of the opportunity to chastise both opponents, saying, "The honor and dignity of these two great offices is insulted and disgraced by their incumbents to a degree that brings the blush of shame to decent and right-thinking citizens in this state." Davidson also reasoned that if she won, Mrs. Ferguson would be further empowered by naming a new attorney general who would support her views. Davidson railed against that circumstance, which he characterized as entirely unfair to the citizens of Texas who had elected Moody. Certainly no Ferguson-appointed attorney general would act as a watchdog to the Ferguson administration as Moody had done. [8]

Moody, expecting criticism, had addressed the frivolous nature of the challenge when he accepted it, saying, "At the outset I want to say that the public offices of Texas are not to be wagered away, or bartered away, or otherwise disposed of than is provided in the Constitution and in the popular will." Some believed that the real reason for Moody's acceptance of the offer was because he believed the dare was a bluff on Ferguson's part, a bluff he intended to call. [9]

The Fergusons were at a disadvantage as they campaigned against the fresh-faced young and energetic man who stood in direct contrast to their blemished records. Still they enjoyed the support of the rural constituency, particularly in East Texas, and a large number of anti-prohibitionists. With no true Klan candidate in the race, Klan members largely split their allegiance between Dan Moody and Lynch Davidson. Using this as a basis, Jim implied that Moody was sympathetic to Klan issues, a suggestion that was entirely unfounded. Jim attacked Moody's war record, calling him a coward. Striking at Moody's religious affiliation, Ferguson alienated a large number of Baptists when he used the term "monkey faced Baptists" in describing a major segment of Moody supporters. Jim later qualified his statement to the satisfaction of few by saying he was referring only to those who believed in evolution. On this subject, Dr. J. B. Cranfill, a physician and prominent Baptist leader, spoke for many when he wrote, "Just why a candidate for governor should offer a gratuitous affront to any religious body will always remain a mystery, though the possible explanation of this blunder of Ferguson's may be that Dan Moody is a Baptist." [10]

At times during the campaign crowds heckled Jim Ferguson. At a July rally in an Austin park hecklers became so boisterous that Ferguson could barely be heard. He invited the unruly men in the audience to a physical fight, but those that tried to make their way to the stage in answer to the challenge, were held back. Ferguson berated the offenders, calling them Ku-Kluxers and ended his speech with this indelicate statement, "Moody has blowed [sic] up and busted." Miriam, for her part, attempted to capitalize on her gender by proclaiming in her very limited number of brief speeches that she represented the rights of women, saying, "If the opposition should succeed in this campaign then the equal rights of women will be set back by a hundred years."[11]

Lynch Davidson directed most of his attacks against Dan Moody, condemning him for supporting oil companies and spending great sums of money in his campaign. Davidson received an interesting telegram from an unlikely source while at a campaign stop in Wichita Falls on June 24. The telegram, from Jim Ferguson's youngest brother, Alex, offered support to Davidson with these words:

"Wish you success and hope the voters who want more business efficiency in public affairs will give active support to your campaign. I cannot support Jim Ferguson, proxy candidate. He is my brother and I know him." [12]

Moody's campaign was largely based on a single theme, that of the complete annihilation of Fergusonism. Most major Texas newspapers liked him and he enjoyed the support of strong political heavy-hitters such as Oscar Colquitt, Martin Crane, Tom Love, and the Hogg brothers, all united under an umbrella of contempt for Jim Ferguson. Colquitt, in particular, put massive energy into the Moody effort when he published a newsletter called the *Free Lance* and distributed it to rural homes in great numbers. Colquitt intended his publication to serve as an antidote to the *Ferguson Forum*, the only news source many rural families read. Moody's forces also campaigned heavily among German and Czech populations, a voter segment that had traditionally backed Ferguson. [13]

Moody's camp turned the tables on the Fergusons, using the *Forum* against them. They reprinted the inflammatory remarks Jim had made against Jews and distributed them along with equally offensive remarks made against the Japanese and Mexican populations. "I would rather have a hundred Japs than a dozen Mexicans in Texas," Jim had written in a 1920 edition of the *Forum*. [14]

In April, Moody married and the associated publicity seemed to further enhance his likability. Ferguson used the occasion as a platform for sarcasm, asserting that Moody's principal assets were his new wife, lipstick, and cigarette smoking. But Ferguson's old-style campaign speeches with their heavy measure of cynicism no longer resonated with voters and the slogan "Dan's the Man" seemed to drown out the "Me for MA" constituency across the state. Another slogan, "No MA for me, too much PA," expressed the growing sentiment of some voters in more precise terms.

Information that trickled out as a result of the road contract investigation and trials indicated that Ouida and her husband, George Nalle, had also benefited from state road contracts. Mrs. Nalle was a partner in the Capital Insurance Exchange, a company that issued surety bonds. One contractor testified that after he was given a state contract, officials directed him to see Mrs. Nalle to obtain his surety bond.

There was further evidence of the financial benefits Ouida gained as a result of her connections to the governor's office. In June of 1926, Ouida's business partner, Ruth Yett, sued her for half of the commission on a bond sale, an amount slightly over $900. The two women had been in business for about five years when Ouida informed Mrs. Yett that she wanted to dissolve the partnership and sever all ties with her. The question before the court was the determination of exactly when that verbal dissolution of the partnership had occurred: before or after the partnership had earned the commission in question. The jury deadlocked and the judge dismissed the case, but not before an interesting point emerged. Mrs. Yett asserted that Ouida had decided to exclude her from the partnership only after her mother's election, "just when the big highway bonds were coming our way."[15]

Lynch Davidson must have realized early in the race that he would emerge third in the primaries. The other candidates, two of them women, received inconsequential numbers of votes while Moody received 409,732 votes to Ferguson's 283,482. Davidson, whose votes would not have changed the end result if Ferguson had received them all, certainly cost Moody a clear majority and a chance to avoid the inconvenience and expense of a runoff election. Moody, less than 2,000 votes short of that goal, held out hope that Miriam would withdraw, especially against such overwhelming odds. The Ferguson defeat was embarrassingly large, including the loss of Bell and Bosque Counties. Even Templeites failed to support their former resident. A large number of county conventions passed resolutions asking for the governor's immediate resignation. [16]

The unique aspects of the election brought national interest to the event. Newspapers around the country could not resist commenting. *The New York Evening Post* declared, "Mrs. Ferguson is rejected because she was not governor herself." [17]

The New York Times printed, "She will lose her office, not as a woman but as an inefficient and disappointing Governor." *The Hartford Courant* reported, "The defeat of Fergusonism in Texas will be well received throughout the country, as the state made a ridiculous exhibition of itself in electing to the governorship the wife of the discredited Jim Ferguson. Her specialty has been giving freedom to prisoners and her administration has not been without scandal. Clearly incompetent, the Texas Governor has undoubtedly injured the cause of the women in politics." And commenting on Ferguson's quest for further vindication for her husband's past actions, *The Courant* also wrote, "Evidently the Texas Democrats do not propose to let the Fergusons' [pursuit of] vindication be a life [long] issue."

The result of the primary, in which Moody defeated Mrs. Ferguson by well over one hundred thousand votes, left team Ferguson obligated to make good on Miriam's promise to resign immediately or appear foolish. She quickly announced that a special session would convene on September 13 to address the validation of road contract bonds, and to allow for the investigation of any state department that the legislature wished to make. She could hardly have done otherwise. The governor declared that in view of the special session, instead of immediately vacating the office, she would resign no later than November 1. She also promised that she was, in fact, withdrawing from the next campaign. She did neither.

The candidates had only two weeks to prepare for the next election. The same tired subjects were revisited—Moody bashing Fergusonism and Jim accusing

Moody of Klan connections, this time accompanied by a scare tactic that a resurgence of Klan activity would follow a Moody victory. The election results seemed to show that voters had replaced their apprehension about the Klan with apprehension about Fergusonism. The inevitable Ferguson whipping came on August 29 when Miriam lost by over 225,000 votes.[18]

Governor Ferguson was busy furiously issuing pardons as her final days as governor slipped by. She issued over 300 pardons in her last days bringing the total for her term to 3,595. The terms of one particular pardon were interesting if not alarming. Mr. Benjamin Hollings, a black man of twenty-six, had served seven years of a ninety-nine-year sentence for murder. Hollings was given a conditional pardon with the stipulation that he live in the Ferguson home for a term of six years at a wage of $15 per month plus board and clothing. Hollings served the Fergusons under the terms of his pardon but returned to the penitentiary in 1941. Another Ferguson pardon attracted the ire of many because it was an obvious personal attack on Dan Moody. Murray Jackson, the convicted Klan member who had brutally flogged and tarred a man in 1923, was serving a five-year sentence after his conviction at the hands of Moody and other diligent prosecuting attorneys. Jackson's conviction, and others like it, had elevated Moody to hero status in the minds of many in 1923. Miriam Ferguson pardoned Murray Jackson, a particularly sinister act given its timing.[19]

Jim Ferguson continued to attribute Moody's victory to the Klan. How he reconciled his own denunciation of the Klan relative to his wife's recent pardoning of the well-known Klan member Murray Jackson is perplexing. Moody's reply to Ferguson's efforts to incite anger by suggesting a fictional Moody-Klan connection was: "The Klan was not an issue [in the election]and Ferguson found it impossible to make it an issue." [20]

The long-awaited special session in September accomplished its goals with the passage of a large number of bills to address past, present, and future issues related to bonds. The House also established a committee to investigate three state agencies: the Highway Department, the Board of Pardons, and the Textbook Commission. Contrary to the terms of her challenge and subsequently revised promise, Mrs. Ferguson was imbedded in the governorship and would remain so until the natural end of her term. In early October, the House, by a close margin, voted to adopt a resolution forcing her to abide by her promise and resign, but the idea met with resistance and eventually died.

The lawsuits against the Hoffman Construction Company would finally end in the State's favor, the last completed in early 1927. Other reports of graft were also exposed, among them the sordid details of the "invisible track" in Bell County. Investigation showed that a staggering $244, 059.22 had been spent for highways in Bell County between January 1 and August 1 of 1915, including the costly project known as the invisible track. The new process, developed by S. B. Moore of La Porte, Texas, was declared experimental when the Texas Highway Commission granted a contract for its use on a five-mile road linking Temple and Belton. In reality, the state of Louisiana had already tested the process with the construction of a half-mile stretch of road near Monroe, Louisiana, and authorities in that state had pronounced it a failure. Even so, Moore was given a job as consulting engineer for the brick and crushed rock road that cost the State of Texas an average of over $49,000 per mile when completed. [21]

Moore was not the only man who enjoyed the financial benefit of the project. Ferguson friend and former appointee to the State Mining Board, Frank Denison, received lucrative contracts to maintain highways in Bell County, including the experimental Temple-Belton road. Denison, who had no experience in road paving, sub-contracted the work to Harold Naylor of the Fort Worth based-General Construction Company, furnishing the supplies and equipment used for the projects from his (Denison's) own hardware store— at a price. A Denison employee later testified that they purchased most of the gravel used in the project from Fred Ferguson, a cousin of Jim's, at a cost of $1.60 per cubic yard when the common rate for such gravel was $1.40. Not surprisingly, the road proved a complete failure. Two strips of bricks positioned to accommodate the width of a car's tires required drivers to keep their wheels within the constraints of its narrow path and proved a ridiculously impractical solution for a busy roadway. [22]

The inferior nature of the highway was not the only questionable issue associated with the infamous invisible track. Though it was new construction, the road was charged to the road maintenance fund rather than the road construction fund. One state employee who questioned certain invoices that contained an inappropriate 10 percent upcharge by the contractor, found himself unemployed soon after. John Ward had been the chief bookkeeper for the highway department since January of 1924, a job that required him to audit and approve for payment highway maintenance account invoices. He testified that his superior had overridden his objections and rejection of certain invoices payable to Denison and Moore. When Ward still refused to approve them, Ward's superior paid the bills without his approval and dismissed him on August 15, 1925. [23]

J. D. Winder, a contractor from Belleville, testified that Jim Ferguson offered to obtain contracts for him in the amount of $75,000 with a stipulation that he, Ferguson, receive a fee of 10 percent payable in five- and ten-dollar bills. When questioned, Jim denied the incident and that he knew or had ever spoken to J. D. Winder. [24]

The state's awarding of textbook contracts fostered questions similar to those raised by the highway contract debacle. Jim's appointment as clerk on the textbook commission, a position that had not previously existed, was the starting point for such questions. Investigations raised nothing actionable and proved nothing beyond the failure on the part of the commission to obtain volume discounts, and the granting of a $600,000 contract to the American Book Company who was, in fact, the *highest* bidder. The prices for the books purchased under that contract were well above what other states were paying for the same books. [25]

The inaugural ceremonies for Dan Moody were clouded with thinly veiled resentment and antagonism on both sides. In her remarks, Governor Ferguson took a jab at the incoming Moody by stating that he was not her choice, a statement that clearly could have gone without saying, except perhaps by a Ferguson. Moody returned fire by saying that he hoped to restore the sacred trust and integrity of the governor's office. [26]

Certainly Miriam wanted to win the election, but the loss was more easily reconciled with her than Jim. It allowed her to leave the scrutiny of public life to enjoy anew the privacy of home and garden. Ferguson colleagues and comrades gifted the couple with a fine piece of property in Austin, where they planned to build a new home. For a few months they lived at Austin's Driskill Hotel followed by a few months in a rented house, pending completion of their new residence on Windsor Road. [27]

Many believed the 1926 Ferguson loss marked the end of Fergusonism as surely as the 1924 election had ended Klan ascension. On January 21, *The Breckenridge Weekly Democrat* wrote, "Texas politicians predict the political career of Jim Ferguson, who in the last fifteen years has been a candidate in eleven elections including races for the President of the United States and the U. S. Senate, has ended."

But those who held that view underestimated the resolve of James Ferguson. His craving to reclaim the power and prestige he possessed in 1915 never left him and nothing short of duplicating that achievement would satisfy his longing. He would not allow the voters of Texas to discount him. He would lie politically dormant for a while, giving his constituency time to miss him, because for some reason, it always seemed to happen that way.

Chapter 20
Coming Back (1927-1932)

D an Moody had begun to fulfill his campaign promise well before he was a candidate for governor. He accomplished his goal of restoring integrity to the state's top office in large part through his tireless efforts initiating investigations and litigation to expose, halt, and correct the effects of the exploitation that had taken place under the Ferguson administration. Moody's administration gave way to stricter attention to state department spending, in particular, ensuring those in charge of letting contracts for textbooks and highways based their decisions on competitive bids for quality products at rational prices. Within Moody's first two months in office, more than thirty positions were abolished within the state highway department. As part of his clean-up efforts, Moody also pushed for laws to restrict wholesale pardoning.[1]

The House Investigating Committee issued its findings in late January when both Fergusons were again private citizens. Though damning, in the collective opinion of the committee members, the charges were not sufficient to warrant criminal prosecution. Jim, as a private citizen, had imposed himself where he had no authority and had used that usurped power for personal gain. Under his direction, the State Highway Commission had let contracts for highway maintenance at outrageously inflated prices and participated in trading favors. But the customary penalty for such offenses was removal from office and Jim Ferguson held no office. That fact, coupled with the committee's assessment that the case did not warrant criminal charges, produced a dilemma for the body charged with offering a recommendation for punishment. They made none, essentially closing the matter. [2]

Jim responded with a predictable denial coupled with insults launched at the members of the committee and a declaration that the entire process was a waste of taxpayer money. "Notwithstanding this committee has spent the big end of $2,500 they did not find one single fact that was not brought out in the campaign," he railed.[3]

In March of 1927 legislators repealed the amnesty bill that Miriam had proudly signed two years earlier. The action did not come easily in the Senate, as evidenced by the four hours of heated debate that preceded the vote. Senator I. D. Fairchild of Lufkin spoke for more than an hour on behalf of the ex-governor, calling him the "greatest man in Texas history." Fairchild further observed, "If no member of this senate that has asked the former governor to help in getting a pardon will vote for this bill, it won't get ten votes." The Senate body was not swayed, and with a vote of 19 ayes to 7 nays and a House vote of 73 ayes and 25 nays, the bill prevailed and overturned the amnesty that would thereafter elude Jim Ferguson. He responded to the news with a personal attack on the Senate which he claimed was "dominated by the oil companies, Ku Klux Klan and prohibition fanatics." [4]

Frank L. Denison, the Ferguson friend and former recipient of lucrative Bell County road maintenance contracts, returned the favor to the ex-governors. In July of 1927, Denison donated a seven-acre tract of land on the east side of Temple with the stipulation that it be made into a city park bearing the Ferguson name. [5]

By January of 1928, the Fergusons' new Austin home was ready for occupancy after a fire during construction delayed its completion. While a school district in Bell County wrestled with foreclosure on Ferguson land for the non-payment of $1,000 in taxes, the couple somehow managed to find the funds to build a fine new home. Ferguson's Bosque Stock Farm received a state contract to supply butter to Austin's eleemosynary institutions in mid-1927, a benefit the Fergusons would enjoy for the following three years as well, but other potential sources of income dried up. The court dismissed, for failure to comply with the rules of cost, a 1926 Ferguson suit that sought $100,000 in damages against the *Dallas Morning News*. [6]

The Fergusons soon faded from journalistic radar. For the better part of the four years covering Governor Moody's two terms, Jim was relegated to endorsing other would-be candidates while simultaneously applying generous amounts of criticism to Moody's administration. Jim delighted in hearing of the struggles that Moody faced in his attempts to get legislators to approve his projects. In particular, four proposed constitutional amendments that Moody supported in the summer of 1927 were fervently panned by Ferguson. All four failed to pass. Ironically, one proposed amendment would have raised the governor's salary, a salary that Ferguson had long criticized as insufficient. Because he used the *Forum* copiously for disparaging the governor and his associates, it was somewhat surprising when, in September of 1928, Ferguson announced that he would cease publication of the weekly. The announcement contained a Fergusonesque caveat: the paper would reappear only under the pressure of multiple requests from friends and subscribers. Whether or not such solicited requests precipitated the newspaper's reemergence, the *Forum* proved as resilient as its founder when it resurfaced a mere 140 days after its cessation. [7]

As benchwarmers in the political game, the Fergusons supported Al Smith for president in 1928, an odd choice with one exception: Smith was a strong opponent of prohibition. Smith was a Catholic and a New Yorker, much to the chagrin of many Texans. Smith lost to Republican Herbert Hoover, a significant election in the Lone Star State because many Texans who had long resisted crossing party lines, registered their distaste for Smith by doing just that. When Moody ran for his second term in 1928, he was probably surprised that neither Ferguson ran against him. To no one's surprise, Jim Ferguson supported Moody's key opponent, Louis Wardlaw, a Fort Worth attorney. There was virtually no contest; Wardlaw had little chance against Moody in spite of Moody's refusal to forsake the Democratic Party in support of Hoover. His reluctant support for Al Smith caused some Texans to turn against him; even so, he won the election in the first primary and effortlessly defeated his Republican opponent. Even so, some believed that a strong showing by several counties that traditionally backed the Fergusons had helped Wardlaw raise nearly 250,000 votes. Though most counties had been won by Moody, Duval had favored Wardlaw by a vote of 1,161 to 28.[8]

The US Senate race was more interesting. In that race, the runoff had Earle Mayfield, the 1922 Klan-backed candidate who had beaten Ferguson for a Senate seat, vying for the nomination against Tom Connally. The professed Klan-hating Jim chose to endorse Mayfield, a move of significance considering the vile remarks Jim had previously made against him. Ferguson's endorsement, whether welcomed or not, did not result in a victory for Mayfield. Jim's response to the election result was nothing short of bizarre, even by Ferguson standards. He claimed that voters failed to elect Mayfield because they had finally realized that the things he said about Mayfield six years prior were true! In the *Forum*, Jim wrote, "In last Saturday's election, they, the people, approved of what I said about Mayfield six years ago." [9]

In October of 1929, the infamous stock market crash jolted the nation and plunged the American economy into economic Hell. Texans would not feel the full effects of the Great Depression for another two years, but the slow advance of the full force of a faltering economy did little to diminish its intensity once it arrived in the Lone Star State.

By early 1930 Jim Ferguson had endured enough peripheral involvement in politics. On April 18, he filed an application to have his name put on the ballot as a gubernatorial candidate, a request that would ultimately be settled through court action. Ferguson's attorneys argued that the amnesty bill of 1925 had effectively pardoned the ex-governor, but the special State Supreme Court that heard the case ruled against Ferguson, announcing its decision on May 22. One week later,

Miriam announced her candidacy in the *Forum*. The recycled resurrection plea for vindication was fodder for newsprint and rendered Texas an easy target for ridicule. One Pennsylvania daily offered these stinging remarks: "The election of his wife would no more wipe out his disgrace than would a majority vote 'vindicate' Benedict Arnold. . . It might mean that the majority of the [*sic*] Texans count themselves no better than the great majority of Americans count Jim Ferguson." [10]

The Fergusons, along with a host of other potential candidates, anxiously awaited Dan Moody's decision regarding the pursuit of a third term. Against the advice of his closest friends and advisors, Moody finally announced his candidacy in late May only to withdraw a few days later. Moody's announced withdrawal came at the state Democratic Executive Committee meeting in Austin, where he denounced both Ferguson and Mayfield. An enraged Jim Ferguson jumped to his feet, shook his finger at Moody, and angrily branded the governor's decision to withdraw from the race, an act of cowardice. [11]

A record-breaking eleven names eventually appeared on the ballot for governor, among them Thomas Love, an ardent Ferguson enemy whom predictors initially placed in the runoff against Mrs. Ferguson. With Miriam running against a long list of other candidates, many feared that vote splitting would afford her a chance to win or at least place second in the primary. There seemed a shared sentiment that Mrs. Ferguson would face one of the other ten in a runoff. If not Love, who? Other hopefuls included Clint Small, Ross Sterling, Barry Miller, and Earle Mayfield. Miller had served as lieutenant governor under Miriam. A prankster named C. C. Moody was also on the ballot. This Moody, calling himself Soapy, drove a laundry wagon and used the coincidence of sharing a name with the governor as a chance to engage in a lark. His silly speeches and mockery of the process went largely unnoticed except by Jim Ferguson who used the occasion to state his opinion that Soapy had more brains and honesty than any other Moody.[12]

It was rather miraculous that a rich man named Ross Sterling emerged late in the race and quickly took the thunder that would cast Love out of a runoff spot. Love's support of Republican Herbert Hoover had cooled the affections of some Texas Democrats towards him, a fact that also caused him a delay in getting his name on the ballot. A newcomer to politics, Sterling was a Houston oil tycoon and newspaper man who stood over six feet tall and weighed in excess of two hundred and fifty pounds. Capitalizing on his recent work as the chairman of the State Highway Commission, a position that he received from Governor Moody, Sterling announced his intentions in late May. He was a capable leader and had made a great contribution to the public good with his efforts in bringing order back to the disheveled, grossly indebted highway department. Sterling's efforts were instrumental in restoring federal aid for highway construction that had been withdrawn under the Ferguson administration due to the highway contract scandal.

The little-known Sterling launched an exhausting campaign. He made ninety-nine speeches in the course of five weeks, garnering name recognition and respect with voters and Texas newspapers. He attempted to emphasize the need for good business training and good judgment over the oratory skills that he believed had elected too many. It was a suitable strategy because the very imposing businessman, Ross Sterling, was anything but a gifted speaker. [13]

Certainly Sterling's recent good work on the State Highway Commission gave him bragging rights but it also influenced his perspective about what constituted the state's greatest needs. At the top of his wish list was the approval of a bond issue of between 3 and 3.5 million dollars to improve state highways. Being an advocate for such large state obligations made Sterling an easy target for other candidates, chief among them Jim Ferguson (on behalf of his wife). [14]

As Election Day approached speculators replaced Thomas Love's name with Clint Small or Ross Sterling as probable contenders against Mrs. Ferguson. It was a correct prediction. In spite of Sterling's appeal for a controversial bond issue, his efforts paid off when he achieved second place in the primary behind Mrs. Ferguson. Sterling had carried fifty-eight counties compared to Mrs. Ferguson's ninety-four. Clint Small placed an impressive third. Once Sterling was the decided runoff candidate, he shifted his focus, and concentrated heavily on the same dominant theme that had worked for Moody. His goal: the complete annihilation of Fergusonism.

In speeches Sterling hammered at the pardon records of team Ferguson, relaying this incident: In Fayette County in South Texas, a man named Langhorne lured two young Bohemian girls out upon a lonely road and made vile proposals to them. When they indignantly resisted his advances, he shot one girl dead and beat and criminally assaulted the other. Authorities arrested Langhorne before he could flee the county. After he made a full confession, he was tried, convicted, and sentenced to die. The Court of Criminal Appeals upheld the verdict of the jurors. When authorities brought Langhorne into court for final sentencing, the judge asked if he had any reason to offer why sentence should not be pronounced. An associate of James E. Ferguson rose and waved a clemency proclamation. Governor Miriam Ferguson had commuted Langhorne's sentence to life imprisonment.

According to Sterling's account, several days before the commutation order was entered upon the docket in the court at La Grange, the county clerk of Washington County filed a deed of trust executed by Langhorne's father, which assigned to James E. Ferguson and an associate, six tracts of land worth about $90,000. The senior Langhorne pledged the land to secure payment of notes he had given to Ferguson and to one other person. Ferguson claimed that the notes and the deed of trust were payments for legal services in a civil damage suit that grew out of the murder and assault case. Sterling backed his charges by saying that he knew the deed of trust was on file because he had seen it. [15]

This public allegation generated no lawsuit from Ferguson. An anonymous party also printed and circulated a two-page pamphlet condemning Ferguson's pardon policy. This circular included a reproduction of Langhorne's signed confession and a reproduction of a deed of trust lien that described more than two thousand acres of land conveyed in trust to secure six promissory notes to James E. Ferguson and a Ferguson friend, T. H. McGregor. Ferguson's camp countered with a statement that the Langhorne boy was mentally ill and a claim that Moody had asked for the commutation of the boy's sentence, but again, no lawsuit.

For his part, Jim Ferguson continued his exhaustive schedule of speeches railing against Sterling's proposed bond issue and taking shots at Governor Moody. At a speech in Whitesboro in early August, Ferguson's declaration that he was poor because he had always been honest preceded a predictable reminder that he had once rendered the prison system profitable. One news reporter's comment on Ferguson's familiar good-deeds speech was amusing. The correspondent claimed that he had heard Jim's good-deeds message so many times that he could write that portion of Ferguson's speech for him "with his eyes shut and his ears closed." [16]

Dan Moody and a host of other notables joined forces to promote Sterling for the final heat of the governor's race. Sterling's grueling efforts to match Ferguson's speaking engagements included an additional fifty-one speeches during the month between the primary and runoff elections. His reward came on Election Day when he defeated Mrs. Ferguson by 89,000 votes. In the Rio Grande Valley counties, Sterling was generally the victor but in Duval County, Mrs. Ferguson had prevailed with 1,153 votes to Sterling's 85. Sterling later defeated the Republican candidate with ease. Governor-elect Sterling did not receive the traditional congratulatory message from the Fergusons. Three days after the election the couple announced retirement saying, "We never expect to seek public office again." They retreated to their Austin home and resumed a life of relative quiet. [17]

By the time Dorrace Ferguson married Earl Stuart Watt, a thirty-two-year-old tire dealer in Austin in June of 1931, Ouida had already been married for thirteen years. The 1930 census showed Watt living with his mother and two adult siblings in Austin and listed his occupation as proprietor of a filling station. True to her nature, Dorrace chose a private ceremony at the Fergusons' Austin home attended only by close family members. The newlyweds took up residence in the Ferguson home on Windsor Road and Dorrace became president of the Bosque Creamery. The business had moved its operations to the outskirts of Austin in Travis County but had, oddly enough, retained the name Bosque Creamery.[18]

Financial problems continued to plague the Fergusons. The Internal Revenue Service examined the couple's personal income tax returns, along with tax returns for the *Forum*, for a period covering several years, and the outcome was not good. The IRS claimed that business and personal funds had been co-mingled, some income was unidentifiable, and deemed that certain deductions and losses used to calculate the couple's taxes were improper. The resulting tax liabilities totaled $15,892. [19]

While the Fergusons passed their days in the relative tranquility of private life, Governor Ross Sterling experienced a troubled term. The full effects of the Depression, which coincided with his taking office, created a unique set of issues for the state's chief executive. The major plank in his campaign platform, highway bonds, certainly lost relevance. A shortfall in state revenues coupled with bank failures, high unemployment, and the falling prices of commodities, upstaged all other concerns. Oil, the lifeblood of the Texas economy, was overproduced, causing the price to plummet. Income from the sale of cotton also suffered from prices that were painfully low for the farmers who relied upon the former "cash crop." Texans, projecting the same distain for many state leaders that they held for Herbert Hoover, were not optimistic about the state's future under the leadership of Governor Ross Sterling. The 1932 race for governor would be a viable one for re-emergence, an opportunity that never escaped the attention of Jim Ferguson. [20]

Miriam, who was fifty-seven in 1932, relished the quiet of private life and enjoyed her beautiful new home in Austin, two grown daughters, and her thirteen-year-old grandson, George Jr. Jim, on the other hand, could not suppress the longing to re-enter the fray. He revealed his sentiments in this entry in his diary in late 1929: "I have many times resolved to quit taking any part in campaigns but there is an irresistible influence that continually draws me into political campaigns. . . I feel a rising desire to again enter a political campaign." [21]

By the spring of 1932, Jim had again used his magic to recruit Miriam and the couple embarked on a new campaign. It would be a bitter ordeal.

The personal wealth of Ross Sterling in contrast to the raw poverty that gripped the state, indeed the nation, did nothing to increase his likeability. Well aware of that great divide, Ferguson was poised to capitalize on it. During the 1930 campaign, Paul Wakefield, Sterling's publicity director and later a secretary in Sterling's staff, observed, "On the other hand was the natural antagonism as between the rich and the poor, and this at a time when the pangs of poverty were keenly felt. Pitched thus, the advantage lay wholly with Ferguson." [22]

Those pangs of poverty to which Wakefield referred had only increased during Sterling's term. Some of the daring measures that the governor took in an effort to increase cotton and oil prices worked against his popularity. His efforts to reduce cotton production and his declaration of martial law in East Texas oil fields were necessary steps to control the supply side of the economic equation, but struggling farmers and oilmen did not see the wisdom in those decisions.

For the most part, the public did not know that Sterling lost much of his own personal wealth to the Depression. Even prior to his taking office, he suffered major losses and by the end of his term economic conditions forced him to sell his bank shares, ranch, and newspaper to pay off debts. Even so, compared to most Texans he was still wealthy and with his prominent girth he appeared gluttonous—causing many to view him as a fat cat—both literally and figuratively.[23]

The Ferguson platform included a promise that Mrs. Ferguson would cut taxes, a pledge that she failed to keep but one that resonated with Depression-weary Texans during the campaign. In contrast, Sterling's campaign pleas against Fergusonism did not have the same sense of urgency that they had held two years earlier.

The primary election should have been enough warning for Ross Sterling to realize the extent of the resolve of Texas voters to unseat him. Miriam received over 400,000 votes to his 296,383 while a third candidate, Tom Hunter, pulled an impressive 220,391. Strategists for the Sterling camp were plentiful; they suggested that the governor consider withdrawing in favor of Tom Hunter. The same apprehensive Sterling supporter lamented, "You cannot win in such a time as this. Thomas Jefferson, George Washington, or Abraham Lincoln, if in office today could not be reelected. The voters of 1932 are as rational as the mob who crucified Christ." [24]

During the five-week period between the primary and runoff race, the State Democratic Executive Committee noted that an examination of voting records for the first primary revealed some alarming statistics. In the case of some 132 counties, primarily in East Texas areas that were traditionally Ferguson-dominated, the number of votes cast greatly exceeded the number of poll taxes paid. This information seemed to raise awareness of the potential for voting fraud, causing Democratic committees and voter officials to announce more oversight at ballot boxes. Ross Sterling was particularly sensitive to the possibility of voter fraud. [25]

Despite the fear in Sterling's camp that Mrs. Ferguson might beat him handily, election day August 27, 1932 brought a vote so close that it could not be called immediately. For several days, the tabulation continued to fluctuate, so much so that at one point tabulators delivered updates hourly. The tension ended with the declaration of a Ferguson victory by fewer than four thousand votes—and a colossal fight. Sterling accused the Ferguson camp of voter fraud and demanded an official investigation. Sterling was convinced that fraud had taken place and, with the help of Texas Rangers, started his own investigation. Sterling and Adjutant General William Sterling (no relation) believed they had specific evidence to prove that fraud had taken place in numerous counties, and that the numbers were sufficient to change the result. They were, however, frustrated by their inability to get anyone to take action in re-examining the count. [26]

Jim countered with his own accusations of voter fraud. However, the district attorney of Webb County, a location Jim cited as corrupt, called what appeared to be Ferguson's bluff by calling a grand jury to investigate the allegations. The grand jury served both Fergusons with subpoenas that required them to appear and testify about the specifics of their charges of voter fraud. Jim responded instead with a quick apology and a retraction. [27]

Convinced the Fergusons had cheated him out of the election and unable to get the Senate to conduct an investigation on his behalf, Sterling filed an injunction to keep Mrs. Ferguson's name off of the ballot in the upcoming general election while his case made its way through the courts. Angry Ferguson supporters promised to write in Mrs. Ferguson's name if necessary. Sterling's suit against Ferguson advanced rapidly to the State Supreme Court. Even so, the court declared that there was insufficient time before the November 8 election to try the case and election officials placed Miriam Ferguson's name on the ballot. After Hoover's disappointing term, Texans were in no mood to consider the possibility of voting for a Republican. Despite Sterling's eleventh-hour appeal to Democrats to cross party lines in an effort to block Mrs. Ferguson, she easily prevailed over her Republican opponent, Orville Bullington.[28]

Team Ferguson was governor-elect once more. According to Ouida, her parents "worked day and night through the month of December interviewing and discussing prospective appointees."[29]

It was a solemn time in Texas history when few Texans were optimistic. Even the inauguration, generally a lavish affair, was less so. Sterling's further attempts to question the election's validity were unsuccessful; intense bitterness remained on both sides and would spill over into the first months of the new administration. It was the last thing needed by state legislators, already struggling with serious issues brought on by the Depression. For his part, Ross Sterling was nothing less than brutally honest when he explained why he took no part in the inauguration and the associated traditions of the day. "I will say to the people of Texas that I do not care to take part in the inauguration of one whom I deem wholly incompetent to occupy the office of Governor and whose husband, who will be the Governor in fact, is ineligible and disqualified to hold any office of trust in the State of Texas, according to the Constitution of the State and decisions of the Supreme Court." [30]

Again, the Fergusons were at a critical crossroads. The chance for perfect revenge against Sterling's stinging remarks lay before them. The *Dallas Morning News* explained it succinctly, saying, "If she and her husband so manage affairs as to justify the trust reposed in them by the people of Texas, Mr. Sterling will be discredited in his judgment upon them." To prove Sterling wrong, they needed only curb their interminable need for revenge and dominance in favor of running a fair, efficient, and effective administration that concentrated on putting the state back on a sound economic footing. After all, such was the essence of Mrs. Ferguson's duty as governor. The public cared little about the personal squabbles and grudges of these politicians. The people needed jobs. [31]

The Fergusons had squandered their first chance for redemption when they failed to put aside the pursuit of personal gain and the use of the spoils systems. The first hint to their future actions appeared in their pre-inaugural activity. After all, they had spent the entire month of December relishing their upcoming appointive power. They cared not what Sterling felt or said—they had beaten him and reclaimed control.

Chapter 21
Twice the Vice

In late November 1932, as Governor Ross Sterling passed his last weeks in office, Jim Ferguson filed suit to freeze state highway construction funds. If the move was an attempt to punish Sterling for his part in further exposing the deplorable conditions within the highway department that had developed under Mrs. Ferguson's watch, it had the added benefit of preserving highway appropriations until the Fergusons would again be in positions to control them. The move immediately made life difficult for the members of the State Highway Commission. Ferguson filed a temporary injunction that was later dissolved. Jim Ferguson appealed the nullification of the injunction, but by the time the case made its way through the courts, the new governor was back in office and in control of the monies—Jim had achieved the desired effect. [1]

Governor Ferguson joined her husband in provoking the Highway Commission when, even before taking office, she accused the department of a one-million-dollar shortage of funds. Indignant members of the commission quickly countered the accusation by presenting specific evidence to the Senate that refuted the governor's charges. Their efforts paid off when Mrs. Ferguson backed down, but the incident represented a rocky start to the relationship between the new Ferguson administration and some members of the Senate. [2]

With the effects of the Depression still daunting the country, Miriam faced the same tough issues that had haunted her predecessor, but her first order of business was making new state office appointments that would ensure a total disbanding of Sterling's influence. Prior to the end of his term, Sterling had submitted the names of three University of Texas regents and three members of the state Board of Education for re-appointment, nominations that created immediate friction between the incoming and outgoing governors. The Fergusons believed that the appointive power in both cases was the prerogative of the new governor. A decision on the disagreement by Attorney General James Allred rendered a victory for each side. Allred ruled that the appointment of regents rested with the incoming governor and the Board of Education openings, which occurred on December 31 while Sterling was still governor, were to be filled by appointees of his choosing, pending confirmation. Mrs. Ferguson proceeded with her nominations of regents and Sterling did likewise with his nominees to the Board of Education, all of which were subject to Senate confirmation. None of this, however, put an end to the controversy. [3]

The first sweep of Ferguson appointments, announced three days prior to the January 17 inauguration, totaled thirty-nine. This action included naming members of the new governor's staff. One surprising nomination was that of Frank L. Denison of Temple, whom the governor nominated as chairman of the Highway Commission. This appointment was particularly brazen, given Denison's background. The long-time Ferguson friend was well-known for his part as a contractor who had engaged in overpricing highway maintenance contracts during the highway scandal of 1925. In particular, Denison was responsible for the infamous invisible track debacle. Given his past, legislators hardly expected to be asked to confirm Denison's appointment to any position. Governor Ferguson's initial show of power also included an act that immediately and completely laid waste to the Texas Rangers when she dismissed the entire forty-four-man force, effective on inauguration day. This action surprised no one. Animosity had long defined the Fergusons' relationship with the Rangers. Sterling's use of Texas Rangers in the investigation he undertook in an attempt to prove voter fraud had further damaged that precarious relationship. [4]

Most members of the House considered A. P. Johnson of Edwards County, a seasoned House member, would be that body's next speaker. But Johnson, an avid Ross Sterling supporter and a very religious man, attracted the ire of Jim Ferguson, a fact that very likely cost him the speakership. Though governors generally try to remain neutral in such matters (there is no precedent for governor spouses in these cases), Jim Ferguson, who seemed never to favor neutrality, took bold steps to block Johnson's election. He approached Coke Stevenson, who had just been elected to his third term in the House, and offering his assistance suggested that Stevenson seek the speakership. It seems that a word from Ferguson to his supporters in the House was enough to seal Johnson's fate; Stevenson rather miraculously won by a vote of eighty-two to sixty-eight. [5]

As Miriam and Jim moved into the Governor's Mansion for the third time in early 1933, Dorrace and her husband, Stuart, stayed in the home on Windsor Road. Dorrace, always the people-pleaser in the family, likely benefited from the separation due to a mutual distaste between her husband and mother. Always close to her mother emotionally, the friction between two people she loved must have been a source of anxiety for Dorrace. Her sister, Ouida, and husband George Nalle were well set when George received a federal appointment as Assistant Secretary of Commerce in charge of aviation. [6]

The generous pardon policy that came to define the Fergusons' governorships was promptly resumed by Mrs. Ferguson, and in the first six months of her term she granted clemencies to 1,055 prisoners. The governor also indulged in a new level of political patronage with the granting of special Texas Ranger commissions. She granted these commissions to anyone who made even a timid case for such an honor. The governor of Pennsylvania, Gifford Pinchot, was among the recipients of this distinction. Amazingly, the governor appointed 2,300 Special Rangers, a few of whom were ex-convicts. [7]

Jim and Miriam again felt the ill effects of their reputation as liberal providers of state jobs. The pair complained bitterly about the army of job seekers who filled the office lobby and kept them away from more important business. "I want them to stop trying to manhandle us and to quit trying to manhandle the legislature, and to let us all alone so we can attend to important problems. They claim they are our friends but I don't believe I saw one of them during the campaign," remarked an exasperated Jim Ferguson. [8]

The appointment process and the battles it generated had scarcely begun. The Senate refused to confirm Frank Denison by a vote of nineteen to eleven, even though the Senate's Committee on Governor's Nominations had given him a favorable recommendation. Governor Ferguson attempted to withdraw the Sterling appointments to the Board of Education, again forcing an intervention by Attorney General Allred. His decision was not to the governor's liking, however. Allred ruled that she could not withdraw Sterling's selections without Senate approval. The parties to the disagreement had exchanged bitter words and wasted valuable time engaged in heated arguments before the squabble ended in a Senate vote of sixteen to eleven in favor of Sterling. In the end, the tug-of-war between ex-Governor Sterling and current Governor Ferguson rendered very little for Sterling. Two of his three appointees were not confirmed and the selections went to Governor Ferguson by default. [9]

On February 1, 1933, Governor Ferguson announced a sweeping second round of appointments. She wiped clear the state Live Stock Sanitary Commission with the removal of 260 men and women. Even the office boy was not spared, replaced with the son of a Fergusonite. Many of the displaced employees took with them the benefit of a ten- to fifteen-year accumulation of experience in their respective jobs. [10]

A few days later, to the astonishment of most senators, the governor again submitted Denison's name, restating her request for his approval as chairman of the Highway Commission. The re-submission of the name of a rejected appointee was unprecedented in Texas and caused an immediate uproar. In particular, Senator Walter Woodward of Coleman balked at the governor's bold move and made serious allegations on the Senate floor. He repeated rumors that coercion, intimidation, threats, and promises had been used to obtain votes for Denison. The Senator cited one particularly galling rumor that senators with state-supported schools in their districts faced a threat of lost appropriations if they failed to support Denison's appointment. Woodward's comments implied that the governor's brazen re-submission was a test to see if Ferguson forces had yet coerced enough votes to seat Denison. [11]

Woodward's revelations spawned four hours of heated debate after which the Senate went into executive session to address the problem. When asked to explain her action, the governor indicated that she had re-submitted Denison's name in response to some confusion and misunderstandings that had accompanied the first submission. This statement did nothing to appease angry senators and it raised additional questions of the appropriateness of her re-nomination. The law required that the initial vote taken in executive session be kept confidential. Senator George Purl demanded to know how the governor knew of any confusion associated with the vote. Another full day of debate followed and the Senate again considered asking the attorney general for a ruling on the validity of re-submission, but the vote to do so did not carry. The debate over Denison's appointment was far from over, and absent the attorney general's intervention, a ruling on the re-submission became the responsibility of Lieutenant Governor Edgar Witt. [12]

Witt's ruling allowed the governor to again tender the name of Denison as a candidate for the Highway Commission chair. On February 22 the Senate, in a closed session, again refused to confirm Denison's nomination, an action that should have ended the debate—but did not. Denison failed to obtain the commonly understood two-thirds' majority required for confirmation, but the Fergusons argued that only a simple majority was necessary and, based on that objection, refused to acknowledge Denison's defeat. Four days later, Denison asserted his power as the chairman of the Highway Commission by ordering the State Comptroller and the State Treasurer to dishonor any payroll or other vouchers from the highway department that did not include his signature. Meanwhile, Mrs. Ferguson requested the results of the vote from the Senate so she could confirm that Denison had received a majority. The Senate refused her request by a vote of twenty-one to nine, citing a Senate rule that votes taken in executive session were privileged. [13]

Denison's fight would not end until May 31 after it reached the Supreme Court of Texas. The high court ruled that Denison was not commissioned because his approval did, indeed, require a two-thirds' majority from the Senate, a vote he had failed to obtain.

The first months of the Ferguson term had been largely unsatisfying to Jim, his disappointments rooted in a number of failed proposals. The Denison battle, finally lost, was a major blow to the Ferguson team as were the failures of three bills that Jim had pushed hard to pass. These bills would have reorganized the Highway Commission, the Board of Control, and the Fish, Game and Oyster Department, centralizing control and giving the governor more appointive power. A 3 percent sales tax sought by the Fergusons was also rejected by legislators, as was a secondary request for a tax on the gross earnings of corporations. The administration had to make deep cuts in appropriations to accommodate the budget shortfall.

While legislators in Austin quibbled about appointments, the Great Depression continued to dominate the lives of Texans. In early 1933 banks across the country began to close with alarming frequency. Those that remained were under extreme pressure, operating under the constant fear that an avalanche of nervous depositors would withdraw their money. By early March, as Americans anxiously awaited the inauguration of the new president, Franklin D. Roosevelt and his New Deal, the worst fears of bankers began materializing as a run on banks began in the eastern part of the country and threatened to spread like wildfire. Governor William Comstock of Michigan declared an amazing eight-day bank moratorium in mid-February, temporarily closing 550 banks in his state. The measure seemed desperate, but other concerned governors followed suit using a more abbreviated closing. By the first of March, seventeen states had used forced bank holidays as a temporary means of addressing the crisis. [14]

Governor Ferguson followed suit when she declared a five-day bank holiday over the period including and surrounding Texas Independence Day on March 2. It was a move meant to allow time for fear and hysteria to subside and proved successful. Once in office, Roosevelt made a similar move on March 6, 1933, closing banks through the ninth of the month. By that time, officials in most banks around the county, including Texas, had placed restrictions on or temporarily closed many banks. With the time bought by these closings, some added restrictions, and a radio address by Roosevelt that offered assurance to the frightened public, officials averted an immediate crisis. Other measures at the federal level, including the establishment of the Federal Deposit Insurance Corporation (FDIC), eased the immediate fears that threatened the banking industry, but high unemployment remained a persistent issue.

Texans were especially enthusiastic about the new administration in Washington in 1933 because the vice president, John Nance Garner, was one of their own. Jim Ferguson was particularly pleased that the new administration pushed for a repeal of the Eighteenth Amendment, the Prohibition law. By 1933, having run a stretch of more than thirteen years, Prohibition had proved sufficiently in the opinions of many that it was not the solution to the nation's social ills. The great experiment had, in fact, spawned other unique and formidable problems. Bootlegging, the perfect enterprise for organized crime, had become widespread during the alcohol ban. Tax revenues lost on bootleg alcohol, coupled with the cost of Prohibition's enforcement, were major problems for cash-strapped governments on all levels.

In May of 1933, a horse racing bill passed both House and Senate and awaited the signature of Governor Ferguson. Lawmakers had banned pari-mutuel betting in Texas in 1909 but the construction of the Arlington Downs racetrack in 1929 had sparked new interest in the prospect of legalizing the sport. Gambling seemed exactly the kind of vice Miriam Ferguson generally found objectionable. However, the strait-laced governor, who abhorred the use of alcohol and tobacco, readily signed the bill. This she likely did with the encouragement of her husband who, according to Ouida, "loved the ponies" and would "bet his last dollar on a long shot." The family enjoyed the races, with the possible exception of grandson George Jr. Ouida expressed her son's sentiments saying, "Daddy's constant losses at the track gave his fourteen-year-old grandson no little worry. A good Scot, and naturally conservative, George, Jr., actually suffered as he sat by and watched his grandfather pick the wrong ponies at Houston." The young man expressed his particular concern at seeing his grandfather lose money at the track and shortly after raise a cry of financial hardship. The legalization of on-track betting signed into law by Miriam Ferguson enjoyed a four-year run before the legislature banished it again in 1937. [15]

In March of 1933 President Roosevelt signed the Cullen-Harrison Act, which sought to ease the rigidity of the Volstead Act by allowing the manufacture and sale of beer and wine with a low alcohol content. The law required that each state pass its own legislation to solidify the change and President Roosevelt urged states to support the repeal. In June, a group of Texans favoring repeal launched their campaign by selecting a committee chairman. After Ferguson opponents voiced strong objections against the idea that he be named chairman, Ferguson withdrew his name from consideration suggesting instead the name of his good friend C. C. McDonald. McDonald became chairman, at least in name. In mid-July, Ferguson and McDonald further solidified their support for repeal when they made a trip to the nation's capital and met briefly with President Roosevelt. [16]

Jim Ferguson hit the campaign trail on behalf of the commission as soon as he returned from Washington. On the eve of the repeal election, Ferguson made a speech that he used as an opportunity to criticize Prohibitionists, saying,

"Pussyfooting prohibitionists [*sic*] had been so self-righteous in the selection of politicians since their prohibition [*sic*] victory that they now have the greatest bunch of peewee politicians ever assembled." Texans eased into the legitimization of alcohol, voting in August 1933 to reinstate the local option election, but only for beer with a low alcoholic content. It was an additional two years before Texas broadened that legalization. [17]

Repeal of the Eighteenth Amendment was only half of the reason that Jim Ferguson embarked on a speaking tour in late July and August of 1933. He also pushed for the passage of a $20 million relief bond issuance known as "bread bonds," the passage of which was necessary for continued financial aid from the federal government. Federal assistance that began in late 1932 and continued in 1933 pumped much-needed relief funds into Texas, but the management and distribution of these funds was a monumental task, and under the supervision of James Ferguson as adviser to the governor, this soon became a problem. The Texas Rehabilitation and Relief Commission, tasked with administering the funds through a system of county boards, was exactly the kind of set-up that attracted Jim Ferguson's interest. Together with Lawrence Westbrook the pair established the county boards and staffed them with Ferguson-friendly appointees. [18]

To keep funds flowing, the Fergusons first pushed the legislature to approve the $20 million bond bill, a bill that was submitted to a public vote. The August 26 vote considered both the bond issue and the repeal of Prohibition. It was a good day for Jim Ferguson when both measures won approval.

With the impending influx of additional relief funds from bonds, some legislators suggested that an alternate agency be established to oversee their disbursement. Rumors circulated about graft in the distribution of the federal relief money including allegations that political influence drove the program and that, in some cases, a disproportionately large percentage of funds went to overhead. For a Senate investigating committee established in late September of 1933, the first order of business was the questioning of Lawrence Westbrook. Although Westbrook and three other state relief commissioners still awaited confirmation of their nominations for positions on the commission, Westbrook had already been active in its meetings for some time.[19]

Westbrook appeared before the committee well prepared and spoke candidly when asked about Jim Ferguson's participation in the committee's meetings. Senator Woodward pointed out that the law automatically rendered Governor Ferguson the ex-officio chairperson of the relief committee. Having established that, the senator asked Westbrook if Governor Ferguson had ever attended any sessions. Westbrook told the committee that while Governor Ferguson had attended none of the meetings of the Rehabilitation and Relief Commission, Jim

Ferguson had presided as chairman at all meetings. Westbrook admitted that certain administrative expenses were out of line and would be adjusted. He further admitted that some acts of fraud and misapplication of funds had, in fact, occurred. In early October, the Senate investigation ended with the establishment of a five-man subcommittee tasked with the responsibility of writing a bill governing the issuance of relief bonds and providing for their distribution. The legislature settled on replacing the Texas Rehabilitation and Relief Commission with a new State Relief Board which would oversee a new organization designed to administer relief funds. Westbrook headed the new commission. Under this arrangement, the governor would vote only in the event of a tie and James Ferguson would have no part in the process. Westbrook's stint as commissioner was short lived. In late January of 1934 he resigned the position to accept a similar post on the federal level. [20]

In early October of 1933, the Texas House directed the appropriations committee to perform an inquiry into the details of a serious allegation presented by Representative Gordon Burns of Huntsville. Burns alleged it was "common street talk" that certain parties were selling state jobs in East Texas. If the committee had any illusions that their assignment would be brief, they were mistaken. A steady stream of witnesses shocked the committee as the full scope of an embarrassing, troubling, and heartbreaking problem came into focus. [21]

Testimony by W. E. Floyd of Gilmer revealed that he had paid $200 to S. J. Waghalter in order to secure a job through Dr. E. F. Jarrell of Tyler. Jarrell was one of three new Live Stock Sanitary commissioners. Under oath, Dr. Jarrell denied any knowledge of job selling or any such conversation with Waghalter. Subsequent testimony, however, convinced the committee of complicity on the part of Dr. Jarrell, who pointed the finger at two brothers, Royce and D. H. Williams of Gilmer, Texas. The brothers pointed fingers right back at Dr. Jarrell, saying he had asked them to find job seekers who were willing to make political contributions in exchange for jobs. When investigators asked W. E. Floyd, the whistle-blower in this affair, if he knew of others in East Texas who had purchased jobs, he replied, "Yes, lots of them." [22]

Authorities called R. H. Burck of Whitney to testify regarding his knowledge of money paid to secure jobs. Burck had worked in the Ferguson campaign during 1932 and admitted that he collected money on behalf of the Fergusons. Victor Krizan of West produced two cancelled checks for $100 each that he claimed represented payments to Burck in exchange for a job that never materialized. Burck maintained that all the money he received was for campaign contributions and claimed that he never made promises related to potential state jobs. When asked about a specific sum he had received from a city commissioner, Burck admitted receiving the money but insisted that he viewed it as a contribution. He later contradicted himself when he claimed that in cases where people believed they had given money in exchange for a job but did not get a job, the money was usually refunded. Krizan, however, had received no refund. [23]

By October 13, 1933, the House Appropriations Committee had heard enough and declared, "It looks as though job selling has developed into a real racket in Texas."

The Committee's report contained these statements:

After an exhaustive inquiry into matters relative to the sale of positions in the Live Stock Sanitary Commission, we are of the opinion that the testimony strongly implicated Dr. E. F. Jarrell in the sales of such positions and evidenced a knowledge on his part of such sales as well as complicity therein; we are convinced that many persons throughout the State paid money under the impression that they were to be given jobs and placed on the State pay roll, but in practically all the instances brought to our attention, no permanent positions were awarded. [24]

Dr. Jarrell tendered his resignation soon after. Waghalter had already been convicted in Upshur County District Court for his part in selling jobs but the related review was not over. The House committee recommended that a special committee be established to continue the probe and that grand juries be selected in the counties where the alleged offenses had occurred. They created a new committee of five, granting them wider authority to investigate any charges of graft, and the investigative work continued. [25]

At the Treasury Department, two former employees told of being pressured to make contributions to the campaign of State Treasurer Charley Lockhart even though he was running unopposed. When asked if he had received the funds in question, Lockhart acknowledged receipt of the money but stated that he considered them "tokens of affection from his employees." [26]

Joe Sims of Whitney testified that he had paid R. H. Burck $100 for a job as a scale inspector and was given a receipt written on a *Ferguson Forum* subscription slip. When the job did not materialize, Sims testified that Burck told him they were awaiting the confirmation of Denison to the Highway Commission and once that happened, Burck assured him, everything would be okay. [27]

Regarding the Texas Game, Fish and Oyster Department, C. P. Miller, assistant state auditor, testified that he had observed Chairman A. E. Wood buying state warrants at a discount, an action that was illegal. He also stated that he had observed Wood using a state-owned car for personal use including a trip out-of-state, that Wood had employed his brother-in-law in the department, and that Wood had used department employees to send campaign materials for his brother-in-law. [28]

More irregularities surfaced. Jim Barber of Dallas testified that he had received and passed money to Royce Williams on behalf of persons wishing to receive jobs as tick inspectors. Barber indicated that the money passed from Williams to Jarrell and that he refunded the money if the jobs were not granted. Barber claimed he was present at a meeting with James Ferguson and D. H. Williams when Williams informed the ex-governor that he had collected money from a large number of job seekers. Barber claimed Ferguson had replied that only a few jobs existed and "they were doing the best they could." [29]

C. A. Loftis, president of the First National Bank of Longview, testified that in connection with several other banks he had paid C. C. McDonald, a member of Ferguson's inner circle, a fee of $1,000 to encourage Governor Ferguson to sign a bill that would benefit his bank. The governor signed the bill, although Loftis stated that he believed she would have signed it regardless of his payment. When asked why he had solicited the assistance of McDonald, Loftis replied, "Because I knew he had influence with the Governor." [30]

More compelling evidence of job selling came from Bert Whisnand of Dallas, a former Texas Ranger, who testified that he had heard of jobs being sold by the Williams brothers from the Adolphus Hotel. Whisnand claimed that when he reported the information to Ranger officials at Austin they advised him to keep quiet. He was later discharged. He also relayed a story about an arrest he had made of a man who had stolen and sold $36,000 worth of goods from trucks. Though the court had convicted and sentenced the man, Whisnand said it was his understanding that the thief gained his freedom by purchasing a pardon. [31]

A boxing promoter named Leon Wilson testified he paid Eugene Smith, another Ferguson insider, $200 to get a promoter's license, which he had been unable to obtain through regular channels. According to Wilson's testimony, Smith had initially asked for a $500 payment. [32]

C. A. Mayberry of Mound testified that he had paid a fee of $25 at the request of Superintendent Nesbit to keep his job at the state Juvenile Training School. He stated that the school engineer also paid a fee to retain his job. When Mayberry lodged a complaint with the Board of Control, he claimed he was fired. [33]

The Committee learned that many anxious people, desperate for employment, had been promised nonexistent jobs. In other instances, the culprits had taken money from several people to whom they had promised the same positions. Some job seekers had collateralized what little property they owned in order to borrow the funds to pay their deceivers, and still held out hope that a job might be forthcoming even long after all positions had been filled. These desperate unemployed men could hardly lodge a complaint when the jobs that they had attempted to buy failed to materialize.

By mid-December, a January 1 end-date for the committee loomed large and necessitated a wrap-up to their investigation. They concentrated their final efforts on the Live Stock Sanitary Commission, where competent men had been released from their jobs and replaced with mostly inexperienced ones. The investigative committee recessed in December, but not before stating that the current laws covering job selling were grossly inadequate. Writing their report between Christmas and the New Year, they recommended tough penalties for future job-selling violators.

About midway through the job-selling investigation, Governor Ferguson announced on November 29, 1933, that the coming year of 1934 would be her last as governor. The following day, Ferguson long-time and close friend, C. C. McDonald, announced his intention to seek the office. Another year in the governorship may have seemed an eternity to Mrs. Ferguson and her daughters, all of whom were anxious to return to a level of anonymity. On the other hand, their family patriarch, who was sixty-two-years old, hearing impaired, and lethargic from excess weight, was hardly ready to step out of the limelight. He would use the coming year to squeeze out the last vestiges of power within his grasp, the power usurped in the shadow of his wife, the governor. He would also cast his lot with C. C. McDonald; doing so offered promise that some semblance of power might still be at his disposal in the future.[34]

Chapter 22
Sunset

For a governor, even a new year in mid-term carries a certain number of expiring appointments and with it the necessity of making new nominations. Frank Lanham, a key player in the highway commission scandal of 1925, had resigned his post on the State Highway Commission in 1926 when an investigation revealed graft within the department, but authorities had brought no charges against him. Governor Ferguson nominated Lanham as a member of the prison board early in her second year, and given the early struggle over Denison's nomination it may have been somewhat surprising that legislators confirmed Lanham's new appointment. By mid-year Lanham would resign that post to take an assignment with the Federal Deposit Insurance Corporation.[1]

In January of 1934, Miriam Ferguson had good reason to regret her past actions against the Texas Rangers and the breadth of her pardon policy. The infamous Bonnie Parker and Clyde Barrow, a daring pair of criminals sometimes joined by other partners in crime, were randomly robbing and assaulting unsuspecting citizens in several central states, including Texas. Members of the Barrow Gang, as they were called, had once included Clyde's brother, Buck, and his wife Blanche, until Buck was fatally wounded and Blanche arrested after a July 1933, shoot-out with police. The other members of the gang eluded capture that day and, after a period of recovery from their wounds, continued their crime spree.

The brazen acts of Bonnie and Clyde captured newspaper headlines and the misplaced admiration of some people who viewed them as clever rebels against the bumbling authorities whose grasp they continually eluded. Robberies of small stores, gas stations, and banks frequently included the theft of an automobile, and at times resulted in the deaths of private citizens and several policemen. With no offensive plan and little coordination between the numerous local law enforcement jurisdictions, police had been unable to control the pair's actions to any degree for over two years, a fact that rendered the criminals' antics a major embarrassment to authorities.

Governor Miriam Ferguson had pardoned Clyde's brother, Buck, permitting his release on March 22, 1933. Buck had immediately reunited with his brother in Missouri where the pair continued their brotherly business of armed robbery. Governor Ferguson was not alone with her ill-fated Barrow pardon. Governor Sterling, whose pardoning policy had also been rather liberal, had pardoned Clyde Barrow in early 1932, a pardon he later tried unsuccessfully to revoke. If Governor Ferguson felt any embarrassment or responsibility for her contribution to the public menace created by the Barrow Gang, she never acknowledged it. [2]

The violence escalated in January of 1934 when a prison escape orchestrated by Bonnie and Clyde at the Eastham prison farm in Texas resulted in the fatal shooting of a prison officer and the escape of five convicts. The event received enough attention and outrage to trigger the involvement of the head of the Texas prison system, Lee Simmons. If law enforcement officers had not been sufficiently humiliated by the capers of Clyde Barrow, Lee Simmons certainly had, and he was determined to do something about it.

Simmons formulated a plan for capturing the outlaws, but the orchestration of that plan required both the authorization and financial support of Governor Ferguson. The essential element of Simmons' recommendation was the hiring of the seasoned, tough, and semi-retired ex-Texas Ranger named Frank Hamer. Simmons felt that Hamer was the man best suited to pull together the fragmented efforts of the scattered authorities. Hamer, a rigid and tough character, had quit the Ranger force in disgust when Mrs. Ferguson won the election in 1932, largely to cheat her out of the pleasure of firing him along with all of the other Rangers. Simmons was resolute about trying his plan but not particularly confident in his ability to get the governor and Frank Hamer, who were mortal enemies, to agree. [3]

However, when approached by Simmons, Governor Ferguson readily agreed to his plan, offering her full support. In February of 1934, Hamer was working as a special investigator for a private business, a job that paid well. When Simmons approached the disinclined ex-Ranger he received the anticipated pushback. Hamer expressed his reluctance to accept the challenge, pointing to his distrust of the Fergusons and the job's low salary as his reasons. Simmons sweetened the deal by offering Hamer his pick of souvenirs from the Barrow cache once he caught the criminals, and further pledged that the Fergusons would support the project for as long as the mission required. With those assurances, Hamer accepted the assignment. [4]

It took only 102 days for Hamer and his hand-picked posse of lawmen to put the Barrow gang out of business, saving taxpayers the expense of a trial in the process. On May 23, 1934, Hamer's planning and persistence paid off along a rural road in Louisiana. There the lawmen surprised and killed the couple who had been betrayed by a former comrade-in-arms and Barrow gang member, Henry Methvin. Methvin had divulged precise details of Bonnie and Clyde's habits that assisted law enforcement in laying the trap that ended their lives. Governor Ferguson received much credit for her part in the mission, including an honorary membership in the Western States Police and Highway Patrol Association. Henry Methvin, whom she had promised a pardon for his cooperation in the project, received that concession in August of that same year. His freedom was short-lived, however; he was soon extradited to Oklahoma where he was tried, found guilty, and incarcerated for crimes committed in the Sooner state. For his part in the mission, Frank Hamer refused interviews and avoided most other opportunities for publicity. [5]

In early May of 1933, Democratic National Committeeman Jed Adams announced that he was leaving his post to take a position in Washington on the Federal Tax Appeals Board. An immediate flurry ensued as Ferguson forces began to push the nomination of Ferguson friend C. C. McDonald to fill the post. Anti-Ferguson forces were desperate to block Ferguson and his close associate from this post, dreading the embarrassment of having a disgraced ex-governor as the Democratic representative from Texas. They knew that power given to McDonald was power that would be shared with Ferguson. National Democratic Chairman James Farley stopped the speculation, at least temporarily, by asking Jed Adams to remain in his position. Adams agreed to stay, but the act was an obvious means of stalling since Adams also kept his new job and could not, in good conscience, hold both positions. By early March of 1934 having pushed the delay tactic to its limits, Farley accepted Adams's resignation, and the clamor erupted anew.

The appropriate means of filling the vacancy was supposed to begin with a nomination from Maury Hughes, the chairman of the Democratic State Executive Committee. That nomination was subject to the approval of the national headquarters. Though Hughes was a Ferguson foe, nineteen of the thirty-one members of the committee were pro-Ferguson and their votes produced a predictable result. By the time the state committee met in Houston on March 24, C. C. McDonald had changed course declaring his intention to enter the governor's race. The pro-Ferguson group dominated the day, ignoring all suggestions made by Chairman Hughes and overwhelmingly choosing Jim Ferguson as their next National Committeeman. [6]

John Nance Garner, the vice president, was an obvious choice to fill the position left open by Adams, but his name had not been considered. Ferguson foes desperately wanted Garner to supplant the ex-governor, but they were powerless to do more than suggest that measure and hope that Ferguson would be rejected at the national level. With speculation high as to what action the Democratic national headquarters might take with respect to Ferguson's nomination, the men anticipated the pivotal 1934 election results. That result would have a huge bearing on the balance of power. C. C. McDonald, the Ferguson choice for governor, was up against some stiff competition. McDonald faced Attorney General James Allred, Tom Hunter, Edgar Witt, Clint Small, and Maury Hughes, but the July primary saw all but Allred and Hunter eliminated. The three ousted candidates immediately put their support behind Hunter and Jim Ferguson did likewise. When Hunter lost the run-off to Allred, Allred wasted no time in announcing his support for John Nance Garner as State Democratic Committeeman.

Ferguson wired the vice president, offering to surrender the nomination for committeeman to Garner if he wanted the post. The reply was affirmative, and on September 10, the State Executive Committee elected John Nance Garner to fill the position, inducing a collective sigh of relief from a hefty number of Texas Democrats. The significance of this power shift was lost on very few political pundits. It marked the end of any major Ferguson influence in Texas politics. Newspapers were quick to point out that sixty-three-year-old James E. Ferguson, who many had considered washed-up many times before, was in fact too old to revive his floundering political career or to garner any measure of power from other officeholders. One Texas paper headlined its story on the election result and Ferguson's failed influence as Ferguson's "Political Obituary." [7]

On the Ferguson home front, a four-year struggle to hold on to the remaining section of Miriam's inherited Bell County property ended in early December. A $40,000 loan that Ferguson had obtained in 1923, using 625 acres as collateral, had first gone into default in 1930. Jim had used every legal tactic he could muster to prevent the loss of the property to the lien holder, the Dallas Joint Stock Land Bank. The bank believed that the property, initially appraised at $137 an acre in 1923, was worth only $50 an acre in 1934. Ferguson challenged the validity of the lien and accused the bank of charging usurious interest rates. He had on several occasions negotiated extensions on the notes on his wife's behalf and subsequently claimed that this action rendered the lien invalid. When those measures failed, Ferguson evoked protection under the mortgage moratorium law, a bill that Mrs. Ferguson, as governor, had signed into law the previous year in an attempt to help struggling farmers save their farms. The law was controversial from its inception, essentially allowing the state to modify the terms of contracts that were already in force, and the state court declared it unconstitutional after several challenges. The Fergusons, having exhausted every means to forestall the foreclosure, finally lost that acreage in December of 1934. [8]

In early December, as the last month of Mrs. Ferguson's term began, Jim again announced that he was retiring from politics. His declaration included a statement that he was going back to farming, publishing his paper, and practicing law, and he assured listeners that rumors of a possible bid for a US Senate seat were untrue. [9]

A flood of pardons consumed the last days of Governor Miriam Ferguson's administration, ending on the eve of the inauguration when fifty-seven convicts received her favor. Incoming Governor Allred would re-examine and revoke several of Governor Ferguson's pardons in his first days in office. One burglar, released prematurely via a Ferguson pardon, was found with a burglary kit in his possession when he was re-arrested under Allred's revocation. [10]

Although the Fergusons were invited to sit on the platform with the other dignitaries on inauguration day, January 15, 1935, James Allred requested that he be introduced by Senator Tom Deberry. It was a snub to the outgoing governor, who traditionally held that honor. Mrs. Ferguson retaliated by failing to provide the customary hot meal for the Allred family and leaving this Bible verse open on the governor's desk: "And the proud shall stumble and fall and none shall raise him up, and I will kindle a fire in his cities and it shall devour all around him" (Jeremiah 50:32).

With his wife out of office and Allred in, Jim's power quickly evaporated. Legislators enacted new state appropriations that raised the governor's annual salary to $12,000, three times the amount that each Governor Ferguson had received. In an effort to retain some small measure of control, Jim announced, in early December, his support for Coke Stevenson in his attempt to retain the Speakership for the upcoming year. Just as he had done two years earlier, Jim threw his influence behind the speaker, influence that had diminished considerably in the interim. [11]

In the early afternoon of January 15, 1935, James and Miriam Ferguson, again private citizens, vacated their state office and the Governor's Mansion for the last time. The move was momentous, representing a turning point in their lives and in the history of Texas politics. Future actions would show that it was not really Jim Ferguson's intent, as he had publicly claimed a month before, to retire from politics. Allred, who immediately adopted the idea of the "fireside chat" that had worked so well for President Roosevelt, became a popular governor who easily won a second term. However, at the close of Allred's terms, Texas would meet a new version of "the people's" politician. This newcomer would put the rural community's long-standing and legendary love affair with Jim Ferguson in serious jeopardy. The only force strong enough to stop James Ferguson was the force that had given him the power in the first place—the ever fickle and unpredictable Texas voter.

Chapter 23
Cross, Double Cross

Returning to the Ferguson home on Austin's Windsor Road in mid-January of 1935 was a relief to Miriam, but the solitude was a burden to the restive Jim. At the family's Bosque Creamery and stock farm outside of Austin, Jim continued to oversee the operation of raising pigs and cows, under the direction of farm manager O. E. Smith. The family still had small holdings in Bell and Bosque Counties as well where hired hands planted corn and tended livestock. But like most Ferguson endeavors, financial difficulties plagued the operations. Jim also held an office in the Nalle professional building in Austin, but with his failed sense of hearing, depleted energy, and a diminished tolerance for the Texas heat, the sixty-four-year-old ex-governor was increasingly forced to spend time at home. When he was able to make the trip to his office, Jim enjoyed the friendship of Jerome Sneed, whose law office was also housed in the Nalle building. In April, Jim again ceased publication of the *Forum* with this bold and unambiguous headline: "WE QUIT."[1]

Stevenson held his position as House Speaker, a feat that allowed him the added distinction of being the first man to succeed himself in that role. It was no cinch; governor-elect Allred had openly supported Robert Calvert for the position. Just how much Ferguson's influence had contributed to Stevenson's triumph was anybody's guess. At least one newspaper suggested that the answer to that question was less than "none," opining, "Stevenson won not in consequence of the Ferguson favor, but in spite of it." A more important concern for some House members was the possibility that Ferguson's support might have earned him some level of influence with the speaker. Stevenson sensed that apprehension and addressed it. After his victory Stevenson addressed members of the House and offered the group assurances that he would not be manipulated or swayed by any outside influence. "You who have served with me know I never have been dominated by any individual or collection of individuals," he said. But Stevenson was still clearly seen as a remnant of the Ferguson-dominated past. One member responded to Stevenson's election, not mincing words. "I like Coke Stevenson but I do not want Ferguson to continue to run the state."[2]

As the gubernatorial campaign of 1936 began, few doubted that Governor Allred, who was popular with both the public and the press, could be unseated. Texas voters had recently accepted an amendment authorizing an old age pension, but the most difficult aspect of the plan—the financing—had not been established. Allred's pleas for revenue-producing taxes had gained no support from legislators. Logically, a remedy for that problem became one of the chief planks of each gubernatorial candidate. Among those candidates was Senator Roy Sanderford of Belton, Ferguson's choice in the race. Sanderford, an anti-prohibitionist, had been in the state Senate for four years and was well-known as a strong Ferguson ally. As a solution to the pension financing problem, he recommended a 3 percent sales tax, even though previous suggestions for a sales tax had drawn heated resistance. Sanderford hoped to convince voters that such a tax could eliminate the need for the ad valorem tax on real estate while raising sufficient revenue to cover the pension plan. [3]

So strong was the Ferguson sentiment in favor of Sanderford that the retired and silenced *Forum* printing press was again dusted off and placed in service. Though he could ill afford it in terms of stamina, Ferguson took to the campaign trail using Ouida and her husband, George, as drivers. The trio drove from city to city where Jim made his impassioned pleas in favor of Senator Sanderford. In Dallas, Ferguson drew laughs from the audience as he ridiculed Sanderford's opponent Tom Hunter. "Tom is honest but he's just as ignorant as he is honest," he joked. To another Sanderford opponent, F. W. Fischer, Ferguson applied a nickname of "Fat Fischer," and offered this comment about Governor Allred: "Allred is squalling like a pig stuck under a gate." The crusade offered Jim a quick fix for his interminable need to be in command of a podium, as well as an opportunity to reminisce with his daughter and son-in-law about days and campaigns gone by, but any support his speeches may have summoned in Sanderford's favor were inconsequential. The election resulted in a landslide for Governor Allred while Roy Sanderford finished in fourth place with an embarrassing 8 percent of the vote. [4]

Over the following year, Jim Ferguson remained relatively quiet. Entries in his 1937 diary paint the picture of a man consumed with five things: his weight, his corn crop, his pigs, the family's dire financial situation, and the prospect of another candidacy for Miriam. Jim seemed to delight in remembering and recording frequent encounters with people who inquired about that possibility. Even small details relative to the prospect seemed worthy of chronicling. A friend named John Boyle "walked across the street" to tell him that "his wife" should run again, he wrote. In a dozen or so similar entries Jim consistently referred to Miriam using the term "my wife." Such references were usually followed with the expressed regret that there was no money for campaigning and that "my wife" has no desire to re-enter politics. W. A. Hanger, Jim's defender and long-time friend, called him in early September to encourage Miriam's candidacy and offer his support in that eventuality, an endorsement that seemed to please Jim. However, on the same day, Jim lamented that Dorrace, who had a great deal of influence over her mother, was advising her against any further political involvement. [5]

In the spring of 1937 plans by former Governor Pat Neff to reunite six former Texas governors along with then-Governor Allred failed to materialize due to the depth of old wounds. Neff had hoped to unite the seven at the dedication ceremony of a new clubhouse at Mother Neff Park, a celebration planned appropriately enough, on Mother's Day. Neff, who had managed to be cordial to the Fergusons in spite of philosophical differences, failed to realize that other governors had not mustered the same degree of tolerance. Governors Sterling and Moody declined the invitation citing the presence of certain other governors as their reason. There is little doubt that the Fergusons were the subjects of the two former governors' objections. For their part, the Fergusons may have anticipated trouble; they declined on the grounds that such a meeting might not be harmonious. [6]

By late 1937, as a potential lead-in to the next gubernatorial campaign, Jim began to heavily promote the Townsend Plan, a liberal and controversial proposal for a federal pension. The Townsend Plan was popular with citizens who were eager to receive a $200 per month pension at age 60, regardless of need. The plan received little serious consideration by the legislature due to the projections of its exorbitant cost, but Jim used the topic to tease the public with the prospect of another Ferguson campaign in 1938. In an article in the resurrected *Forum*, he referenced support for the Townsend Plan as one of his "planks," and further teased *Forum* readers when he declared that the *Forum* would name no candidate allegiance in the early stages of the election. [7]

There was, of course, one major problem with any serious plan for a future candidacy. Mrs. Ferguson had stated without ambiguity that she had no desire to run for a third term. It was no ruse. Jim had repeatedly logged entries into his personal diary in 1937 stating his quandary; he was certain that Texans wanted "his wife" but she was adamant in her resolve to remain retired. Getting her back into the race required a major scheme on Jim's part. In January of 1938, Jim, through Texas newspapers, set his plan in motion suggesting that public demand for Miriam's candidacy would impose on her a duty to enter the race.

This declaration carried a dual purpose: it elicited a certain number of telegrams in support of another Ferguson term, and, he hoped, it would place a burden of guilt on Miriam's shoulders should she fail to respond to voters' pleas. [8]

In April of 1938, Miriam demonstrated that she would not succumb to public or spousal pressure to run for the '39–'40 term, announcing unequivocally that she was not physically or financially able to make the race. This did not, however, preclude the announcement of a Ferguson candidate. On May 4, James Ashley Ferguson, a sixty-eight-year-old Belton farmer and cousin to Jim, declared his intentions to run for the governorship. No sooner had the original "Farmer Jim" come out publicly in support of the new "Farmer Jim" than "Cousin Jim" experienced a change of heart and excused himself from the race.[9]

The campaign of 1938 shared an unfortunate issue with the previous gubernatorial election. The pension plan that was in need of funding in 1936 remained without remedy and created an escalating problem. Not only had no source of revenue been established, but the cost of the plan had been grossly underestimated and it had generated a surprising $13,000,000 deficit. Astute voters demanded a solution for that crisis from 1938 gubernatorial candidates. [10]

Thirteen men filed as candidates for the '39–'40 term as governor for the Lone Star State, chief among them Ernest O. Thompson, Tom Hunter, and Attorney General William McCraw. Among those initially believed to be less viable was Wilbert Lee O'Daniel, an executive in his own newly formed flour business. O'Daniel had a long history as a flour salesman whose credentials included a successful radio show promoting his product via a hillbilly band. O'Daniel and his band, the Light Crust Doughboys, and later the Hillbilly Boys, delighted a growing following with their western-swing style music. A little advising and preaching thrown into the mix only heightened O'Daniel's appeal and the show's popularity. Born in Ohio, O'Daniel had moved to Texas in 1925 from Kansas. Not only had he contemplated no political aspirations prior to his decision to run for governor in 1938, he readily confessed that he had never even voted. He seemed an improbable political candidate but with his increased popularity came suggestions that he run for governor. After an avalanche of requests, O'Daniel finally announced his intention to secure the nomination on May 1, 1938. [11]

While Jim Ferguson threw his support to Attorney General McCraw, O'Daniel and his hillbilly band hit the campaign trail in their custom-fitted bus, complete with an innovative, crowd-drawing loudspeaker. The campaign, which was little more than an extension of his radio show, drew large crowds. "Pappy," a nickname that inspired the same kind of affection that "Ma" and "Pa" had in the past, became O'Daniel's tag. The label originated from an advertising slogan, "Pass the biscuits, Pappy," but the message was one of an implied pseudo-kinship.

Many Texans quickly found favor with more than O'Daniel's music and biscuits. His promises of no poll tax, pensions for the aged, and economy in government, were just what voters wanted to hear and his omission of any plan to pay for the pensions seemed inconsequential. Declaring that the Golden Rule and the Ten Commandments guided his actions, O'Daniel surprised the press, other predictors, and even himself with his rapid ascent.

The other candidates were understandably frustrated with the legitimacy that O'Daniel's campaign seemed to garner despite the limited substance of his platform. Exasperated opponent William McCraw expressed this sentiment: "A businesslike farmer does not employ a field hand because he is a good crooner, nor does a sick man select a doctor because he is a good tap dancer... One candidate is offering thirty dollars a month pensions without pretending to show how to raise the $40,000,000 a year or more to pay them." [12]

O'Daniel captured an astounding 51 percent of the votes in the primary and easily defeated his Republican opponent in the general election. He had taken 231 out of 254 counties in the primary with only his wife for a campaign manager and no political experience. The election results made two facts abundantly clear: the advent of the radio had largely redefined campaigning, and voters who had traditionally backed the Fergusons had found a new favorite.

The 1938 election also saw an advance in the career of Coke Stevenson who sought and won the office of lieutenant governor. Again newspapers pointed to the loss of O'Daniel's Ferguson-backed opponent (McCraw) as an indication that Ferguson's endorsement might actually constitute a negative effect. Jim had little means for rebuttal, his *Forum* newspaper having been discontinued again in July of 1938, this time permanently. With O'Daniel in office, Jim settled in for another wait.

For those like Jim Ferguson who watched the new governor's every move with displacement in mind, O'Daniel was a joy to behold. His every action was fodder for ridicule, his blunders beginning well before he took office. The Hillbilly Band, complete with the governor, continued its weekly radio broadcasts from the front porch of the Governor's Mansion. O'Daniel was immediately at odds with the legislature, where his total lack of protocol earned him nothing but disrespect and scorn and assured him little cooperation. Any trace of leadership ability was also absent. A vow to end the death penalty in Texas became a broken campaign promise when his push for repeal of capital punishment found few backers. Yet despite his unfulfilled campaign promises and his severe shortcomings as a leader, Governor O'Daniel was enormously popular with Texans at large.[13]

A diversion from politics and the looming war in Europe came to the Ferguson family in 1939, and it was a wonderful sort of distraction. The first

Ferguson grandson, George Nalle, Jr., had enjoyed the distinction of being the only Ferguson grandchild for nineteen years but he welcomed a cousin, James Stuart Watt, on August 4, 1939. This baby boy would be Dorrace's only child and the last grandchild for Miriam and Jim.

Berating Governor O'Daniel in anticipation of opposing him in a future race required no exaggeration and very little research. Jim Ferguson predicted that O'Daniel faced a bumpy road to re-election due to his failure to produce the higher pensions he had promised voters two years earlier. Ferguson reminded voters that while they were hoping for tax reductions, only a tax increase would allow O'Daniel to honor his promise of increased pensions. When asked about Mrs. Ferguson's intentions as a candidate, Ferguson told newsmen that many had requested that she run but he added, "She will not get into politics."[14]

Over the following three months however, Miriam began to soften her resolve. On March 24, Mrs. Ferguson repeated a favorite Ferguson tactic when she announced that she would run—**if** enough people asked her to do so. Journalists had a field day with the announcement, one newspaper referring to Jim as the "governor-once-removed." A newspaper editorial summarized the situation in this way: "Mrs. Ferguson asks you to send a post card if you want her to run for Governor. In effect, she wants to draft you to draft her to run… Oh we Texans have handled our government as if it were a farce at somebody else's expense. We've been pretty silly about it all, and that's a fact which we cannot deny. But surely it has not been so bad that we actually deserve the Fergusons again."[15]

Three days after Mrs. Ferguson's timid plea in support of the very *notion* that she run, O'Daniel upstaged her. In a case of pure mimicry, Governor O'Daniel announced the launching of his own political newspaper that he titled the *W. Lee O'Daniel News*. He offered a trial subscription covering four months for twenty-five cents and promised no advertisements in his publications. He further promised that any profit generated by the publication would be donated to the Red Cross. On April 6, 140,000 copies of the paper—complete with two pictures of O'Daniel—rolled off the presses in Fort Worth. [16]

On April 27, Mrs. Ferguson opened her campaign in Waco. Reminiscent of her first campaign in 1924, she spoke briefly and then deferred to Jim. Leading her campaign pledges was an assurance that she would be loyal to President Roosevelt and his agenda. A secondary Ferguson pledge advocated a pension to qualified persons over the age of sixty-five funded by a gross receipts tax.

Mrs. Ferguson took to the airwaves in an attempt to level the playing field and counter the showboat antics of her fiercest competitor. Though radio time was expensive, the growing popularity of the medium put any candidate who failed to use it at a severe disadvantage. Two mornings each week, the Fergusons participated in a reversal of roles as Jim deferred to his wife who used the new medium to speak of her agenda. The radio was not a good fit for the man whose strength had always been in face-to-face fiery speeches with responsive audiences. Miriam was comfortable with her radio campaigns, but without a gimmick she could not compete with O'Daniel for the capricious affection of Texas voters. As he had done in his first race, O'Daniel again easily took the nomination, this time by way of a 55 percent vote. Mrs. Ferguson placed an embarrassing fourth in the race.

Forced to retreat, Jim continued his harsh criticism of O'Daniel. Out of the spotlight but itching to rejoin, Jim looked for opportunities to inject himself into the political arena, even peripherally. In early April of 1941, such an opportunity presented itself when US Senator Morris Sheppard, author of the Eighteenth Amendment (enacting Prohibition), died from a stroke. Ouida described the immediate flurry that ensued in this way: "Senator Sheppard's body was hardly cold before the politicians' pots began boiling in Texas over his political carcass."[17]

Governor O'Daniel was certainly on that list of plotters. His choice of a temporary replacement to fill Sheppard's seat was a calculated one. The near eighty-seven-year-old Andrew Jackson Houston, the only surviving son of Sam Houston, was encumbered even beyond his advanced years. Houston's health was tenuous, a fact that was certainly not lost on O'Daniel. Knowing that Houston would offer no obstacle to his own aspirations for the seat when the election for a permanent replacement came, the governor appointed him. Indeed, Houston was no hindrance; the elderly gentleman died soon after his arrival in Washington. O'Daniel quickly set a date for a special election and the flurry of plotting began anew.

Though Ouida was critical of the connivers, her father was chief among the schemers who busied themselves calculating how the vacancy might best advance each man's own agenda. Jim Ferguson considered running for the position himself, forgetting or ignoring his wife's intense dislike of Washington winters and her declaration that she would not live there. He teased the public with a statement to newspapers on April 29 that one of his planks would be an opposition to national Prohibition, *should* he decide to run. On May 10 he offered an unusual explanation for his decision against making the race—he simply did not want to run. That notion seems unlikely, however. A more plausible explanation might be that pressure from Miriam, a slim chance for success, and an absence of funds, decided his fate.

Twenty-seven candidates eventually completed the list of hopefuls for the Senate seat, O'Daniel being one of the last to file. He based his delayed declaration largely on his unfinished business as governor. He offered the legislature a five-point program that he encouraged them to address before he would "consider" entering the Senate race. This attempt to hurry through some key elements that

215

the governor wanted, failed when the Texas Legislature ignored most of his wishes. He stalled until he could stall no longer, and finally on May 19, announced his candidacy using his favorite venue, a radio address.

Certainly no one expected Jim Ferguson to support Governor O'Daniel's aspirations for a Senate seat after the remarks that both Fergusons had made on O'Daniel's inability to govern. But Ferguson had a dual purpose for the sudden change of allegiance he adopted. O'Daniel was becoming a threat to the beer industry in Texas with suggestions that certain restrictions be placed on its sales. For this reason Ferguson and other anti-prohibitionists wanted to get him out of the state. The other factor motivating Ferguson to support of O'Daniel had to do with a juggling of positions that he hoped might bring him closer to the inner circle of power in Austin. Lieutenant Governor Coke Stevenson was positioned to immediately become governor should O'Daniel win the open Senate seat. Fresh on Jim Ferguson's mind was the support he had lent Stevenson in 1933 and 1935.

Though Lieutenant Governor Stevenson had been in Texas politics for some twenty-five years, he was still a rising star. He had moved up the ranks in politics, although somewhat reluctantly because he did not especially like the process, his personality not well suited for "politicking." A reserved and prudent man who never spoke without considerable forethought, Stevenson was uncomfortable in social settings. He preferred doing something more productive, such as the back-breaking work he frequently engaged in on his sprawling ranch in Hill County. Friends and other supporters had drafted him into many of the political offices he held, but through them he had earned a reputation as a natural leader and a man of considerable integrity. A most capable and sought-after lawyer, Stevenson was an avid reader who abundantly loved and understood the law. He had given ten years of distinguished service to the Texas House, where, after two terms as House Speaker, he had turned down the offer of a third. Few doubted that Stevenson would make a fine governor if O'Daniel prevailed in a bid for the open Senate seat but probably few wanted that more than Jim Ferguson. [18]

O'Daniel's election to the US Senate was by no means guaranteed. In the year since Mrs. Ferguson had campaigned against him, O'Daniel's popularity had waned somewhat, or so it seemed, and there was a lot of competition hoping to capitalize on that notion. Among them, thirty-two-year-old Lyndon Johnson seemed a viable candidate, as did Attorney General Gerald Mann and Congressman Martin Dies, chairman of the House Committee for the Investigation of un-American Activities. [19]

Campaigning against Lyndon Johnson may have been as awkward for the Fergusons as campaigning *for* O'Daniel. Johnson and his father, Sam Ealy Johnson, had been lifelong and passionate Ferguson supporters. Sam had served for twenty years in the Texas House of Representatives and young Lyndon had grown up watching and admiring the Fergusons. In 1937, Lyndon Johnson had campaigned for and won the vacated seat of James P. Buchanan in the US House of Representatives. He was re-elected in 1938 and 1940. When Sheppard's US Senate seat became available, Johnson was eager to advance his career by winning that seat.

The ambitious and shrewd Lyndon Johnson had a talent for campaigning, but he knew that he would test those talents in his attempt to take the Senate seat. The escalating war in Europe attracted the attention of Americans who speculated that the nation's involvement in the war was probably inevitable. Playing to that dread, Johnson crafted a sentiment that turned it to his favor and made him very popular with voters. The young congressman promised anxious Texans that he would join their sons on the battlefield in the event of America's participation in the war. Johnson had another advantage, at least in the eyes of those who found favor with the New Deal. He could boast the enthusiastic support of President Franklin Roosevelt. [20]

If it was uncomfortable for Jim Ferguson to sing the praises of a man he had one year earlier labeled an "ignoramus" and a "slick haired banjo player," he did not betray the emotion. Jim appeared comfortable in supporting the idea that the man he had accused of being the reason for elderly Texans being without adequate pensions—a man he said had Republican leanings and no tax plan—had somehow morphed into a good senatorial candidate.

Unfortunately, during the days of hand-written ballots, election fraud and manipulation were sometimes a part of campaign strategy available to unprincipled campaigners in Texas. When it came to Johnson and O'Daniel, each side had his respective pockets of influence where the possibilities existed for "negotiated" votes. Johnson's stronghold encompassed the San Antonio area and the southern counties under George Parr's influence, while O'Daniel's strength was a block of mostly rural East Texas counties. On the night of June 28, Election Day, the vote was close in Johnson's favor, but not so close that Johnson had confidence in the win. The second day following voting, the Johnson lead advanced and congratulations began filtering in, but the fourth day brought shocking changes that rendered those congratulatory messages premature. Late reports coming from remote counties in East Texas overwhelmingly favored O'Daniel and eventually produced a victory for him by a slim margin of 1,300 votes. [21]

Johnson was caught completely off-guard. He had purchased or otherwise bargained with George Parr and other forces with the ability to manipulate election results, for what he believed to be sufficient votes to secure the nomination. A confident Johnson had allowed those kingmakers to release the results on

Election Day, inadvertently giving the O'Daniel camp time to scurry up, with late tabulations and "corrections," just enough votes to steal the election back from him. In reality, O'Daniel had few connections from which to scrape together additional votes in East Texas, but James Ferguson certainly did. Only in a very close race could the Ferguson influence have had such a decisive effect and only with the added twist of Johnson's early release of South Texas vote counts could the "fix" have been completed. [22]

A study done after the election showed clearly that O'Daniel owed his win in large part to the votes of farmers, this likely attributable, at least in part, to Ferguson's influence. Without this margin-narrowing support during campaigning, there would have been no need to pull together those final critical votes. The exact means used to obtain those belated votes and the extent of Ferguson's involvement remains a mystery. [23]

This shenanigan proved Jim Ferguson's last major show of muscle in Texas politics, and carried with it a double irony. The absurdity rests in the fact that Ferguson made an error in believing that Coke Stevenson would acknowledge any debt to the ex-governor for his part in elevating Stevenson to the governorship prematurely. Ferguson's support for O'Daniel had been an indirect benefit to Stevenson and was almost certainly unsolicited. Governor Stevenson was successful in his own right, his popularity later demonstrated during the 1942 and 1944 primaries that he won handily without the necessity of a runoff. He was confident in his own talents and probably had no desire to test the theory that Ferguson's influence might prove negative.

Miriam would later express a disdain for Coke Stevenson for what she believed was a display of ingratitude to her husband for his part in supporting Stevenson's career advances. It was Miriam's claim that the governor had failed to visit Jim when he was ill and that he had also failed to embrace Jim when he had visited the governor. We can only speculate at Stevenson's reasons for avoiding the Fergusons, if in fact he did so. Without question Stevenson knew that Ferguson's support for both O'Daniel and himself was disingenuous and that Ferguson's backing was ultimately for the protection of alcohol and a desire to earn future favors. Perhaps it was Mrs. Ferguson's own philosophy, projected on others, that distorted her view. She likely found it inconceivable that Stevenson did not subscribe to the "reward and punishment" philosophy that had long dominated her decision-making and that of her husband. [24]

Stevenson's personality was a key factor that deserves consideration in this discussion. Robert Caro, describing Stevenson's relationship with the powerful Duval County bosses, explained Stevenson's relationship in this way: "Money was never a factor in the Valley's support of Stevenson—he treated the 'jefes' with the same indifference and independence that he displayed toward other powerful political figures." [25]

Indifference—that was likely the emotion (or lack of emotion) that Stevenson exhibited toward Jim, a reaction the Fergusons found highly objectionable. Regardless of his treatment of Jim Ferguson, the astute governor certainly knew that Ferguson was not trustworthy and that any association with him might call his own reputation into question in the minds of the public and other legislators. Indeed, Ferguson was not to be trusted. In his 1989 biography of John Connally, author James Reston tells this story: "During those critical hours when the election win was seesawing between Johnson and O'Daniel, Connally, who was working at the Johnson campaign headquarters, received a telephone call from none other than Jim Ferguson. According to Connally, Ferguson offered to stop stealing votes in a certain East Texas district in exchange for money. A shocked Connally claims that he took great offense at the proposition and hung up the phone." [26]

Therein rests the second irony. Assuming Connally's version of events is true, Jim Ferguson's support for O'Daniel, his passion to keep alcohol legal, and his wish to see Coke Stevenson in the governor's chair were all for sale in the final hour.

Johnson knew O'Daniel forces had outmaneuvered him but could scarcely afford to ask for an investigation in light of his own purchased votes. He quietly returned to Washington to his position in the House of Representatives a little wiser. Six months later, on December 7, 1941, the attack on Pearl Harbor abruptly cast the United States into the Second World War. His previous promise to join the ranks of men in combat forced Lyndon Johnson into making a decision. He had to honor that pledge or face certain scorn that had the potential of seriously damaging his political career—and Lyndon Johnson was certainly not one to put any aspect of his political aspirations at risk.

Chapter 21
The Last Act

Nineteen-hundred and forty-two found the nation consumed with the war effort and James Ferguson in a continuing state of failing health. The Fergusons sold the Temple home in August 1941 for $3,200 even though they had paid $4,250 for the double lot in 1907. The cash infusion did little to alleviate the couple's financial stress. Jim's poor health forced Ouida to assume the responsibility for oversight of the operations at the dairy and pig farm, a task for which she was admittedly ill-equipped. The financial situation was so daunting that she soon determined that the best course of action was to close the business and submit the remaining assets to auction. From his sickbed, Jim wrote a letter of thanks to his daughter for her efforts, which included a lengthy thesis on how she might take steps to raise heartier swine. This gesture, so indicative of his personality, proved that even from a sickbed, Jim Ferguson was not meant to be a bystander. He was unaware that Ouida had already sold the pigs out of financial necessity.[1]

Lyndon Johnson was already a lieutenant commander in the Naval Reserves when the war intruded upon the safety of his desk job in Washington D. C. He could ill afford to avoid entirely some semblance of combat duty in fulfillment of the campaign promise he had made earlier in the year. Johnson made several successful attempts at delaying deployment by securing non-combative domestic assignments within the Navy until, with the help of President Roosevelt, he finally received orders to deploy to Australia in late May 1942. His duty as part of a three-man team was to survey the war effort in the Southwest Pacific and report those observations to Washington. His short-lived military service was over by mid-July 1942 when President Roosevelt called all national legislators out of active duty. Some chose to resign their offices while others, like Johnson, left the military and returned home.[2]

Lyndon Johnson was among those who visited the ageing Fergusons in their Austin home, both before and after his short stint in Australia. His friendship with the Fergusons might have seemed curious in light of Jim's efforts to sabotage Johnson's 1941 campaign in favor of W. Lee O'Daniel, but Johnson was known for befriending previous opponents and was even better known for seeking the advice of older, more experienced politicians. Leaving no stone unturned when it came to gaining a political advantage, Johnson knew better than to discount any potential Ferguson stimulus. From years of observing the pair, he was well aware that the couple's influence would not die entirely until they did, but it seems he had a less complicated reason for befriending them; he simply liked them. John Connally, Johnson's close friend, explained the future president's admiration for Jim Ferguson this way: "There were men who knew how to overcome scandal through the force of their personalities," explained Connally, "the power of their oratory, [and] the solidity of their political friendships." To Johnson, Ferguson personified that kind of man.[3]

Jim's health had been failing for several years but went into a rapid decline following a stroke in February of 1944. He died the following September 21, at his Austin home under a vigil by Miriam and hired medical assistants. The death certificate listed the cause of death as Parkinson's disease. Even though Ouida had auctioned off all of the assets of the failing dairy and pig farm in April of that year, there was little money in the Ferguson household. Friends contributed to the funeral expenses and later established a Ferguson Memorial Foundation to ensure the ex-governor received a grand monument suitable for a statesman.

The passing of the key political player in the Ferguson family certainly diminished the surviving family members' interest and involvement in politics, yet this ebb included one far-reaching and enduring statement from the Ferguson family. Ouida Ferguson Nalle's rendering of the lives of her famous father and mother—titled *The Fergusons of Texas, or Two Governors for the Price of One*—was published in 1946. The book, which sold for three dollars, did not make a profit for the San Antonio-based publisher, but its subsequent contribution to the inside story of the Ferguson legend has been invaluable to researchers who can filter through its biases and inaccuracies. The most enduring features of the book to the family are its permanence and a title that carries the Ferguson name.[4]

A common theme Mrs. Nalle used in her writing was that of blaming Ferguson enemies for the problems that beset the family. Among the more objectionable interpretations in her book is Nalle's labeling of the members of the committee that impeached her father as a "kangaroo court," a characterization that insults the integrity of capable men who undertook that difficult task. Nalle further stated that "As the trial progressed, our fair-weather friends began to quit us." While it is true that a number of Ferguson friends, such as Misters Hudspeth, Bee, Bailey, Page, and Harley, began as staunch defenders of Ferguson, they almost certainly changed their opinions based on the strength of the evidence. The notion that volumes of compelling evidence altered the opinions of these men seems never to have occurred to Mrs. Nalle—or perhaps she believed that friendship trumped evidence. In the case of Archie Parr, that seems to have been the case. Parr voted "no" on every charge and for his loyalty Ouida Nalle described him as one whose name "is engraved upon our heart." Archie Parr's endorsement was hardly a laudable one; in investigations that occurred before and after his death, Parr was suspected or linked to extortion, theft of public funds, intimidation, election fraud, and murder.[5]

By 1948, after ten years in the House of Representatives, Lyndon Johnson was more than impatient to advance to the Senate, a move he viewed as crucial to his political future. By that time, former Governor Coke Stevenson was enjoying the quiet of his ranch in Hill County, although it was a little too quiet for his liking. Stevenson's beloved wife, Faye, had succumbed to cancer on January 3, 1942, and had died in the Governor's Mansion, and his only son was an adult. Stevenson had served as governor for the entire period of World War II and was immensely popular, astute, and effective, having taken the state from a thirty-million-dollar shortage to a thirty-five-million dollar surplus during his tenure.[6]

The backdrop for the unusual features that came to define the race can best be explained by examining the state of mind of the men as they entered the race. Stevenson, never a fan of politics, was motivated by a strong belief in his ability to provide a valuable service to Texans, and was confident that his past record would sustain him in his pursuit. With that point of view, he refused to engage in the gimmickry and showboat campaigning that had served W. Lee O'Daniel so well. Johnson, on the other hand, driven by a feeling of self-imposed desperation, believed that his political life and future rested with the success of the 1948 election. With this mentality, and the financial backing of Houston's Brown and Root Construction Company, he was poised to launch a zealous campaign using every tactic at his disposal. As the campaign began, Johnson happily accepted the endorsement of former Governor Miriam Ferguson.

The campaigning was fierce, laden with name calling, dirty tricks, and the widespread use of inventive campaign gimmicks, but unlike most other elections, the use of these rash tactics was entirely one-sided. Johnson had no qualms about making statements against Stevenson that were entirely baseless, so much so that he even astonished his own aides with the level of maliciousness he employed. Using the novel helicopter, Johnson moved quickly and conspicuously from town to town, where a pre-arranged band drew crowds in anticipation of his arrival. Johnson tapped his connections with the likes of the agent of the Boss of Duval County, George Parr, where the parties consummated agreements for "support." George

Parr, son of Archie Parr, a Ferguson friend, had taken over the family business well in advance of his father's death in 1942. George Parr liked Johnson, who had helped him obtain a pardon in 1946 for a conviction on income tax evasion. Stevenson had also once had a friendly relationship with Archie Parr; he had even been an honorary pallbearer at the elder Parr's funeral. More recently, though, he had angered the "Boss," George, by not honoring his request to appoint a friend to the vacated post of Laredo's District Attorney in 1944 while Stevenson was governor.[7]

For his part, Stevenson campaigned the old-fashioned way, traveling by car and speaking to those who gathered with little or no prompting. He believed that "right" would always prevail, and for a time it did. In the primary, Stevenson fared well, especially considering that another conservative, George Petty, was also in the race and his presence pulled votes from Stevenson. In the primary, Stevenson took 40 percent of the vote, Johnson 36 percent, and Petty 20 percent. Assuming that most, if not all, of Petty's 20 percent share was from moderates and would go to Stevenson in the runoff election, it seemed certain that Stevenson would take the US Senate seat.[8]

This result only heightened Johnson's sense of apprehension. Having used every stunt in his political playbook during the first heat, he was hard pressed to find new tactics for harvesting more votes. His 98 percent vote in Duval County had not been enough to overcome Stevenson's share, nor had his 90 percent average in Parr's neighboring counties. He could hardly ask to increase those percentages since they were already grossly disproportionate to other areas of the state. Furthermore, as demonstrated in the result of the primary, purchased votes could only be used successfully to supplement a very close count, a fact that Johnson understood well.[9]

The Johnson camp continued spreading lies about Stevenson, lies so blatant that the very act of repeating them was repugnant. A favored tactic was sending hired Johnson "missionaries," as they were dubbed, into bars and courthouse squares, to start casual conversations with unsuspecting citizens, conversations that included dropping negative innuendos about Stevenson's character. These whispered character assassinations included insinuations that Stevenson was a communist, a sensitive subject in post-World War II America.[10]

Generally, Stevenson refused to respond to the attacks on his character, but his silence became a disadvantage as he continuously refused to refute the charges that Lyndon Johnson launched against him. By the time Stevenson took a defensive stance, which eventually escalated into a greater offensive stance as well, it was almost too late. Polls showed that the margin between the contenders had narrowed significantly.

What had appeared an easy win for Stevenson only a month prior ended as the closest political race in Texas history. As Election Day approached, it appeared that Johnson's efforts to narrow the margin had been successful. He had secured a great number of votes in the San Antonio area by negotiation and he had George Parr poised to do his part within his sphere of influence. This, he hoped, should close an anticipated small gap. But, to the bitter end, it was still either man's game.[11]

In the early morning hours of August 29, the Texas Election Bureau closed for the night. The statewide spread between candidates was an amazing 854 votes in favor of Stevenson who dared not celebrate. The customary late votes and corrections continued coming in, and on the fourth day election officials declared Stevenson the winner by an astonishing 362 votes. But additional amended counts kept coming, the most suspicious of these from the town of Alice in Jim Wells County. Not coincidentally, Jim Wells was a neighboring county to Duval and one over which George Parr held sway. In the end, a mere 200 new votes for Johnson decided the election in his favor with a margin of 87 votes. Curiously, the 200 "new votes" from Wells County were later found to be written in alphabetical order and all of the same handwriting. Duval County had rendered a 99 percent vote in Johnson's favor and the combined Parr-controlled surrounding counties had given him a staggering average of 93 percent of the vote.[12]

Stevenson had no intention of accepting the lost election without an investigation into the dubious circumstances that clouded it. He first sent two lawyer friends who were former FBI agents to Jim Wells County to investigate. What they found was damning, but without the cooperation of the county authorities they were unable to obtain enough evidence to prove fraud. Next, Stevenson himself made an investigative trip to Alice, Texas, with the help of famed ex-Texas Ranger Frank Hamer. Once there, the two men found that obtaining evidence was nearly impossible and attempts at finding witnesses who were willing to talk was hopeless. The men found convincing signs that fraud had decided the outcome of the race, but a local election official blocked them from taking any records that could prove their case. Johnson, desperate to stop their investigation, filed for an injunction in the local court of Jim Wells County. His friendship with Parr assured him the cooperation of local judges and the injunction he sought was summarily granted, bringing the investigation to an abrupt halt.[13]

Convinced that Johnson had won the election fraudulently, Stevenson took what few legal remedies were available to him and had a federal restraining order issued, which temporarily kept Johnson's name off of the runoff election ballot. The restraining order was later set aside and the general election proceeded. Not surprisingly, Johnson easily beat his Republican opponent and headed back to Washington.

Coke Stevenson never found the justice he sought. The Texas Democratic Executive Committee, charged with certifying the runoff vote, failed to support his efforts to have the election declared illegal and the US Supreme Court ultimately blocked his efforts to obtain justice. Meanwhile, the voting list for the infamous ballot box 13 had mysteriously gone missing. An embittered Stevenson retired from politics, returning to the ranch and lifestyle where he was most comfortable. He continued his law practice, remarried, had another child, and lived to the age of eighty-seven, but his battered sense of fair-play never recovered.

The commotion surrounding the ballot box 13 controversy, which followed LBJ all the way to the White House, suddenly resurfaced with a vengeance in 1977, two years after the deaths of both Coke Stevenson and George Parr. Seventy-eight-year-old Luis Salas, a Duval County election judge in 1948, confessed that under directions from George Parr 202 votes (Salas said he added two votes for Stevenson for appearance's sake) had indeed been fraudulently added to the total tally well after election day. Salas also admitted that he had lied about the vote tampering during subsequent investigations. Once a tough and sturdy character, Salas had in his youth ridden for two and a half years with Pancho Villa's revolutionary army in Mexico before moving to the United States. Serving as a deputy sheriff in three counties under Parr's control, he had also served as an enforcer for the Duke of Duval for ten years. His stories about the extent of Parr's control were nothing short of disturbing.[14]

There were certainly those who then and now doubt the confessions of the aging Salas, particularly his assertion that Johnson met face-to-face with George Parr during those critical days of tabulation. Due to the disappearance of ballot box 13, the mystery will never be solved with certainty, but the cover-up, the sordid history of the Parr machine and the fact that the critical box went missing, are compelling reasons to believe that fraud decided that 1948 race.

Miriam Ferguson's initial assistance to the Johnson campaign was in the form of letters of endorsement, signed in her hand and mailed by Johnson campaign workers. She had also supplied the Johnson camp with the names of the Ferguson faithful, extracted from her little black book of record. More importantly, she offered advice in the form of the names of the South and East Texas precincts that were most likely to sell or otherwise negotiate votes. This occurred fourteen years after her last term in office, so the effect that these gestures actually had on the election result is impossible to measure but likely negligible. Certainly, Lyndon Johnson, who began his political career when he ran a carefully crafted campaign in 1937 and took the vacated congressional seat of James Buchanan, needed little advice on campaigning in Texas. At the very least, however, Miriam's influence was useful in narrowing that critical margin that kept Johnson's presence in the Senate race viable.

Close Ferguson family friend Jerome Sneed revealed in interviews many years later that Miriam extended her assistance to Johnson forces still further on that critical election night. Though Ferguson grandson James Watt was only nine years old in 1948, he too later supported Sneed's recollection of events that night. Sneed recalled that Miriam Ferguson placed a call to George Parr on election night in an attempt to help Lyndon Johnson. Sneed believed that Parr's 200 vote "discovery" was a result of that phone call and Sneed had no qualms about saying that Miriam placed it as an act of revenge against Coke Stevenson.[15]

However, Sneed's conclusion that Miriam's election-night phone call solidified the win is illogical and likely grossly overstates Miriam's impact in Johnson's campaign. She made her call four days before the 200 vote "adjustment." Certainly, George Parr had a plan in place well in advance of Election Day and was prepared to deliver the votes Johnson needed to ensure his win. Luis Salas admitted that he had changed many votes for Stevenson to Johnson's favor during the initial count, well before the 200-vote addition. The disproportionately high percentages of Johnson votes in Parr-controlled counties during the primary proved that Parr was delivering to the best of his ability. Unable to reasonably report 100 percent margins, he strained the boundaries of reasonableness by delivering 99 percent of the vote to Johnson. Parr had benefitted from a valuable lesson learned in the 1941 election. He knew that it was necessary to wait until the last possible hour to make final vote "adjustments," and that is precisely what he did. A phone call from Miriam Ferguson on election night was almost certainly inconsequential.

Largely unscathed, George Parr's political machine in Duval County survived isolated attempts to dislodge it, including a 1950s investigation that produced over 650 indictments against the group. These indictments saw some Parr cronies punished, but Parr himself dodged any serious penalty. A larger investigation in 1975 ended with another sentence for income tax evasion. Parr, facing certain jail time, cheated justice by committing suicide.

The family and friends of Miriam Ferguson may not have realized the implications of their disclosure when they revealed the details of her phone call to George Parr. Boasting that his friend Miriam had a pivotal role in Johnson's election, correct or not, Sneed actually exposed a guarded truth. Miriam's call to Parr confirmed a close relationship with the "Boss of Duval" and further supports the notion she felt confident that she had a significant level of influence with him. The fact that she relayed information to the Johnson campaigners concerning which South and East Texas counties could be purchased, has the same resonance. Even though that information may have been common knowledge among Texas politicians, her action amounted to a sanction of such unethical and illegal tactics, a sentiment she knowingly passed to the next generation of public servants.

Regardless of the actual impact her efforts had on the election, Miriam's attempt to help Johnson use fraudulent tactics speaks to her character, as does her motive. Driven by an acrimonious desire to punish Coke Stevenson for a perceived slight, she set aside her duty to promote the common good for the people of Texas when she attempted to steal from them the benefit of a fair election.

Miriam lived out her remaining years in the quiet of her Austin home with the physical support of a small staff and financial support from her older grandson. In August of 1952, after a four-month hospital stay, elder Ferguson daughter, Ouida, died of cirrhosis of the liver at the age of fifty-one, a shattering loss to her mother and sister.

The obscure aspects of Miriam's later years were briefly interrupted in 1955 when friends honored her with a lavish dinner banquet commemorating her eightieth birthday. Attended by Senator Lyndon B. Johnson and other dignitaries, the function marked the ex-governor's last notable public appearance. She died of heart failure in June of 1961 at the age of eighty-six and was buried beside Jim in the Texas State Cemetery in Austin. Dorrace Ferguson Watt was left to carry the Ferguson banner until her own death on March 18, 1991.

Fast Forward

In 1977, Dr. May Paulissen, co-author of the biography *Miriam, the Southern Belle Who Became the First Woman Governor of Texas*, had a remarkable stroke of luck. While visiting a friend in an Austin nursing home, she discovered to her amazement and delight that the ninety-one-year-old woman in the next room possessed a remarkable past. This lady, Mrs. Nola Wood, had been a secretary and clerk in the Texas governor's office for a period that encompassed the terms of four governors. More specifically, she had been in charge of drawing up criminal pardons under Mrs. Ferguson. [16]

Dr. Paulissen, having a passion for the details of the Fergusons' lives, sprang into action and secured a borrowed tape recorder and permission from Mrs. Wood to conduct an interview.

Although she had been called Nola all of her life, the woman's real name was Frances Lee Norah Wood, but she invited Dr. Paulissen to call her "Woody." Indeed, Woody had a story to tell, and in 1977 the magnitude of it may have been lost on many, but fortunately, was not lost on Dr. Paulissen. A long suspected and controversial accusation that the Fergusons had sold pardons had survived both Ferguson administrations and several minor investigations. Solving that mystery on that day was surely beyond the scope of Dr. Paulissen's expectations when she began her interview with the elderly Frances, aka Nola, aka "Woody."

It seems that the luck involved in the chance meeting of these two distinguished ladies that day was not entirely on the side of Dr. Paulissen. Nola had picked a most unlikely time and place to come clean about her troubling past. She finally felt safe to speak of secrets she had harbored for many years. She spoke of those years quite clearly, sometimes repeating herself, as if to emphasize a point.

She explained her relationship with the Fergusons saying, "I went through mental agony working for them. At nighttime I had an awful time going to sleep at night [*sic*]. Lord, forgive me for what I was a party to. Took me a long time after they were out to get over and sometimes I suffer now; tonight I will. Just talking about it . . ."

In that fateful interview, Nola told of much personal pain. She had borne five children with only two surviving, and her husband had left her for another woman when the children were young. These disappointments left her determined on two fronts. She vowed that she would maintain a good relationship with her ex-husband for the sake of her son Maurice and daughter Mary, and that she would earn a living for them. Her introduction into an office environment began when she took a job working for a lawyer in Belton, Texas. The lawyer was later elected to the state Legislature, and after moving to Austin he sent for Nola to join him there as his secretary. She never named the legislator or the year, but the move eventually led to her advancement in the form of a job in the governor's office.

Nola's characterization of Jim was complex and contradictory. She described him as both likable and mean, but also labeled him a "crook." She spoke of his frightful temper and propensity to use his fists when men angered him, and of his determination to place his friends in positions of influence. "When the governor went in, all his friends came with him," Nola told Dr. Paulissen, explaining that the applications for government jobs were altered to accommodate the applicant's qualifications. "He wanted his friends in there and some of his friends couldn't qualify by answering all of the questions," she explained.

The most interesting element of Nola's story related to the issue of pardons. She told of "fellows" coming in with great wads of cash under their hats, money concealed further by a newspaper wrapping. In the back room, the men spread the cash on a table, counted it, and settled on amounts. She processed the paperwork rapidly while the money was re-wrapped and put into a basket marked "personal" inside a fire-proof vault.

"I've seen money piled up on that desk, great piles of it ... I issued so many proc-lamations so fast and furious [*sic*] that I couldn't keep count of them," she confessed.

The elderly Nola told of the anger and resentment that Jim held toward those responsible for his impeachment. "If there had been any way in the world he could have gotten back at them, he would." While Nola's confession was sprinkled with references to her children and her need for her job, no excuse could account for the last detail of her confession. She told of being called before an investigating committee on two or three occasions, confessing that she had failed to convey the truth through lies of omission. As she put it, "they just did not ask the right questions," and she volunteered nothing. A second inquisition followed these appearances before fact-finding committees. Governor Miriam later drilled her about the committee's questions and, more importantly, her responses.

While her decision to withhold the truth from an investigating committee is inexcusable, it is no less profound. Her actions could well have reshaped the course of Texas history, resulting in a second impeachment and other indictments. For her crime of silence, she suffered punishments the extent of which we may never understand. Nola confided in Dr. Paulissen that she feared for her very soul.

There are surely those who would doubt the utterances of a ninety-one-year-old woman who waited forty-three years to break her silence. On the other hand, it seems that there could be no stronger motive than the cleansing of one's soul for revealing a belated truth.

Chapter 25
Not Your Average Ma and Pa

Nola Wood's serendipitous story emphasizes the dark shadow of influence that was cast by the Fergusons when, from positions of immense influence, they abused their authority, thereby establishing administrative climates where deception and fraud cascaded down the chain of command. In such an environment, integrity and conscience become disadvantages. If the governor's shadow describes the sphere of influence that surrounds the chief executive, the Fergusons' realms were dark ones that loosely encompassed two casts of characters: those who understood and endorsed the unseemliness, and those unfortunates who were simply caught in the crossfire. Within the Ferguson gubernatorial shadow, innocents like John Lomax and Edward Blackshear and unsuspecting players like H. C. Poe became collateral damage, the public protection expected from the penal system was sold, the judicial system was undermined, taxpayer money was squandered or stolen, cronyism flourished, and—perhaps—souls were compromised.

Now, with a larger collection of puzzle pieces, we may better understand how this unusual phenomenon called Fergusonism registered itself so thoroughly in Texas's political history and we can more accurately evaluate its impact. The best starting point might be to re-evaluate the couple's existing legacies and to challenge some information (or perhaps *misinformation*) that has long endured.

Governor James Ferguson has been given much credit, appropriately so, for the promotion and advancement of education, particularly rural education, which was the focus and recipient of new regulations under his watch. His administration gave life and substance to a compulsory attendance law, easier access to local funds for the use of textbooks, and a million-dollar allocation for rural school districts. Perhaps even more importantly, his administration established awareness for the critical need for educational appropriations, which likely influenced subsequent governors and legislators, many of whom also made education a legislative priority.

His second administration's most meritorious act was the establishment of a much-needed State Highway Commission, a fact largely overshadowed by the 1925 scandal that resulted from his oversight of the funds at its disposal. The James Ferguson administration's accomplishments came with the aid of a cooperative legislature, a benefit that not all governors experience. Even so, Governor Ferguson is certainly due credit.

But Ferguson's support for education was not collective. Though his espousal of a generous appropriation for the University of Texas may have given the initial impression that he was supportive of its goals, his immediate and severe demands for the allegiance of the school's staff and faculty casts suspicion on the true motive for his generosity. Some believed that Ferguson's animosity for the university grew out of his poor relationship with the institution, but the truth appears to be the exact opposite. The following statement from a newspaper article suggests that Ferguson's bias against the institution of higher education was apparent early: "The fact is that, consciously or unconsciously, Mr. Ferguson is under a prejudice against the whole cause of higher education. He betrays this prejudice in several places in his message. . ." There is nothing profound about this statement until you consider its date. Published on January 22, 1915: a mere four days after James Ferguson took office, the article refers to his first official message as governor. [1]

James Ferguson is probably best known as an advocate for farmers and the poor, but that theory certainly overstates the facts. His campaign promise of a remedy for the plight of the tenant farmer produced an ill-conceived tenant law, one that had little effect and was later found unconstitutional. The percentage of tenant farmers continued to increase and the plight of the rural poor did not improve under his watch. Other than his efforts at tick eradication, and his support for rural education, there is little of merit to hold up as an example of his help to farmers or the poor during his administration. His flagrant use of the spoils system offers ample evidence that his greatest interest in helping others was largely limited to those who were in positions to reciprocate. [2]

Any credit for compassion that might otherwise be associated with the plethora of pardons that both Fergusons granted is surpassed by the near certainty that financial gain and reduced prison expenses incented the pair in that regard. Although the Fergusons claimed that their plentiful sanctions to prisoners stemmed from compassion, that theory is suspect. They seldom passed the greater test of a forgiving nature: the granting of leniency to those who displeased them.

Excessive pardons were harmful on many levels. Every criminal pardon represented a blatant override of another's authority, a disrespect and disregard for the juries and judges who had carefully weighed evidence and made decisions in favor of incarceration. Considering that there were fewer than 4,000 people in Texas prisons in 1915, Jim's 2,253 pardons from 1915–1917 is nothing short of astounding. Mrs. Ferguson was even more liberal with her pardoning powers.

The impression that Jim Ferguson was a prudent, self-made businessman and a capable lawyer is erroneous in view of the incontestable evidence that contradicts these notions. Though he is still recognized by most writers as having been an accomplished businessman by virtue of his most ambitious business venture, the founding of the Temple State Bank, we now know the extent of mismanagement the institution suffered under his guidance. Using the institution as his personal piggy bank, Ferguson indulged himself and friends to a degree that crippled its ability to operate. In her writing, daughter Ouida certainly overstated the amount of ownership in and the success of her father's early business pursuits. There is no evidence that any of his undertakings were profitable with the possible exception of some of his livestock sales. Most of his undertakings were short-lived and distressed, often beginning with grandiose plans meant to attract capital, followed with little or no sound management.

There has been a general consensus that James Ferguson was successful until he entered public service where unfortunate circumstances, including the low governor's salary, altered his prosperous course. In reality, well in advance of his first campaign he was disguising his debts from other bank stakeholders by listing them in the names of other parties. As early as 1913, and again in 1914, he claimed to have had "not one cent" in cash. Among his poor choices was a decision to reduce the bank's capital with a 50 percent distribution of paid-in-capital and the payment of annual dividends, resource reductions that the young undercapitalized institution could ill afford. This Ferguson did because, even with the infusion of assets from his wife's substantial inheritance and a bounty of other business interests, Jim Ferguson was in desperate need of cash. His refusal to write off the bank's bad debts, and his need to tap state monies for deposits soon after he took office, suggest that his bank's books were in serious need of buttressing well before he handed them off to H. C. Poe. Charles Maedgen's 1916 public challenges to Ferguson also offer evidence that he and another vice president at the Temple State Bank had witnessed Ferguson's abuses of bank resources at least two years before Poe's arrival.

Ferguson is often credited with having overcome the ill effects of a limited education but that point is largely moot. A compulsive nature precluded his making decisions to proceed with caution when entering new business ventures. His daring and overconfidence compelled him to take on challenges that were often disproportionate with his ability and his deficient character and poor judgment, rather than his limited education, doomed those undertakings. His decision to leave school is simply an early example of a bullishness that never lessened. He used little or no discernment when it came to making sound decisions but his audaciousness made him averse to taking advice from others. However, he and his family forever blamed his enemies, the state (for his low salary) and the legislators who impeached him for his failures and the family's interminable financial troubles.

A look at the Fergusons' 1915 federal tax return and the accompanying worksheet points succinctly to debt at high rates of interest as the main source of his financial problem. That year the Fergusons' gross income was an impressive $80,024.50, over half of which came from the sale of livestock. But interest payments of a staggering $18,250 crippled the family purse. Even though this amount of interest is painfully disproportionate to the amount of income it generated, it represents only the interest actually paid, not accrued. We know from Poe's testimony that Jim Ferguson was not paying many of his debts in 1915, so the actual amount of interest he accumulated was probably much higher. These numbers were taken from 1915 records; Jim Ferguson continued thereafter to buy land with money borrowed at high rates of interest even though his debt level (including his sizable overdrafts), was dangerously high. Much of that mortgaged land sat idle. [3]

By the end of 1917 Jim Ferguson had amassed debts in the form of personal notes totaling $434,042. That debt was comprised of thirty-five notes payable as follows: six notes payable to insurance companies, fifteen notes payable to individuals, nine notes payable to banks and mortgage companies, three notes payable to banks where he was a stockholder, and three notes payable to Texas brewers. The total did not include accrued interest, property taxes, or liabilities of the Bell-Bosque stock farm. Jim Ferguson was drowning in the debt that he had spent many years accumulating. [4]

By his own admission Jim Ferguson was not a particularly capable attorney. During testimony, he professed an aversion to the practice of law as a profession and a decidedly limited (his word, *elementary*) understanding of its principles.

The Fergusons were well aware of the meager $4,000 annual salary that Texas governors received and also keenly aware of their inability to survive on that level of income when they begged to reclaim the job in 1924. Ouida confessed that her parents stayed at her home until they could occupy the Governor's Mansion because they could not afford a hotel. These facts coupled with the pair's immediate launch of several money-making schemes after Mrs. Ferguson's second election, suggest that a plan for exploiting the power and prestige of the office in pursuit of financial infusions was an integral part of the Fergusons' strategy in seeking office.

The couple, primarily Mrs. Ferguson, has long been given significant credit for the fall of the Ku Klux Klan, but closer examination of the facts also renders that assessment an exaggeration. In fact, the Fergusons may have inadvertently helped the Klan. When Jim tried to take a Senate seat in 1922, the Klan was the topic de jour just as the liquor and tenant issues had been in 1914. These polarizing subjects were vote catchers; attaching himself to them gave Jim an immediate base of support and a source of cash from which to build his candidacy. Certainly Jim knew that as an impeached governor, he was damaged goods and, therefore, not a strong contender. But because his real agenda was re-emergence, he refused to make a realistic assessment of the race. If he had been a thoughtful champion of the anti-Klan cause, his best contribution to the Senatorial election of 1922 would have been to have stayed out of it. Absent Ferguson's insidious attacks on Charles Culberson's health, the senator might well have retained his seat. This would have been no loss to Ferguson's pet issues since Culberson also held anti-prohibition and anti-Klan sentiments. There is no question that Mayfield's win in that race was a significant coup for the Klan and it is widely believed that many prohibitionists voted for Mayfield, not because they had Klan sympathies, but because they detested Ferguson. Culberson or another anti-Klan candidate might very well have produced a different result and hastened the reversal of escalating Klan influence.[5]

Again, in the gubernatorial race of 1924, Miriam's presence took votes from other capable candidates. Certainly Miriam's anti-Klan sentiment was genuine, but she was hardly a protagonist for any cause. Her true agenda was not the annihilation of the Klan but the annihilation of her husband's disqualification penalty. A number of capable anti-Klan men were eliminated in her favor, any one of whom would almost certainly have been the victor in her absence. Klan power, which was already disseminating well before her election, would certainly have continued on that path under another's similarly positioned leadership.

This brings to mind a critical element of the story, one that cannot be overemphasized. We must indict, to a large degree, Texas voters of the day who repeatedly gifted the Fergusons with the public trust when each succeeding circumstance was less explicable than the last. With every trust betrayed, Texas voters remained faithful in sufficient numbers to keep a Ferguson presence in Austin often. We can only speculate about the reason. Certainly rural voters trusted Jim; he spoke to them through the *Ferguson Forum* and sometimes it was the only "news" they accessed. Is it reasonable to attribute the popularity of the Fergusons to the growing pains of the state as it transitioned from rural to urban? Or do the subsequent successes of Lee O'Daniel and the positive response voters had to other campaigns with carnival-inspired antics offer another glimpse into the minds of voters? Were they simply indulging themselves in the entertainment value of politics? [6]

The Ferguson story teems with irony. In many ways Jim Ferguson's early fortuitous political success burdened the green politician with responsibility for which he was ill-equipped. Some of his early mistakes could certainly be attributed to this inexperience, but his repeated failures to learn from those missteps sent his career into a downward spiral. He seemed incapable of setting boundaries on any aspect of his life including his emotions or the use of the power he amassed. This power evaporated under the weight of his nefarious actions, taking with it any advantages he had gained for his core political interests. The suffragist and prohibitionist forces galvanized against him when he was most vulnerable, but it was a self-inflicted vulnerability caused by his refusal to soften his autocratic style and to rein in his explosive temper. Without question, it was Ferguson's departure in disgrace that gave clearance for suffrage and prohibition endorsement under the Hobby administration.

The pivotal election of 1924 that paired husband and wife brought hope for a balancing effect that was not to be. Mrs. Ferguson, who was a quick-study under the tutelage of her ethically challenged spouse, continued to abuse every gift. She was an active player in the political maneuvering that employed deceit, power, intimidation, and the heavy use of reward and punishment to accomplish Ferguson goals. Her attempts to disrupt Dan Moody's efforts to cancel usurious highway contracts and her pardoning of Murray Jackson are but two examples of actions she took as governor that were wholly contrary to the public's benefit.

The enfranchisement of women, which Jim Ferguson so adamantly opposed for the greater part of his political career, rescued the disgraced governor from obscurity when it helped to clear a path for Miriam to seek and secure the office on his behalf. Yet Miriam only damaged the women's cause; this she did indirectly as a result of the poor example she set as governor. Miriam's decision to give her husband the gift of a governorship, then turn a blind eye to his conduct, was at the expense of all other Texans, but particularly those females who were eager to gain acceptance in positions that had been traditionally held by men. Her greatest failing may have been to her own daughters whose names she had evoked in a plea for a second chance to prove the Ferguson name honorable.

The essence of the Ferguson story is one of opportunity lost. At the pinnacle of Jim's popularity with the public, the Democratic Party, and the Texas legislature, the blossoming young governor held immense promise. But his great potential went unfulfilled when his character deficiencies dominated his reasoning and impaired his ability to make altruistic decisions. Miriam's misused opportunity to bring a semblance of honor back to the family name was also unfortunate but more egregious was her betrayal of the public trust in view of her keen awareness of potential problems and her promises to avert them. Jim's insatiable desire to feel relevant, to be heard, to dominate those around him and punish his detractors, and Miriam's limitless need to appease her husband's every whim, led them to actions that were entirely self-serving.

James Ferguson's blunders demonstrated both his shrewdness and his immaturity. He was clever and bold enough to stack boards with those who would do his bidding, allowing him to circumvent a system that otherwise did not allow him to remove capable people in the middle of their terms, but he was equally flippant about those unprincipled tactics. His failure to take inventory of his political skeletons before he embarked on a prolonged battle with the University of Texas and its powerful allies was a critical error. In that conflict that amounted to a test of wills, Jim Ferguson gambled and lost everything. In his descent, he took with him the things he loved most in life: his family and the political issues that had once empowered him. Only his ego remained unscathed, this demonstrated by his outrageous bid for the office of president of the United States. Never again elected to any office after the 1917 impeachment that ended his governorship, Jim Ferguson's influence and authority thereafter were either borrowed or stolen from others, yet he abused even this arrogated power until age and illness rendered him incapable.

Some might characterize the Fergusons' inappropriate behavior as "politics as usual." He certainly did not commit his unscrupulous acts alone nor were his dissenters without fault. However, a blanket judgment of all public servants precludes a proper acknowledgement due the men who acted to hold Ferguson accountable. Absent the balancing effect of a viable two-party system in Texas, these mostly conscientious and courageous men collectively undertook with vigilance the painful task of impeaching a member of their own party and—in many cases—their friend. After granting Jim Ferguson every concession, a fact that was evident by the abbreviated depth of the first investigation, they were subsequently compelled to expel him under the weight of the indisputable evidence of his wrongdoing. Even with that drastic measure taken, Ferguson critics found it necessary to work continuously to hold Ferguson's power in check after his wife reclaimed the governorship on his behalf.

For those men who may well have had an election stolen from them, we re-victimize them if we fail to concede that crimes of election fraud almost certainly went unacknowledged and unprosecuted, some abetted by the Fergusons.

Without question, Dorrace Ferguson was the family member whose life was least entrenched in politics. Like her mother, she craved a level of privacy that generally eludes the families of high-ranking politicians. Even so, she carried the banner for dignity in memory of her family when she felt the occasion required it. In 1975 Dorrace, the remaining member of the immediate Ferguson family, responded to an author's letter of inquiry about her parents with these cautionary words:

> I wish to call your attention to the fact that "Ma" and "Pa" are not proper names. These names originated during the 1924 campaign by news reporters and were used only for campaign purposes. My mother and father were never called Ma and Pa by any of the family, and they were called "Governor Miriam" and "Governor Jim" by their friends, co-workers, servants, etc. I do not think that your excessive use of an improper name will lend dignity or respect to the article which you are preparing about my mother. [7]

Dorrace Ferguson's plea on behalf of her parents is commendable. However, in defense of Bryant Messer, the writer whom she rebuffed for calling the Fergusons by their campaign-inspired nicknames, we should remember that "Governor Miriam" and "Governor Jim" were the reputed people's people. They were forever friends to the common man such as Mr. Messer, or so they professed. There certainly was a time when the Ferguson family heartily embraced those monikers and the voter appeal they propagated. Any criticism from the Ferguson family directed at people who did not interpret the boundaries of that campaign device in a way that corresponded with their own, is unfortunate.

The Fergusons were lucky that they held office at a time when no reporter or writer dared ask the tough questions. Imagine the interrogation an investigative reporter of this century might have imposed upon Dorrace Ferguson Watt if she had agreed to an interview about her parents' gubernatorial terms. Shielded by the custom of the day, the ex-governors and their immediate family were never called to answer key questions, a fact that helped them re-write history. Just as Jim had done in 1914 when he altered the story about his travels west, omitting the fact that he left his mother to wonder about his fate, so too did the Fergusons craft a sanitized version of their lives for the public record—a version of life so squeaky clean that they perceived an overuse of nicknames as a threat to the degree of respect they believed was due them. This may at first seem a trivial point, but it highlights a larger and more critical truth. It demonstrates how distorted the Fergusons' view of reality became. It reveals how completely they compartmentalized and minimized their acts of malfeasance, and how they fully expected the public to do likewise.

A final irony deserves mention.

One hundred years have elapsed since Jim Ferguson entered Texas politics and time has eroded familiarity with the Ferguson name. Most inquiries made to Texans about ex-Governors James and Miriam Ferguson bring a blank stare until the names "Ma" and "Pa," are added. These appellations have endeared the duo in the minds of the public. The Fergusons' individual and collective failure to put duty above self has, to a large degree, been overshadowed *by those enduring nicknames*. These tags have become an indelible part of the Ferguson legacy and still have the ability to conjure up, in the minds of many, pleasant pictures of home-spun, innocuous, down-home folks like Ma and Pa Kettle.

If these campaign-inspired names keep the Ferguson personas alive in the memory of Texans, and if this kind of whimsy distracts from the unpleasantness of their misconduct and Jim's removal from office, it is a cinch that Governor Miriam and Governor Jim would approve. Given the choice between obscurity and being tagged "Ma" and "Pa," certainly Jim Ferguson would feel that there could be no fate worse than being forgotten or considered irrelevant, and Miriam, without question, would echo his sentiment.

The final comment belongs to the gifted writer Roy Bedichek who, in an open letter to Governor Jim Ferguson in 1917, made this profound statement about the office of governor: "The mantle of high office may sit gracefully upon the shoulders of one, giving him an added dignity and increasing the respect in which he is held by his fellows. Upon another, the same mantle may dwarf and render contemptible the object which it clothes. . ." [8]

Perhaps the greatest honor we can bestow upon the many who give their best in public service is to hold accountable those who do not.

Notes

Abbreviations:

Investigation Transcripts = Transcripts from *Proceedings, Investigation Committee, House of Representatives, Thirty-fifth Legislature, Charges against Governor James E. Ferguson together with Findings of Committee and Action of House, with Prefatory Statement and Index to Proceedings.*

Impeachment Transcripts = *Record of Proceedings of the High Court of Impeachment on the Trial of Hon. James E. Ferguson, Governor.*

Introduction

1. *Dallas Morning News*, August 20, 1930.

2. One example of dishonesty in Nalle's writing can be found in her description of the report on the initial investigation of her father's questionable acts. Nalle wrote, "Nothing had been found to be irregular." The investigating committee's comprehensive report stated unequivocally that James Ferguson had misapplied certain state funds, which they ordered him to repay. Further, the committee reported that his actions, as they related to his bank, were "Deserving of the severest criticism and condemnation." Ouida Ferguson Nalle, *The Fergusons of Texas, Two Governors for the Price of One*, 122; *Investigation Transcripts*, 390.

Prologue

1. *El Paso Herald*, August 11, 1914.

2. Norman D. Brown, *Hood, Bonnet and Little Brown Jug*, Introduction, 4. Brown characterized the choices facing voters in this way: "For anti-Klan, anti-Ferguson Democrats the election represented the evil of two lessors, but a majority chose the old gray bonnet." *The Houston Post* printed this opinion: "Many will vote for Ma Ferguson, but no one, not even the editor of the Chronicle, will vote for her because he thinks she is more capable than Dr. Butte."

3. Roy Bedichek to Robert Marquis, October 29, 1924, "While it does not stand to reason that Butte can be elected, still I believe he is going to get a vote which will scare the Fergusons into a fit. I shall certainly violate whatever pledge participation in the primary may have imposed upon me, and vote for Butte." Bedichek, a writer, folklorist, and newspaper editor, was at odds with Jim Ferguson over the UT controversy but reviled the Klan so much that he voted for Miriam in the primaries. He would vote for Dr. Butte, the Republican candidate, in the general election. William A. Owens and Lyman Grant, editors, *Letters of Roy Bedichek*, 106.

Chapter 1

1. George W. Tyler, *History of Bell County*, Information about Tyler, vii–ix, Gifts of Nature, xii–xiii, Trouble with Indians, 56–75; Bertha Atkinson, "History of Bell County" (Note: There are two sources, one book and one thesis, with the same title, *History of Bell County*, by different authors). Atkinson wrote that the cost of some Bell County land was a low as twenty-five cents per acre, and as late as 1880, some land still sold for as little as $1.50 per acre. See Atkinson, 84.

2. Tyler. The book names Reverend Ferguson and Joseph Wallace as early pioneers of the county on pages 86, 160, 269, 288, and 297.

3. Quotation about Belton, A. Bryant Messer, *The Prairie Queen and Her Choo Choo Train (It's about Temple, Texas, and Then Some)*, 99.

4. Tyler, 350–351.

5. Tyler, 359. Tyler said this about Salado's growth: "The village of Salado had now grown from one family in 1859 to some one hundred and fifty families, within a radius of three miles from the College. . ." within a period of about ten years. See also Atkinson. The author said this of the citizens of early Salado: "The Saladon-ions were, to a great extent, a cultured people of high moral character. The cul-ture was largely due to the influence that the school had there," 80. This book also made mention of the importance of the early mills: "If a settlement contained a mill, it was sure to thrive," 20.

6. Atkinson, 65 and 66. Gra'Delle Duncan, Bell County Historical Commission Newsletter, "Dirty Politics Nothing New in Texas," Winter, 1992.

7. Quotation regarding Civil War, Tyler, 201. Atkinson's thesis puts the exact number of Bell County enlistees at 1037. See page 85.

8. Nalle, 3. Confirmed through census records. Tyler, 297, confirms Ferguson's pur-chase of the mill in 1867.

9. Names and ages of Eliza's daughters, listed as stepchildren in the Wallace home found in the 1870 census records. Michael W. Kelsey and Nancy Graff Kelsey, local authors and historians, visited Wesley Ferguson's isolated grave in Decem-ber of 2008. The occupant of the nearby home, Mrs. Jones, told the couple that Ferguson's descendants had confirmed that he was buried away from other family members because of his Union sympathies.

10. Atkinson, 74.

11. Possessions confiscated, Tyler, 248–250.

12. Charles C. Alexander, *The Ku Klux Klan in the Southwest*, preface, 1.

13. Messer, 167–168. Messer's statement regarding Reverend Ferguson and the Klan: "One day in 1869 he [Reverend Ferguson] went atop of his water-powered grist mill with his neighbors. Here he organized Central Texas' first Ku Klux Klan." The notion that the elder Ferguson may have started or even joined the early Klan is not particularly significant. It is, however, interesting considering his son's destiny that would be largely impacted by the reemergence of the Klan in Texas about 1920.

14. Tyler, 263.

15. Ibid., 265.

242

Notes

16. Nalle, 9; Atkinson, 51; *Dallas Morning News*, "Letter of Ferguson's Father, Circuit Rider, Gives Glimpse of Early Texas Experiences," October 5, 1924; *The Houston Daily Union*, "Death of Rev. J. E. Ferguson," Feb. 2, 1871; "Wife, Children and Friends," March 13, 1871.

17. *The Houston Daily Union*, "Wife, Children and Friends," March 13, 1871.

18. Nalle, 9; E. F. C. Robertson diary, University of Texas at Arlington.

19. Probate Records, Bell County Clerk's Office, Belton, Texas.

20. *Dallas Morning News*, "Wild Bill Throws James E. Ferguson," May 3, 1914. Details about Sam Sparks and James Ferguson's political differences are explained in chapter 3 of this work. Jim's elementary school teacher J. G. Fouts taught the young man at Live Oak Chapel School. Mr. Fouts proclaimed that young Jim "scrapped a lot," but added that the youngster did not lie about it and didn't play hooky often. *Dallas Morning News*, June 25, 1916; Messer, 163. The author states that Jim wrestled with Negro boys.

21. Stats on school attendance in 1900, *The Belton Journal*, July 15, 1900.

22. An historical marker in front of the Anderson home in Salado tells of Jim Ferguson's lodging there while he attended Salado College. The story of Jim's expulsion was taken from his daughter Ouida Ferguson Nalle's book. Details of the story could not be verified. See Nalle, 12–13. Ferguson himself would later describe his education as a sixth grade equivalent. See *Impeachment Transcripts*, 742.

23. Jim's trip west is described in Nalle, 15–16. In testimony at his impeachment trial, Jim also described his trip and the many odd jobs that he undertook beginning with picking cotton in Collin County, Texas. At that time, he made no mention of whether or not his family knew of his whereabouts. *Impeachment Transcripts*, 492.

24. Handwritten copy of original Blum speech, James E. Ferguson File, The Dolph Briscoe Center for American History, The University of Texas at Austin, Box 3P46.

25. In a March 1916 visit to Colorado when Jim Ferguson was governor of Texas, he told Colorado's governor, George Carlson, that he had once lived and worked in Colorado as a young man. The newspaper article explained that Ferguson had worked at the Windsor Hotel in 1888 and at the Arcade restaurant as a waiter where he received a tip of $10 from prizefighter Jack Dempsey. (Jack Dempsey was born in Colorado but not until 1895.) *Fort Worth Star Telegram*, March 8, 1916.

26. Ferguson described his legal training in this way: "I got some knowledge of the elementary principles of law as best I could from my own reading." See *Impeachment Transcripts*, 492. During Ferguson's 1914 campaign, John Robinson, by then a District Judge, told of sharing legal notes and briefs with Jim Ferguson. *Cleburne Morning Review*, July 5, 1914; *Dallas Morning News*, March 21, 1914.

27. Blum speech, James E. Ferguson file, The Dolph Briscoe Center for American History, The University of Texas at Austin, Box 3P46. The account of Ferguson's

question-free exam was taken from Nalle, 19 and 20. The story could not be otherwise substantiated. An expert on legal history in Texas, Michael Ariens, wrote: "Admission to the bar throughout the nineteenth century was extraordinarily easy, sometimes in spite of the official rules." He confirms that an oral exam by other attorneys was the early method used to test bar applicants. Michael Ariens, *Lone Star Law, A Legal History of Texas*, 182.

28.   Nalle, 20.

29.   A former neighbor of the Wallace family told of her childhood trips to the Wallace farm for water. *Temple Daily Telegram*, May 18, 1930; Bell County Museum, Belton, Texas.

30.   *Temple Daily Telegram*, February 10, 1899; (Obituary) Mike and Nancy Kelsey's private collection. Author's note: Ferguson daughter, Ouida Ferguson Nalle put the date of Joseph Wallace's death at January 1898 and states that the cause of death was meningitis. Nalle, 37 and 38.

31.   Nalle also stated on page 38: "It was to her husband's nephew, Jim Ferguson that Eliza Wallace turned for legal advice." In reality Jim was her FIRST husband's nephew.

32.   Bell County Probate Records, Bell County Clerk's Office, Belton Texas, Volume M, page 353. The records include the wording from Joseph Wallace's will.

33.   Ouida Ferguson Nalle stated that Jim's first proposals of marriage to Miriam were rebuffed. Nalle, 39.

34.   Susan Wallace's College records are in the name of "John" Wallace. Information courtesy of University of Mary Hardin-Baylor, Belton, Texas. List of early Bell County marriages, compiled by Rick Miller, Bell County Museum, Belton, Texas.

35.   Date and cost of Belton lot, Deed Records, Bell County Clerk's Office, Belton Texas.

Chapter 2

1.   *Fort Worth Morning Register*, May 12, 1901. *Dallas Morning News*, January 4, 1902, January 28, 1904, and February 19, 1902. Nalle, 48. In her book, Nalle referred to the opera house as "His opera house" and the lending business as, "His loan and trust company," with no mention of other owners. See note 3 below for more information. When the trust company was later accused of charging usurious rates, Jim Ferguson diminished his role and defended himself saying, "If there was any crime about that, I want it to be remembered that I was only the secretary-treasurer of the company." "Ferguson Denies Charge of Usury," *Fort Worth Star Telegram*, May 26, 1914.

2.   *Fort Worth Star Telegram*, February 19, 1905; *Dallas Morning News*, February 19, 1905; *San Antonio Express*, February 20, 1905; Nalle, 46.

Notes

3. Nalle, 46. A newspaper account reported the purchase of the Belton opera house by five individuals including Ferguson (Campbell, Peyton, Ray, and Pendleton). At the time the men purchased it, the troubled business had defaulted on mortgage bonds, forcing the sale. *San Antonio Express*, March 11, 1903; *Dallas Morning News*, September 16, 1903; Kristin Henn, Thesis, "The Opera House of Belton Texas," 50–51; Lena Armstrong Public Library, Belton, Texas.

4. "Ferguson Denies Charge of Usury," *Fort Worth Star Telegram*, May 26, 1914.

5. *Dallas Morning News*, September 26, 1905; *Fort Worth Star Telegram*, September 19, 1906.

6. Messer, 113 and 256; *Fort Worth Star Telegram*, "Temple Is Growing," January 1, 1907; Temple and Belton 1900 population stats, Tyler, 340.

7. Robert A. Ozment, *Temple National Bank, A History*; *Dallas Morning News*, "Temple State Bank, Finally Chartered and to Open for Business May 1," April 9, 1906. The reason for the caveat, "finally," we do not know. Ferguson's 1915 percentage of ownership taken from *Impeachment Transcripts*, 756.

8. Nalle, 50. Bell County recorded a transfer of deed from James and M. A. Stanton to James and Miriam Ferguson on March 22, 1907, at a cost of $4,250 (a very high price in 1907). See Book #175, page 617, Bell County District Clerk's Office, Belton, Texas. Another source who wrote about life in early Temple stated that Jim Ferguson bought Jim Stanton's house and then built a mansion on the site. Ferguson apparently moved or destroyed the existing house. The existence of maid's quarters to the rear of the mansion suggests that the Stanton house may have been moved to the back of the lot and used for that purpose. Messer, 164.

9. Number of acres conveyed to the Wallace offspring, Deed Records, vol. 158, pages 384–385 and vol. 180, pages 495–496, found in Bell County District Clerk's office, Belton, Texas. The exact amount of cash and/or securities that Miriam inherited is not known. In a 1916 personal financial statement Jim supplied to a bank where he was attempting to secure a loan, he listed the family assets, which included Miriam's inherited property. At the bottom of the page, almost as a footnote, he added to the family's net worth an amount of $75,000, which he labeled "net worth, wife." Clues also abound in daughter Ouida Ferguson Nalle's writing suggesting that Miriam received a fair amount of cash or other assets as part of her inheritance. In her writing, Ouida relayed a story about Jim's family's belief that Miriam's spending habits were excessive. In defense of her mother, Ouida responded: "It was her money she was spending and not Jim's." This quotation leaves us to surmise that Miriam's inheritance included enough cash to render her comfortable in spending it freely; see Nalle, 48. Ouida made another reference to her mother's money saying, "Mama paid for her social secretary out of her own pocket and Daddy's," Nalle, 107. Actually, records in evidence at the investigation of Jim Ferguson showed that Miriam's social secretary was also paid by the State of Texas. At the initial investigation, Jim Ferguson said that his wife's inherited land was 717 acres. *Investigation Transcripts*, 279.

10. Ferguson's quotation is from his first political speech in Blum, Texas. James E. Ferguson file, The Dolph Briscoe Center for American History, The University of Texas at Austin, Box 3P46. Ferguson friend Alexander Dienst described Jim's relationship with the church in this way: "He is only a brother-in-law to the church, his wife being a member," Temple Daily Telegram, July 6, 1914. Found in James E. Ferguson file, The Dolph Briscoe Center for American History, The University of Texas at Austin, Box 3P45. Former Ferguson law partner, John D. Robinson endorsed Jim in 1914, saying that while Ferguson was "A member of no church," he was "in sympathy, a Methodist." The Cleburne Morning Review, July 5, 1914. Miriam's social involvement in Temple described in Nalle, 55.

11. Ouida Ferguson Nalle's quotation, Nalle, 51. In an interview with Ferguson grandson James Watt in or about 1995, Mr. Watt told his interviewer, Dr. May Paulissen, that his mother Dorrace and his aunt, Ouida, "did not get along." Notes from Dr. Paulissen's private collection.

12. Nalle, 50, 54–59. Story of Jim Ferguson's brother Alex's home came from an interview with Temple resident Charles Harrell. Mr. Harrell lived near the Alex Ferguson home when he was a child and was in that home on many occasions. The home has since been torn down.

13. *Dallas Morning News*, September 1, 1909. *Temple Daily Telegram*, April 4, 2011. Marian Cones, of Houston, spoke to the newspaper about the Brass Rail, an establishment that was owned by her great-grandfather, and of Jim Ferguson's unpaid tab. "He ran up a tab that he never paid. When my grandfather died in 1917, it amounted to quite a bit of money."

14. Nalle, 54. Laura Simmons, whose grandfather worked for Jim Ferguson on his Bosque ranch in 1915 and 1916, said that Ferguson paid better than most men, $32.00 per month plus house, water, wood, and all the cow milk one wanted. "He gave us pigs to grow our meat, and feed to raise the pigs." Laura Simmons, *Out of Our Past, Texas History Stories*, 78.

15. *Temple Daily Telegram*, March 7 and 8, 1911.

16. *Temple Mirror*, December 17, 1911, copy in Michael and Nancy Kelsey's private collection.

17. Ibid.; *Temple Daily Telegram*, July 1915.

18. Michael Kelsey and Nancy Kelsey, *Images of America, Temple*. The professional offices of many prominent doctors and surgeons occupied the space in the upper floor of the new bank building, 26 and 40. *Dallas Morning News*, April 27, 1912. The building that originally housed the Temple State Bank belonged to A. J. Jarrell; see Robert A. Ozment, *Interfirst Bank Temple, 1910–1985, A History*, 3; *Dallas Morning News*, April 27, 1912.

19. *Dallas Morning News*, December 11, 1912; *Cleburne Morning Review*, November 24, 1912.

20.   Number of acres of land, *Investigative Transcripts*, 246.

21.   The 1915 Temple phone directory listed the Temple Electric Co. with this brief description, "Electricians, Electrical Supplies, Construction and Repairing." It identified James E. Ferguson as Vice President. See *Dallas Morning News*, March 13, 1909, August 29, 1909, May 10, 1910, May 28, 1912 and June 27, 1912.

22.   Information about Alexander Dienst, The Handbook of Texas Online, http://www.tshaonline.org/handboo/online/articles/fdi1

        Quotations regarding Dienst, Messer, 151.

23.   *Temple Daily Telegram*, July 6, 1914; James Ferguson file, The Dolph Briscoe Center for American History, The University of Texas at Austin.

24.   Messer, 261. Jim Ferguson knew two men with the name Frank Denison who were father and son. Frank L. Denison was Ferguson's neighbor and friend in Temple while Frank W. Denison, the son of Frank L., was a Ferguson business partner who lived in Bastrop, Texas. Ferguson and Frank W. Denison partnered in purchasing the Bastrop Lignite Coal Company, a partnership that was not prosperous, at least not during the time that Jim was involved in it. A balance sheet for the company dated only 1916 (month not given, assume December 31), is reproduced in *Investigation Transcripts*, page 248.

Chapter 3

1.   *Dallas Morning News*, February 20, 1912.

2.   Ibid., April 18, 1912, July 4, 1912, and September 1, 1909; Lewis L. Gould, *Progressives and Prohibitionists: Texas Democrats in the Wilson Era*, 130–131; Seth McKay and Odie B. Faulk, *Texas after Spindletop, The Saga of Texas: 1901–1965*, 42–42.

3.   *Fort Worth Star Telegram*, December 4, 1910.

4.   *Texas Pythian Banner-Knight*, April 1915, The Dolph Briscoe Center for American History, The University of Texas at Austin; *Austin American*, 1917, "Who's Who in Texas and Why," The Dolph Briscoe Center for American History, The University of Texas at Austin; *Dallas Morning News*, March 24, 1912.

5.   Wilbourn E. Benton, *Texas, Its Government and Politics*, 4. Sam Houston won the election in 1859 with the support of the Know-nothing party and insurgent Democrats. The pattern of Democratic dominance in Texas continued until 1978 when William Clements was elected governor. O. Henry's quotation in George Fuermann, *Reluctant Empire*, 57.

6.   Gould, 6 and 7; Randolph B. Campbell, *Gone to Texas*, 338.

7.   Kenneth E. Hendrickson Jr., *The Chief Executives of Texas*, 156.

8. 51.7 percent of Texas farmers were tenants in 1910. See Robert Calvert, Arnoldo DeLeon, Gregg Cantrell, *The History of Texas*, 254 and 255.

9. Ibid., 260; *Dallas Morning News*, January 22, 1915.

10. Clarence R. Wharton, *History of Texas*, 446 and 447.

11. Seth McKay, *Texas Politics 1906–1944*. McKay says that voters were almost equally divided on the alcohol issue at the time (1911–1914) that Colquitt ran for office immediately prior to Ferguson, 24.

12. Gould, 122–125; *Dallas Morning News*, March 20, 1914; McKay, *Texas Politics, 1906–1944*, 55.

13. Ibid.

14. Nalle, 69. Ouida Ferguson Nalle, speaking of her father's first speech said: "Daddy now spent many days and winter evenings writing his platform and his opening speech. When he finished the platform, he read it aloud to us, and although I remember that it was entirely over my head, we were all as proud as a new grandmother." The tablet containing the original copy of Ferguson's Blum speech is in the James E. Ferguson Papers, The Dolph Briscoe Center for American History, The University of Texas at Austin, Box 3P46.

15. Gould, 131; *Dallas Morning News*, March 21, 1914; Nalle, 64 and 65.

16. Nalle, 65. Ouida Ferguson Nalle's version of this story is interesting. She claimed that she was surprised to have read the story in the newspaper because the notion of her parents taking a trip overseas was ridiculous. It seems not to have occurred to her that her father might have concocted the story for political reasons. *Dallas Morning News*, March 21, 1914.

17. Benton, 69. Ferguson later submitted an itemized list of campaign expenses totaling $31,424.63. The newspaper article that printed this information was unnamed and undated. Found in James E. Ferguson file, The Dolph Briscoe Center for American History, The University of Texas at Austin, Box 3P46.

18. *Fort Worth Star Telegram*, April 26, 1914; *Cleburne Morning Review*, July 5, 1914.

19. Gould, 136. An interesting note on the topic of liquor in the 1914 campaign was furnished by David Ball Jr., the grandson of Thomas Ball, many years later. According to David Ball, Jim Ferguson sent Thomas Ball a bottle of bourbon as a Christmas gift, an insinuation that Ball drank privately while publicly disclaiming the use of alcohol. The elder Ball smashed the bottle in disgust. See *Houston Chronicle*, April 8, 1996.

20. Hendrickson, 148–151.

21. Marjorie Spruill Wheeler, ed., *One Woman, One Vote*; Judith N. McArthur, "Minnie Fisher Cunningham's Back Door Lobby in Texas: Political Maneuvering in a One-Party State," 320; Gould, 137; McKay, *Texas Politics 1906–1944*, 59.

22. *Dallas Morning News*, July 3, 1914.

23. *Cleburne Morning Review*, July 5, 1914.

24. *Temple Daily Telegram*, July 6, 1914, James E. Ferguson file, The Dolph Briscoe Center for American History, The University of Texas at Austin. Shettles' accusations, Shettles to Dienst, July 18, 1914, Texas State Library and Archives, Austin (accessed online). https://www.tsl.state.tx.us/exhibits/suffrage/comesofage/shettles-1.html

25. *The Huntsville Item*, ca. June, 20, 1914, found in The Dolph Briscoe Center for American History, The University of Texas at Austin, Texas, Box 2D58.

26. *The Fort Worth Star-Telegram*, July 31, 1914.

27. McKay, *Texas Politics 1906–1944*, 57 and 58.

28. *Cleburne Morning Review*, August 14, 1914.

29. *Dallas Morning News*, December 2, 1914.

Chapter 4

1. Poe was an interesting choice to succeed Ferguson as bank president. His youth prompted one newspaper to announce him with the headline, "Ferguson's Banker Successor is Baby Money President." See *Fort Worth Star-Telegram*, January 4, 1915. Though technically Poe had to be elected to the position of bank president, with Ferguson being the bank's founder and majority stockholder, his choice was likely not questioned. Poe was elected on or about January 11, 1914. See *Investigation Transcripts*, 98. Ferguson testified that Poe had come to Temple at his (Ferguson's) request and that their agreement contained elements that were been both verbal and written. *Investigation Transcripts*, 212.

2. Poe's credentials taken from his testimony under oath, *Investigation Transcripts*, 80. *Texas Pythian Banner-Knight*, April, 1915, copy found in The Dolph Briscoe Center for American History, The University of Texas at Austin.

3. *The Bartlett Tribune*, January 1, 1915. This article contains details of the agreement between Poe and Ferguson including the lease of the Ferguson house. The article states that Poe purchased 150 shares of stock and leased the Ferguson house for "a term of years understood to be four." Ferguson testified in 1917 that he believed that Poe had purchased only 50 shares. See *Investigation Transcripts*, 212. Poe's 1917 draft registration and a 1917 Temple city directory list his address to be that of the Ferguson mansion on North 7th Street in Temple. See City Directory at Temple Public Library, Temple, TX.

4. A newspaper article (*Fort Worth Star Telegram*, December 16, 1914), reported the reduction in capital at the Temple State Bank. The testimonies of both Poe and Ferguson were also in agreement on this point. Poe's testimony in *Investigation Transcripts*, 100.

5.   Regarding the initial bank meeting, testimony from Poe and Ferguson as found in: *Investigation Transcripts.* 81–82, 212–213. Their respective testimony regarding this meeting was similar. Both Ferguson and Poe testified in depth to the details of their relationship as it related to the bank. As it turned out, it was information that was *omitted* from that critical first meeting that led to many of the problems that the two men later experienced.

6.   *Dallas Morning News,* January 18, 1915.

7.   Trouble with the Texas Store per Poe's testimony, *Investigation Transcripts,* 330–331. Poe could not remember the exact amount of the Texas Store note; he testified that it was either $21,000 or $23,000. Ferguson did not dispute Poe's version of events related to the Texas Store. In his 1917 testimony, Ferguson made this statement: "The Texas Store was not a success as a financial undertaking and Mr. McKay severed his connection with the store about November 1913." *Investigation Transcripts,* 207. Alexander Dienst, in an endorsement he wrote for Ferguson's bid for the governorship in 1914, had claimed that Jim's bank building had never had a vacancy. He failed to elaborate on the facts surrounding that statement. Most of the businesses renting those spaces, the bank, the electrical supply company, the Square Drug Store, and the Texas Store, were all businesses in which Ferguson was a stockholder or partner and at least two of the businesses had been established for the purpose of supplying a renter.

8.   *Dallas Morning News,* January 16, 1912.

9.   *Investigation Transcripts,* 330.

10.   Ibid., 331. The Texas Store was still in bankruptcy court at the time of Poe's testimony. He estimated the bank's $16,000 loss. Poe's feelings and reactions have been summarized using various elements of his testimony and letters between Poe and Ferguson.

11.   Amount of Ferguson's initial debt taken from bank clerk Blum's testimony in *Impeachment Transcripts,* 84.

12.   *Investigation Transcripts,* 100 and 101.

13.   *Investigation Transcripts,* 88–90; *Dallas Morning News,* August 30, 1915.

14.   James E. Ferguson to H. C. Poe, December 24, 1915, *Impeachment Transcripts,* 76.

15.   Ibid.

16.   Poe's discovery of loans in other people's name will be explained in a later chapter. Regarding hostile resistance, Poe testified in the initial investigation, "Well I wrote to Mr. McKay and told him his indebtedness was entirely too heavy and that I wanted him to pay at least half of the note, and he didn't like my letter and wrote me a pretty hot letter, I guess, from what I found out about. He phoned Mr. Hughes to get the letter out of the office and not let me see it." Regarding another of these notes, Poe testified, "Well I got after Mr. Spryor and he came in all swelled up about it and said it was not his note." *Investigation Transcripts,* 83. H. C.

Poe to Dr. W. L. Crosthwait of Waco on Temple State Bank letterhead. The letter stated: "If there is any differences [*sic*] between you and Governor Ferguson you will have to settle the matter with him. I know nothing about differences between you gentlemen and neither is this bank interested in same. Unless you send me a check covering the amount you are due the Temple State Bank in the next two or three days I will pass your note to our attorneys for suit." Found in James E. Ferguson file, The Dolph Briscoe Center for American History, The University of Texas at Austin, Box 3P45.

17.   *Investigation Transcripts*, 134.

18.   Ibid., 86. Ferguson later secured two notes with the Houston National Exchange bank in 1916. In June he was able to borrow $7,500 and the following month, another $11,000. *Impeachment Transcripts*, 87.

19.   *Investigation Transcripts*, 87 and 88; *Dallas Morning News*, January 30, 1916.

20.   H. C. Poe to Ferguson, July 27, 1916, *Investigation Transcripts*, 135.

21.   Ferguson's Blum speech, Ferguson file, The Dolph Briscoe Center for American History, The University of Texas at Austin, Box 3P46.

22.   *Dallas Morning News*, March 21, 1914.

Chapter 5

1.   Information regarding Poe's family history obtained from various census records.

2.   *Texas Pythian Banner-Knight*, April, 1915, copy found in The Dolph Briscoe Center for American History, The University of Texas at Austin; *Dallas Morning News*, September 27, 1916. Article announces Poe's election as vice president of the American Bankers Association. *Bartlett Tribune*, April 30, 1915 and July 2, 1915, attest to Poe's community involvement including the program for young would-be farmers. *Temple Mirror*, December 19, 1915, from Michael and Nancy Kelsey's private collection; *Texas Bankers Journal*, July, 1916, from Michael and Nancy Kelsey's private collection.

3.   Ferguson to Poe, February 13, 1916, *Impeachment Transcripts*, 77.

4.   *Investigation Transcripts*, 208 and 310. Ferguson testified, "Mr. Love owes the bank on that note, I do not owe the bank on that note." Love supplied an instrument that stated: "Mr. Ed Love, this is to acknowledge that note of $3,750.00 to Temple State Bank, due July 7, 1915, is our joint obligation and I agree to pay one-half of same or any renewal thereof, which you may execute. James E. Ferguson." The note had originally been for $3,000.00 but had been renewed to include accrued interest.

5.   *Investigation Transcripts*, 310.

6.   J. H. Davis, Jr. to Temple State Bank on behalf of Ferguson, May 22, 1916, *Impeachment Transcripts*, 393.

7.   The State Bank Examiner's report dated June 8, 1916, *Investigation Transcripts*, 170–171.

8.   James E. Ferguson to DeWitt Dunn, Cashier at the Union National Bank of Houston, April 26, 1916 and copy of Ferguson's personal balance sheet (not dated). Found in James E. Ferguson File, The Dolph Briscoe Center for American History, The University of Texas at Austin, Box 3P46.

9.   Ibid.

10.   *Investigation Transcripts,* 101–105*; Impeachment Transcripts,* 36 and 59.

11.   *Texas Bankers Journal,* July 1916; *Investigation Transcripts*, 104.

12.   Ibid., 106

13.   *Dallas Morning News,* July 16, 1916. Mr. Maedgen resigned his position at the Temple State Bank in early February 1915 about one month after Poe took over as president. News clipping, name of paper unknown, February 4, 1915, in private collection of Michael and Nancy Kelsey, Belton, Texas.

14.   *Dallas Morning News*, March 21, 1914.

15.   *Dallas Morning News,* July 20, 1916.

16.   *Investigation Transcripts*, 175–176; *Dallas Morning News*, September 21, 1916; *Fort Worth Star Telegram*, February 9, 1917; *The Temple Mirror,* February 11, 1917; James E. Ferguson file, The Dolph Briscoe Center for American History, The University of Texas at Austin, Box 3P45.

17.   Ibid., 113.

18.   Ibid., 125.

19.   Ferguson and Patterson, among others, incorporated the First State Bank of Moody in 1907. See *Dallas Morning News,* July 28, 1907.

20.   *Fort Worth Star Telegram*, November 1, 1916.

21.   *Investigation Transcripts*, 335.

22.   Ibid., 126 and 127.

Chapter 6

1.   Ferguson's inaugural speech http://www.lrl.state.tx.us/scanned/govdocs/James%20 E%20Ferguson/1915/IA_Ferguson_1.19.15.pdf. James A. Clark, *The Tactful Texan*, 46, 49 and 51; Harmony with the Legislature, McKay, *Texas Politics 1906–1944*, 60–61.

2.   Gould, 154 and 155. Colquitt had won the 1912 election by a slim 40,000 votes in "the hardest campaign he had ever waged." See McKay, *Texas Politics 1906–1944*, 44, 50

Notes

and 52.

3. So strong was the Fergusons' belief in the reward/punishment system that Jim and Miriam kept an accounting of friends and favors in a leather-bound book. Even though the book was tan in color, they dubbed it "the little black book." After their deaths, the book was in the possession of their grandson George Nalle, Jr. See Paulissen and McQueary, 116 and 319. Details regarding Alexander Dienst's appointment as postmaster, *Fort Worth Star Telegram*, October 23, 1914. Ferguson would also secure an appointment as Belton's postmaster for his brother Alvah in 1916. Letter from James Ferguson to Alvah Ferguson, September 9, 1916, James E. Ferguson file, The Dolph Briscoe Center for American History, The University of Texas at Austin, Box 3P45.

4. Gould, 157; Campbell, 350; *Dallas Morning News*, July 7, 1915.

5. Ibid., "The Governor's Sort of Spoils Politics," March 25, 1915. The statement, "you have removed worthy men from the state's service to gratify your hunger for spoils," made in 1917 by a journalist, shows that Ferguson's reputation for punishing those who opposed him was well understood. Owens and Grant, eds., *Letters of Roy Bedichek*, 50.

6. *Fort Worth Star Telegram*, May 27, 1915.

7. *Cleburne Morning Review*, January 31, 1915; *Dallas Morning News*, April 9, 1915.

8. Nalle, 82.

9. *Dallas Morning News*, March 8, 1915; Nalle, 83 and 107; Pearle Cashell Jackson, *Texas Governors' Wives*, 151.

10. Nalle, 145; *Dallas Morning News*, March 8, 1915; Mansion Payroll Records, *Investigation Transcripts*, 501, 505, 508, and 509.

11. Nalle, 83.

12. Jackson, 155; Nalle, 84 and 85. Dorrace claimed that her father's rural association earned her the name of a "potato digger" at school.

13. *Montgomery Advertiser*, October 15, 1915.

14. Jean Houston Daniel, Price Daniel, and Dorothy Blodgett, *The Texas Governor's Mansion*, 143, 144 and 148; Friends of the Governor's Mansion, eds., *The Governor's Mansion of Texas, A Historic Tour*, 119 and 125.

16. *The Texas Governor's Mansion*, 151–152.

17. *Dallas Morning News*, January 11, 1915; *Cleburne Morning Review*, January 7, 1915.

18. McKay, *Texas Politics, 1906–1944*, 44; Gould, 117 and 146–148.

19. Robert Calvert, Arnoldo De Leon, and Gregg Cantrell, *The History of Texas*, 288.

20. Walter Prescott Webb, *The Texas Rangers: A Century of Frontier Defense*, 484–486.

21. Ferguson's quotation, Robert M. Utley, *Lone Star Lawmen: The Second Century of the Texas Rangers*, 28.

22. Ibid., 27, 28, 42, 43 and 69.

23. *Dallas Morning News*, November 24, 1915.

24. Gould, 165 and 223.

25. Rick Miller, *Bloody Bell County*, 171–178; *Fort Worth Star Telegram*, July 31, 1915.

26. Southern lynching was not uncommon and perpetrators generally went unpunished. *Oregonian*, "Slow Rising Against Lynchers," July 31, 1916. Texas ranked an embarrassing third nationally in the lynching of Negros between 1900 and 1910. Calvert, DeLeon and Cantrell, 261. Governor Pat Neff (1921–1924) also took no action against people who performed several lynchings while he was governor. Brown, 81.

27. *Fort Worth Star Telegram*, April 2, 1915.

28. *Fort Worth Star Telegram*, November 12, 1915; *Dallas Morning News*, November 12, 1915.

29. *Fort Worth Star Telegram*, December 26, 1915.

30. Wharton, 447; Gould, 167; *Dallas Morning News*, February 5, 1916.

31. *Dallas Morning News*, May 26, 1915

32. Ad valorem tax rate, Handbook of Texas Online. http://www.tshaonline.org/handbook/online/article/ffe5.html.

33. Judith N. McArthur, "Saving the Children: The Women's Crusade Against Child Labor 1902–1918," *Women and Texas History*, 60.

34. *Dallas Morning News*, July 15, 1915.

35. *Dallas Morning News*, August 22, 1915.

36. Prisons profitable: http://www.tshaonline.org/handbook/online/articles/jjp03

Interestingly, Ferguson and his attorney made sure to inject into the governor's testimony the fact that the prison system was profitable. It had no bearing on the charges. *Investigation Transcripts*, 195. Purchase of additional land described in *Dallas Morning News*, October 8, 1915, and November 24, 1915. Also *Fort Worth Star Telegram*, July 2, 1916.

37. *Fort Worth Star Telegram*, October 17, 1915.

Notes

38.   *Fort Worth Star Telegram*, March 22, 1914.

39.   Senator Quintus Watson made the referenced statements and further stated, "Ferguson is the Moses who will lead us out of the wilderness, and into the promised land of a cash basis government, improved educational institutions and a bettered penitentiary system," *Dallas Morning News*, August 8, 1915.

Chapter 7

1.   Utley, 45.

2.   *Fort Worth Star Telegram*, May 13, 1917.

3.   Webb, 514–517.

4.   Gould, 171 and 172.

5.   Judith N. McArthur, "Minnie Fisher Cunningham's Back Door Lobby in Texas: Political Maneuvering in a One-Party State," 319.

6.   In 1924, Miriam said, "we have lost the [*sic*] most of our earthly possessions in these years of trouble. . ." *Dallas Morning News*, June 18, 1924. See Jim Ferguson's testimony in which he blamed the investigation, impeachment and low salary for his financial woes. *Impeachment Transcripts*, 747 and 749. Also see Ferguson's testimony at the initial investigation. He said, "Then after I came to Austin, like all men in public life, paying the expenses of the Mansion, such as the government does not pay. . ." *Investigation Transcripts*, 203. Ferguson's personal financial statements dated December 1, 1916, were in evidence at the 1917 investigation. They showed debt of $170,000 secured by land, $100,000 secured by stock, $40,000 secured by cattle and $25,000 as "other liabilities." The incorporated Bell-Bosque farm statement showed an additional $80,000 in liabilities, $50,000 of which was secured by livestock.

7.   James E. Ferguson to James Talley, Memorial Baptist Church of Temple, April 11, 1916, James E. Ferguson file, The Dolph Briscoe Center for American History, The University of Texas at Austin, Box 3P46.

8.   James E. Ferguson to John T. Land, August 15, 1916, James E. Ferguson file, The Dolph Briscoe Center for American History, The University of Texas at Austin, Box 3P46.

9.   James E. Ferguson to A. F. Bentley, President, Kings Daughters Hospital Association, October 18, 1916, James E. Ferguson file, The Dolph Briscoe Center for American History, The University of Texas at Austin, Box 3P46.

10.   Telegram from James E. Ferguson to A. S. Burleson, August 28, 1916,; James E. Ferguson to Jake Wolters, July 14, 1916,; James E. Ferguson to A. F. Ferguson, September 9, 1916, all found in James E. Ferguson file, The Dolph Briscoe Center for American History, The University of Texas at Austin, Box 3P45.

11.   *Investigation Transcripts*, 131.

12.   Testimony regarding the sale of the bank stock, Ibid.

13.   Hendrickson, 160; *Fort Worth Star Telegram*, July 2, 1916; *Dallas Morning News*, July 14, 1916.

14.   *Fort Worth Star Telegram*, December 28, 1916.

Chapter 8

1.   *Impeachment Transcripts*, 742. In his final plea against impeachment, Ferguson made a lengthy speech. He referenced his past popularity saying, "The people of Austin thought I was the biggest man that ever sat in the Governor's chair, and, notwithstanding I had never been past the sixth grade in school...."

2.   Gould, 190.

3.   John Lomax, *Will Hogg, Texas*, ix

4.   Hogg to Ferguson, September 22, 1915, Hogg Papers, The Dolph Briscoe Center for American History, The University of Texas at Austin, Box 2J314.

5.   Ferguson to Hogg, September 25, 1915, Ibid.

6.   Gould, 192.

7.   *Dallas Morning News*, Oct 27, 1915, and April 26, 1916; Gould, 193.

8.   Vinson's credentials: *Impeachment Transcripts*, 174.

9.   Jim Nicar, *The Alcalde*, "The Defenders, 1913–1926," 2010. The true source of Ferguson's objection to the certain faculty members was their failure to support his ideas. This fact was evidenced by a letter of September 25, 1916, from Ferguson to Rabbi Faber and again in the Governor's dismissal of Dr. S. J. Jones on May 29, 1917. In the letter to the Rabbi, Ferguson made this reference, "When you continue on a board of an institution that permits its professors to go down to a ward convention and join with those who opposed the endorsement of my administration, after it has stood the criticism of having given the University the biggest appropriation in its history. . ." In Ferguson's proclamation dismissing Dr. Jones, he cited this reason, "Whereas, the said S. J. Jones, since his appointment and during his incumbency in office, has openly manifested an utter lack of harmony with the views and purposes of the present administration. . ." *Impeachment Transcripts*, 152. Law professor R. E. Cofer, one of Ferguson's targets, had taken part in political activity Ferguson found objectionable. See Gould, 193.

10.   *Impeachment Transcripts*, 191.

11.   *Impeachment Transcripts*, 192.

12. Ferguson would later enlist the services of an auditor to find items that might cast suspicion on the service of the men he found objectionable. This was done in September, well after his objections in June. It seemed to suggest that Ferguson had no legitimate charges against the men when he initially suggested their dismissal. Owens and Grant, 48–49.

13. *Impeachment Transcripts*, 192.

14. Ibid., 192–193.

15. Ibid., 150.

16. Ibid., 150–151.

17. Gould, 197. Gould characterized Brents as Ferguson's friend and political cohort. Details of the Fergusons-Brent trouble are from *Impeachment Transcripts*, 140–150.

18. Transcriptions of the October meeting of the Board of Regents were read at the impeachment trial. *Impeachment Transcripts*, 211.

19. *Fort Worth Star-Telegram*, December 17, 1916.

20. Owens and Grant, eds., xxv–xxviii.

21. Ibid., 49.

22. Ibid., 46 and 47.

23. *Dallas Morning News*, February 18, 1917 and March 6, 1917.

24. All charges detailed, *Investigation Transcripts*, 3–7.

25. Nalle, 129.

26. *Fort Worth Star Telegram*, March 3, 1917.

Chapter 9

1. http://www.tshaonline.org/handbook/online/articles/fcr04 Texas State

2. Bruce Rutherford, *The Impeachment of Jim Ferguson*, 44.

3. *Investigation Transcripts*, 8 and 241.

4. Poe's entire statement, Ibid., 7–15.

5. Ibid., 15.

6. Ibid., 27.

7. Ibid., 31.

8.   Ibid., 32.

9.   *Fort Worth Star Telegram,* June 13, 1915.

10.   *Fort Worth Star Telegram,* June 14, 1916.

11.   Terrell's testimony, *Investigation Transcripts,* 38–54.

12.   Achilles testimony, Ibid., 68–73.

13.   Sayers testimony, Ibid., 77–79.

14.   *Investigation Transcripts,* 53; *Dallas Morning News,* July 16, 1916; *Fort Worth Star Telegram,* February 9, 1917.

15.   *Temple Telegram,* July 20, 1916. The details of Maedgen's story were allegations he made against Jim Ferguson. They were never proven.

16.   Ibid.

17.   Ibid.

18.   Crane's comments, Ibid., 79.

Chapter 10

1.   Poe's testimony under Crane's questioning, *Investigation Transcripts,* 80–97 and 126–169.

2.   Poe's quotation, Ibid., 113.

3.   Ibid., 96.

4.   Committee's reaction, Ibid., 97.

5.   Ibid., 80.

6.   Poe's testimony under Hanger's questioning, Ibid., 97–126

7.   Ibid., 140.

8.   Poe's letter to Ferguson, Ibid., 140–143.

Chapter 11

1.   Ferguson testimony, *Investigation Transcripts,* 187–288, and 342–344. Also *Impeachment Transcripts,* 299. Ferguson's good work, *Investigation Transcripts,* 195.

2.   On March 22, Ferguson wrote a letter to the Supreme Court judges specifically calling their attention to the *Middleton vs. Terrell* case. In that letter the governor

reminded the judges of a law that he felt gave legislators the right to raise revenue for all incidental expenses. The letter was introduced as evidence in Ferguson's impeachment trial. *Impeachment Transcripts, 299.*

3.   Ferguson quotation, *Investigation Transcripts,* 199.

4.   Ferguson quotation, Ibid., 201.

5.   Ferguson quotation, Ibid., 205.

6.   Ferguson quotation, Ibid., 205. Census records show a John W. *Spires* in Bell County. In the transcripts the name is sometimes spelled Spires but also spelled "Spryors" and "Spyers" at times.

7.   Ferguson quotation, *Investigation Transcripts,* 206–207. Though Ferguson testified that McKay had been six or seven thousand dollars over his allotted $30,000 campaign budget, in his required disclosure of campaign expenses filed with the county judge, Ferguson had submitted an itemized list of expenses totaling $31,424.63. The newspaper article that printed this information is un-named and undated. Found in James E. Ferguson file, The Dolph Briscoe Center for American History, The University of Texas at Austin, Box 3P5.

8.   Crane quotation, Ibid., 215.

9.   Ferguson quotation, Ibid., 221.

10.   Ferguson quotation, Ibid., 231.

11.   Ferguson quotation, Ibid., 235.

12.   Financial statements, Ibid., 246.

13.   Ferguson quotation, Ibid., 236.

14.   Ferguson quotation, Ibid.

15.   Ibid., 332.

Chapter 12

1.   *Investigation Transcripts,* 166. Poe's testimony regarding his meeting with Mr. Austin included this: "When I came to see him with reference to these affairs of the Governor he asked me not to make up the usual annual report and have the Directors sign it and send it in, and I told him that I would think the matter over. He said that when Mr. Patterson died they were keeping the records from the Temple State Bank under lock and key, and Mr. Patterson was carrying the key so no one would have access to them, and he was still keeping them so no one could see them. That the Temple State Bank was in the most serious condition of any State Bank in Texas, and that he did not want the report to come in over the signature of the Directors and be filed."

2.   Mr. Austin's testimony, *Investigation Transcripts,* 295–307.

3.   Ibid., 302–303.

4.   Ibid., 306.

5.   Ibid., 252.

6.   Ibid., 254.

7.   Ibid., 260.

8.   Ibid., 265.

9.   Ibid., 343.

10.   Ibid., 276.

11.   Ibid., 310. Mr. Love testified that the note had been paid and he had not paid it. He assumed that the governor, the only other interested party, had done so. There is another interesting point about the Square Drug Store: while Jim had invested a total of $2,500 capital in the store according to his testimony, the personal financial statements he supplied to the committee showed his investment in the Square Drug Store to be $700. Ibid., 246.

12.   Ibid., 328.

13.   Ibid., 328.

14.   Ibid., 335.

15.   Ibid., 326.

16.   Ibid., 170–171.

17.   Ibid., 172.

18.   Ibid., 168.

19.   Ibid., 343.

20.   *Fort Worth Star Telegram*, March 17, 1917.

Chapter 13

1.   Entire Report. *Impeachment Transcripts*, 384–390.

2.   Invoices for stock feed: *Investigative Transcripts*, 406, 417, 418, 424, 444, 474, 478, 489, 499 and 500. Also paid from the fund were numerous invoices for gasoline, car repairs, and dry cleaning.

3.   Testimony and evidence at the impeachment trial would show that Ferguson had only temporarily moved the debt to another bank until the investigation was over. For more details, see chapter 14.

4.   *Dallas Morning News*, February 18, 1917. Copy of statement from bank officials as published in the *Temple Daily Telegram*, February 18, 1917, The Dolph Briscoe Center for American History, The University of Texas at Austin, Box 3P45. Lawrence Heard's address in Temple City Directory of 1917 shows the Ferguson home address.

5.   *The Bartlett Tribune*, April 27, 1917.

6.   Court Documents File DCCRM49, Cause number 9146-9148, Bell County District Court, Belton, TX.

7.   Ibid., Cause number 9148.

8.   *The Bartlett Tribune*, March 8, 1918.

9.   Information about Poe obtained through census records. Poe's new bank announced: *Bartlett Tribune*, March 18, 1917; *Fort Worth Star Telegram*, December 4 and December 15, 1918.

10.   Paulissen and McQueary, 76.

11.   http://www.rootsweb.ancestry.com/~txeastla/cemeteries/Longbranch.html

12.   *Impeachment Transcripts*, 301, 302.

13.   Jim Nicar, *The Alcalade*, "The Defenders, 1913–1926," Month unknown, 2010.

14.   Nolan Porterfield, *Last Cavalier, The Life and Times of John A. Lomax*, 214. Ferguson's quotation: *Fort Worth Star Telegram*, June 14, 1917; Veto Message: James E. Ferguson Papers, The Dolph Briscoe Center for American History, The University of Texas at Austin, Box 3P46.

15.   *Dallas Morning News*, July 6, 1917; Gould, 205.

16.   Porterfield, 195, 203 and 211.

17.   A sample of the large and lengthy ads signed by the "Ex-Students Committee" can be seen in *Dallas Morning News*, July 6, 1917 and *Fort Worth Star Telegram*, June 27, 1917. An example of Hogg's speeches made in support of the university, *Dallas Morning News*, July 29, 1917. The reprint of the transcripts of the initial investigation as reproduced by the University of Michigan Libraries, includes, at the beginning of the book (page not numbered), a copy of the dedication that Will Hogg wrote and circulated in his reprints of the transcripts. It also contains the list of Ferguson quotations that Hogg found most objectionable, iv and v. Examples of letters from public to Hogg regarding the dispute as well some letters of response, Hogg Papers, Dolph Briscoe Center for American History, The University of Texas at Austin. Box 2J314. Brown, 166; Gould, who states, "While his opponents organized and criticized, Ferguson took his case to the people," 206 and 207.

18.   Gould, 209 and 212. *Fort Worth Star Telegram*, July 29, 1917.

19.   *Dallas Morning News,* July 29, 1917.

Chapter 14

1.   *Fort Worth Star Telegram,* August 1, 1917; *Dallas Morning News*, August 15, 1917.

2.   Rutherford, 59.

3.   Rutherford, 67, 68 and 71. The details of each charge, *Impeachment Transcripts,* 11–16; *Dallas Morning News*, August 26, 1917.

4.   *Impeachment Transcripts,* 11, 13, 98, 138, 139, 257-258, 426, 427, 581, 582.

5.   Article 13, the charge that outlined Ferguson's failure to repay the inappropriate expenses as required in the investigation, stated that the amount was "several thousand dollars." However, Ferguson later stated that he had paid about $2,400 to settle his obligation with the state. *Impeachment Transcripts*, 13 and 25.

6.   Ibid., 36–38, 43–44, 46–47, 59, 70, 582.

7.   Ibid., 87 and 96.

8.   Ibid., 412.

9.   Ibid., 12, 43, 70.

10.   Ibid., 18, 47.

11.   Ibid., 651–682. Among the ideas that were suggested to force Jim to divulge the details of the loan, was this potential plan written in a letter to Col. R. M. Johnston from Will Hogg: "A motion will be made to adjourn the case until he does testify, thereby leaving him suspended from office indefinitely." Hogg to Johnston, September 14, 1917, Hogg papers, The Dolph Briscoe Center for American History, The University of Texas at Austin, Box 2J314.

12.   *Impeachment Transcripts,* 87–89.

13.   Opinion based upon reading Vinson's testimony. *Impeachment Transcripts,* 174–227.

14.   *Fort Worth Star Telegram,* September 15, 1917.

15.   *Impeachment Transcripts,* 235–250.

16.   Ibid.

17.   Ibid., 302–303.

18.   Nalle, 129.

19.   *Impeachment Transcripts,* 734.

20.   Ibid., 733.

21.   Ibid., 740, 742 and 744.

22.   Ibid., 763.

23.   Ibid., 763-764.

24.   *Fort Worth Star Telegram*, September 21, 1917.

25.   *Tulsa World*, September 26, 1917; *Dallas Morning News*, September 27, 1917.

26.   Senator O. S. Lattimore to Hogg, September 24, 1917, Hogg Papers, The Dolph Briscoe Center for American History, The University of Texas at Austin, Box 2314.

27.   The three senators, Bee, Page, and Hudspeth, requested and received permission from the Senate to make public statements of their views regarding Ferguson's comments. *Fort Worth Star Telegram*, September 26, 1917.

28.   John E. Clark, *The Fall of the Duke of Duval, A Prosecutor's Journal*, 23.

29.   Ibid., 27–33.

30.   Ibid., William Sessions' statement is in the introduction to John Clark's book, page vii. Evan Anders, *Boss Rule in South Texas, The Progressive Era*, ix. Duval County and Archie Parr's election fraud became infamous in Texas history. Parr's own re-election to the Texas Senate in 1918 was highly contested under allegations of election fraud. Though there is little doubt that fraud occurred, Parr managed to survive the investigation and keep his Senate seat. His tactic for securing the close race was the late release of an amended vote count. Anders, 258–263.

31.   In the 1914 election Ferguson had easily taken the primarily Mexican-controlled counties in South and Southeast Texas. His appeal seemed lost to this group after the impeachment as was evident in his attempt to take the governorship from Hobby in the following election. Most Mexican counties had deserted him with the exception of Duval County, which gave him a favorable vote of 284 to 15. McKay, *Texas Politics 1906–1944*, 82.

32.   Chester Terrell to Hogg, October 3, 1917, Hogg papers, The Dolph Briscoe Center for American History, The University of Texas at Austin, Box 2J314.

Chapter 15

1.   *Dallas Morning News*, August 1, 1917; *Messenger*, August 2, 1917; *Tulsa World*, August 2, 1917.

2.   Nalle, 144.

3.   *Fort Worth Star Telegram*, August 20, 1922. James Bowmer, transcripts from a speech to the Temple Ladies Federation Club meeting made on March 13, 1984, on file

at the Bell County Museum, Belton, Texas. Mr. Bowmer's parents were lifelong Ferguson friends and his father was a partner in a law office on the second floor of Ferguson's bank building. Ferguson had appointed the senior Bowmer, whose first name was Dewitt, to the position of District Attorney in Killeen when he was only twenty-three years old. Bowmer later represented Ferguson in lawsuits for libel against newspapers. In his speech, James Bowmer described the harsh treatment that the Fergusons received in Temple after the impeachment, repeating stories that his parents had relayed to him.

4.   Paulissen and McQueary, 85.

5.   *Fort Worth Star Telegram*, September 26, 1917.

6.   A large collection of the *Ferguson Forum* editions are held at the Bell County Museum in Belton.

7.   *Ferguson Forum*, November, 8 and 17, 1917, Bell County Museum, Belton, Texas. Ferguson had stated his opinion before the Board of University Regents that the Department of Journalism was a waste of money. In view of that, it is interesting that he would start his own newspaper, employing his daughter in that business. *Dallas Morning News*, June 28, 1917.

8.   Hogg to Hamilton, December 17, 1917, Hogg Papers, Dolph Briscoe Center for American History, The University of Texas at Austin, Box 2J314; *Dallas Morning News*, June 28, 1918; *The Bartlett Tribune*, July 23, 1918.

9.   Nalle, 149.

10.   Gould, 230–233.

11.   Ibid., 233; Judith N. McArthur, *Creating the New Woman, The Rise of Southern Women's Progressive Culture in Texas, 1893–1918*, 137–138.

12.   *Fort Worth Star Telegram*, June 29, 1918.

13.   *Dallas Morning News*, July 26, 1918; *Fort Worth Star Telegram*, July 24, 1918.

14.   *Dallas Morning News*, July 3, 1918.

15.   *The Weekly Corpus Christi Caller*, July 25, 1918.

16.   Gould, 256.

17.   Campbell, 357.

18.   Ferguson had managed to obtain 217,012 votes to Hobby's 461,479. McKay, *Texas Politics 1906–1944*, 82.

19.   *Albuquerque Journal*, August 2, 1918; *Dallas Morning News*, August 3, 1918.

20.   *Fort Worth Star Telegram*, August 2, 1918, and August 8, 1918.

21.   *Dallas Morning News*, October 17, 1918.

22.   Texas Historical Marker #5027003398. This marker stands on the Sparks prop-
       erty where Miriam grew up. It states that the property was mortgaged in 1917 to
       support Jim's political expenses. Ouida Ferguson Nalle (on page 157) wrote about
       a comment her father made to Miriam in 1919, saying that he had no money and
       would be lucky to save her family farm.

Chapter 16

1.   *Investigation Transcripts*, 285; *Fort Worth Star Telegram*, August 22, 1917. For details
       about the land sale and escrow money, refer to chapter 14.

2.   A newspaper ad titled, "A Wild Cat," pitched the prospect to would-be investors.
       The ad offered the endorsement of 41 citizens, some of whom were Ferguson
       relatives. The amount of money the ad generated is not known. *Fort Worth Star
       Telegram*, January 27, 1919; *Fort Worth Star Telegram*, Ad for Kokernot Oil Company,
       January 16, 1921. Don Biggers also wrote of Ferguson's oil speculations. Don Big-
       gers, *Our Sacred Monkeys; or, 20 Years of Jim and Other Jams, (Mostly Jim) the Outstanding
       Goat Gland Specialist of Texas Politics*, 51 and 55.

3.   Sale of Lignite Coal, *Fort Worth Star Telegram*, September 2, 1920; Ferguson's talk
       with bank board, *Investigation Transcripts*, 235.

4.   A 1916 balance sheet for the coal company was entered into evidence in the
       March 1917 investigation. *Investigation Transcripts*, 248. Testimony revealed that
       L. Adoue of the Galveston Brewing Company held $150,000 in lignite company
       bonds while Hugh Hamilton of Magnolia Brewing Company held about $25,000
       of the same investment. *Fort Worth Star Telegram*, September 12, 1917. Under ques-
       tioning at the impeachment trail Jim first claimed that he could not remember
       who had purchased Lignite Coal Company's bonds. When pressed, he admitted
       that two persons with brewery connections were among the investors. *Impeachment
       Transcripts*, 359–360.

5.   Silliman to Hogg, June 28, 1917, Hogg Papers, The Dolph Briscoe Center for
       American History, The University of Texas at Austin, Box 2J314; *Dallas Morning
       News*, December 8, 1917.

6.   Nalle described the speed at which the money generated by the lawsuits was spent
       saying, "It melted like a snowball in the Texas Sun." Nalle, 146. In a speech before
       Temple's Ladies Federation club in 1984, Jim Bowmer, attorney and the son of a
       personal friend of Ferguson's, relayed the stories his mother had told him about
       the use of the money from the settlements. The elder Bowmer, an attorney, had
       represented Jim in one of the suits against a newspaper and upon receiving pay-
       ment both Bowmer and Ferguson went up and down Temple streets, paying off
       debts. Transcript of Bowmer's speech, Bell County Museum, Belton, Texas.

7.   There are many references in Nalle's book to the lack of money in the Ferguson
       household following the impeachment. This reference hints that Miriam might
       have been ashamed to travel to Austin because of her clothing. Ouida claimed
       that 1919 represented a turning point in Miriam's attitude about family finances,

and thereafter she gave the subject a great deal of attention. Nalle, 157 and footnote 182.

8.   *Fort Worth Star Telegram*, April 22, 1920.

9.   Ibid., April 25, 1920.

10.   American Party Broadside, Claude Elliott Collection, Box 3, University of Houston Special Collection, Houston, Texas.

11.   Regarding American Party Convention, *Fort Worth Star Telegram*, August 9 and 19,
1920. Ferguson's quotation, *Dallas Morning News*, October 3, 1920.

12.   *Fort Worth Star Telegram*, May 4, 1921.

13.   The statistics on Ferguson's debts were revealed in a radio address by Thomas
Love who campaigned on behalf of Ross Sterling. This writer could not verify the
information. There was no public denial or lawsuit from Ferguson regarding it.
Love's statement was printed in full in the *Dallas Morning News* the following day.
Dallas Morning News, August 21, 1932.

14.   *Dallas Morning News*, July 21, 1921.

15.   *Ferguson Forum*, October 20, 1920.

16.   Alexander, 1, 2, 18, 19 and 50.

17.   Brown, 72.

18.   The prospect of Miriam's senatorial candidacy is particularly interesting in view
of her vehement opposition to her husband's pursuit of a Senate seat. Not a fan
of cold weather and fearing the high cost of living, she dreaded the possibility of
moving to Washington D. C. in the event of his victory. Even so, she allowed her
husband to put her name on the ballot. Nalle, 161. *Dallas Morning News*, May 28,
1922; *Fort Worth Star Telegram*, June 28, 1922.

19.   McKay, *Texas Politics, 1906–1944*, 119; *Fort Worth Star Telegram*, July 9, 1922; *Dallas
Morning News*, August 22, 1922.

20.   *Fort Worth Star Telegram*, June 22, 1922. Ferguson challenged Culberson to come to
Texas and "show himself to the people," knowing that the senior senator was too
ill to make the trip. Ferguson offered to resign immediately if Culberson would
make the trip to Texas and convince voters that he was capable of discharging his
duties.

21.   McKay, *Texas Politics, 1906–1944*, 116; *Dallas Morning News*, July 26, 1922.

22.   McKay, *Texas Politics, 1906–1944*, 124–125; Brown, 121–125.

23.   McKay, *Texas Politics, 1906–1944*, 125 and 127; *Dallas Morning News*, August 29,
1922.

24.   *Fort Worth Star Telegram*, December 20, 1922. Little information exists about this short-lived partnership if, in fact, it was ever consummated. Daughter Ouida's writing is silent on any details during this time period. Ferguson was only in Dallas for a few months before he returned to Temple with the *Forum* in tow.

Chapter 17

1.   *Dallas Morning News*, January 25, 1923 and January 26, 1923.

2.   Ibid., February 10, 1923, and May 16, 1923; Nalle, 165–166.

3.   Biggers, 62–63; Brown, 215.

4.   Brown, 216; *Ferguson Forum*, January 3, 1924, February 28, 1924, and July 31, 1924. Bell County Museum, Belton, Texas.

5.   Brown, 182, 183.

6.   *Dallas Morning News*, January 20, 1924.

7.   McKay, *Texas Politics 1906–1944*, 131; Brown, 223.

8.   *Dallas Morning News*, June 18, 1924. Miriam also made an obvious admission when she said, "I know I can't talk about the constitution and the making of laws and the science of government like some other candidates, and I believe they have talked too much, but I have a trusting and abiding faith that my Redeemer liveth and I am trusting in him to guide my footsteps. ..." Miriam's comments about Jim's lack of religion, *Ferguson Forum*, June 26, 1924.

9.   McKay, *Texas Politics 1906–1944*, 133.

10.   Brown 224. Robertson's campaign manager, Larry Mills, received a nomination for an appointment to the State Board of Education from Governor Miriam Ferguson in 1933, which he declined. He later supported her in her unsuccessful bid for governor in 1940.

11.   Nalle, 177. Miriam would later report the contributions for her second leg of the race as $1,963. It seems a small amount to be characterized as a "gulf tide" of donations. *Dallas Morning News*, September 6, 1924.

12.   *Dallas Morning News*, August 28, 1924.

13.   *Dallas Morning News*, April 13, 1955; Fred Gantt Jr., *The Chief Executives of Texas*, 285. Gantt credits newspaperman Frank Gibler of the *Houston Post* with Miriam's nickname. Her full name was too long to fit the space available for the headline, causing Gibler to use Mrs. Ferguson's initials. The creation of a nickname was unintentional.

14.   Crane's admission to the support offered to Mrs. Ferguson in 1924 was part of a review of Ferguson misdeeds, including her failure to abide by the terms of the agreement, subsequently presented by Crane. *Dallas Morning News*, August 26, 1932.

15. *Dallas Morning News*, August 2, 16, and 24, 1924. Though the Fergusons' grandson gave the family's collection of *Ferguson Forums* to the Bell County Museum, copies of editions with these and other offensive remarks are conspicuously absent in the collection. It seems to be another means of censorship imposed by some unknown party since the most egregious editions are consistently missing. The information about the *Forum* article was obtained in Brown, 234–235.

16. *Dallas Morning News*, August 18, 1924.

17. McKay, *Texas Politics 1906–1944*, 137 and 138.

18. *Ferguson Forum*, August 28, 1924; Robertson's support of Ferguson in 1914, *Fort Worth Star Telegram*, July 14, 1914.

19. Brown, 243.

20. Brown, 246; *Dallas Morning News*, September 16, 1924, and October 21, 1924.

21. The family later rented the Bosque property and attempted to reclaim it on credit in 1926, an action that failed. *Dallas Morning News*, January 3, 1926.

22. *Dallas Morning News*, October 24, 1924.

23. Ibid., November 4, 1924.

24. McKay, *Texas Politics 1906–1944*, 141 and 142.

25. Nalle, 180. The home in Temple was kept by the Fergusons and rented for a number of years even though the family built a new home in Austin. In 1938, six years prior to his death, Jim wrote Judge Few Brewster, who lived in the home across the street from the Temple mansion, asking him if he would like to make a trade. The letter stated: "How would you like to trade your home for my wife's place across the street from where you live? I think my wife would be willing to take your place and you pay a difference of $3,000.00. I will be glad to have you write me if you would be interested." It is curious that Jim referred to the home as Miriam's place. It is equally curious why he wanted to trade the home for one across the street. He may have been simply trying to raise cash. We can assume that Judge Brewster had no interest in the swap since the trade was not made. Jim Ferguson to Few Brewster, October 18, 1938. Letter courtesy of the Bell County Museum, Belton, Texas.

Chapter 18

1. *Dallas Morning News*, January 4, 1925.

2. *Dallas Morning News*, January 20, 1925, and January 21, 1925; *Greensboro Record*, January 20, 1925. Dorothy Blodgett, Terrell Blodgett, David L. Scott, *The Land, the Law, and the Lord: The Life of Pat Neff*, 147.

3. *Dallas Morning News*, February 6, 1925; *Trenton Evening Times*, December 6, 1925; Brown, 277.

4.   *Dallas Morning News*, January 12, 1925.

5.   Ibid., January 7, 1925.

6.   Ibid., January 22, 1925, and January 25, 1925.

7.   Blodgett, Blodgett, and Scott, 97; Gantt, 151.

8.   Brown, 255–257.

9.   In 1917, at the initial investigation of the governor, Jim Ferguson testified that his brother-in-law, F. M. Morton, *might have* paid off a portion of his debt in an effort to help with his mounting liabilities. This had been done at the request of Jim's brother Joe Lee. Jim's uncertainty about the details possibly angered his sister who may have seen Jim's clouded memory as ingratitude or she may have felt that her husband's financial assistance constituted Jim's share of the couple's fortune. See *Investigative Transcripts*, 239; Nalle, 123.

10.   Details of Kate's death and details of her will and the subsequent lawsuit, *Dallas Morning News*, March 12, 1925, April 5, 1925, and December 10, 1931.

11.   *Dallas Morning News*, February 21, 1925. Senator Woodward, the author of the amnesty bill, would later regret his part in the process and would publicly apologize for it. While speaking on behalf of Ross Sterling in 1930, Woodward asked listeners not to throw anything at him when he admitted that he had supported the amnesty bill. Paul Wakerfield, *Campaigning Texas*, 1932.

12.   Brown, 258–259; Gantt, 201; *Dallas Morning News*, April 7, 1925.

13.   During the impeachment trial, Ferguson admitted that he had told Will Hogg that he objected to Mayes because, according to Ferguson, Mayes had "Skinned me from Hell to breakfast" in his newspaper. Quoted in *Impeachment Transcripts*, 535 and 634; Brown, 263–264.

14.   *Dallas Morning News*, September 26, 1923; Ken Anderson, *You Can't Do that, Dan Moody*, 38–47; McKay, *Texas Politics 1906–1944*, 146–147.

15.   *Dallas Morning News*, May 8, 1925; Brown, 270 and 271; Nalle, 189–191.

16.   *Dallas Morning News*, April 26, 1925, and April 28, 1925; Brown, 270.

17.   *Dallas Morning News*, July 3, 1925. Amon Carter, the publisher of the *Fort Worth Star-Telegram*, was certainly chief among the drinkers the Fergusons targeted with her offer of a specifically worded reward. Mrs. Ferguson detested Carter. The reward was offered in November, soon after Carter had embarrassed the governor at a football game by shouting "Hurray for Dan Moody," in her presence. She also demanded that Carter resign from his position as a regent for Texas Tech, a demand he refused to heed. The university did not ask Carter to resign and the subject was eventually dropped. See Brown, 271–272.

18.   *Dallas Morning News,* January 4, 1927; Brown, 278 and 279.

19.   Louis Kemp Papers, State Highway Department File, The Dolph Briscoe Center for American History, The University of Texas at Austin, Box 2R-217; *Dallas Morning News,* October 21, 1926.

20.   *Cronista del Valle,* January 13, 1926; *Dallas Morning News,* November 9, 1926; Brown, 280.

21.   Biggers, 68; Brown, 281–287. Frank V. Lanham was an unsuccessful candidate for mayor of Fort Worth in 1910. He had been a long-time supporter of Jim Ferguson. In 1917, Lanham's Fort Worth paving company, Bramley-Lanham Company, had been involved in some controversy over paving contracts with the city of Dallas. The city had rescinded the contracts that they believed were priced exorbitantly. Lanham threatened the city with court action stating that as the lowest bidder, his company was entitled to the contracts. *Dallas Morning News,* October 12 and 27, 1917.

22.   Louis Kemp Papers, State Highway Department File, The Dolph Briscoe Center for American History, The University of Texas at Austin, Box 2R-217; Biggers, 67–70; Brown, 284–287.

23.   *Dallas Morning News,* September 19, 1925; Brown 284–287.

24.   Louis Kemp Papers, State Highway Department File, The Dolph Briscoe Center for American History, The University of Texas at Austin, Box 2R-217; *Richardson Echo,* October 23, 1925. It is interesting to note that the *Echo* waited a full month to run the story. Brown, 289–290.

25.   *Dallas Morning News,* October 8, 1925.

26.   *Dallas Morning News,* October 18, 1925 and October 26, 1925.

27.   *Dallas Morning News,* October 25, 1925 and November 6, 1925; Brown, 290.

28.   *Dallas Morning News,* December 15, 1925.

29.   *Dallas Morning News,* October 27, 1925 and October 28, 1925; Brown, 292.

Chapter 19

1.   *Dallas Morning News,* February 28, 1926. With this statement Miriam took the emphasis off of her broken promise and put it on her "enemies," that is to say, those who opposed her. Few knew that she was also breaking an agreement she had made with certain powerful Democrats, including Martin Crane, who had helped her get elected in 1924.

2.   McKay, *Texas Politics 1906–1944,* 151; *Dallas Morning News,* March 7, 1926; Brown, 300.

3.   *Dallas Morning News,* January 6, 1926.

4.   *Dallas Morning News,* January 27, 1926, January 30, 1926 and November 9, 1926.

5.   Details of the lawsuit, *The Bartlett Tribune*, February 5, 1926. Reverend Atticus
        Webb had also been critical of Mrs. Ferguson's pardon policy in 1925, saying,
        "When Mrs. Ferguson pardons a murderer, and she had pardoned many, she
        does violence to the right of every widow and every orphan made so by these
        murderers." Webb suggested that Mrs. Ferguson concentrate instead on personal
        forgiveness for those who she felt had wronged her. *Dallas Morning News*, May 31,
        1925. The Rangers' disapproval of and disappointment in Texas governors was
        not limited to the Fergusons. They also accused Colquitt and Hobby of using the
        Ranger Force for political purposes. Utley, 107, 110, 112 and 118.

6.   *Dallas Morning News*, October 29, 1929.

7.   McKay, *Texas Politics, 1906–1944*, 150.

8.   *Bartlett Tribune*, May 28, 1926.

9.   *Dallas Morning News*, May 23, 1926.

10.   *Dallas Morning News,* July 28, 1926. This letter from Cranfill was printed in the
        "Letters from Readers" section of the newspaper. *Dallas Morning News,* July 24,
        1926 and June 23, 1926.

11.   *The Bartlett Tribune and News,* June 25, 1926.

12.   Brown, 324.

13.   Ibid.

14.   Ibid.

15.   *Dallas Morning News,* June 26 and 28, 1926.

16.   McKay, *Texas Politics 1906–1944*, 151–152.

17.   Quotations from other newspapers, "As the Editors View Texas Primary Election"
        section of the *Dallas Morning News*, August 2, 1926.

18.   McKay, *Texas Politics 1906–1944*, 156.

19.   *The Bartlett Tribune and News*, October 22, 1926; *Breckenridge Weekly Democrat,* January
        20 and 21, 1927. Mrs. Ferguson's private secretary, Ghent Sanderford, claimed in
        an interview many years later, that it was he who granted the pardon to Jackson
        without realizing the significance of the act until it was completed. He had made
        this specific pardon without the knowledge of Mrs. Ferguson, he stated. However,
        the disclosure that Governor Ferguson delegated the pardoning power to a subor-
        dinate is perhaps more troubling than the pardon itself. Also disconcerting is the
        careless nature of the process given that Sanderford did not initially realize who
        he was pardoning. This writer doubts that Sanderford was telling the truth. He
        may have confessed to granting the pardon after Mrs. Ferguson received a great

deal of criticism for the act. Paulissen and McQueary, 155–156.

20.   *Dallas Morning News*, August 30, 1926.

21.   Louis Kemp Papers, The Dolph Briscoe Center for American History, The University of Texas at Austin, Box 2R-217.

22.   Ibid.; *Dallas Morning News*, November 12, 1926.

23.   *Dallas Morning News*, November 9, 1926.

24.   *Dallas Morning News*, October 19, 1926.

25.   Brown, 289.

26.   *Dallas Morning News*, January 19, 1927.

27.   Nalle, 206.

Chapter 20

1.   McKay, *Texas Politics 1906–1944*, 159; *Dallas Morning News*, March 20, 1927.

2.   Brown, 345.

3.   *Dallas Morning News*, January 25, 1927.

4.   Quotation from *The Bartlett Tribune*, February 20, 1927; *Dallas Morning News*, March 22, 1927.

5.   *Dallas Morning News*, July 15, 1927. Ferguson Park remains in use as of 2013.

6.   Regarding the financing of the house, in *Miriam*, page 171, Paulissen and McQueary wrote, "Jim did not tell Miriam the details about the financing of this Mediterranean-style house on 1500 Windsor Road, but referred to it as 'a gift from friends.'" *Dallas Morning News*, December 20, 1927, January 26, 1928, August 31, 1928.

7.   Biggers, 80; *Dallas Morning News*, July 22 and 26, 1927.

8.   McKay, *Texas Politics 1906–1944*, 160–163.

9.   *Dallas Morning News*, August 30, 1928.

10.   *Dallas Morning News*, May 9, 1930; *Dallas Morning News* quotes the *Charleston News and Courier*, August 12, 1930.

11.   Ross Sterling and Ed Kilman, *Ross Sterling, A Texan*, 96–97.

12.   McKay 187–189; *Dallas Morning News*, July 24, 1930.

13. Paul L. Wakefield, *Campaigning Texas*, 35, 99, 100 and 130.

14. McKay, *Texas Politics 1906–1944*, 191–192.

15. Wakefield, 131.

16. *Dallas Morning News*, August 10, 1930.

17. *Dallas Morning News*, August 29, 1930.

18. *Dallas Morning News*, June 7, 1931.

19. *Dallas Morning News*, February 6, 1934. (1934 is correct.)

20. Hendrickson, 190–191.

21. Jim's diary entry from Nalle, 212.

22. Wakefield, 148.

23. Sterling and Kilman, 128.

24. McKay, *Texas Politics 1906–1944*, 234.

25. *Dallas Morning News*, August 17, 1932; McKay, *Texas Politics 1906–1944*, 237.

26. Sterling and Kilman, 204; William Warren Sterling, *Trails and Trials of a Texas Ranger*, 264–269.

27. *Dallas Morning News*, October 19, 1932.

28. Sterling and Kilman, 209–211.

29. Nalle, 219.

30. *Dallas Morning News*, January 17, 1933.

31. Ibid.

Chapter 21

1. Ross and Kilman, 220; *Dallas Morning News*, November 27, 1932 and January 8, 1933.

2. *Dallas Morning News*, February 17, 1933.

3. *Dallas Morning News*, January 12, 1933 and January 22, 1933.

4. Utley, 337; *Dallas Morning News*, January 15, 1933.

5. Gantt, 240; Sterling and Kilman, 221; *Dallas Morning News*, January 9, 1933.

6.   *Dallas Morning News*, February 13, 1933; Paulissen and McQueary, 283–284.

7.   *Dallas Morning News*, July 17, 1933. The Handbook of Texas Online, http://www.tshaonline.org/handbook/online/articles. The Great Depression. Also Official Texas Ranger Hall of Fame and Museum Website: http://www.texasranger.org/history/BriefHistory2.htm

8.   *Dallas Morning News*, January 22, 1933.

9.   *Dallas Morning News*, January 25, 1933.

10. *Dallas Morning News*, February 2, 1933.

11. *Dallas Morning News*, February 10, 1933.

12. Ibid.

13. *Dallas Morning News*, February 24, 1933.

14. *Dallas Morning News*, February 16, 1933; Robert A. Caro, *The Years of Lyndon Johnson, The Path to Power*, 250.

15. Nalle, 230–231; *Dallas Morning News*, May 19, 1933.

16. *Dallas Morning News*, July 7, 1933.

17. *Dallas Morning News*, August 25, 1933.

18. http://www.tshaonline.org/handbook/online/articles/npg01

19. *Dallas Morning News*, September 21, 1933.

20. *Dallas Morning News*, September 21, 1933, and January 30, 1934.

21. *Dallas Morning News*, October 11, 1933.

22. Ibid.

23. *Dallas Morning News*, October 11, 1933 and October 13, 1933.

24. *Dallas Morning News*, October 14, 1933.

25. *Dallas Morning News*, October 11, 1933.

26. *Dallas Morning News*, November 2, 1933.

27. *Dallas Morning News*, November 5, 1933.

28. *Dallas Morning News*, November 22, 1933.

29. *Dallas Morning News*, November 25, 1933.

30. *Dallas Morning News*, December 17, 1933.

31. Ibid.

32. *Dallas Morning News*, November 3, 1933.

33. *Dallas Morning News*, December 17, 1933.

34. *Dallas Morning News*, November 30, 1933.

Chapter 22

1. *Dallas Morning News*, January 6, and July 11, 1934.

2. Ibid., July 23, 1933.

3. Jeff Guinn, *Go Down Together: The True, Untold Story of Bonnie and Clyde*, 254.

4. Ibid.

5. Utley, 161–164.

6. *Dallas Morning News*, March 9, March 24, March 25, and March 27, 1934.

7. Ibid., September 7, 1934, "The State Press, Reprints article from the Canyon News."

8. *Dallas Morning News*, March 4, 1934, and December 1, 1934.

9. Ibid., December 1, 1934.

10. Ibid., January 15, 1935.

11. Governor's new salary: Daniel, Daniel and Blodgett, 182.

Chapter 23

1. *Ferguson Forum*, April 11, 1935.

2. *Dallas Morning News*, January 9, 1935 and January 15, 1935.

3. McKay, *Texas Politics 1906–1944*, 295–296.

4. Nalle, 239; Ferguson quotations, *Dallas Morning News*, July 22, 1936; McKay, *Texas Politics 1906–1944*, 301–302.

5. Jim Ferguson's 1937 Diary, Claude Elliott Collection, Box 3, University of Houston Special Collection, Houston, Texas. Even in a note of thanks to daughter Ouida in 1943, Jim had referred to Miriam as "my wife." This odd habit seemed to prove that Jim had a hard time seeing any identity for Miriam apart from her relationship to him. See Nalle, 260.

6. Blodgett, Blodgett, and Scott, 213.

7. *Dallas Morning News*, December 10, 1937.

8. Ibid., January 9, 1938.

9. Ibid., May 15 and May 17, 1938.

10. McKay, *Texas Politics 1906–1944*, 306 and 308.

11. Ibid., 310; L. Patrick Hughes, "Only in Texas: Ma, Pa, and Pappy," University of Texas Continuing Education, http://www.austince.edu/lpatrick/his1693/mapa.htm

12. McKay, Texas Politics *1906–1944*, 316.

13. Hughes, "Only in Texas: Ma, Pa, and Pappy."

14. *Dallas Morning News*, January 19, 1940.

15. *Dallas Morning News*, Lynn Landrum, "Thinking Out Loud," March 26, 1940.

16. Ibid., March 27 and April 8, 1940; McKay, *W. Lee O'Daniel and Texas Politics 1938–1942*, 269.

17. Nalle, 255.

18. Robert Caro, *The Years of Lyndon Johnson: Means of Ascent*, 156, 164.

19. McKay, *Texas Politics 1906–1944*, 346–348.

20. Caro, *Means of Ascent*, 19.

21. McKay, *W. Lee O'Daniel and Texas Politics 1938–1942*, 365.

22. Caro, *Means of Ascent*, 189.

23. McKay, *W. Lee O'Daniel and Texas Politics 1938–1942*, 490.

24. Miriam's statements about Stevenson in Paulissen and McQueary, 250–254.

25. Caro, *Means of Ascent*, 190.

26. James Reston, Jr., *The Lone Star: The Life of John Connally*, 66.

Chapter 24

1. Nalle, 260. The Temple home was sold to Minnie Cope. See Bell County Clerk's records, Belton, Texas.

2. Caro, *Means of Ascent*, 33.

3. Reston, 40.

4. In *Ross Sterling, Texan*, the editor notes that, during Ed Kilman's search for a pub-

lisher, he was told by Naylor Publishing that they had lost money on a book they published in 1946 the subject of which was the Fergusons, 239.

5.   Nalle, 116, 122 and 124; Tracy Campbell, *Deliver the Vote*, 223–224; John Clark, 22–41.

6.   Richard Morehead, *50 Years in Texas Politics*, 66.

7.   Caro, *Means of Ascent*, 190, 191, and 210.

8.   Ibid., 265–266.

9.   Ibid.

10.   Ibid., 287 and 288.

11.   Ibid., 305.

12.   Ibid., 311, 312, 317.

13.   Ibid., 326, 327; John Clark, 52.

14.   *Dallas Morning News*, August 4, 1977.

15.   Paulissen and McQueary, 280 and 330.

16.   All of the information and quotations from Nola Wood were taken from the transcripts of the 1977 interview that was conducted by Dr. Paulissen and discussions between Dr. Paulissen and this writer. This document is from Paulissen's personal collection.

Chapter 25

1.   *Dallas Morning News*, January 22, 1915.

2.   James Ferguson was not alone in failing the rural poor. In *Progressives and Prohibitionists: Texas Democrats in the Wilson Era*, Gould states, "The inability to improve the conditions of the rural poor was a major failing of reform in Texas before 1921." The weight of this failing falls more squarely on Ferguson because he was elected on a promise to help farmers. Gould, 285.

3.   Ferguson's tax returns and other financial information, Claude Elliott Collection, Box 3, University of Houston Special Collection, Houston, Texas. Ferguson's 1915 tax return was audited but the changes to that year's return resulted in an assessment of only $356.21 suggesting that the income and expenses were fairly accurate as initially filed.

4.   Ibid.

5.   In *Hood, Bonnet and Little Brown Jug*, Brown wrote, "The *[Dallas Morning] News* concluded, 'That a good many thousand prohibitionists who have no sympathy with the Ku Klux Klan and its works voted for its senatorial candidate'" (117).

Jim Ferguson's aversion to those who had Klan connections was not absolute. Ferguson awarded one of the state road contracts to his friend and former railroad commissioner Charles Hurdleston in 1925. Hurdleston was a Klan member but resigned when offered a contact by the governor's advisor. See Brown, 283.

6.   Brown wrote of Moody's campaign and his efforts to offset the effects of the *Forum* on rural voters. He theorized that many rurals read nothing else. Brown 302–308.

7.   Messer, 165.

8.   Owens and Grant, 50.

Books:

Alexander, Charles C. *The Ku Klux Klan in the Southwest.* Norman: University of Oklahoma Press, 1995.

Anders, Evan. *Boss Rule in South Texas: The Progressive Era.* Austin: University of Texas Press, 1982.

Ariens, Michael. *Lone Star Law, A Legal History of Texas.* Lubbock: Texas Tech University Press, 2011.

Benoit, Patricia K. *Historic Temple, An Illustrated History.* San Antonio, TX: Historical Publishing Network, 2009.

Benton, Wilbourn E. *Texas, Its Government and Politics.* Englewood Cliffs, NJ: Prentice-Hall, 1972.

Biggers, Don H. *Our Sacred Monkeys; or, 20 years of Jim and other Jams, (Mostly Jim) the Outstanding Goat Gland Specialist of Texas Politics.* Brownwood, TX: Jones Printing Company, 1933.

Blodgett, Dorothy, Terrell Blodgett, and David L. Scott. *The Land, the Law, and the Lord: The Life of Pat Neff.* Austin, TX: Home Place Publishers, 2007.

Bowmer, Daurice, and Jim D. Bowmer. *The Unknown Bell County*. Self-published, 1980.

Brown, Norman D. *Hood, Bonnet and Little Brown Jug.* College Station: Texas A&M Press, 1984.

Calvert, Robert A., Arnoldo De Leon, and Gregg Cantrell. *The History of Texas.* 3rd ed. Wheeling, IL: Harlan Davidson, 2002.

Campbell, Randolph B. *Gone to Texas: A History of the Lone Star State.* New York: Oxford University Press, 2003.

Campbell, Tracy. *Deliver the Vote: A History of Election Fraud, An American Political Tradition, 1742-2004.* New York: Carroll & Graff Publishers, 2005.

Caro, Robert A. *The Years of Lyndon Johnson: Means of Ascent.* New York: Alfred A. Knopf, Inc. 1990.

————. *The Years of Lyndon Johnson: The Path to Power.* New York: Vintage Books, 1990.

Clark, James A., with Weldon Hart. *The Tactful Texan: A Biography of Governor Will Hobby.* New York: Random House, 1958.

Clark, John E. *The Fall of the Duke of Duval.* Austin, TX: Eakin Press, 1995.

Daniel, Jean Houston, Price Daniel, and Dorothy Blodgett. *The Texas Governor's Mansion.* Austin: Texas State Library and Archives Commission and the Sam Houston Library and Research Center, 1984.

Friends of the Governor's Mansion, eds., *The Governor's Mansion of Texas, A Historic Tour*, published by Friends in Austin, 1985.

Fuermann, George. *Reluctant Empire.* Garden City, NY: Doubleday & Company, 1957.

Gantt, Fred Jr. *The Chief Executives of Texas: A Story of Gubernatorial Leadership.* Austin: University of Texas Press, 1964.

Gould, Lewis L. *Progressives and Prohibitionists: Texas Democrats in the Wilson Era.* Austin: Texas State Historical Association, 1992.

Guinn, Jeff. *Go Down Together: The True, Untold Story of Bonnie and Clyde.* United Kingdom: Simon and Schuster, 2009.

Hendrickson, Kenneth E. Jr. *The Chief Executives of Texas from Steven F. Austin to John B. Connally, Jr.* College Station: Texas A & M University Press, 1995.

Jackson, Pearl Cashell. *Texas Governors' Wives.* Austin, TX: E. L. Steck Publishers, 1915.

Kelsey, Michael, and Nancy Kelsey. *Images of America, Temple.* Charleston, SC: Arcadia Publishing, 2010.

LeFan, Michael. *Temple in Vintage Postcards.* Charleston, SC: Arcadia Publishing, 2004.

Lomax, John. *Will Hogg, Texan.* Austin: University of Texas Press, 1956.

McArthur, Judith N. *Creating the New Woman: The Rise of Southern Women's Progressive Culture in Texas, 1893–1918.* Urbana: University of Illinois Press, 1998.

————. "Minnie Fisher Cunningham's Back Door Lobby in Texas: Political Maneuvering in a One-Party State." In *One Woman, One Vote: Rediscovering the Woman Suffrage Movement*, edited by Marjoire Spruill Wheeler. Troutdale, OR: New Sage Press, 1995.

————. "Saving the Children: The Women's Crusade Against Child Labor." In *Women and Texas History*, edited by Fane Downs and Nancy Baker Jones. Austin: Texas State Historical Association, 1993.

McKay, Seth S. *W. Lee O'Daniel and Texas Politics 1938–1942*. Lubbock: Texas Tech University Press, 1944.

————. *Texas Politics, 1906–1944*. Lubbock: Texas Tech University Press, 1952.

McKay, Seth S., and Odie B. Faulk. *Texas After Spindletop, The Saga of Texas: 1901–1965*. Austin, TX: Steck-Vaughn Company, 1965.

Messer, A. Bryant. *The Prairie Queen and Her Choo-Choo Train (It's about Temple, Texas, and Then Some)*. Temple, TX: M & M Publishing Company, 1976.

Miller, Rick. *Bloody Bell County: Vignettes of Violence and Mayhem in Central Texas*. Waco, TX: Nortex Press, 2011.

Morehead, Richard. *50 Years in Texas Politics*. Burnet, TX: Eakin Press, 1982.

Nalle, Ouida Ferguson. *The Fergusons of Texas: Two Governors for the Price of One*. San Antonio, TX: The Naylor Company, 1946.

Owens, William A., and Lyman Grant, eds. *The Letters of Roy Bedichek*. Austin: University of Texas Press, 1985.

Ozment, Robert A. *Temple National Bank: A History*. Salado, TX: Anson Jones Press 1974.

————. *InterFirst Bank Temple, 1910–1985: A History*. Salado, TX: Anson Jones Press, 1985.

Paulissen, May Nelson, and Carl McQueary. *Miriam: The Southern Belle Who Became the First Woman Governor of Texas*. Austin, TX: Eakin Press, 1995.

Porterfield, Nolan. *Last Cavalier: The Life and Times of John A. Lomax*. Urbana: University of Illinois Press, 1996.

Proceedings, Investigation Committee, House of Representatives, Thirty-fifth Legislature, Charges against Governor James E. Ferguson Together with Findings of Committee and Action of House, with Prefatory Statement and Index to Proceedings. Originally published Austin, TX: C. Baldwin and Sons. Reprinted by The University of Michigan Library, nd.

Record of Proceedings of the High Court of Impeachment on the Trial of Hon. James E. Ferguson, Governor. Hathi Trust Digital Library. Accessed June 2010 http://babel.hathitrust.org/cgi/pt?id+mdp.39015030830684

Reston, James, Jr. *The Lone Star: The Life of John Connally.* New York: Harper and Row, 1989.

Rutherford, Bruce. *The Impeachment of Jim Ferguson.* Austin, TX: Eakin Press, 1983.

Shanklin, Felda Davis. *Salado Texas: Its History and Its People,* Belton, TX: Peter Hansbrough Bell Press, 1960.

Simmons, Laura. *Out of Our Past: Texas History Stories.* Waco, TX: Texian Press, 1967.

Sterling, Ross, and Ed Kilman. Edited and revised by Don Carlton. *Ross Sterling, A Texan.* Texas: University of Texas Press, 2007.

Sterling, William Warren. *Trails and Trials of a Texas Ranger.* Norman: University of Oklahoma Press, 1959.

Tyler, George. *History of Bell County.* Belton, TX: Village Press, 1936.

Utley, Robert M. *Lone Star Lawmen: The Second Century of the Texas Rangers.* New York: Berkley Books, 2008.

Wakefield, Paul L. *Campaigning Texas.* Self published, 1932.

Webb, Walter Prescott. *The Texas Rangers: A Century of Frontier Defense.* Boston, MA: Houghton Mifflin Company, 1935.

Wharton, Clarence R., *History of Texas.* Dallas, TX: Turner Co., 1935.

Wheeler, Marjorie Spruill, ed. *One Woman, One Vote: Rediscovering the Woman Suffrage Movement.* Troutdale, OR: New Sage Press, 1995.

Articles:

Gra'Delle Duncan, Bell County Historical Commission Newsletter, "Dirty Politics Nothing New in Texas," Winter, 1992.

Newspapers:

Bartlett Tribune, Bartlett, Texas

Belton Journal, Belton, Texas

Breckenridge Weekly Democrat, Breckenridge, Texas

Cleburne Morning Review, Cleburne, Texas

Cronista del Valle, Brownsville, Texas

Dallas Morning News

El Paso Herald

Ferguson Forum

Fort Worth Morning Register

Fort Worth Star Telegram

Greensboro Record

Houston Chronicle

Houston Daily Union

Houston Post

Huntsville Item, Huntsville, Texas

Messenger, Ft. Scott, Kansas

Montgomery Advertiser, Montgomery, Alabama

Oregonian, Portland, Oregon

Richardson Echo, Richardson, Texas

San Antonio Express

Temple Daily Telegram, Temple, Texas

Temple Mirror, Temple, Texas

Tulsa World, Tulsa, Oklahoma

Theses, Manuscripts and Transcripts:

Atkinson, Bertha. "History of Bell County." M. A. Thesis, University of Texas, Austin. 1929.

Bowmer, James D. Transcript from speech. "The Eagle is Here!" Presented to the Ladies Federation Club luncheon in Temple, Texas on March 13, 1984: Copy of transcript courtesy of Bell County Museum, Belton, Texas.

Claude Elliott Collection, The University of Houston, Special Collection, Houston, Texas.

Crane, Martin. Crane Papers. Dolph Briscoe Center for American History, University of Texas, Austin.

Dienst, Alexander. Dienst Papers. Dolph Briscoe Center for American History, University of Texas, Austin.

Ferguson, James. Ferguson's first campaign speech in Blum. Copy at Dolph Briscoe Center for American History, University of Texas, Austin.

————. Biographical File. Dolph Briscoe Center for American History, University of Texas, Austin.

————. Veto Message, June 2, 1917. Dolph Briscoe Center for American History, University of Texas, Austin.

Ferguson, Miriam A. Biographical File. Dolph Briscoe Center for American History, University of Texas, Austin.

Ferguson, James, and Miriam Ferguson. Biographical File. Bell County Museum, Belton, Texas.

Henn, Kristin. "The Opera House of Belton, Texas." M. A. Thesis, Southwest Texas State University, San Marcos, May 1998.

Hogg Papers. Dolph Briscoe Center for American History, University of Texas, Austin.

Tyler, George. Tyler Papers. Bell County Railroad and Heritage Museum, Temple, Texas.

Wood, Nola. Transcripts from 1977 Interview by Dr. May Paulissen. Courtesy of Dr. Paulissen.

Other

The Alcalde, Publication of Texas Exes.

Ancestry.Com. Internet site, various census records.

Genealogybank.com. Multiple newspaper articles.

Longbranch Cemetary website, Eastland County, Texas, http://www.rootsweb. ancestry.com/-txeastla/cemetaries/Lon   Accessed 2011

Texas Bankers Journal, July 1916.

Texas Pythian Banner-Knight, April, 1915, copies found in James E. Ferguson Collection, Dolph Briscoe Center for American History, University of Texas, Austin.

Interviews Conducted by Author

Dr. May Paulissen.

Charles Harrell, childhood neighbor of Alex Ferguson (James Ferguson's brother) 2011.

Priscilla Heard, widow of Lawrence P. Heard, Jr. T. H. Heard, President of the Temple State Bank from 1917 to 1918, was Lawrence P. Heard Jr.'s grandfather.

Index

A

Achilles, W. A., 87–88, 99, 114, 258

Adams, Jed C., 205–206

Adolphus Hotel, 200

Alexander, Charles C., on the Ku Klux Klan, 5, 242, 266, 279

Alice, Texas, 225

Allred, James V., 191–193, 206–211

American Bankers Association, 47, 251

(The) American Party, 142, dissolved, 144

American National Bank, 108, 124

American National Insurance Co. of Galveston, 100

American Printing Company, 173

Anderson, James (historic home in Salado, TX), 7, 243

Anti-Saloon League, 28

Archer County Bond Issue, 172

Arlington Downs, 196

Atkinson, Bertha, 4, 241, 242, 243, 284

Austin American Statesman, 173

Austin, Charles O., accusations against Poe, 94; appointed commissioner by James Ferguson, 54; appointed commissioner by Miriam Ferguson, 160; charge against him, 81; criminal indictment, 133; defends actions, 109–110; deposits state funds in Temple bank, 126; first meets with Poe, 53; judgment against, 114; notes, 259, 260; testimony, 104–107; un-cooperative with Crane, 94

Austin, Dave T., 165–166

Autry, R. L., (VP of Houston Ice and Brewing) 32

B

Bailey, Joseph Weldon, 34, 68, 141, 144

Baldwin, Captain B. C., Texas Ranger, 173

Ball, Thomas, 1914 gubernatorial candidate, 28–29; 31–34, 56–57, 60, 248

Bandit Wars, 67

Barber, Jim, 200

Barrow, Blanche, 203

Barrow, Buck, 203–204

Barrow, Clyde, 203–205, 248, 280

G

M

N

Nolansville or Nolanville (later Belton), 2

O

O'Daniel, Wilbert Lee, 212–219, 222–223, 235, 276, 281

Opera house of Belton, lost in a fire, 15–16

Opera house in Temple (proposed), 22

Ousley, Clarence, 28, 31

P

Parker, Bonnie, 203–205, 254, 280

Parr, Archie, 130–132, 149, 223–224

Parr, George, 132, 217, 223–227

Patterson, John, 45, 53–54, 105, 111, 126

Paulissen, Dr. May, 228–230

Peddy, George E. B., 147–148

Pendleton, D. R., 12, 15–16, 31, 245

Pershing, General John, U.S. Army, 67

Pinchot, Gifford, 193

Plan of San Diego, 60

Poe, Hosea C., arrest and trial, 115–116; born 1881, 47; contacts Commission of Insurance and Banking, 53–54, ; death, 117; efforts to improve bank, 47–48; open letter, 81, 83–84; regarding Maedgen's allegations, 51–52, takes over Temple State Bank, 37–38; trouble with bank, 40– 46, 48–51; trouble with Texas Store, 38–40

Porterfield, Nolan, 119, 261

Prairie View Normal and Industrial College, 56

(The) Presbyterian Theological Seminary of Austin, 75

Prohibition, 20, 23, 25–29, 32–34, 63–64, 68, 136, 141–142, 151–152, 154, 156, 182–183, 196–197, 215, 235–236

Purl, George C., 194

R

Ramos, Basilio, Mexican rebel, 60

Ramsdell, Charles W., Compiled *History of Bell County*, 1

Ransom, Henry, Captain in the Texas Rangers, 61

Reconstruction, 1, 4, 5, 26

T

U

Underwood, Oscar W., 151

Union National Bank of Houston, TX, 49–50, 124, 252

University of Mary Hardin-Baylor, x, 11, 244

University of Texas, Austin, TX, xvi, 23, 38, 56, 58, 59, 64–65, 71, 73, 74, 76, 78, 79, 80, 114, 117, 119, 120, 136, 140, 147, 156, 163, 191, 232, 237

University of Texas at Austin Ex-Students, 74, 118, 161, 120, 261

V

Villa, Pancho, 67, 226

Vinson, Robert E., trouble with Governor Ferguson, 75–77, 79, 118–119, 127, 129, 256, 262

W

Wallace, Eliza, 3–4, 9, 11–12, 18, death, 58; 244

Wallace estate, 11

Wallace, Joseph, 4, 9–11, 242, 244

Wallace, Miriam, see Ferguson, Miriam

Wallace, Susan Priscilla, nicknamed John, 9, 11, 34

Wallace, Warner, born 1871, 9

Wallace, William, born 1873, 9, 41, 92, 101

War preparedness plan of Woodrow Wilson, 61

Ward, John, 166

Wardlaw, Louis J., 183

Washington State, 8

Watson, T. R., owner of Teague, TX bank, murderer of John Patterson, 53–54

Watson, Q. U., 138, 255

Watt, Ruby Dorrace Ferguson, accompanied mother in campaigning, 155; birth of, 12;, called "potato digger" at school, 253; childhood, 19–20; death, 228; denounces use of "Ma" and "Pa" 237–238; employed at *Forum*, 135; discourages political involvement, 211; gives birth, 214; personality traits, 19, 24; president of Bosque creamery 186; pride in father, 29; weds, 186

Watt, Earl Stuart, 186

Watt, James Stuart, 214, 227, 246

Webb, Atticus, 173, 271